WHERE THE BIRDS ARE

WHERE THE BIRDS ARE

A Travel Guide to **Over 1,000**
Parks, Preserves, and Sanctuaries

Robert J. Dolezal
With the editors of BIRDS & BLOOMS

Reader's Digest

The Reader's Digest Association, Inc.
Pleasantville, New York • Montreal

For Reader's Digest

U.S. Project Editors: Barbara Booth, Kimberly Casey

Canadian Project Editors: Jim Hynes, Pamela Johnson

Consulting Editor, Birds & Blooms: Heather Lamb

Project Designer: Jennifer Tokarski

Associate Art Director: George McKeon

Executive Editor, Trade Publishing: Dolores York

Manufacturing Manager: John L. Cassidy

Director of Production: Michael Braunschweiger

Associate Publisher: Rosanne McManus

President & Publisher, Trade Publishing: Harold Clarke

Library of Congress Cataloging-in-Publication Data

Dolezal, Robert J.
   Where the birds are : a travel guide to over 1,000 parks, preserves, and sanctuaries / Robert J. Dolezal.
      p. cm.
      ISBN 13: 978-0-7621-0860-2
      ISBN 10: 0-7621-0860-6
      1. Bird watching--North America--Guidebooks. 2. North America--Guidebooks. I. Title.

QL681.D65 2007
598.072'347—dc22

2006051803

The photo credits that appear on pages 278–279 are hereby made a part of this copyright page.

For Dolezal & Associates

Project Manager: Robert J. Dolezal

Consulting Editor: Cynthia Rubin

Layout Art: Barbara Dolezal

Contributing Designer: Jennifer Tokarski

Production Manager: Barbara Dolezal

Photoshop Artist: Jerry Bates

Writer: Robert J. Dolezal

Principal Photographer: John M. Rickard

Researchers: Jerry Bates, Robert J. Dolezal, Barbara Dolezal, John M. Rickard

Cartography: Hildebrand Design, San Francisco, California

Indexer: Albie Celf

Note to our Readers

The information for this book was gathered and carefully fact-checked by Reader's Digest researchers and editors. Since site information such as dates and hours is always subject to change, you are urged to check with the sites you are planning to visit to avoid any inconvenience.

We are committed to both the quality of our products and the service we provide to our customers. We value your comments, so please feel free to contact us.

The Reader's Digest Association, Inc.
Adult Trade Publishing
Reader's Digest Road
Pleasantville, NY 10570-7000

For more information about Reader's Digest, visit:
   www.rd.com (in the United States)
   www.readersdigest.ca (in Canada)

For more information about Birds & Blooms, visit:
   www.birdsandblooms.com

This book is printed on environmentally friendly paper, certified by the Forest Stewardship Council (FSC).

Printed in China

1 3 5 7 9 10 8 6 4 2

About This Book

Millions enjoy nature and bird-watching—and they are the reason this book was written. With routes that cover birding sites in North America—from Hawaii, Alaska, and British Columbia to Quebec, Texas, and Florida—this guide shares the most interesting and exciting places for bird-watchers looking to visit hot spots close to major destination gateways.

Divided into four sections—the Western Region, the Rocky Mountain Region, the Central Region, and the Eastern Region—the 35 tours found in *Where the Birds Are* take you to places that are known by birds and birders alike. The routes and stops were selected with aid from state tourism offices; birding groups; the National Forest Service; national, state, and provincial park staffs; and countless birding experts in every region of the land. Each drive route presents a trail of popular birding sites—over 1,000 refuges, preserves, parks, and sanctuaries—along with detailed directions and the site's key features. The location of each of these sites is pinpointed on a specially designed map with a red line depicting the route and red dots to mark each stop.

Map insets give greater detail in cities or show areas outside of the main map.

Both on the road and in the comfort of your home, you'll find *Where the Birds Are* a welcome companion for birding travel.

Abbreviations Used in This Book

IBA	Important Bird Area
NF	National Forest
NG	National Grassland
NHP	National Historical Park
NM	National Monument
NP	National Park
NPS	National Park Service
NWR	National Wildlife Refuge
SHP	State Historical Park
SNA	State Natural Area
SP	State Park
SRA	State Recreation Area
USDA	U.S. Dept. of Agriculture
USFS	U.S. Forest Service
USFWS	U.S. Fish and Wildlife Service
WMA	Wildlife Management Areas

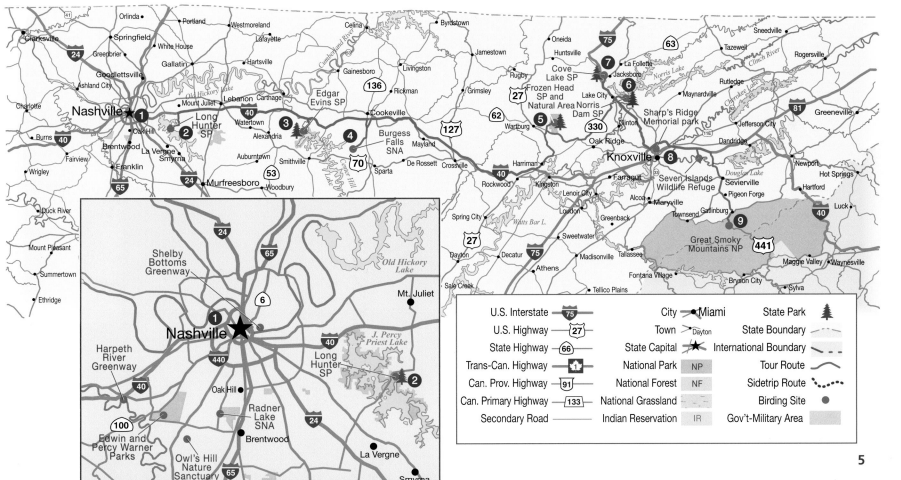

The Western Region

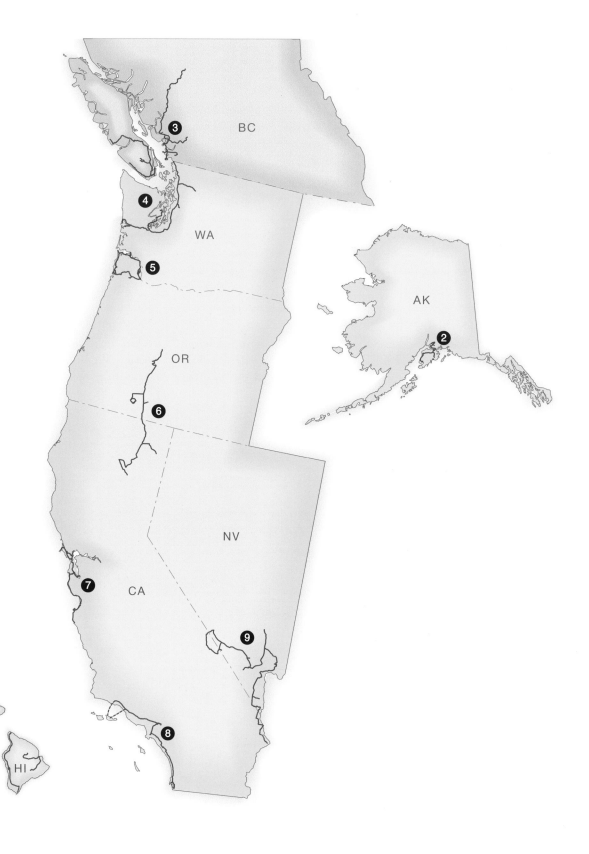

Page 14

The Rocky Mountain Region

Page 84

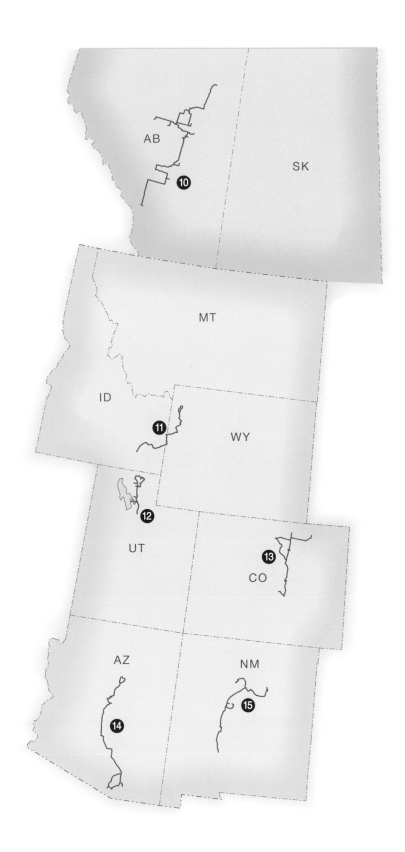

The Central Region

Page 124

Page 186

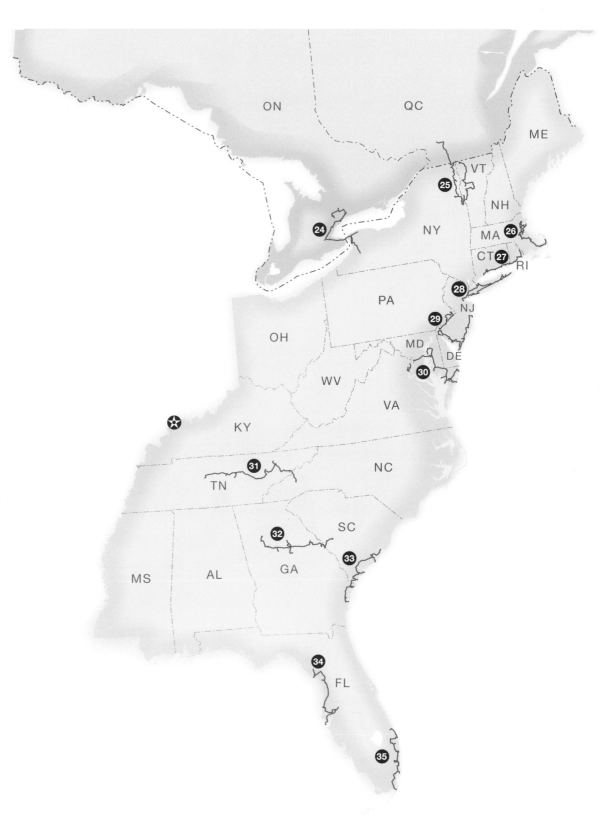

Introduction

"Those little nimble musicians of the air, that warble forth their curious ditties."

—Izaac Walton, *The Compleat Angler*

This book is for everyone who loves nature, birds, and wildlife. It resulted from having leftover time to fill during trips taken to distant cities. The problem wasn't having something to do; it was filling time with something that satisfied a craving for seeing the wild places. There are a surfeit of activities in every major city, but digging out birding pearls from the dross takes time and planning.

Today's world is often busy, hectic, and filled with responsibilities. Finding time to enjoy one's interests is a constant challenge. Why not simply enjoy some really great birding when a sales call ends, before or after a meeting, when family obligations are met, or when a theme park or shopping has lost its allure? The birding routes found in these pages will fill the needs of amateur and experienced bird-watchers faced with time during a holiday or business visit to one of the major cities across Canada and the United States.

Look for a major destination in the United States and Canada and it will be found here, along with suggestions of where to go in and around that city or farther afield. These birding routes have been carefully planned to make an enjoyable outing over several days, or they can be divided into day trips taken over many seasons and return visits. Birders with a schedule in mind can pick and choose destinations based on solid birding knowledge from experts on the ground.

Since seasonal changes are constant in birding populations, each route brings new sightings and discoveries at each visit. Sites were selected because they offer an excellent birding experience or they had nature centers, boardwalks, viewing towers, tours, trails, canoe paths, or blinds to enhance the bird-watching experience. For those with family and jobs that keep them closer to home, perhaps paging through the great birding sites found across this continent will inspire a special bird-watching trip or bring back thoughts of local favorites.

Is this an exhaustive list of the top 100 birding sites to visit or some other exclusive guide to the very best bird-watching sites in North America? No, it isn't. There are locations omitted here that experts agree are among the very best for bird-watching in the continent, but for good reason: They simply aren't close to the major destination gateways. If time and passion permit, those sites will be found anyway, because the expert staff at the sites included will suggest them as additional options. The routes are intended to be convenient, representative, and provide as wide a range of birding experiences as is possible within a given geographic region. Favorites—personal or those of our editors—were left out if they didn't fit these standards.

There are over 900 species of birds found in the United States and Canada. Region by region and season to season, each bird-watching trip will differ. A reader who visits all of the more than 1,000 sites in this book will stand an excellent chance of seeing many or most of them, but even that dedicated birder would still have a new experience on each and every trip—that's the lure of bird-watching.

Birds seen in the North often have different plumage than those same birds seen in the South, and eastern bird species vary from related western birds. Take, for example, the bluebird: eastern, western, and mountain bluebirds are quite different in their appearance. Part of the fun and reward of birding is learning these differences, discovering new information, and sharing it with friends. So take a more relaxed approach by making the birds the experience rather than filling out a checklist or compiling a daily total. Note the many festivals and special stops recommended, become part of the birding community, and learn new things from experienced hands.

Like any hobby or pastime, birding has a few terms and conventions that may seem strange at first, but they are easily mastered. Wonder what an IBA is, for example? It's a designation that a site has a special habitat that makes it an *Important Birding Area* for one or more species and experts have agreed that it should be recognized and preserved. Wherever possible, the book includes a straight explanation of these common acronyms, abbreviations, descriptive terms, and other bird-watching words that may seem unfamiliar at first. Within a few pages, for instance, you'll know that a passerine is a fancy word for birds that perch and that neotropical birds spend their winters in Central and South America.

Finally, to paraphrase the words of famous conservationists, walk softly on the land, take only pictures and memories, and leave the trail better than it was found. Here are some tips to follow that will make a visit to any birding site more enjoyable and productive:

Listening skills. Listen and hone the skill of identifying birds by their songs and calls. Start by associating calls of birds being watched, then listen for the songs that don't fit. With a little effort, bird songs will become second nature to seeing the birds and will enhance the entire experience.

Boats and birding. Use a canoe, a kayak, or a boat with an electric trolling motor to silently glide along waterways and view the wildlife that resides there. Birds seen by boat include waterfowl, as well as wading birds and shorebirds, birds that feed on insects or fish, and those in search of a refreshing drink or bath.

Automobiles as blinds. This technique is best practiced and only recommended on birding drives provided in refuges, preserves, or other wildlife management areas, or in situations where a car can be parked safely out of traffic without creating a personal or public hazard. Using the car as a blind avoids disturbing nesting and migrating birds and sometimes makes a close approach possible.

Trail precautions. Stay on marked trails to prevent damage to plants and habitat and to stop erosion. Always clean shoes and clothing before entering and after leaving a birding area; this necessary step avoids spreading to sensitive areas contaminating parasites, germs, or invasive seeds that cling to muddy soles or clothing.

Photography blinds. Blinds allow birds to go about their normal activities of feeding, caring for young, and resting without being disturbed. The photographic opportunities abound in such structures. It is usually a prerequisite to reserve blinds prior to arrival and to be in position at a set time before dawn or dusk. This courtesy extends to other birders who have timed their arrival accordingly, since birds are most active at these periods.

Observation towers. Looking out over a site from a high vantage point makes it possible to see into tall grasslands and waterways. Some viewing towers raise the observer to the tree canopy, where boreal birds—birds of the forest—are most active.

Guided tours. This may bring back to mind the ranger-led nature tours of one's youth, but experienced naturalists make ideal guides.

A yellow warbler waits in the pine forests for a binocular-toting nature lover to hear its song.

A number of professional guides also provide birding tours; the choice to tour with others is an individual one with both economic and experiential considerations, but for birders traveling alone—especially in unfamiliar urban or rural areas—tours are recommended for personal safety; read more about this in "Birding Safety" on the next page.

Often, local chapters of the Audubon Society, birding clubs, and others offer free or inexpensive guided birding tours; check chapter websites for more information. Other expert tours are offered by the staff at national wildlife refuges and state, provincial, and national parks. Some private preserves and refuges have similar tours.

Another touring option is Birdingpal (**www.birdingpal.org**). It encourages private exchanges of the services of local birders for similar guiding favors when one's guide visits a former guest's home area.

A more formal way to bird is with a professional guide hired to lead a group on a set itinerary and share expert knowledge. Inclement weather, seasonal changes, fires, flooding, spills, and other unforeseeable events can change an otherwise good birding site to a less-than-pleasurable experience. Professional guides make it their business to know about the birding conditions for the areas they travel. Use of guide services certainly lessens the chance of disappointment and goes a long way to guaranteeing good results. Using such services may make sense when the destination is remote and unfamiliar.

Birding safety. Because many of the birding sites are within city parks in large metropolitan areas, always be city-smart and personally safe. Regardless of the birds, remain aware of surroundings and always go in pairs or groups. Even the most city-savvy person can be caught unaware and vulnerable when loaded with camera equipment and concentrating on an interesting bird.

Practical preparation. Remember to apply sunscreen, take plenty of drinking water and snacks, and lock valuables in an automobile's trunk. Avoid birding in hunting areas during hunting season.

Bring along a map and a GPS device and pay attention to routes, landmarks, and distances to avoid becoming lost. Be sure to carry a cellular phone to summon quick aid if necessary.

Hiking shoes, boots, or waders are at the top of the list. Make sure they are broken in, comfortable, waterproof, and suitable for the site and conditions.

Dress in layered clothing appropriate to the weather and season. When venturing out for a full day of birding, be prepared for changes in the weather, especially in areas known for sudden thunderstorms, flash floods, strong winds, hail, or other inclement conditions that could result in hypothermia or distress.

Sometimes tall grasses, wetlands, forests, rivers, or beaches hold hazards. It may be as innocuous as a bite from a mosquito carrying the Rocky Mountain spotted fever or West Nile virus; annoying as a biting fly, stinging fire ant, or bee; or as serious as encountering a Lyme disease–carrying tick. Of course, there are other hazards, such as wild animals: bears, wild pigs, raccoons, rattlesnakes, and alligators, to name just a few. Use insect repellent and wear site-appropriate hats, long-sleeved shirts, and pants. Read warnings on informational kiosks and postings at visitors centers with area safety cautions.

Finally, always disclose your travel plans to a trusted contact and notify them upon return.

Birding equipment. Equipment quality and features are very important, and they can enhance or detract from the experience.

When choosing binoculars for birding, splurge a little and get a pair best suited to the individual. The physical size of the binoculars has little to do with their magnification power or clarity:

- 10X is the upper limit for handheld binoculars, and many bird-watchers prefer 7X or 8X with wider fields of view.
- Image stabilization is practically a necessity for high-power magnifications; this has become an affordable option that makes it possible to handhold wide-field, high-magnification binoculars.
- Choose large-diameter quality lenses with antireflective coatings to allow for maximum light transmission.

- Eyeglass wearers should choose binoculars with eye cups that accommodate their glasses yet still provide a full field of view.
- Select a waterproof nitrogen-filled model; it prevents fogging, simplifies cleaning, and avoids costly replacement.

Angle spotting scopes are preferred by many birders since they allow for stable high-magnification viewing on a tripod and are more comfortable than straight-line spotting scopes, avoiding painful neck strain and bending.

Wild-bird photography requires a film or digital camera with a moderate telephoto zoom lens that can be held without shaking, such as the equivalent of a 90-mm to 200-mm lens on a 35-mm camera.

A bird field guide is useful for identification. Obtain a bird checklist from the site to learn which birds are present. What starts as a casual bird-watching hobby may change over time to an avocation memorialized in a bird life list.

Birding festivals. Many festivals celebrating birds are held each year in every locale. They are a great way to meet other birders, learn from experts, share stories, and support local birding organizations.

Join up. The Audubon Society, Bird Studies Canada, The Nature Conservancy, Ducks Unlimited, local birding clubs, and others have turned the tide on endangered bird species, helped in efforts to conserve vanishing habitats, and are devoted to educating the public. Become a member, meet like-minded friends, and make a difference.

A great blue heron prepares to land at Lake Shastina in northern California. Will the branch hold its weight?

The Western Region

Restless wayfarers, by night crossing the face of the full moon or at midday soaring along the flanks of mighty volcanoes, the birds of the Pacific Flyway travel the entire Western continent. From the Cascades of British Columbia and mountains ringing the northern Pacific in Alaska to the Sierra Nevada range and deserts of the South, some journey as far west as the Hawaiian Islands, fly south to Tierra del Fuego, or cross the Pacific's vast emptiness to Asia.

The West is everywhere influenced by the sea. Ocean-borne winds carry moisture to the mountains, creating rivers that flow back to the coast. From these lush habitats rise forests, lakes, and grasslands that offer nesting areas and feeding grounds for the West's many birds, while its open ocean is a welcoming home to seafaring birds, from gulls and tropicbirds to cormorants and frigatebirds. Come west and revel in the region's avian bounty.

Birding in Hawaii means island-hopping back through time. The Big Island was the most recent to form, and its hot magma spills from several active volcanoes, adding new land with every flow sent into the Pacific. Each island northeast is more ancient; memory of its fiery origins fades, mountains erode, the sea encroaches, and vegetation becomes more complex. Finally, travelers arrive in Kauai—the oldest of the major Hawaiian Islands—a starting point for bird-watching in a tropical setting that provides an experience quite unlike the mainland. Choose one or more favorite islands and enjoy a mix of exquisite avian offerings, natural beauty, crystalline waters, and sparkling sunlight.

Hawaiian Islands

Born of volcanic fires and the ocean's waves, these Polynesian jewels bob mid-Pacific, serene and majestic in their isolation. Craggy cliffs of hardened lava and varied habitats are home to myriad birds of the sea and rare land dwellers.

Kilauea Point NWR is home to a pair of diminutive nene—Hawaiian geese—found only in the Hawaiian Islands.

Kauai—Hawaiian moorhens are abundant in the Garden Island's lagoons.

❶ Island of Kauai

Kilauea Point NWR is the place to view seabirds such as albatross, boobies, frigatebirds, tropicbirds, shearwaters, and golden Pacific plover. Turn off Hwy. 56, the Kuhio Hwy., at the entrance to Kilauea and follow signs to Kilauea Lighthouse on

Lighthouse Rd. A fee is charged, and it is open daily except major holidays. Be sure to take in the view of soaring birds riding updrafts along the cliffs, others roosting and nesting in the sheer rock face, and still others in the lush grass near the lighthouse. This grassy lawn area is the

most likely place to see rare, endangered nene geese, Hawaii's state bird.

Kilauea Point NWR
Hwy. 56 and Lighthouse Rd.
Kilauea, Kauai, HI 96754
(808) 828-1413
www.fws.gov

Kauai

Haena SP
Na Pali Coast SP
Koke`e SP
Waimea Canyon SP
Hanalei NWR
Hanalei
Kilauea
Kilauea Point NWR
Alaka`i Swamp
1
56
Kapaa
Wailua
Wailua River SP
Mana
Kekaha
Russian Fort Elizabeth SHP
50
Kaumakani
Eleele
Omao
Lihue
Poipu

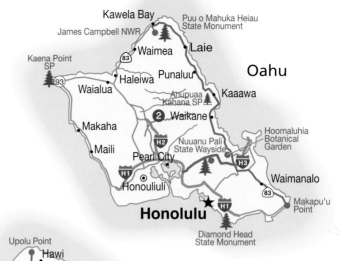

Oahu

Kawela Bay
Puu o Mahuka Heiau State Monument
James Campbell NWR
Waimea
Laie
Kaena Point SP
83
Haleiwa
Punaluu
Waialua
Ahupuaa Kabana SP
Kaaawa
93
Makaha
2
Waikane
Hoomaluhia Botanical Garden
Maili
H2
Nuuanu Pali State Wayside
Pearl City
H3
H1
Waimanalo
Honouliuli
83
Makapu'u Point
Honolulu
H1
Diamond Head State Monument

Maui

Kapalua
Kaanapali
Waihee
Halekii-Pihana Heiau State Monument
Haiku
Wailuku
Kanaha Pond
360
30
Olowalu
Kahului
Pukalani
Wailua
Kaumahina State Wayside
Hosmer Grove
Wai'anapanapa SP
**3**
Kihei
Waiakoa
Waikamoi Preserve
Kaeleku
Kealia Pond NWR
Haleakala NP
31
Makena
Ulupalakua
Haou
Makena SP
31
Kaupo

Hawaii (inset)

Hawaii

Upolu Point
Hawi
Lapakahi State HP
Kahua
270
250
Honokaa
Kalopa Native Forest SP and Recreation Area
Puukohola Heiau State Historic Site
19
Waimea
Ookala
Papaaloa
Puako
Weloka
190
Waikii
Akaka Falls SP
Honomu
Kekaha Kai SP
Puuanahulu
200
Mauna Kea SP
Hakalau Forest NWR
Papaikou
19
19
Wailoa River SP
Kaloko-Honokohau NHP
Kalaoa
Hilo
Kailua
4
200
Kahaluu
Honalo
Keaau
Mountain View
130
Captain Cook
Kepuka Puaulu
Lava Tree SP
Puuhonua o Honaunau NHP
Kealia
Volcano
Pahoa
Thurston Lava Tube
Kilauea Crater
Opihikao
Hawaii Volcanoes NP
Hawaii Volcanoes NP
Kalapana
11
Miloli'i
Manuka SP
Pahala
11
Naalehu
Punaluu
South Point

Travel west on Hwy. 56 past Princeville Shopping Center, where a roadside overlook peeks into **Hanalei NWR.** The refuge is closed to the public but home to 49 species of birds. Bring a spotting scope or binoculars to see Hawaiian stilts, ae`o, and other waterfowl from the road.

The highway ends a few miles west at the hauntingly beautiful Na Pali Coast— sheer green cliffs washed by a stream of endless combers.

Retrace the outbound route from Lihue back to Wailua and **Wailua River Valley.** Common moorhens, laughing thrushes, and Japanese bush warblers call this meandering river home.

Check current trail conditions, stay on trails to keep from getting lost, and return well before dark. Carry ample drinking water, food, rain gear, and a first-aid kit. Wear appropriate footwear. Sunscreen and mosquito repellent are recommended. Avoid areas with ground-nesting wasps. Visitors with open wounds should avoid entering streams and ponds; harmful bacteria such as *Leptospirosis* are present.

Frigatebirds are often found on Kilauea Point NWR on Kauai.

Drive south on Hwy. 56 through Lihue to Hwy. 50, around Kauai's south end, and up its west coast, turning onto Hwy. 550 at Waimea.

Nestled in the Na Pali—seen earlier from the island's east side —**Koke`e SP** is a prime place to find rain forest birds. During the ascent to the park on Hwy. 550, take a peek within **Waimea Canyon SP**, where it's possible to sight white-tailed tropicbirds. In Koke`e plan a stop at **Alaka`i Swamp** trailhead off Mohihi Rd., within the extinct throat of Kauai's tallest volcano, just beyond Alaka`i Shelter picnic area. From the parking lot follow the trail 3.5 miles (5.6 km) on an old military road and board-walk—stay on the trail to protect

the many fragile plants that live here—and arrive at Kilohana Lookout. The rain forest here receives 460 inches (1,168 cm) of rain annually. The reward for this slosh is the chance to see many rain forest birds plus possible glimpses of puaiohi and i`iwi and kaua`i creepers. `Elepaio, `amakihi, `anianiau, `apapane, and `akepa are often seen here.

Dept. of Land and Natural Resources: Div. of State Parks
P.O. Box 621
Honolulu, HI 96809
(808) 587-0400
www.hawaii.gov/dlnr/dsp/kauai.html

❷ Island of Oahu

Home of Honolulu and most heavily impacted by humans, Oahu abounds with natural places for bird-watching.

Drive the Pali Hwy. across Oahu's mountains to **Nuuanu Pali State Wayside.** Strong winds frequently carry seabirds across the island here. Continue over the Pali to the **Hoomaluhia Botanical Garden,** good for seeing perching birds.

Makapu`u Point, the island's easternmost promontory and a prime place to view seabirds, is accessible by trail from Hwy. 72.

James Campbell NWR, tucked in a valley near Waialua in the north, hosts guided public

tours from fall to spring; the refuge closes the rest of the year to protect nesting Hawaiian stilts. Many far-ranging migratory species dwell in the refuge while it is open. Call for reservations. Hawaii Audubon Society guides refuge field trips in fall.

O`ahu NWR Complex
66-590 Kam Hwy., Rm. 2C
Haleiwa, HI 96712
(808) 637-6330
www.fws.gov

❸ Island of Maui

Kealia Pond NWR, found on the south shore of Maui's isthmus, is tops for wetland birds— and don't miss seeing whales in the nearby offshore waters. These marshes preserve the last Hawaiian Island wetlands. Over 30 species of shorebirds and waterfowl frequent the lagoon, including Hawaiian stilts and Pacific golden plovers. A similar habitat lies a few miles north on the opposite side of the isthmus at **Kanaha Pond.**

Maui NWR
P.O. Box 1042
Kihei, HI 96753
(808) 875-1582
www.fws.gov

To find tropical forest birds, take a drive up Haleakala Hwy. to **Hosmer Grove,** 0.5 mile (0.8 km) from the gate to **Haleakala NP.** Admission fees, open daily.

Hosmer Grove is open to the public, and park staff also guides twice-weekly hikes (reservations) to The Nature Conservancy's **Waikamoi Preserve,** otherwise closed to the public. It's common to see `i`iwi, `apapane, `amakihi, and Maui creepers, and even rare `akohekohe and Maui parrotbills in the preserve.

Haleakala NP
P.O. Box 369
Makawao, HI 96768
(808) 572-4400
www.nps.gov/hale/

❹ Island of Hawaii

Pu`uhonua o Honaunau NHP, south of Kailua-Kona on Hwy. 11, holds attractions ranging from pelagic birds to historical sites. Turn on Hwy. 160 toward the sea at Honaunau Post Office. The road leads to the park. Admission fees, open daily.

Pu`uhonua means refuge, and priests here absolved those who broke the ancient island kapu laws. A park handout describes the area's many local birds and plants.

Pu`uhonua o Honaunau NHP
P.O. Box 129
Honaunau, HI 96726
(808) 328-2288
www.nps.gov/puho/

Upolu Point, on the northernmost point of the Big Island, and **South Point,** directly south,

Hakalau Forest NWR, a wild-forest preserve high on Mauna Kea, is the best place to see rare Hawaiian native birds.

are other good places to view seabirds. Accessing South Point can be a challenge because of rough lava fields that make the trail difficult.

The adventurous can access a remote and primitive Malulu tract of **Hakalau Forest NWR** from Hilo by four-wheel-drive vehicle, traveling west on Hwy. 200 to Mauna Kea Observatory Rd. Turn right and drive up to Keanakolu Rd., turning right again. Malulu tract is the only section of the refuge open to visitors, and only on weekends; make reservations a week in advance

to obtain a key to enter. Despite the obstacles, it is the best place on the Big Island to see eight endangered native birds, including the very rare `akias pola`aus, akepas, and crested honeycreepers.

Big Island NWR Complex
32 Kino`ole St., Ste. 101
Hilo, HI 96720
(808) 933-6915
www.fws.gov

Before visiting **Hawaii Volcanoes NP,** make a stop at the visitors center for a map showing **Kilauea Crater, Thurston Lava Tube,** and **Kepuka Puaulu.** Look for common Hawaiian forest birds, such as hawks and white-tailed tropicbirds, even occasional appearances by nene geese.

Timing Is Everything

Late winter and spring are best for viewing rain forest birds: Hawaiian owl, 'i'iwi, amakihi, palila, 'apapane, elepaio, and anianiau. If these names seem unfamiliar, it's all the more reason to go bird-watching in the Hawaiian Islands.

Most seabirds visit from March through September. They include great frigatebirds, white-tailed and red-tailed tropicbirds, white terns, wedge-tailed shearwaters, and red-footed boobies.

Wetland birds such as Hawaiian stilts, common moorhens, and black-crowned night-herons are found year-round.

Migrating winter visitors include Pacific golden plovers, sanderlings, wandering tattlers, and ruddy turnstones.

Consult **www.hawaiiaudubon.com,** the Hawaii Audubon Society website, for rare bird sightings and guided tours.

Anchorage and the Kenai Peninsula

Minutes from Alaska's largest city is wilderness worthy of both interest and respect. Situated on Cook Inlet between the Gulf of Alaska and the vast Alaskan interior, the region abounds with migratory birds of every species, size, color, and habitat.

As spring breaks over most of North America—indeed, even as winter clamps down hard in distant Patagonia—the migratory birds become increasingly restless and begin their long travels north. Their shared destination: long daylight-filled hours in forests, marshes, meadows, and shorelines of Alaska and the Canadian arctic. From May until the snows begin to fall in late September, slowly descending in a white line down the Chugach Mountains that tower in majesty above Anchorage, America's 49th state is a birding paradise. Start a bird-watching tour north of town in the Matanuska Valley—a fertile plain with meandering rivers—and peruse the south-central region on a tour that ends in Resurrection Bay.

Eagle River Nature Center may seem miles from civilization, but it's just an hour's drive from Anchorage's city limits. The center has numerous bird-watching facilities and trails.

Discover arctic terns in Kenai NWR between Portage and Soldatna.

❶ Palmer

Begin the birding tour driving north 38 miles (61 km) from Anchorage on the Glenn Hwy. (Hwy. 1), to the Parks Hwy. (Hwy. 3), and on to the town of Wasilla. In Wasilla follow Goose Bay Rd. 2.6 miles (4.2 km) southwest to Hayfield Rd., turn left and drive to West Edlund Rd., turn left again and follow that road until it turns into East Fairfield Loop Rd., then make a final left. Paths lead south from this road to Weinie, Dinkel, and Reedy lakes and to fields and bogs along Palmer Slough, all part of the **Palmer Hay Flats State Game Refuge,** a 28,000-acre (11,331-h) area that comprises the Knik and Matanuska rivers' brackish intertidal delta.

Many tens of thousands of dabbling ducks, at least three species of geese, and both tundra and trumpeter swans fly

Eagle River Nature Center is located in a fjordlike cleft cloaked by the boreal forest of the Chugach Mountains just north of Anchorage. Visit in the evening to hear and see owls or in the morning to watch river birds.

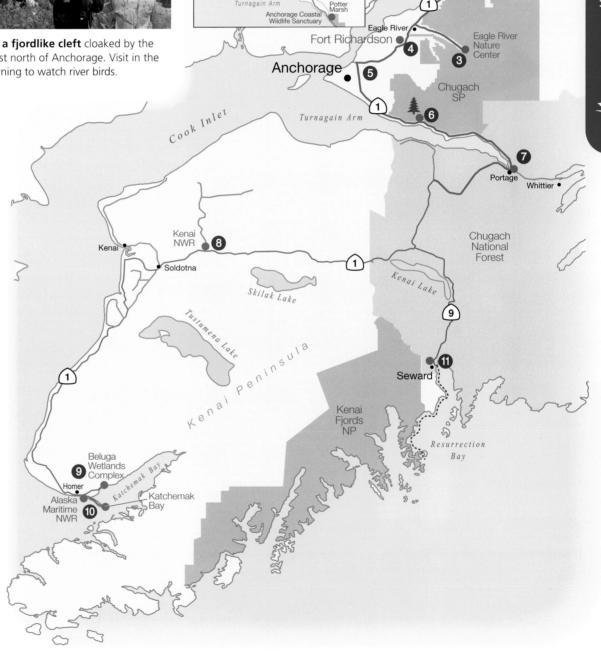

through these Palmer hay fields, arriving in late April and either remaining all summer or continuing north to the state's interior. Nesting birds are seen in the margins between marsh and scrub brush. Look for lesser Canada, greater white-fronted, and snow geese, plus plentiful pintail, mallard, green-winged teal, wigeon, canvasback, and common goldeneye ducks.

In fall the cycle repeats as the northern travelers return to Palmer's hay flats before flying across the Gulf of Alaska in their southern migration.

Waterfowl congregate at the slough in marshes and bogs created by land subsidence after the great 1964 earthquake or in the hay flats that gave their name to the refuge.

If time permits, also look for birds in the riparian habitats at Wasilla and Cottonwood creeks and Rabbit Slough. The trick on weekends is finding the birds among the numerous coho and sockeye salmon fishermen who frequent these popular waters.

Comical and delightful, horned puffins live together, condo style, in rocky crevices

ADF&G/Wildlife Conservation
1800 Glenn Hwy., Ste. 4
Palmer, AK 99645
(907) 746-6300
**www.wildlife.alaska.gov/index
.cfm?adfg=refuge.palmer_hf**

❷ Knik River

Depending on the season, more than 200 species of birds frequent the gravel bars, shorelines, and clouded waters of the Knik River. Fine rock, ground to powder by glaciers, makes the river appear milky in color.

To reach a good viewing area, retrace the outbound route on the Parks and Glenn highways, cross over the Knik River, and take the South Old Glenn Hwy. exit, traveling 3.8 miles (6.1 km) east to a slough of the Knik River. An unpaved road leads west along the north edge of the slough. Observe perching birds in the brush along its shoreline, waterfowl and wading birds on the river's margins, and raptors in summer. It's also a likely place to see gulls, American pipits, northern wheatears, and gray-crowned rosy finches.

❸ Eagle River Nature Center

The next stop on the route is to the south past **Mirror Lake State Wayside**—check the marsh along its north end for wading birds—near the town of Eagle River. Exit on North Eagle River Access Rd. and follow Eagle River Rd. to its end, going 12 miles (19 km) through town and into the heart of **Chugach SP**'s boreal forest. (Eagle River Rd.'s name becomes Cumulus Rd. about 2 miles [3.2 km] before it reaches **Eagle River Nature Center.**)

This environmental center on the famous Iditarod Trail has a network of hiking and walking paths through its extensive grounds. Concentrate on those that lead to the swampy tributaries and main channel of the Eagle River. Watch the trees and listen intently as dusk nears for sightings of owls, including great horned, northern hawk, boreal, and northern saw-whet owls; their calls echo in ghostly whispers through the trees. Look at water's edge for wading birds and waterfowl, then scan the willows to see songbirds of every description.

Eagle River Nature Center
32750 Eagle River Rd.
Eagle River, AK 99577
(907) 694-2108
www.ernc.org

❹ Fort Richardson

Returning to Eagle River and Hwy. 1, turn south toward Anchorage. The route passes 62,100-acre (24,767-h) **Fort Richardson** and 13,095-acre

(5,299-h) **Elmendorf AFB.** Both bases have excellent birding habitats, but access is sometimes limited for security reasons. Turnouts and waysides adjacent to these facilities may reveal such birds as bald eagles, ring-necked ducks, Bohemian waxwings, gadwalls, and black-headed and three-toed woodpeckers.

Fort Richardson
U.S. Army Alaska Public Affairs
Attn: APVR-RPO
724 Postal Service Loop #5900
Fort Richardson, AK 99505
(907) 384-2019
www.usarak.army.mil/pao/

❺ Anchorage

The urban core of Alaska's largest city remains remarkable for its natural setting and birdlife. Creeks flowing from the Chugach Mountains create nearly continuous greenbelt habitats that attract more than 200 species of resident and migratory birds within view of the city's high-rise offices.

Start a city bird-watching tour at Goose and Hillstrand lakes in **Anchor Park,** on E. Northern Lights Blvd. The two lakes are connected by a paved bike trail. Goose Lake is a great spot to view nesting loons, mew and Bonaparte's gulls, various geese and ducks, and numerous songbirds.

Next, visit **University Lake Park,** adjacent to the University of Alaska at Anchorage, another facility along Chester Creek. Watch nesting red-necked grebes and songbirds while walking the looping lake trail.

Complete a visit to Anchorage's northeast section at **Campbell Creek Science Center** off E. 68th Ave., in Far North Bicentennial Park. Here, closer to the foothills of the Chugach Range, a slight change in elevation brings the sight of boreal songbirds. In late spring migratory birds pass through the center in great numbers, peaking in May.

For entirely different habitats and topographies, move northwest to **Westchester Lagoon,** where Minnesota Dr. becomes W. 15th Ave. At this spot on Cook Inlet, tidal currents rage past and exceptionally high tides—29 feet (8.8 m) or more—force birds near the trail; bring binoculars or spotting scopes at other points in the tidal cycle. Look for yellowlegs, dowitchers, plovers, western and semipalmated sandpipers, surfbirds, and godwits, as well as grebes and loons on the lagoon proper.

Off Raspberry Rd. near Anchorage International Airport lies **Kincaid Park,** a great birding hot spot. The long days of summer are a good time to find spruce grouse, three-toed woodpeckers, white-winged crossbills, northern shrikes, and boreal chickadees, among other uncommon sights. In late May most birds are in breeding plumage and calling.

Finish the sampling of Anchorage's many birding delights by traveling south on Hwy. 1, the Seward Hwy., to the edge of town and **Potter Marsh,** site of the **Anchorage Coastal Wildlife Sanctuary.**

The tidal flats, marshes, and alder-bog forests of Turnagain Arm hold the greatest diversity of birds found in Anchorage. Peak concentrations of migrants occur in late April to mid-May, then repeat in July and August as birds congregate before traveling south. Besides geese and many duck species, look for arctic terns, alder flycatchers, common snipe, scaup, tree swallows, northern phalaropes, and yellowlegs.

Anchorage Convention & Visitors Bureau
524 W. Fourth Ave.
Anchorage, AK 99501
(907) 276-4118
www.anchorage.net

❻ Chugach NF and SP

Nowhere else on the North American continent but the Bay of Fundy does the sea wage such a savage struggle with the shore as in Cook Inlet's Turnagain Arm. Tidal bores—standing waves—as tall as 12 feet (366 cm) regularly roil the inlet's waters as the tides change, all under the eye of many thousands of shorebirds and waterfowl. Exposed mudflats

are covered in minutes at a speed that astonishes visitors to this natural wonder, forcing the birds toward the bed of the Alaska Railroad near the ski resort village of Girdwood.

On the other side of the railroad and Hwy. 1, the mountain range to the east and south of Girdwood is part of the vast **Chugach NF,** while to the northwest is **Chugach SP,** the third-largest state park in America.

Three general zones for birdwatching are worth exploring at every opportunity: coast, birch/spruce forest, and alpine. In this far north region, alpine conditions and tree line are just 1,000 feet (305 m) from sea level.

In the coastal zone look for migratory waterfowl, wading birds, and gulls. The forest zone is a breeding ground in summer for waterbirds and perching birds, both the migrants and the residents. The alpine meadows host

Puffins are best seen from boats.

Remote Alaska Maritime NWR, at the tip of the Aleutian Peninsula, has its headquarters in Homer on Katchemak Bay. Interpretive staff at the facility provide information about its unique maritime habitat, birds, and wildlife.

ptarmigan, ravens, raptors, harriers, magpies, eagles, and many songbirds. Take advantage of the many turnouts, side roads, and trails that occur along the Seward Hwy. to see a truly amazing variety of birds. The best time to visit is from late April until September. Remember that this region of Alaska isn't a zoological park. Throughout the entire area, even in the city, wild animals are common. Give all moose, caribou, bears, and foxes respect by keeping safely away from them and never leaving food in cars.

AK DNR/Parks & Recreation
550 W. 7th Ave., Ste. 1260
Anchorage, AK 99501
(907) 269-8400
www.dnr.state.ak.us/parks/ units/chugach/index.htm

❼ Portage and Whittier

The southeast tip of Turnagain Arm is the village of **Portage,** situated on a glacial moraine left by the retreating Portage glacier and site of the Begich, Boggs Visitor Center of Chugach NF, open daily except major holi-

days. Located 50 miles (80 km) southeast of Anchorage, the visitors center faces Portage Lake, a good birding spot with outlet streams and trails worth walking for the chance to see boreal forest birds. Large concentrations of bald eagles and osprey fish the lake and inlet, nesting in trees nearby. Look for arctic and yellow warblers, juncos, black-billed magpies, thrushes, and even the rufous hummingbirds. In the fall huge flocks of geese, cranes, and ducks funnel through the narrow pass as they fly to the Gulf of Alaska.

Located 8 miles (12.9 km) east of Portage down a gravel road is the village of **Whittier,** an Alaska Marine Ferry port; take a brief side trip to gaze at the many seabirds on its rugged fjord. The route continues west on Hwy. 1 around the inlet's end.

Chugach NF
301 C St.
Anchorage, AK 99503
(907) 743-9500
www.fs.fed.us/r10/chugach/

❽ Kenai NWR

En route to the next stop, the road climbs from Cook Inlet through twisting mountain valleys, past rugged, glacially carved terrain. Pause along the way to see boreal and alpine birds, such as ptarmigan. These well-camouflaged grouse are

easiest to view in early spring while they still have their white winter plumage.

Where Hwy. 1 parts with Hwy. 9, it becomes the Sterling Hwy. Continue on Hwy. 1 to the shores of **Kenai Lake,** less than 1,000 feet (305 m) above sea level, with an alpine feel. It is one of the best spots in the region to see arctic terns feeding.

The route enters **Kenai NWR** at milepost 55. At milepost 60 a visitors center is open from Memorial to Labor Day (the main headquarters are in Soldotna). This nearly 2-million-acre (809,000-h) refuge has representative habitats that make it an Alaska in miniature. It also has dense vegetation, so choose viewing spots wisely: Sure bets are Seven Lakes Trail at Kelly Lake for songbirds, the Kenai River between Kenai and Skilak lakes for bald eagles and trumpeter swans, and the Kenai River flats for nesting sandhill cranes and snow geese.

To experience more of the refuge, drive Swanson River Rd. north or charter a drift boat to see the river's birds, including many forest-nesting shorebirds such as common snipe, killdeer, long-billed dowitchers, and greater and lesser yellowlegs.

Kenai NWR
P.O. Box 2139
Soldotna, AK 99669
(907) 262-7021
http://kenai.fws.gov/

❾ Soldotna and Kenai to Homer

West of the refuge are the Kenai river towns of **Soldotna** and **Kenai,** which merit a brief side trip on Kenai Spur Hwy. Follow the river to its mouth on Cook Inlet, where it's possible to see five volcanoes—four active and one dormant—from Kenai's beaches. The river's mouth is the spot to see seabirds, shorebirds, and migrants feeding on the salmon runs heading upriver.

Drive south on Bridge Access Rd., cross the Kenai River, and turn right at Kalifornsky Beach Rd. to parallel the inlet a short distance, then join the Sterling Hwy. for an 80-mile (129-km) drive to **Homer.** There's seashore to view along the way; the best places for birding are the many beach side roads and waysides.

Homer is recognized worldwide for its bald-eagle population and birding along its prominent sand spit. Eagles by the hundreds crowd the spit, and close-up photo opportunities abound.

Homer's bird visitors include some otherwise-rare species such as fork-tailed storm-petrel, common eider, whimbrels, various murrelets, and diving and dabbling ducks. It's common to see Asiatic accidentals here; lost birds follow the Aleutian Island chain to the Alaskan Peninsula and cross the strait to Homer.

Just north of the spot where the spit joints the shore, at the town's airport, lies a 280-acre (113-h) Critical Habitat Area, **Beluga Wetlands Complex.** More than 200 species have been recorded at this site from April to June, including the rare Aleutian tern and many exciting raptors. Watch the action from the viewing platform, across the street from the airport passenger terminal.

While in Homer, also visit the headquarters of **Alaska Maritime NWR,** a valuable resource for knowledge about the 40-million-plus avian residents of Alaska's southwest peninsula and islands.

Alaska Maritime NWR
5 Sterling Hwy., Ste. 1 MS 505
Homer, AK 99603
(907) 235-6546
alaskamaritime.fws.gov

❿ Katchemak Bay

Maritime birds are best viewed from Homer's spit—or by chartering kayaks or taking birding tours from its small boat harbor; many operators service the area. **Katchemak Bay** is the west gateway to **Kenai Fjords NP** and a terminal for the Alaska Marine Ferry System serving Kodiak, the Aleutian Islands, and southeast Alaska.

Seabirds, shorebirds, and bald eagles share the bay's many jutting rocks and islets from spring to summer, making it a great spot to see tufted and horned puffins, pigeon guillemots, black-legged kittiwakes, murres, and other pelagic birds.

Homer Chamber of Commerce
201 Sterling Hwy.
Homer, AK 99603
(907) 235-7740
www.homeralaska.org

⓫ Seward and Kenai Fjords NP

No birding visit to the Kenai Peninsula would be complete without backtracking to Hwy. 9 and driving 171 miles (275 km) to Seward. En route the road passes Upper Trail Lake and both ends of Kenai Lake, then descends to the fjordlike coastal plain at Resurrection Bay.

Seabirds and nesting shorebirds abound in the alder woods at the bay's north end, but the real attraction is **Kenai Fjords NP.** Charter tours take full-day trips to the scenic and heavily populated birding area in Aliaik Bay, departing from Seward's docks. Besides birdlife, these tours typically show porpoises, great and lesser whales, sea otters, seals, and sea lions. Look for the common birds of Alaska's Gulf: bald eagles, black- and red-legged kittiwakes, common and thick-billed murres, horned and tufted puffins, gulls, guillemots, and storm-petrels.

Seward Chamber of Commerce
2001 Seward Hwy.
Seward, AK
(907) 224-8051
www.sewardak.org

Parakeet auklets roost on the cliffs and rocks of Kenai Fjords NP, a remote park accessible by charter boats from Homer and Seward.

Vancouver and Vicinity

Picturesque and nestled on the temperate shores of the Strait of Georgia, Vancouver and its surroundings are a playground for waterfowl, wading birds, and marine species. It is also a summer nesting and feeding area for river and forest birds of all types.

An oceanside city carved out of tractless forests and mountains, Vancouver's the mainland destination of birders from across the breadth of Canada and host to visitors from the United States. The rich, protected waters of the Strait of Georgia teem with fish, invertebrates, crustaceans—even magnificent marine mammals. And it's an approachable shoreline, accessible from city streets and parks as well as shoreline-hugging highways. Nearby sites are fruitful spots for birdlife, from Pemberton Lake and Whistler in the north to the marine ferry at Nanaimo on Vancouver Island. Plan to spend extra time in this sophisticated, welcoming city, a location where birds are found at every vista point.

Great blue herons are motionless hunters of the shore.

Stanley Park, in North Vancouver, has bird-friendly shores with a backdrop of high-rise office buildings. Look for waders and waterfowl here on day outings.

❶ Pemberton

Begin the birding tour by car, driving north 100 miles (160 km) on Hwy. 99 (Sea-to-Sky Hwy.), along scenic Howe Sound and up a fjordlike valley toward Pemberton, passing Squamish and Whistler, and skirting the northern edge of **Garibaldi**

Provincial Park. On the right side of the road and southern outskirts of Pemberton, find **One-Mile Lake,** a city park. Trumpeter swans, Canada geese, great blue heron, common loon, and turkey vulture are likely in summer on this lakeshore, along with numerous ducks, grebes, and mergansers. Paths lead to a boardwalk over the wetlands along the lake's north side, popular for birding.

Note the prominent osprey nest south of the park boundary —adult birds feed their young on fish from the lake. Watch the woods for plentiful songbirds and hummingbirds that forage the slopes of towering Mount Currie, backdrop to this alpine village. If time permits, the town's hotels, inns, and B&Bs are great base camps for birding the nearby, much larger **Lillooet Lake** and valley region south of Pemberton.

Village of Pemberton
P.O. Box 100
Pemberton, BC Canada V0N 2L0
(604) 894-6135
www.pemberton.ca

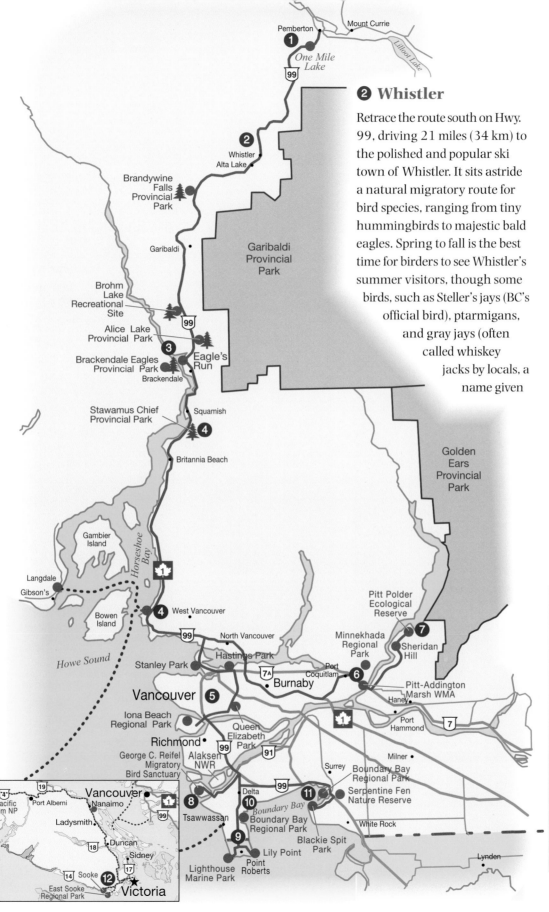

② Whistler

Retrace the route south on Hwy. 99, driving 21 miles (34 km) to the polished and popular ski town of Whistler. It sits astride a natural migratory route for bird species, ranging from tiny hummingbirds to majestic bald eagles. Spring to fall is the best time for birders to see Whistler's summer visitors, though some birds, such as Steller's jays (BC's official bird), ptarmigans, and gray jays (often called whiskey jacks by locals, a name given by lumberman), are found year-round—they are curious birds and may return a close look.

The Squamish, Mamquam, and Cheakamus rivers draw birders seeking bald eagles. The eagle concentrations peak from November to March when birds winter here, but they fish these waters and nearby Howe Sound all summer. Be sure to visit Lost Lake Park across Fitzsimmons Creek, with its wetland viewing platform. A looping trail connects to Green Lake and downtown, making for outstanding cross-country birding.

Tourism Whistler
4010 Whistler Way
Whistler, BC Canada V0N 1B4
(888) 869-2777
www.tourismwhistler.com

Whistler's and Brackendale's main attraction is the bald eagle. They winter on nearby lakes and rivers.

Pitt Polder Ecological Reserve is a breathtaking glimpse into a tidal marsh and its varied birds. Visitors hope to be lucky enough to catch the sight of an osprey diving head- and talons-first into the water, then rising majestically and flying to its nest to feed and care for its young (see page 36). The site features covered observation platforms and towers, first-class accommodations for a day of birding.

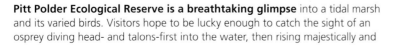

❸ Brackendale Eagles Provincial Park

Resume the tour by traveling south on Hwy. 99, passing first **Brohm Lake** and then **Stump and Alice lakes**—all excellent birding sites. About 19 miles (30 km) south the valley widens and the Squamish River becomes braided near its namesake town and the head of Howe Sound. To the west, mostly across the Squamish River, is Brackendale Eagles Provincial Park. Bald eagles visit Brackendale in large numbers, drawn by heavy runs of chum salmon each fall and winter. It has long been considered among the very best places worldwide to observe these striking birds. The eagles are most numerous from November through February, though some nesting pairs are seen during the summer in the forests near the river where they fish.

Exit Hwy. 99 at Mamquam Rd. and drive northward to Government Rd., leading to **Eagle Run,** a viewing area located outside the park. Access to park lands is difficult and frequently restricted, so this dike is the best bird-watching spot. An interpretive sign notes many features of the bald eagles found nearby.

While wintering eagles are the main attraction, nearly 150 other species of birds frequent the Squamish River valley. Look for songbirds and others in the brushy river margins.

A number of private tour operators in Squamish offer float trips and rafting trips on the Mamquam, Cheakamus, and Squamish rivers to see the eagles. In winter dress appropriately in waterproof layered clothing for protection from the cold and rain.

Tourism British Columbia
510 Burrard St., 12th Fl.
Vancouver, BC V6C 3A8
(800) 435-5622
www.hellobc.com

❹ Howe Sound

Just south of Squamish on Hwy. 99, the river meets the sea at Howe Sound, a natural inlet of the Strait of Georgia. Howe is a good place to pull into a shoreline turnout or beach access and begin to sample the vast array of seagoing and shorebirds of British Columbia.

Bounding Sea-to-Sky Hwy. and the sound on the south near its head is **Stawamus Chief Provincial Park.** The park is named—together with its looming 2,300-foot (700-m) granite monolith overlooking the inlet—for a nearby native village and is a favorite destination for rock climbers and hikers seeking lofty sea views. From March to July it's also a critical nesting site for peregrine falcons. These majestic birds are frequently seen fishing the sound in breathtaking high-speed

dives followed by a splash, grasp of the fish, and a powerful climb to a nearby treetop roost to dine (they rarely miss). Closures of trails protect the nesting birds from intrusion, so the best views are found at Howe Sound.

Continue south along the shore of Horseshoe Bay on Hwy. 99 en route to the car ferry terminal, passing Petgill Lake and three provincial parks on Howe Sound: **Murrin, Cove,** and **Cypress.** Reservations are necessary (www.bcferries.com) for the frequently departing round-trip passages across the bay to the town of Langdale or to the bay islands of Bowen, Keats, or Gambier. A ferry ride is a fun diversion that brings close contact with the many species of seabirds and waterfowl found in Horseshoe Bay. Overnight stays on the islands are worthwhile, affording visitors many more opportunities to see the seabirds and wading birds amid rugged and scenic coast and its adjacent primeval conifer forests.

After returning to the mainland on the ferry, travel south on Hwy. 99. Just around the corner are the outskirts of the bustling and modern city of Vancouver.

Tourism British Columbia
510 Burrard St., 12th Fl.
Vancouver, BC V6C 3A8
(800) 435-5622
www.hellobc.com

❺ Vancouver

The compact metropolitan area of Vancouver is an embarrassment of riches when it comes to birding. Nearly every street ends in a vista, and parks abound. Take several days to explore this first-class Canadian city's waterfront and parks.

Make **Stanley Park** a first stop in West Vancouver, found just 9 miles (15 km) southeast of the prior stop. Take the Taylor Way exit from Hwy. 1, turning south and following Taylor to Marine Dr. (Hwy. 1A). Turn right on Marine, then right on Bridge St. Stanley Park is the first exit after the Coal Harbour bridge. The park is a summer breeding ground for ducks, geese, swans, and other birds.

A peregrine falcon perches on a snag overlooking Pitt Lake at Pitt Polder Ecological Reserve, east of metropolitan Vancouver.

Visit the shoreline following a paved 6-mile (10-km) seawall walk, and see Beaver Lake and Lost Lagoon, nesting hot spots for waterfowl.

Stanley Park is the site of **Blue Heronry,** the oldest bird sanctuary in this region. The tall, stately birds can be seen in great numbers hunting along the shore, in marshes, and, at twilight, roosting in the trees where they build their nests. From mid-March to July more than 110 heron nests may comprise this high-rise condominium complex.

Another site worth a birding visit is **Hastings Park,** found in northeast Vancouver above and adjacent to Bedwell Bay just off East Hastings St. Its hidden secret is a spacious sanctuary pond replete with visiting waterfowl and a marshy margin filled with songbirds, all easily watched from encircling paths that twine through the park.

Reifel Migratory Bird Sanctuary has sandhill cranes worthy of respect.

BEWARE OF SANDHILL CRANES. THEY ARE VERY AGGRESSIVE. BEWARE

Southward, in the heart of Vancouver and situated atop the city's highest point on Cambie St. south of downtown, **Queen Elizabeth Park** is a heavily visited but meticulously groomed haven for bird-watching set on 130 acres (52 h) of transformed stone quarry. In April and May the park is among the very best of spots in Vancouver to see migrant passerines, especially in early mornings and in late afternoons. Visit the park on overcast days following stormy periods of rain for the greatest chance to observe these birds in the foliage.

Outdoor birding is just one possible pursuit at Queen Elizabeth Park. For a break, the spacious dome of Blodel Floral Conservatory is the right place to closely watch exotic and native birds (open 9 A.M. to 8 P.M. weekdays, 10 A.M. to 9 P.M. weekends, modest fee). Over 100 colorful bird species fly freely within the structure's varied climate-controlled habitats, ranging from desert to tropical rain forest.

Vancouver Park Board
2099 Beach Ave.
Vancouver, BC Canada V6G 1Z4
(604) 257-8400
www.city.vancouver.bc.ca/ parks/index.htm

While local birding organizations list more than 40 sites in Vancouver to watch birds, perhaps none captures the heart of wilderness lurking behind the sophisticated urban heart of this Pacific maritime city quite like **Iona Beach Regional Park,** nestled on Sea Island between a sandy peninsula of Vancouver International Airport, the Fraser River, and the Strait of Georgia. More than 300 species of birds feed and rest at Iona throughout the year, and watching eagles, falcons, waterfowl, seabirds, and waders at sunset is a majestic experience. The park gates close at sunset, but feel free to leave cars outside the park, walk in, and watch the birds fly home to roost in the island's marshes as dusk settles and stars fill the inky sky. Iona is close to the lights of the city, but if it's spring or fall and the moon is full, there's a good chance of seeing Vs of geese and ducks fly across its face.

Greater Vancouver Regional District
4330 Kingsway St.,
Burnaby, BC Canada V5H 4G8
604-432-6200
www.gvrd.bc.ca/parks/ IonaBeach.htm

Reifel Migratory Bird Sanctuary's easy-access observation deck is a comfortable, sheltered place to relax and watch waterfowl as they go about their daily routine of foraging for food and caring for their young nestlings without disturbing the resident and visiting birds.

➏ Minnekhada Regional Park

Crossing Vancouver east to Coquitlam on Hwy. 7, turn north onto Coast Meridian Rd. After 2.2 miles (3.5 km) turn right again onto Victoria Dr., which becomes Quarry Rd., and leads to the main parking lot of **Minnekhada Regional Park,** on the road's right side.

The onset of summer brings many migratory passerine birds to the deciduous woods in this hemlock-studded forest, including a variety of thrushes, western tanagers, flycatchers, and warblers. Both ruffed and blue grouse are found in the forest-meadow margins.

Follow the marsh-encircling trails from Quarry Rd. or retrace the path by car on Quarry Rd. back to Gilley's Trail, turn left, and left again onto Oliver Rd., leading to Minnekhada Lodge and the short Fern Trail to the lookout over **Pitt-Addington Marsh WMA.**

In springtime this prolific wetland adjoining the diked Pitt River hosts as many as 50 bird species, including green heron, sandhill cranes, raptors, gulls, American bittern, and numerous other waterfowl. The sandhill cranes nest in grassy hummocks found in the marsh, standing vigil over their clutches of one to three eggs. During nesting season the preserve is closed. Observe cranes from the lookout and avoid coming near their nests; they are fiercely protective of their eggs and young. Many bears also frequent the trails of this park, so remain aware of the surroundings at all times, especially in autumn. Access to the marsh is subject to closures during sandhill nesting season, April to June.

Greater Vancouver Regional District
4330 Kingsway St.
Burnaby, BC Canada V5H 4G8
(604) 432-6200
www.gvrd.bc.ca/parks/ minnekhada.htm/

➐ Pitt Polder Ecological Reserve

Pitt Polder is only a short distance from Minnekhada, but getting to it means finding bridges over the Alouette and Pitt rivers. It's well worth the trip. Return to Coquitlam and Hwy. 7 and turn east. Shortly after the highway crosses the Pitt River, Dewdney Trunk Rd. splits left. Follow Dewdney 1.4 miles (2.3 km), turn left on Harris Rd., cross the Alouette River, and turn right on McNeill Rd. A final left turn at Rennie/ Neaves roads leads for 6 miles (10 km) to the remote dike trails that follow the tidal boundaries of the Pitt River and Katsie Marsh.

Keep an eye open once Rennie Rd. meets the Pitt River; its margins are a good spot for gray catbirds. Ospreys nest on the pilings in the Pitt River, while sandhill crane frequently hunt the open fields on both sides of Rennie Rd.

After viewing the margins of the Pitt River, walk the dike around Katsie Marsh or view birds such as American bittern, Virginia rail, and sora from one of several observation towers and platforms. There are swans to see in winter and, in harsher weather, snow buntings and common redpoll right on the dikes. This area is a haven for waterfowl, amphibians, and aquatic mammals, including beaver and muskrat.

A female wood duck and her young ducklings relax on a streamside log.

On the return south from Pitt, pass **Sheridan Hill,** a woodland that is a good spot to see rufous hummingbirds, flycatchers, vireos, warblers, and cedar waxwings.

BC Environment, Lower
Mainland Region
10470 152nd St.
Surrey, BC Canada V3R 0Y3
(604) 582-5200
http://wlapwww.gov.bc.ca/sry/

⑧ Reifel Migratory Bird Sanctuary

Across Vancouver and south of suburban Richmond, **George C. Reifel Migratory Bird Sanctuary** nestles in the delta islands of the Pitt River. From Hwy. 99S, look for Ladner, take Ladner Trunk Rd. to 47A St., turning into River Rd., and drive west 1.8 miles (2.9 km). Turn right, cross the Westham Island Bridge, and drive 3 miles (4.8 km) on Westham Island Rd. to the sanctuary gates and parking lot. The facility's dikes, marshes, and wetlands are heavily visited, and an admission fee is charged. The site adjoins the **Alaksen NWR,** once part of the Reifel farm, which is planted each autumn to cover and forage crops.

Reifel hosts 280 known species of resident and migratory birds, easily viewed from a two-story observation tower. The best times to visit are April to May and August to October, the peak migration season for waterfowl, shorebirds, sandhill cranes, passerines, and raptors. Beginning in November, visitors will be thrilled to see flocks of up to 20,000 snow geese as they rest during their journey south from Siberia and Alaska.

BC Waterfowl Society
5191 Robertson Rd.
Delta, BC Canada V4K 3N2
(604) 946-6980
www.reifelbirdsanctuary.com

⑨ Point Roberts

Returning to Hwy. 99, turn south, exit on Hwy. 17 to Tsawwassen, and drive south on 56th St. to reach Point Roberts, a cutoff enclave of the United States. South of the border post, the street continues as Tyee Dr. Follow it and turn right at APA Rd. to **Lighthouse Marine Park,** or turn left and drive east a short distance to **Lily Point**—park at the graveyard and follow a short path to the point.

Either spot is excellent for viewing seabirds. The best season is late autumn to spring, when gulls, common murres, rhinoceros auklets, and ancient murrelets mingle with myriad shorebirds until temperate spring weather arrives in late February and allows them to return to the open sea.

Lighthouse Point in winter is a good spot to look for rare species. Birds such as rock sandpipers, black turnstones, and pigeon guillemots have been seen along the shore at the park, especially in late fall and winter. The highlights of the park are an extensive boardwalk and a viewing platform, 30 feet (9 m) tall, with sweeping views of the Strait of Georgia. Scan the waters for migrating and resident whales and orcas, as well as the many rafts of waterfowl and flying shorebirds on the water.

Lighthouse Marine Park
811 Marine Dr.
Point Roberts, WA 98281
(360) 945-4911
www.co.whatcom.wa.us

⑩ Boundary Bay Regional Park

Northeast of Point Roberts is Boundary Bay, a south-facing inlet surrounded by sand dunes, salt marshes, shallow flats, and brackish lagoons—in other

Serpentine Fen has two observation towers to make viewing easy.

A great blue heron shares the waterways with cargo ships and other vessels near Vancouver's shoreline.

words, rich habitats for all manner of birds. The west side of the bay is the site of a regional park and wildlife reserve. To reach it, retrace the route north on Tyee Dr. across the international border and north on 56th St. At 12th Ave., turn right and make another right onto Boundary Bay Rd. Note and obey posted closing times for dusk visits, or park outside

the park and walk in. There is an admission fee.

Boundary Bay Regional Park hosts Canada's largest population of wintering raptors, and it is a rest stop in spring and fall for many thousands of migrating shore, pelagic, and songbirds, as well as numerous waterfowl. It has been designated an Important Bird Area (IBA) by Canadian Audubon Society.

Boardwalks and trails wend through the dikes that divide the wetlands from the shore, leading south along the edge of the wildlife refuge. The trail is 0.9 mile (1.5 km) long, with many excellent viewing stops. Birding Boundary Bay is best from September to late March, with migrant numbers peaking in early October. Work the inland reserve while moving south, then concentrate on the bay during the return to the starting point.

A second marked trail is due south of the park entry—and provides the best location for raptor viewing.

Boundary Bay Regional Park
Greater Vancouver Reg'l. Dist.
4330 Kingsway
Vancouver, BC V5H 4G8
(604) 432-6200
www.gvrd.bc.ca

⑪ Serpentine Fen and Blackie Spit Park

Across Boundary Bay from the prior stop are **Serpentine Fen Nature Reserve** and **Blackie Spit Park,** respectively a tidal estuary and its nearby sandy outlet. To reach Serpentine Fen, retrace the outbound path to rejoin Hwy. 99 and turn south —actually east at this spot— then turn off at White Rock, going east on Hwy. 99A, the King George Hwy. Park at the bridge over the Serpentine

River—near the wooden observation tower—or on nearby 44th Ave., a crossroad.

This is Serpentine Fen Nature Reserve (for those who are geologically inclined, fens are ranked midway between swamps and bogs), a prime birding site. Follow the looping trails around the fen's ponds, muddy river edges, and stands of trees to check for shorebirds, waterfowl, passerines, and raptors, or climb the tower—there's another a short distance to the north—to look down on the reserve. Canals and ditches in the reserve are also good locations to see hunting herons and bitterns.

After viewing the estuarine fen, drive south on King George Hwy. to Crescent Rd., turn right and continue for 3.1 miles (5 km) into the town of Surrey, bear right on Sullivan St., turn right on McBride Ave., and follow it to

Vancouver lies in clear sight from this viewing deck, with interpretive signs identifying common birds.

Blackie Spit Park. This shoreline park has many trails as well as other visitor facilities and is regarded among the most scenic in the Surrey area.

Time visits to Blackie Spit to coincide with high tide. The incoming water pushes waterfowl and shorebirds from nearby Mud Bay into the shoreline, concentrating their numbers. Various species of tern frequent these beaches in summer, such as Caspian and common. In late summer shorebird populations increase, while migrating visitors begin appearing in September. A number of rare sightings have occurred in the park, including Lapland longspur. Also walk the wooded dike bordering the south side of Farm Slough to look for perching bird and songbird species.

These birding hot spots on Boundary Bay and the Strait of Georgia are the final highlights for Vancouver and vicinity, but many other nature areas, parks, and preserves beckon. Check with local birding organizations to identify further spots worth visiting in coastal British Columbia's magnificent setting.

Tourism British Columbia
510 Burrard St., 12th Fl.
Vancouver, BC V6C 3A8
(800) 435-5622
www.hellobc.com

A Vancouver western seagull has a starfish for its lunchtime snack.

Ospreys **construct their nests** high atop prominent trees or posts and **always near water**

⑫ Vancouver Island

The nearby town of Tsawwassen—a name meaning "looking toward the sea" in coastal Salish—is another terminal of the British Columbia Ferry System and a gateway to the Strait of Georgia's Gulf Islands. If time permits, this offshore archipelago's queen, Vancouver Island, is worth an entire birding trip of its own.

Start the trip by close observation while traveling on the car ferry between Tsawwassen and Swartz Bay: There are cormorants, bald eagles, numerous gulls, loons, and various fishing raptors to see. Once at the ferry docks, drive south to the island's principal city, Victoria.

• Victoria

Over 240 different species of birds have been noted in Victoria, and the nearby habitats and surrounding areas add another 140. It's common for birders to add 100 or more to their life lists while visiting Vancouver Island. The best months to come are during spring and fall migrations, though the island is bird-rich all year round thanks to its maritime temperate climate and the rich ocean waters. Look for rare skylarks (the only location in North America), varied cormorants, eagles, falcons, and shorebirds; pelagic species such as marbled murrelet, tufted puffin, and other alcids; even such occasional upland game birds as California quail.

Start a visit at the **Ogden Point Breakwater,** gateway to the waterfront between Ogden Point and east to Clover Point. The jetty thrusts out into the sound, making it a good platform to view deepwater seabird and shorebird species. Use it as a spot to view rare migrants, surfbirds, and wandering tattlers,

as well as many species of northern Pacific gulls.

Other top spots for watching seabirds in Victoria are Gonzale, Cattle, and Ten Mile points.

Midway between the Ogden and Clover points and inland a few blocks is **Beacon Hill Park,** the place in Victoria to see Anna's hummingbirds and warblers. Farther north find **Mount Tolmie**, one of Victoria's best passerine birding locations. Migrant fallout can be spectacular here in spring as exhausted birds fill the oaks and rest on the ground after their long transoceanic flights. Note the many flycatchers, occasional lazuli buntings, and frequent raptors, eagles, and peregrine falcons.

A last spot to visit on the outskirts of town in the Saanach District is the Swan Lake Christmas Hill Nature Sanctuary, located northwest of Mount Tolmie off of Patt Bay Hwy. Here, trails wind through forest and along the lakeshore, offering birders views of hummingbirds, towhee, bushtits, sparrows, wrens, owls, and raptors, as well as shorebirds and waterfowl.

• Sooke and East Sooke Regional Park

From Victoria follow Hwy. 14 west to **Sooke Harbor** and take a walk on the spit dividing this protected bay from the sea. The wide, sandy promontory is a nesting site for kildeer and a resting spot for cormorants, gulls, pelicans, and other birds. Across the inlet the rugged shoreline marks the site of **East Sooke Regional Park.** To reach it, retrace the outbound path on Hwy. 14 to East Sooke Rd. and turn right, following the road to the park, which overlooks the Strait of Juan de Fuca. Visible from park headlands on clear days is Washington State's Olympic Peninsula, as well as great kettles of

hawks and vultures in late September. South-bound migrants of all species stage at this spot before crossing the strait.

• Nanaimo to Tofino

Extend a birding trip on Vancouver Island by driving north 72 miles (116 km) and just over two hours from Victoria to **Nanaimo** on the Trans-Canada Hwy. (Hwy. 1). Nanaimo is the gateway to **Qualicum Beach** and the trip across the island to remote **Tofino.**

The hot spots in Nanaimo are near the airport (vesper and Savannah sparrows): Colliery Dam Park/Morrell Nature Sanctuary (perching birds, owls, and raptors), Haslam Rd. Marsh (redwinged blackbirds, waders, ducks, and geese), and Hemer Park off Cedar Rd. (try for a grand slam of red-breasted sapsuckers, flickers, in combination with downy, pileated, and hairy woodpeckers).

Drive northwest another 28 miles (45 km) from Nanaimo to Qualicum Beach, home to over 250 recorded bird species and site of the annual Brant Wildlife Festival in early April. The town celebrates the Pacific black brant, a small maritime goose that rests here en route to Alaska from Mexico.

Finally, branch off Hwy. 1 onto Hwy. 4 and cross the island to Tofino, watching along the way for woodland and river bird species.

Tofino is built on a long, sandy peninsula of land—reaching it means driving through the length of **Pacific Rim NP.**

Explore the Pacific side with its ocean birds, the sheltered eelgrass mudflats to the east, or the intervening cedar and spruce forests. Visits to the peninsula after rainstorms mean many rare birds seldom seen elsewhere.

A male fox sparrow sings a song of spring as it tries to attract a mate.

Seattle and Puget Sound

While the Pacific Northwest holds many natural attractions, for birders the multitude of migratory and resident species found around Puget Sound is its drawing card. Spend time here with seabirds, shorebirds, waterfowl, and birds of the forest.

From its start a short distance below the Canadian border to its finish at Grays Harbor on the wild Pacific coast, the Seattle-area route, situated on the Pacific Flyway, is a magnet for birds of all types. Its skies fill with V- and W-shaped flocks of geese and ducks twice a year. Less visible but even greater in number are coastal shorebird and boreal migrants en route to and from their nesting areas in the far north. Spring and autumn are the right times to visit—rain and fog are less likely than in winter or midsummer—but to enjoy the spectacle of bald eagles and osprey filling a river, the time to go is in the dead of winter, when the salmon runs peak and every stump and snag on the Skagit River fills with fish-sated birds. Whatever the season, birds abound in Puget Sound's protected waters.

Grays Harbor boardwalk offers unparalleled birding thrills during spring and fall migration, when a million shorebirds travel the Pacific Flyway. Counts at Grays Harbor top 365 species, over 75 percent of all birds seen in Washington State.

A snowy plover at Grays Harbor

❶ Drayton Harbor and Semiahmoo

Start the birding tour in the town of Blaine at **Drayton Harbor.** Exit I-5 on Blaine Rd., duck under the freeway, and turn south. After 0.5 mile (0.8 km) turn right on Drayton Harbor Rd., follow it past a golf course, and turn right again on Semiahmoo Pkwy, which leads to **Semiahmoo County Park** on the spit.

Visit as the tide floods while mudflats are still exposed, pushing shorebirds to the park and the Semiahmoo channel. In winter many waterbirds fly through the harbor entrance and down the shipping channel. In spring shorebirds pass through the harbor. Equally good views can be had from the Blaine side of the channel, and at Blaine's pier the number of birds can be truly phenomenal. Most of the

Skagit River at its mouth in Skagit Bay—and especially upriver near Marblemount—attracts large numbers of bald eagles from December through February. They are drawn to the river by the salmon runs and feed on dead fish carcasses.

land along the neck of the harbor is public. Scope the bay's shoreline for birds on sandbars or bobbing in rafts.

Look for red-throated loons, brant, all three species of scoter, double-crested cormorants, common and Barrow's goldeneyes, greater scaup, mergansers, and nearly every other western duck species. Also note alcids, great blue herons, and gulls.

Bald eagles frequently nest at the base of Semiahmoo Spit. Shorebirds commonly include large flocks of dunlin in winter, together with greater yellowlegs, black-bellied plovers, western sandpipers, sanderlings, and black turnstones.

Blaine Chamber of Commerce
728 Peace Portal Dr.
Blaine, WA 98230
(800) 624-3555
www.blainechamber.com

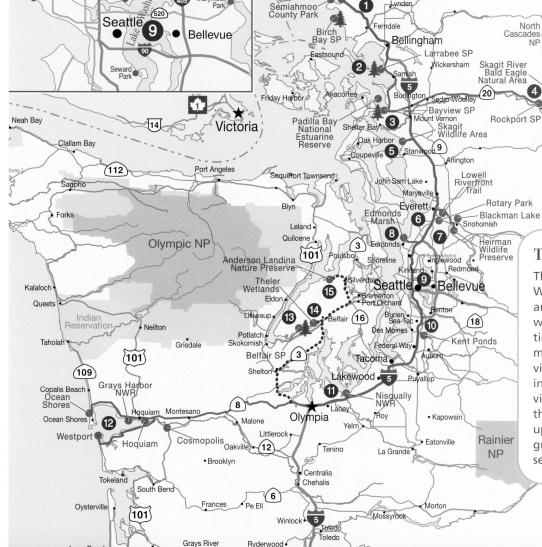

Tides and Bird-Watching

The tides affect the birds seen along Washington's coast. At high tide, mudflats and sandbars are submerged, and seeing wading birds is unlikely. At extreme low tide the shallows will drain, and birds will move with the receding water far from view. Start a trip at low water as the rising tides push birds up the shore and into view. In the channels the roiling water that accompanies the changing flow stirs up feed and draws bait fish on which gulls, pelicans, diving ducks, and other seabirds feast.

Tree swallows prefer a **cozy birdhouse** **or a hollow tree** for raising their young

❷ Larrabee SP

From Blaine travel I-5 south 30 miles (48 km) beyond Bellingham to **Larrabee SP.** Take the Hwy. 11 exit, turn west onto Old Fairhaven Pkwy., drive 1.3 miles (2.1 km), and turn south onto Chuckanut Dr. Continue straight 4.9 miles (7.9 km), turning right into the park. An admission fee is charged.

Larrabee SP is a good year-round birding spot, 2,683 acres (1,086 h) of varied habitat, including hills, saltwater coves, lakes, forests, and tide pools.

At the coast watch for harlequin ducks, double-crested and pelagic cormorants, glaucous-winged gulls, bald eagles, and great blue herons along the shoreline. Common loons and mew gulls visit during winter.

In the park's uplands see western screech-owls, northern pygmy-owls, and great horned and barred owls. These forests are also home to pileated woodpeckers and red-breasted sapsuckers.

Follow Fragrance Lake Rd. to its namesake for more shorebirds and boreal birds.

After visiting, follow scenic Chuckanut Dr. south to the next waypoint; the road becomes FTM 237 at Edison.

WA State Parks & Recreation Commission
P.O. Box 42650
Olympia, WA 98504
(360) 902-8844
www.parks.wa.gov

❸ Padilla Bay National Estuarine Reserve

Traveling south from Larrabee on FTM 237, turn right at Josh Wilson Rd. to enter Bayview, with a right again at Bayview-Edison Rd. before going north to enter **Bayview SP.**

This park is a tiny outpost in 10,000-acre (4,047-h) **Padilla Bay National Estuarine Reserve,** which protects mud flats, offshore eelgrass beds, salt marshes, beaches, and forests.

The best times to visit are winter, spring, and autumn, when the bay fills with brant, pintails, wigeons, scaups, and other ducks and geese, plus grebes, loons, and green herons. (In summer the park becomes crowded with human visitors.)

Shorebirds here include dunlins, yellowlegs, sanderlings, and western sandpipers. In winter it's also common to see peregrine falcons fishing.

Consider bird-watching on the 2-mile-long (3.2-km-long) Padilla Bay Shore Trail, accessed from a trailhead located 0.5 mile (0.8 km) south, or visiting the Breazeale Padilla Bay Interpretive Center just north of the park. The staff has birding information.

WA State Parks and Recreation Commission
P.O. Box 42650
Olympia, WA 98504
(360) 902-8844
www.parks.wa.gov
www.padillabay.gov

❹ Skagit River

Follow FTM 237 south from Bayview to the junction with Hwy. 20, turning left toward the town of Sedro-Wooley, 8.5 miles (13.7 km) east on the Avon Cutoff. Continue east on Hwy. 20, following the river past Hamilton and Concrete to **Rockport SP** and the threshold of one of the Pacific Northwest's greatest autumn birding shows: bald eagles at Skagit River.

Rockport to Marblemount has been designated **Skagit River Bald Eagle Natural Area,** an 8,000-acre (3,237-h) preserve. Wintering eagles peak in December to early February, when the river fills with the birds.

They are drawn to spawned-out salmon; the fish die after laying their eggs in the river's gravel, and the eagles feed on their protein-rich flesh.

To view eagles, start at the interpretive center in Rockport, with docents and staff offering bird-watching advice, directions, and guided interpretive walks.

Visit at dusk to see roosting birds on the branches of old-growth trees along the river. Otherwise, the best viewing takes place between dawn and 11 A.M. on cloudy days. Eagles are more active and disperse when the sun is bright.

Consider taking a guided raft trip to see the eagles and other river birds; half-day trips can be arranged in Rockport and Marblemount.

North Cascades NP is about 25 miles (40 km) east of Rockport on Hwy. 20. Visit this scenic park with many places to view birds on good trails.

Each February the interpretive center hosts a bald-eagle festival with activities, guided tours, and eagle viewing.

Skagit WSR
10 State Rte. 20
Sedro-Woolley, WA 98284
(360) 856-5700
www.fs.fed.us/r6/mbs/skagit wsr/overview/wildlife.shtml

❺ Skagit Wildlife Area

Retracing Hwy. 20 down the river, join I-5 south for 8 miles (12.8 km) and take exit 221, following Fir Island Rd. west 3.2 miles (5.1 km). Turn left at the WDF&G sign to Fir Island Farm and Hayden Reserve in the 11,000-acre (4,452-h) **Skagit Wildlife Area.**

This is a four-season birding opportunity, best in winter to fall. Among birds seen here are bald eagles, northern harriers, ducks, swans, snow geese, dunlins, plovers, sandpipers, peregrine falcons, and owls.

Tree swallows abound at Marymoor Park.

Nisqually NWR has an easy-access boardwalk that spans large areas of marsh and forest, a favorite habitat for boreal birds and shorebirds.

Walk the dikes to the overlook and other viewing sites.

Skagit Wildlife Area
21961 Wylie Rd.
Mt. Vernon, WA 98273
(360) 445-4441
**http://wdfw.wa.gov/lands/
r4skagit.htm**

⑥ Everett

From Fir Island rejoin I-5 and drive 16 miles (26 km) south to Everett. Take exit 192 and turn east onto 41st St. At the first light turn right on S. 3rd Ave. and drive 1 mile (1.6 km) to Lenora St. Turn left and enter **Rotary Park** and **Lowell Riverfront Trail.**

This all-access trail leads 1.8 miles (2.9 km) along the Snohomish River through cottonwoods filled with owls, Bullock's orioles, pine siskins, spotted towhees, ruby-crowned kinglets, yellow-rumped warblers, fox sparrows, and Cooper's, redtailed, and sharp-shinned hawks —even occasional bald eagles.

Everett Parks & Recreation
802 E. Mukilteo Blvd.
Everett, WA 98203
(425) 257-8300
www.everettwa.org

⑦ Snohomish

Travel east 5 miles (8 km) on Lowell-Snohomish Riverfront Rd. to Snohomish. Cross the river on the Hwy. 9 bridge, turn right onto 2nd St., then turn left at Ave. D, which leads to Ferguson Park Rd. and **Blackman Lake.**

This city lake has good spots in spring and winter to see dabbling and diving ducks, mergansers, grebes, and cormorants. Walk its margins for juncos, chickadees, spotted towhees, and red-breasted nuthatches.

South of town 2.3 miles (3.7 km) on Hwy. 9 from the Snohomish River, take Broadway Ave. left 0.8 mile (1.3 km), then fork left at Connelly Rd. to **Heirman Wildlife Preserve.** The riverside preserve is a good year-round spot to see forest and river birds.

Snohomish Co. Tourism Bureau
909 S.E. Everett Mall Way, C300
Everett, WA 98208
(425) 348-5802
www.snohomish.org

⑧ Edmonds Marsh

Retrace the outbound path to I-5, turn south, take exit 177, and follow the signs to the Edmonds/Kingston Ferry until Hwy. 104 crosses Dayton St. Turn left on Dayton and drive to the wharfside parking lot. The 23-acre (9.3-h) **Edmonds Marsh** (across Admiral Way), fishing pier, and beach to the north host over 200 recorded species of birds.

Year-round residents include marbled murrelets, pigeon guillemots, harlequin ducks, and pelagic cormorants. In spring migration look for greater and lesser yellowlegs, western and solitary sandpipers, long-billed and short-billed dowitchers, even rhinoceros auklets.

In fall migrating common terns rest with common murres, brant, and white-winged, black, and surf scoters; they transition to ancient murrelets as the calendar turns to November.

Snohomish Co. Tourism Bureau
909 S.E. Everett Mall Way, C300
Everett, WA 98208
(425) 348-5802
www.snohomish.org

Visit these sites along the way on the nearby Kitsap Peninsula...

⑬ Belfair SP
410 N.E. Beck Rd.
Belfair, WA 98528
(360) 275-0668
www.parks.wa.gov/parks

This park on 63 acres (25 h) has 0.7 mile (1.1 km) of saltwater shore at the Hood Canal. From Olympia go north 11 miles (18 km) on Hwy. 8 and Hwy. 101 to Hwy. 3, and drive 33 miles (52 km) to Belfair; turn left on Hwy. 300 and drive to the park. Boreal and waterbirds abound.

⑭ Theler Wetlands Nature Preserve
22871 N.E. Hwy. 3
Belfair, WA 98528
(360) 275-4898
www.thelercenter.org

Found 3 miles (5 km) north at the south end of Belfair is Mary E. Theler Exhibit Building, with a trailhead behind it. All-access trails and a long floating boardwalk, plus interpretive kiosks, interactive displays, and nature exhibits.

⑮ Anderson Landing Nature Preserve
Warren Rd.
Silverdale, WA 98383
(360) 337-5350
www.kitsapgov.com/parks

A 68-acre (28-h) nature preserve on Hood Canal with trails along the mudflats. Drive from Belfair to Silverdale on Hwy. 3, take NW Anderson Hill Rd. 3.5 miles (5.6 km) to Warren Rd., turn right, and drive to this shorebird hot spot's trailhead.

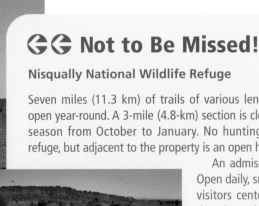

Nisqually NWR facilities are accessible to bird-watchers of all ages and abilities. Magnification scopes make watching the antics of its barn swallows easy to follow for children.

❾ Seattle

Washington's queen city holds a wealth of riches for birders. Start with 534-acre (216-h) **Discovery Park,** located 3 miles (4.8 km) northwest of downtown off W. Emerson St., accessed by Metro bus lines 19, 24, and 33.

The park features seacoast shorelines, freshwater wetlands, meadows, streams, and mixed forests with more than 270 species of birds. View upland and boreal birds on the 2.8-mile (4.5-km) Loop or waterbirds on the North Beach or South Beach trails accessible from parking lots at the wastewater treatment plant. Obtain maps at the Environmental Learning Center on W. Government Way.

Birding former landfills may seem dubious, but birds and birders alike sing the praises of **Union Bay Natural Area,** a restored wild island in an urban setting near University of Washington. It's just south of N. 45th St. on Mary Gates Memorial Dr.

Famed for its many microhabitats, the site is visited by over 200 species of birds, such as American bitterns, yellow-headed blackbirds, American pipits, merlins, peregrine falcons, and both rufous and Anna's hummigbirds. Its ponds attract waterfowl, Wilson's phalaropes, least and solitary sandpipers, as well as dowitchers.

In suburban Redmond **Marymoor Park** on the outlet river from Lake Sammamish boasts riparian stands of black cottonwood, willow, and alder, mixed with thickets of brush and bunchgrass. Follow the signs to the South Lot and walk the trail west toward East Meadow by the Sammamish River with its boardwalk and lake-viewing platform.

Dozens of species reside in the park, but even more nest here. Visit in summer for nesting hummingbirds, sapsuckers, flycatchers, wood-pewees, warblers, vireos, grosbeaks, and thrushes. In winter see sharp-shinned and Cooper's hawks, cackling geese, various gulls, scoters, grebes, mergansers, Wilson's snipes, northern shrikes, and fox and many other sparrow species.

Finally, complete a visit to Seattle at these birding hot

↰↱ Not to Be Missed!

Nisqually National Wildlife Refuge

Seven miles (11.3 km) of trails of various lengths, most of them open year-round. A 3-mile (4.8-km) section is closed during hunting season from October to January. No hunting is allowed in the refuge, but adjacent to the property is an open hunting area.

An admission fee is charged. Open daily, sunrise to sunset. The visitors center is open Wednesday through Sunday, 9 A.M. to 4 P.M., closed on holidays.

Exhibits, information desk, and bookstore is located in the visitors center.

The Boardwalk Trail is a 1-mile (1.6-km) loop open year-round at the visitors center. It includes Twin Barns Observation Platform, pictured here with viewing scopes for watching nesting barn swallows and birds in nearby fields.

A longer, 5.5-mile (8.8-km) loop trail along the tops of dikes visits Riparian Forest Overlook, an observation platform, a seasonal observation tower, and two photography blinds.

Guided nature and bird walks, as well as those teaching digital wildlife photography, are conducted April through September.

Grays Harbor has observation decks for viewing coastal birds and migrants traveling north in spring and south in fall on the Pacific Flyway.

fowl, songbirds, and raptors visit this marshy delta to feed and rest. In March bald eagles and spring migrant birds begin to nest. The best times for viewing are early mornings and late afternoons; periods following storms are particularly good.

Nisqually NWR
100 Brown Farm Rd.
Olympia, WA 98516
(360) 753-9467
www.fws.gov

spots found on central Seattle's Lake Washington:
- **Juanita Bay Park** in Kirkland for Virginia rail and hooded mergansers.
- **Seward Park** on the lake's southwest shore off South Orcas Ave.
- **Warren G. Magnuson Park** and bird blind at Promontory Point on the northwest shore.

Seattle Convention & Visitors Bureau
701 Pike St., Ste. 800
Seattle, WA 98101
(206) 461-5840
www.seeseattle.org

⑩ Kent Ponds

Near SeaTac Airport off I-5 is **Kent Ponds.** Take exit 152 and follow Orillia Rd. east until it turns and crosses Russell Rd. Turn south along the river to reach the parking lots and trails leading to a series of reclaimed wastewater ponds.

See shorebirds nesting in summer, or view migrants and raptors from October to April.

City of Kent Public Works
220 4th Ave. S
Kent, WA 98032
(253) 856-5500
www.ci.kent.wa.us/publicworks/specialprograms/grnra.asp

⑪ Nisqually NWR

At the southern tip of Puget Sound on Nisqually Bay, just off I-5's exit 114, lies **Nisqually NWR,** a visitor-friendly reserve with 7 miles (11.3 km) of trails, observation platforms with telescopes, boardwalks, and photo blinds. Admission is charged.

Each winter to spring many thousands of geese and water-

⑫ Grays Harbor

A final waypoint is Grays Harbor, found 61 miles (98 km) to the west via I-5 to Hwy. 101, Hwy. 8, and Hwy. 12. Grays Harbor has four towns: Cosmopolis, Hoquiam, Ocean Shores, and Westport, each a rich destination for birding and bird-watching.
- **Cosmopolis** on the east has very good bird-watching locations along the Chehalis River on S.W. Front St. and at Mill Creek Park, located just off 1st St.

Hooded mergansers at Nisqually NWR are among several diving ducks found in Pacific Northwest waters.

- **Hoquiam,** across the river, is home to 1,500-acre (607-h) **Grays Harbor NWR,** found adjacent to Bowerman Airport on Paulson Rd. off Hwy. 109. It is a world-famous spot for watching feeding and nesting shorebirds.
- **Ocean Shores** on the north spit has 300 recorded species of birds, including transhemispheric migrants. Start at the game range, jetty, and Damon Point at spit's end.
- **Westport** on the south spit and jetty is equally endowed with birds. Charter boats leave from Westport and offer pelagic bird-watching in a species-rich environment.

Grays Harbor Tourism
P.O. Box 1229
Elma, WA 98541
(800) 621-9625
www.graysharbortourism.com

Canada geese **show off** their
fuzzy goslings to binocular-toting visitors

Portland and North Coast Oregon

Birders sample scenic grandeur along the Pacific Flyway and drive a loop through mountains, forests, and seashores, from Portland on the banks of the Columbia River to the waters of the Oregon Coast and back.

Cosmopolitan yet always lovely, Portland—the City of Roses—invites bird-watchers to its refuges, reserves, and parks before they begin an easy trek down the Columbia River to Astoria. With each mile traveled, the river becomes broader and the birds more varied, until the route breaks through the fog to reveal the sparkling waters of the Oregon coast. Here pelagic seabirds bob alongside gulls, pelicans, and other shorebirds, while river species mix with traveling migrants flying to and from their wintering and nesting grounds. Turn south toward Tillamook Bay, then press inland over the coastal range to return to the starting point.

Gulls rest in flocks on the sandbars near Fort Stevens SP.

Cape Meares's lighthouse stands sentinel on a crag overlooking the boundless Pacific. Waters below the cape are rich with murres and murrelets.

❶ Portland

Nestled between low, rolling mountains and the Columbia River, Portland is a focal point for birds flying the river, those found in hardwood and conifer forests, and migratory species wending north on the Pacific side of the Cascades. The result is a bird-watcher's paradise within a city-dweller's grasp.

Start the birding tour inside the city limits at **Oaks Bottom Wildlife Refuge** in southeast Portland by taking Macadam Hwy. 43 off I-5 and crossing the Selwood Bridge. Once on the river's east side, turn left on S.E. 7th Ave., go left on S.E. Spokane St., and enter the park on S.E. Oaks Park Way. The refuge has several trails and natural areas; the best viewing areas are at the north end of the park adjacent to the lake, floodplain, and marsh. Visit in spring or in fall through midwinter for best results.

The refuge is the premier spot to see great blue herons, Portland's official bird. They feed here and nest at a rookery on nearby Ross Island. Note all the other wading, shore, and boreal birds on the site; it's also a rest stop for migratory waterfowl and raptors.

The next must-see birding spot is **Audubon Society of Portland Nature Sanctuary,** in the northwest city. From I-405 take the N.W. 14th Ave. exit and drive north to N.W. Lovejoy St., turn left, and drive west 0.8 mile (1.3 km), where Lovejoy becomes N.W. Cornell Rd. and veers right. Continue 1.5 miles (2.4 km) through two tunnels; the sanctuary is past the second tunnel.

The 143-acre (58-h) preserve is free to the public and open

Portland's Oaks Bottom Wildlife Refuge is a wetland bird haven in sight of metropolitan Portland.

dawn until dusk, with 4.5 miles (7.2 km) of trails that include Wildwood Trail to Forest Park, the next waypoint.

In the sanctuary's mixed-conifer forest and by Balch Creek, see warblers, Steller's jays, chickadees, varied thrushes, mourning doves, and barred owls, as well as juncos, swallows, and hawks.

Stretching northwest from the sanctuary nearly 6 miles

(9.7 km) is **Forest Park,** the largest natural urban forest area in the United States, at 5,100 acres (2,064 h). It is home to 112 species of birds.

Sample the park by driving west on N.W. Connell Rd. and turning right on N.W. 53rd Dr. At its end, turn right again on N.W. Forest Ln., the main road to the park's center. Other access is from Hwy. 30 along the Columbia River's Multnomah Channel. The park has 30 miles (48 km) of trails, great for upland and forest-dwelling birds of all types.

These stops just dip into the rich birding opportunities in Portland. Expand a visit by adding additional destinations.

Portland Parks and Recreation
1120 S.W. Fifth Ave., Ste. 1302
Portland, OR 97204
(503) 823-7529
www.portlandonline.com/parks

An osprey's call is a single or series of sharp, shrill whistles.

❷ Sauvie Island Wildlife Area

Sauvie Island is 8 miles (12.9 km) northwest of I-405 on Hwy. 30 in Portland, a route following the Multnomah Channel of the Columbia River. Note signs to the Sauvie Island Bridge and Sauvie Island Rd. Nearly 12,000 acres of land on the island are preserved as **Sauvie Island Wildlife Area,** managed by the Oregon Department of Fish and Wildlife (ODFW). Open mid-April through September; off-road areas are closed to the public during the winter breeding season. The island has limited facilities, so fuel vehicles before crossing the bridge. Access fee charged (Sam's Cracker Barrel Market, by the bridge).

Make a stop at Howell Lake in **Howell Territorial Park,** 1 mile (1.6 km) north of the bridge, then continue north on Sauvie Island Rd. to a series of lakes, lagoons, and sloughs. Several trails lead east to **Steelman, Sturgeon,** and **Crane lakes** from the road.

Return east on Sauvie Rd. to Reeder Rd., turn left, cross the island to the Gillhan/Reeder

fork, and bear left. Reeder Rd. traverses the island's north edge and the riverbank, with many spots for birding. On the road's left side, 3 miles (4.8 km) from the fork, an observation platform has excellent views of the nearly 250 species that visit this wetland island. Noted species include waterfowl in autumn and spring, bald eagles in winter, plus wading birds and shorebirds.

Multnomah Co. Information
1221 S.W. 4th Ave.
Portland, OR 97204
(503) 823-4000
www.co.multnomah.or.us

❸ Puget Island and Cathlamet

Return to Hwy. 30 and drive about 54 miles (87 km) north to Westport, Hwy. 409, and the Wahkiakum Ferry crossing the Columbia to **Puget Island** and **Cathlamet,** Washington.

On Puget Island drive Welcome Slough Rd. to skirt the sloughs that divide the island; make stops along the dikes to observe shorebirds and water-birds. Scan the skies for hawks, kites, and other birds of prey over the wetlands before looping back to Hwy. 409 and proceeding over the bridge to Cathlamet. Drive 6.3 miles (10.1 km) west on Hwy. 4 to Steamboat Slough Rd., making a left turn. The off-shore islands hold **Lewis and Clark NWR** and **Julia Butler**

Hanson Refuge for Columbian white-tail deer, reached by charter boat from Cathlamet or by private craft launched from ramps on Steamboat Slough. There's an abundance of birds to see on the mainland along Steamboat Slough or Brook's Slough Rd. These sites have bald eagles, osprey, peregrine falcons, tundra swans, geese, ducks, and many species of shorebirds, including heron and wading birds. Best times to visit are in spring and fall migration, when waterfowl number many thousands and the skies fill with birds.

Lewis and Clark NWR
46 Steamboat Slough Rd.
Cathlamet, WA 98612
(360) 795-3915
www.fws.gov

❹ Lower Columbia

Return to Hwy. 30 in Oregon by bridge and ferry and drive 10 miles (16 km) west to **Twilight Eagle Sanctuary** at Cathlamet Bay. A viewing platform overlooks mudflats, wetlands, the John Day Channel, and islands previously seen from Washington at the last stop. Interpretive panels describe the wetlands, bald eagles that congregate here in late January, and Lewis and Clark's 1805 visit to the area.

Go 25 miles (40 km) west on Hwy. 30 to **Astoria,** gateway to the Columbia's mouth and the site of several birding spots worth a visit. Located on the river just 7 miles (12 km) from the ocean, the **6th Street Pier** and viewing tower are good spots to view gulls, pelicans, and birds ranging from

Wahkiakum Ferry to Puget Island on the Columbia River.

Twilight Eagle Sanctuary features a viewing platform overlooking Cathlamet Bay on the lower Columbia.

bald eagles to diving ducks. Other piers are found at riverside on 14th and 17th streets. Both charter and tour boats ply the riverfront, offering excellent birding views of this port's avian residents and seasonal migrant visitors.

From Astoria join Hwy. 101 and drive south across Young's Bay Bridge. At Ridge Rd. turn right and drive onto **Clatsop Spit,** a sandy promontory projecting north into the river and leading to **Fort Stevens SP,** the jetty, and the river's mouth. The broad, shelfing beach, sand

dunes, and jetty all have many coastal and pelagic birds, but perhaps the best spot for birding is a cleverly hidden blind near parking lot D in the park—look for a concrete "gun emplacement" topped by plantings of beach grass.

The best times to visit the spit and park are July and August, when shorebirds migrate along the coast and the Pacific teems with anchovies and herring. Walk the jetty to see sooty shearwaters and brown pelicans, or visit parking lot C for roosting shorebirds at high tide.

Following a visit to the spit, drive Ridge Rd. north to 6th St. and turn right. It turns into Ft. Stevens Hwy. 104. At N.W. 13th St. turn left, drive to the end circle, and park. Trails lead south to **Alder Creek,** offering an entirely different bird-watching experience. During March and April large numbers of migrating rufous hummingbirds gather here to sip nectar from salmonberry flowers. The trail also has good views of the adjacent wetlands and tidal flats. The lower Columbia River is worth several days of birding.

Astoria-Warrenton Area Chamber of Commerce
111 W. Marine Dr.
Astoria, OR 97103
(503) 325-6311
www.oldoregon.com

❺ Seaside to Cannon Beach

Just a few miles' drive south from the Columbia River on Hwy. 101 is **Necanicum River Estuary,** the next birding area in north Seaside. A good access point is found at G St. Go west, cross an

49

Viewing a dense nesting colony of common murres atop a crowded rocky islet requires one of the telescopes found at Cape Meares

estuary, veer north on Neacoxie Dr., left on E St., and follow it to its end, a trailhead that leads to the dunes and ocean beach. Bird south from the trail along the sandy shore to the Necanicum River mouth, then work inland along tidal flats to the wooded margins.

Necanicum Estuary and the north spit are designated IBA sites and nesting grounds for snowy plovers, sandpipers, and semipalmated plovers. Also look for whimbrels, long-billed curlew, and western sandpipers during spring and fall migration seasons. Bald eagles nest in the spruces to the east.

Seaside Visitors Bureau
989 Broadway
Seaside, OR 97138
(503) 738-3097
www.seasideor.com

From Seaside, continue the drive south on Hwy. 101 and follow the Cannon Beach signs to **Ecola SP.** This world-renowned scenic destination is capped by Haystack Rock, an offshore seastack island. There's an observation platform at Cannon Beach with good birding views. A close look at the similar rocks found to the north off Chapman and Ecola points reveals tufted puffins and brant geese, as well as pelagic cormorant and common murre colonies that gather to nest and rear their young in June. Also watch the beaches for shorebirds and gulls.

Oregon Parks and Recreation Department
725 Summer St. NE, Ste. C
Salem, OR 97301
(503) 986-0707
www.oregonstateparks.org

⑥ Tillamook Bay

Heading south on Hwy. 101, the route passes through **Oswald West SP** and **Nehalam Bay SP** before nearing Tillamook Bay, 29 miles (47 km) in all.

At the north end of the bay, **Barview Jetty Park** provides beach access and RV camps, with a mix of seabirds and forest species, including double-crested and Brandt's cormorants, all three species of scoters, rock sandpipers, black turnstones, and black-legged kittiwakes (late fall), plus chestnut-backed chickadees, wrentits, winter and Bewick's wrens, golden-crowned kinglets, Steller's jays, red crossbills, and Townsend's warblers.

Just 2 miles (3.2 km) south, the fishing village of **Garibaldi** is a gateway to the bay. Minutes from the open ocean, the narrow channel often fills with rafts of seabirds and waterfowl.

Another 4.5 miles (7.2 km) south on Hwy. 101 is **Bay City.** Follow Hayes Oyster Dr. to the breakwater for excellent views of seabirds and shorebirds. A wastewater treatment pond complex visible from Hwy. 101 just to the south attracts waterfowl,

Cape Meares highlights a birding tour along the northern Oregon coastline. The best seasons to visit are spring and fall; in summer the coast is often blanketed in dense fog.

including rare tufted ducks and emperor geese, along with gulls.

Continue 5.6 miles (9 km) south to **Tillamook,** nestled at the bay's head. South of town near the airport, short-eared and barn owls fly at dusk. Also visit the open fields and sinuous estuaries northwest of town along 3rd St. and beyond on Bayocean Rd. to see hawks, white-tailed kites, and cattle egrets in winter, along with

great blue herons, stilts, and other wading birds. Follow Bayocean Rd. along the southwest edge of Tillamook Bay to the south spit and **Meares Lake,** both good places to see thousands of hungry migrant shorebirds in spring and fall. Included are four kinds of sandpipers, several plovers, sanderlings, dunlins, and godwits—together with hawks, kites, peregrine falcons, and the occasional bald eagle.

Tillamook Chamber of Commerce
705 Hwy. 101 N
Tillamook, OR 97141
(503) 842-7525
www.tillamookchamber.org

Where Bayocean Rd. meets Meares Lake, the road name changes to Cape Meares Loop and it turns south. Follow it 1.7 miles (2.7 km) to **Cape Meares State Scenic Viewpoint** and turn right into Lighthouse Rd.

The cape is an unmatched place to see nesting peregrine falcons, along with thousands of seabirds: Brandt's and pelagic cormorants, common murres, tufted puffins, western gulls, pigeon guillemots, black oyster-catchers, migrating loons, and grebes. Two viewing decks offer glimpses into three offshore national wildlife refuges and two national wilderness areas, plus a 0.2-mile (0.4-km) walk to the historic lighthouse (open April to October). From the

Fowl-in-Focus

VAUX'S SWIFTS
Chaetura vauxi

Length 4.75 in. (12 cm)

What to look for Cigar-shaped body with short, squarely blunt tail; deep gray body with pale gray throat; shorter wings than chimney swifts.

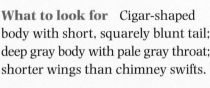

Habitat Usually found in forested areas and river valleys. Feeds in flight, scooping up swarms of insects with its bill. Both males and females build nests and care for young, in colonies or solitary pairs. Migrates from Mexico and Central America to Oregon and north to British Columbia. Though ornithologists claim Vaux's swifts seldom roost in chimneys, they do in Eugene (see Join In, on this page).

bluffs, view one of the largest nesting colonies of common murres on Oregon's coast.

Oregon Parks and Recreation Department
725 Summer St. NE, Ste. C
Salem, OR 97301
(503) 986-0707
www.oregonstateparks.org

❼ Forest Grove

From the previous waypoint, return to Tillamook and drive inland 22 miles (35 km) on Hwy. 6, turning left into **Tillamook Forest Center** 0.2 mile (0.3 km) before it reaches North Fork Rd.

The center has numerous trails leading through forest recovering from the 1930s Tillamook burn fire, and it is an excellent place to look for forest birds, including the reclusive spotted owl.

Tillamook Forest Center
45500 Wilson River Hwy.
Tillamook, OR 97141
(503) 815-6800
www.tillamookforestcenter.org

Continue east on Hwy. 6 and turn onto Hwy. 8 to the town of Forest Grove, 40 miles (64 km) east. Hwy. 8 becomes 19th Ave. as it enters Forest Grove; follow it through town to Maple St., turn right, and drive south until the road crosses Hwy. 47 and its name changes to Fernhill Rd. **Fernhill Wetlands Research**

Join In

Welcome back the swifts, first in April and again in September

See thousands of Vaux's swifts entering Agate Hall chimney to roost for the night on the University of Oregon campus in Eugene.

- Arrive about a half hour before sunset and watch the swifts swarm over the smokestack in a twirling funnel that appears to suck them down into the chimney. Those that miss go back up to the top of the flock to try again. It's unforgettable. Bring a comfortable chair and enjoy.

Find out more from the Lane County Audubon Society: www.laneaudubon.org, or call (541) 485-2473.

and Education Center is 0.2 mile (0.3 km) beyond, adjacent to a wastewater facility.

Best visited from fall through spring, the diked ponds and wetlands attract migratory waterfowl, trumpeter swans, greater scaups, wood ducks, Eurasian wigeons, and hooded mergansers, as well as migrating bald eagles, peregrine falcons, and merlins. They are a good spot in summer to see Virginia rails and sora.

Return to Hwy. 47, turn west, and drive 3.4 miles (5.5 km) to

Spotted towhee (above) and cute Canadian goslings (right) take in some spring sunshine.

Not to Be Missed!

The Willamette Valley from Salem to Eugene

Oregon's Willamette Valley is equal parts prime farmland, pristine habitats, and expanding cities. In this mix are some great birding sites, including three national wildlife refuges.

Minot-Brown Island Park in Salem, though no longer a true island, has 5 miles (8 km) of paved biking paths dotted with birding observation platforms. Make a visit to **www.cityofsalem.net/export/departments/parks/index.htm** for more information.

Nearby **William L. Finley, Ankeny,** and **Baskett Slough NWRs** provide a wintering habitat for dusky Canada geese, found only in the Willamette Valley and at Alaska's Copper River. The refuges are generally closed to public entry during nesting season: November 1–April 30. The FWS website has details: **www.fws.gov/willamettevalley/**.

- **Baskett Slough NWR** is west of Salem on Hwy. 22. Its kiosk offers good views and has a spotting scope, interpretive panels.
- **Ankeny NWR** is at the intersection of Ankeny and Wintel roads, 12 miles south of Salem and 1.5 miles (2.4 km) west of exit 243 from I-5, with boardwalks, blinds, overlooks, and kiosks.
- **William L. Finley NWR** is 10 miles (16 km) south of Corvallis on Hwy. 99W, milepost 93. It has a headquarters building, trails, kiosks, and a viewing pond. Two county roads in the refuge are open to the public year-round.

Extend a visit to the Willamette area with a stop at **Jackson-Frazier Wetlands Preserve** on Lancaster Street in Corvallis. A 0.7-mile (1.1-km) raised boardwalk with interpretive signs winds through the wetlands. Obtain information at **www.co.benton.or.us/parks/jfraz.htm**.

Drive south on I-5 from Eugene to Hwy. 58 and southeast, for a total of 17 miles (27 km), to 847-acre (343-h) **Elijah Bristow SP,** with meadows, woodlands, and wetlands along the Willamette River. View osprey, herons, and bald eagles. See **www.oregonstateparks.org**.

Fern Ridge Reservoir, located about 7 miles (11 km) west of Eugene on Hwy. 126, is an Important Bird Area (IBA) with over 200 species. The best place to view ospreys' nests is Perkins Peninsula Park, which has a nice view of the reservoir.

Scroggins Valley Rd. Turn right for 3.5 miles (5.6 km) and follow the signs to **Henry Hagg Lake.** Access fee charged; full-access facilities and trails throughout.

The lake park is open from March to November, a loop road circles the water, and the northwest half of the lake is reserved for hand-powered vessels. Several creeks flow into the basin, making them good birding habitats.

Over 15 miles (24 km) of trails wind through meadows, scrub brush, and mixed conifer and hardwood forests filled with woodpeckers, warblers, vireos, wrens, and other songbirds, as well as a host of migrant travelers and waterfowl.

The best times to visit Henry Hagg Lake are from the site's opening to the end of the spring migration and again in the late fall. Look for boreal birds typical of the Pacific Northwest mixing freely with subtropical migrants. Large predator and scavenger birds include eagles, falcons, and turkey vultures.

Northern saw-whet and long-eared owls are common in these forests. At water's edge find brown creepers, wrens, and band-tailed pigeons.

Complete the birding loop by returning to Portland on Hwy. 8 via Hwy. 47 through Beaverton.

Bend, Oregon, to Mt. Shasta, California

South-central Oregon and northern California skirt the high desert and the Cascades Range. Freshwater lakes, wetlands, grassy meadows, and mixed forests mean a combination of habitats that draw abundant bird life, both residents and migrants.

Open-sky country and vistas of towering volcanic peaks denote an inland flyway populated by millions of flying birds from fall to spring. Nearly 45,000 acres (18,211 h) of wetlands and freshwater marshes are critical habitats for waterfowl, shorebirds, gulls, and other species. Rivers, grasslands, sagebrush desert, and mixed conifer forests are home to upland game birds, raptors, songbirds, and visiting migrants. Begin the route in Bend, near Oregon's center point, then travel south to see the spectacle of the Klamath Basin NWR Complex, six refuges remarkable for bird-watching and scenic grandeur.

Double-crested cormorant at Lake Shastina

Mt. Shasta, seen here from Lake Shastina's tiny islands, is an amazing gathering spot for aquatic birds such as gulls, American white pelicans, double-crested cormorants, great blue herons, and a few Canada geese.

❶ Bend

Centrally located on Hwy. 97, **Bend** is rich with birding sites. Spend a day within the city limits viewing migratory and river birds. The best starting point is **Tumalo SP** on the Deschutes River, 5 miles (8 km) north of town on Hwy. 20. It has many easily accessed hiking trails for birding. Open daily year-round. Admission fee charged.

Tumalo State Park
64120 O.B. Riley Rd.
Bend, OR 97701
(541) 388-6055
www.oregonstateparks.org

Robert W. Sawyer Park (62999 O.B. Riley Rd.) is a 45-acre (18-h) area straddling both banks of the Deschutes River. A footbridge leads to Deschutes River Trail. A few blocks south find **Riverview Park** (Division St.), with paths to the river's edge. **Drake Park** (N.W. Riverside

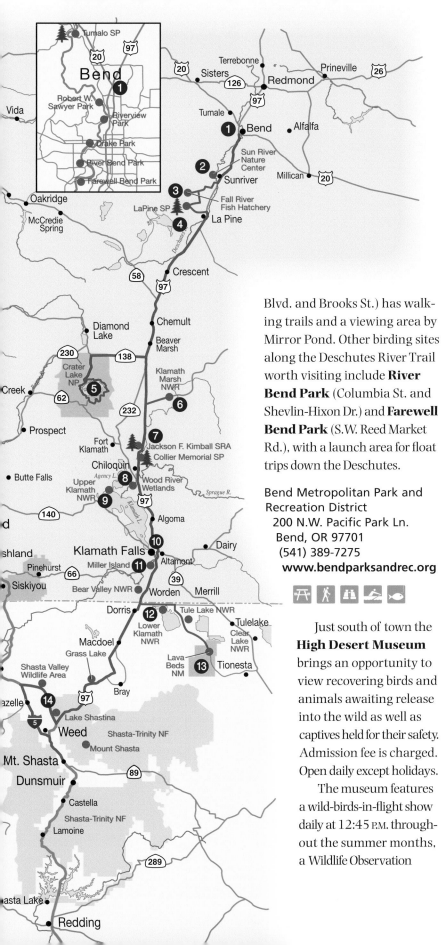

Blvd. and Brooks St.) has walking trails and a viewing area by Mirror Pond. Other birding sites along the Deschutes River Trail worth visiting include **River Bend Park** (Columbia St. and Shevlin-Hixon Dr.) and **Farewell Bend Park** (S.W. Reed Market Rd.), with a launch area for float trips down the Deschutes.

Bend Metropolitan Park and Recreation District
200 N.W. Pacific Park Ln.
Bend, OR 97701
(541) 389-7275
www.bendparksandrec.org

Just south of town the **High Desert Museum** brings an opportunity to view recovering birds and animals awaiting release into the wild as well as captives held for their safety. Admission fee is charged. Open daily except holidays.

The museum features a wild-birds-in-flight show daily at 12:45 P.M. throughout the summer months, a Wildlife Observation Pavilion with displays, and many wildlife viewing areas on its spacious grounds.

High Desert Museum
59800 S. Hwy. 97
Bend, OR 97702
(541) 382-4757
www.highdesertmuseum.org

❷ Sunriver Nature Center and Observatory

Drive 16 miles (26 km) south on Hwy. 97, turn west onto S. Cascade Hwy., drive 1.5 miles (2.4 km) to Abbot Dr., and turn right at the traffic circle, left at the next, and left again onto River Rd. to reach this private nonprofit nature center. It features paths through lodgepole pine forests and marshes on a 0.3-mile (0.4-km) nature trail by Lake Aspen. Observatory tours here reveal the sun by day and stars and planets by night.

Sunriver Nature Center
P.O. Box 3533
Sunriver, OR 97707
(541) 593-4394
www.sunrivernaturecenter.org

❸ Fall River Trail and Fish Hatchery

From Sunriver follow Hwy. 97 south to milepost 155, turn west on Forest Rd., drive 1 mile (1.6 km), and turn left on S. Century Dr. The entry to **Fall River Fish Hatchery** and five trailheads are 6 miles (9.7 km) south. Open May to September.

Fall River runs just 12 miles (19 km) but has large numbers of wading birds, birds of prey, songbirds, and waterfowl. Best time to visit is in fall. The 3.5-mile (5.6-km) north-side trail passes through old-growth ponderosa pines. A short trail on the south side has a footbridge and leads to the Fall River Campground.

Fall River Fish Hatchery
5055 S. Century Dr.
Bend, OR 97707
(541) 593-1510
www.dfw.state.or.us

❹ LaPine SP

Follow S. Century Dr. north to Huntington Rd., turn south, drive 3.2 miles (5.1 km) to State Recreation Rd., then make a right turn and drive 2.4 miles (3.9 km) to **LaPine SP.** Admission fee is charged.

The scenic Deschutes River park has 10 miles (16 km) of looping trails. Watch for red-tailed hawks, Steller's and other jays, boreal birds, and migrants. Along the river, note wood ducks, waterfowl, heron, and wading birds.

LaPine State Park
15800 State Recreation Rd.
LaPine, OR 97739
(800) 551-6949
www.oregonstateparks.org

Tule Lake NWR attracts many birds including, American avocets (left). Trails, blinds, and observation areas make for a great day of birding (above).

❺ Crater Lake NP

Return to Hwy. 97 and follow it south to Hwy. 138, turning west. The road leads 12 miles (19 km) to the north entrance of 249-square-mile (645 km²) **Crater Lake NP.** Roads in the park are subject to snow closures in winter, but snowstorms sometimes also occur during the summer. Admission fee charged.

The park's 33-mile (53-km) Rim Dr. provides spectacular views of varied terrain and many feathered residents, such as hairy woodpeckers, mountain chickadees, dark-eyed juncos, great horned and spotted owls, red-breasted nuthatches, brown creepers, Clark's nutcrackers,

and bald eagles—watch for them on snags by the rivers. The park features overlooks, picnic areas, and hiking trails, such as Rim Village Visitor Center trail, 2.6 miles (4.2 km) round-trip, and Crater Lake Lodge's 3.4-mile (5.5-km) round-trip trail.

Crater Lake National Park
P.O. Box 7
Crater Lake, OR 97604
(541) 594-3000
www.nps.gov/crla/

❻ Klamath Marsh NWR

Exit Crater Lake NP to the north and follow Hwy. 138 back to

Hwy. 97. Turn south for 9.5 miles (15.3 km), and east 6 miles (9.7 km) on Silver Lake Rd. The road bisects the 16,400-acre (6,637-h) wetlands of **Klamath Marsh NWR.** Public access is limited to wildlife auto routes, viewing areas, and—July to September—the canoe trail at Wocus Bay off FS Rd. 690, found 4 miles (6.4 km) south of the forest-marsh boundary on Silver Lake Rd.

Klamath Marsh is an important breeding area for waterfowl and colonial nesting birds, such as American white pelicans, sandhill cranes, and herons. Scan the sky for osprey, peregrine falcons, and bald eagles. From fall through spring, migrants rest in the marsh along with black terns, yellow rails, and great gray owls.

Klamath Basin NWR Complex
4009 Hill Rd.
Tulelake, CA 96134
(530) 667-2231
www.fws.gov

❼ Collier Memorial SP and Jackson F. Kimball SRA

Return to Hwy. 97 and drive south about 15 miles (24 km) to **Collier Memorial SP** and the confluence of Williamson River and Spring Creek. A 10-mile (16-km) trail connects the park to **Jackson F. Kimball SRA** on the Wood River. Admission fee charged.

Besides many river, wading, and boreal birds, a museum displays historic logging equipment. Keep an eye open for wood ducks.

Collier Memorial SP
46000 Hwy. 97
Chiloquin, OR 97624
(541) 783-2471
www.oregonstateparks.org

❽ Wood River Wetlands

Drive south on Hwy. 97 for 3.2 miles (5.1 km), turn right on Hwy. 422, and go about 3 miles

(4.8 km). Cross the Crater Lake Hwy., turn left on Modoc Point Rd., and drive 0.5 mile (0.8 km) south. Turn left at the sign into **Wood River Wetlands**.

Among the birds to be seen at the 3,000-acre (1,214-h) wetland are American bitterns, wood ducks, Forster's, Caspian, and black terns, yellow-headed and tricolored blackbirds, warblers, Bullock's orioles, great and snowy egrets, American avocets, sandhill cranes, peregrine falcons, Wilson's phalaropes, American white pelicans, and many other species of water birds.

BLM/Klamath Falls
2795 Anderson Ave., Bldg. 25
Klamath Falls, OR 97603
(541) 883-6916
www.or.blm.gov/Lakeview/kfra

❾ Upper Klamath NWR

West and south of the Wood River Wetlands is **Upper Klamath NWR,** another unit of Klamath Basin NWR Complex. Its main access is across Upper Klamath Lake. To reach it, drive south on Modoc Point Rd. and turn onto Levee Rd. Follow Agency Lake's perimeter, which holds many shorebird and waterfowl viewing opportunities. After traveling south and west, Levee Rd. turns north and its name changes to Fourmile Canal Rd. Follow the road to Brown Rd., turn left, and drive to Westside Rd. Malone Springs canoe launch is about 1.1 miles (1.8 km) south.

Watercraft are a must to fully experience this refuge, its 9.5-mile (15.3-km) self-guided canoe trail, and many eagles, white pelicans, ospreys, western and eared grebes, black terns, great blue herons, and snowy egrets.

Klamath Basin NWR Complex
4009 Hill Rd.
Tulelake, CA 96134
(530) 667-2231
www.fws.gov

❿ Klamath Falls

Within Klamath Falls are several sites on the Klamath Birding Trail. Putnam's Point Park is reliable in mid-May for mating western and Clark's grebes. Take Hwy. 97 to the Oregon Ave. exit west onto Lake Shore Dr. Cross the Link River Bridge and turn into the park. It's also a good spot for snowy egrets, green herons, Barrow's goldeneye, hooded mergansers, tree swallows, and in spring, migrating warblers. Next, visit Moore Park Marina and the Link River Trail by continuing on Lake Shore past Putnam Point Park. The 1.5-mile (2.4-km) trail connects Upper Klamath and Euwana lakes. Look for hooded mergansers and Barrow's goldeneyes (winter) and black-crowned night-herons roosting in the trees near Lower Klamath Lake.

Great Basin Visitor Association
205 Riverside Dr.
Klamath Falls, OR 97601
(800) 445-6728
www.klamathbirdingtrails.com

⓫ Miller Island

A 2.5-mile (4-km) loop is open year-round at the **Miller Island** unit of Oregon's Klamath Wild-

Lower Klamath NWR is a nesting ground for American white pelicans and other water and shorebirds.

A great blue heron's landing can be somewhat precarious, yet fascinating

life Area. Take Hwy. 97 south of Klamath Falls and turn west on Miller Island Rd.; the refuge is just across the railroad tracks. Nesting sandhill cranes perform mating dances here, and bald eagles are common February to March. Up to 35,000 snow geese visit the island during their annual migrations.

Klamath Wildlife Area
1850 Miller Island Rd. W
Klamath Falls, OR 97603
(541) 883-5734
www.dfw.state.or.us/wildlife
area/klamath_wa.htm

⑫ Klamath Basin NWR Complex

Several of the earlier waypoints were units of this far-ranging collection of bird refuges; south of Klamath Falls is the mother lode for migratory birding.

Start at **Bear Valley NWR,** a closed-to-the-public facility reputed worldwide for its bald-eagle flyouts during winter. The unit is on Hwy. 97 about 7 miles (11.3 km) farther south. Turn west onto Keno-Worden Rd. just south of Worden. A short distance after the railroad crossing turn left on an unpaved road for about 0.5 mile (0.8 km) and park along the shoulder near the refuge boundary. Plan a visit on overcast or rainy days, arriving a half hour before sunrise. Scores of bald eagles lift from their roosts, swooping past the spot en route to their nearby river and lake hunting grounds.

A few miles south, across the Oregon-California border, take Hwy. 161 east 4 miles (6.4 km) to the start of a 10-mile (16-km) auto tour of **Lower Klamath NWR.** The route has interpretive signs and photography blinds strategically placed for early morning photography.

Continue east on Hwy. 161 to Hill Rd., turn right, and drive south 4 miles (6.4 km) to the complex's visitors center. Hiking trails that follow the dikes from the center reward birders with waterfowl, pelicans, wading birds, raptors, eagles, and falcons. A short distance south are roadside viewing areas. **Tule Lake NWR** has photography blinds, a canoe trail, and overlooks. Look for white-faced ibis, pelicans, peregrine falcons, grebes, terns, and tricolored blackbirds, along with countless geese, ducks, swans, herons, and other migratory species.

The complex also oversees **Clear Lake NWR,** a unit closed to the public, east of Hwy. 139, nearby on FS Rd. 136.

Klamath Basin NWR Complex
4009 Hill Rd.
Tulelake, CA 96134
(530) 667-2231
www.fws.gov

⑬ Lava Beds NM

Continue south on Hill Rd. to the boundary of **Lava Beds NM,** a maze of cinder cones, lava flows, grasslands, and pine forests. Admission fee is charged.

The monument road has viewing pullouts likely to yield sightings of American kestrels, calliope hummingbirds, Say's phoebes, ash-throated flycatchers, loggerhead shrikes, and green-tailed towhees.

⑭ Mount Shasta Country

A final stop on the birding route is **Mount Shasta,** towering to the southwest. Retrace to Hwy. 97, turn south, and follow the road past **Grass Lake** to **Lake Shastina,** a desert lake populated by shore and migratory birds off Big Springs Rd.

North about 20 miles (32 km) near Montague on Big Springs Rd. is **Shasta Valley Wildlife Area,** another migrant bird area.

South of Weed on I-5 are vast tracts of **Shasta Trinity National Forest,** home to 200 species of forest and grassland birds, including jays, nuthatches, finches, and warblers.

Siskiyou Co. Visitors Bureau
P.O. Box 1138
Mount Shasta, CA 96067
(530) 926-3850
www.visitsiskiyou.org

Double-crested cormorants, nesting condo style, in the trees at Lake Shastina, form gregarious colonies.

San Francisco to Monterey

While the largest estuary found on California's Pacific Coast is San Francisco Bay and the Sacramento/San Joaquin delta, Monterey Bay is perhaps its most scenic. The Bay Area is a bird-watching haven filled with varied habitats and avian visitors.

Birds leave more than their hearts in San Francisco; well over 475 species visit the region to feed, rest, mate, nest, and rear their young. From ocean shorelines to golden hilltops and from forests to wetland fields, the region attracts seabirds, coastal migrants, neotropical wayfarers, shorebirds, songbirds, waders, predators, and scavengers both diverse in species and numbering many thousands. Competitive birders rack up daily counts of 170 species and higher in the avian-rich area. Start in the north at Point Reyes, pass through the bird-friendly bay counties, and wind down the coast to Monterey while experiencing this sampler of northern California's birding bounty and scenic beauty.

Monterey Bay, with its sandy beaches stretching for miles to the north, is home to willets and other sandpipers.

A western gull surveys its lunchtime possibilities from atop a piling in the Monterey Bay's harbor.

❶ Point Reyes NS

Point Reyes National Seashore has an astonishing count of 490 recorded bird species. Its 70,000 acres (28,328 h) of estuaries, grasslands, coastlines, and forests account for the site's numerous feathered visitors, as does its prominent location on the Pacific Flyway.

Reach the seashore by taking Hwy. 101 north from San Francisco, crossing the Golden Gate Bridge, taking Shoreline Hwy. (Hwy. 1) exit, heading west under the freeway, and driving about 18 miles (29 km) to the coast and past **Bolinas Lagoon** (worth a stop for wading birds and waterfowl), then 11 miles (17.7 km) to Bear Valley Rd. Turn left and drive 1.5 miles (2.4 km) to a red barn on the left, Bear Valley Visitors Center. Pick up bird lists, brochures, and maps, then proceed into Point Reyes sprawling park.

Routes of particular interest to birders include Bear Valley Trail for warblers, sparrows, kinglets, thrushes, wrens, woodpeckers, and hummingbirds. Follow Estero Trail among the old pines to find long-eared and great horned owls. In the estero (Spanish for lagoon) proper, see egrets, herons, and loons.

Above the bluffs on the rolling grasslands, look for hawks. Abbotts Lagoon is the best locale for wintering ducks and raptors, such as black-shouldered kites. Its beaches are also nesting sites for endangered western snowy plover—walk carefully and avoid trampling eggs and young during the spring and summer. In winter ring-necked ducks, green herons, hooded mergansers, and grebes visit Five Brooks

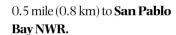

Black skimmers' have a top bill that is notably shorter.

Pond. En route, look in the trees for pileated woodpeckers, swallows, hawks, warblers, and thrushes. Save as a finale Point Reyes Lighthouse and its cliffs, which host brown pelicans and Brandt's cormorants, common murres, pigeon guillemots, loons, and surf scoters in fall. Rocky beaches below sport black oystercatchers all year, while in spring or early summer occasional tufted puffins visit. Return via **Drakes Bay** to see loons, grebes, cormorants, scaups, and scoters.

Point Reyes National Seashore is worth a full day's birding or more. If time allows, the marshes at the head of Tomales Bay—smack atop and a result of the notorious San Andreas Fault—are good bird-viewing spots.

Point Reyes National Seashore
1 Bear Valley Rd.
Point Reyes Station, CA 94956
(415) 464-5100
www.nps.gov/pore/index.htm

❷ San Pablo Bay NWR

Return to Hwy. 1 and turn south. Turn left a short distance later on Sir Francis Drake Blvd. and drive over the coast range 23 miles (37 km) through Fairfax to San Rafael. Join Hwy. 101 north for 9 miles (14.5 km) to Hwy. 37, turn east, and drive 5.4 miles (8.7 km) past Lakeville Hwy., turn right, and continue

0.5 mile (0.8 km) to **San Pablo Bay NWR.**

The refuge is located on the bay's northern shore with open water and tidal marshes. See waterbirds, dabbling and diving ducks, shorebirds, and raptors. Starting in May, it's a nesting place for black-necked stilts, mallards, gadwalls, barn swallows, and Caspian terns. Large heron and egret rookeries are also worth a look.

At **Tolay Creek,** 2 miles (3.2 km) east near the junction of highways 37 and 121, a 4-mile (6.4-km) hiking trail gives limited access for viewing birds.

The refuge is open year-round during daylight hours but has no site facilities; its headquarters are in Vallejo, well to the east.

San Pablo Bay NWR
7715 Lakeville Hwy.
Petaluma, CA 94954
(707) 769-4200
www.fws.gov

❸ Richardson Bay Audubon Center and Sanctuary

Return to Hwy. 101, turn south, and drive approximately 15 miles (24 k m) to the Tiburon exit. Cross over the freeway, drive east 0.7 mile (1.3 km) to

Richardson Bay Audubon Center & Sanctuary's overlook has a weatherproof field guide for handy reference (above). Lyford House (right) displays artwork by John James Audubon. It is open to tours by appointment. Look for the entrance sign (far right) on Greenwood Cove Rd.

Greenwood Cove Rd., turn right, and follow Greenwood Cove Rd. to **Richardson Bay Audubon Center and Sanctuary.** They have 911 acres (369 h) of land and offshore waters, closed to boating half the year.

The center has a 0.5-mile (0.8-km) trail, platforms with viewing scopes, a redwood grove, a native plant garden, a pond, a hummingbird garden, and scenic Richardson Bay shoreline.

Richardson Bay Audubon
Center & Sanctuary
376 Greenwood Beach Rd.
Tiburon, CA 94920
(415) 388-2524
www.tiburonaudubon.org

❹ Golden Gate NRA–Marin Headlands

Return to Hwy. 101 south. Just north of the Golden Gate Bridge, take the Conzelman Rd. exit and drive southwest about 2 miles (3.2 km), looking for the Hawk Hill sign. **Marin Headlands** is the area's most famous hawk-watching site, with thousands of raptors passing over during the peak months of September and October. The Hawk Hill name was bestowed by local birders.

Conzelman Rd. continues to overlook the Golden Gate—the entrance to San Francisco Bay whose name predates its landmark bridge—and a lonely lighthouse on the headlands. Walk its many-stepped path to see raptors, seabirds, and gulls riding the strong updrafts. This locale also provides a glimpse out into the Pacific Ocean far to the distant west of the Farallon Islands, isolated rocky crags that provide nesting grounds for a dozen species of rare and endangered seabirds and a roosting spot for tens of thousands of common species. Birding tour operators in Sausalito and San Francisco offer boat trips offshore to see the site. Return to Hwy. 101, cross the bridge back into the city, and prepare to enjoy bountiful urban birding.

Golden Gate National Parks
Fort Mason, Bldg. 201
San Francisco, CA 94123
(415) 561-4700
www.nps.gov/goga/

❺ San Francisco

This former Gold Rush port is now a sophisticated metropolis surrounded on three sides by salt water—the Pacific in the west and San Francisco Bay to the north and east. Urban transport on bus, trolley, train, or the singular experience of the cable car brings birding sites at every street corner and stop.

Begin with a visit to **Golden Gate Park,** 45 city blocks and 1,013 acres (410 h) bounded by Lincoln Way on the south, Fulton St. on the north, Stanyan St. on the east, and the Pacific Ocean at the west—the largest man-made city park in the world. As in any city parks, it's best to bird in pairs or groups for personal safety.

Within the park Stow Lake has an 0.8-mile (1.3-km) path with two footbridges to Strawberry Hill Island, encircling it. This reservoir attracts mallard and ring-necked ducks plus green-winged and cinnamon teal in winter. On the island's west side note a heronry of black-crowned night-herons. In the trees surrounding the lake, watch for migrating warblers, flycatchers, and tanagers.

S.F. Recreation and Park Dept.
501 Stanyan St.
San Francisco, CA 94117
(415) 831-2700
www.parks.sfgov.org

Exiting the park and heading north on the Great Pacific

Hwy., past Point Lobos and the Cliff House, the road turns at Geary Blvd. Follow it east to 34th Ave., turn left, and enter **Lincoln Park,** where it becomes Legion of Honor Dr. (There's good birding along the cliffs below the museum.) The route now follows part of a scenic drive marked by blue signs bearing seagulls, leading via El Camino del Mar and Lincoln Ave. to Golden Gate NRA's Presidio Unit. As Lincoln Ave. passes Bowley St. beyond the Sea Cliff neighbor-

hood, 0.5-mile (0.8-km) Lobos Creek Valley Trail leads to a boardwalk along the last of San Francisco's natural streams, one of the best spots for songbirds in the Presidio. Note also the parking areas for **Baker's Beach,** another good seabirding site during early morning hours; later in the day the beach fills with people. This parking lot is a trailhead for Mountain Lake Trail, with a 2.4-mile (3.9-km) path leading to the Broadway gate on the Presidio's other side.

Drive north on Lincoln, cross under Hwy. 101, and turn left 0.2 mile (0.3 km) from the underpass on Long Ave. This road leads to Fort Point, with good views of gulls and seabirds by the Golden Gate Bridge. At its intersection with Marine Dr., turn east and join Mason St., which leads to the **Crissy Field Wetlands** and 100 acres (40 h) of shoreline and lagoon, with ample wading and shorebirds. Crissy Field Center overlooks the marsh, providing full-access facilities.

Crissy Field Center
603 Mason St.
San Francisco, CA 94129
(415) 561-7690
www.crissyfield.org

(415) 561-4449
www.presidio.gov

❻ Don Edwards San Francisco Bay NWR

Leaving San Francisco, drive south on Hwy. 101 about 30 miles (48 km) to Dumbarton Bridge exit (Hwy. 84). Turn east, cross the bridge, exit at Thornton Ave., and drive south 0.8 mile (1.3 km) to enter **Don Edwards San Francisco Bay NWR.** Follow Marshlands Rd. to the stop sign and parking lot.

Besides its 280 known bird species, the refuge has a visitors center, trails, and 30,000 acres (12,141 h) of open waters, salt ponds, tidal marsh, and mudflats ringing the entire southern end of San Francisco Bay. Tens of thousands of shorebirds and waterfowl visit the refuge during spring and fall migration,

Golden Gate NRA—Marin Headlands gives visitors striking views of the scenic bay entrance and, on clear days, the Pacific Ocean stretching to the Farrallon Islands. During summer it's equally likely that the narrow Golden Gate strait will be cloaked in dense and fast-moving blankets of bone-chilling fog. The best times to visit are in spring and fall, when clear skies and moderate temperatures reveal hundreds of sea and shorebirds on the water, roosting on cliffs and offshore rocks, or flying overhead.

Barn swallows use mud to build their nests on bridges, piers, garages, and, of course, barns

Don Edwards San Francisco Bay NWR provides a raised walkway over fragile salt marsh, allowing close-up views of birds that are visiting the wetlands.

such as black-bellied and endangered snowy plovers. Its resident species include endangered California clapper rails and, infrequently, Virginia rails.

Use the raised boardwalks and dike trails to approach the tidal flats and estuaries filled with shorebirds. Several provide full access.

Don Edwards San Francisco Bay NWR
1 Marshlands Rd.
Fremont, CA 94552
(510) 792-0222
www.fws.gov/desfbay

❼ Palo Alto Baylands Nature Preserve

Return across the Dumbarton Bridge on Hwy. 84 to Hwy. 101 (westbound toll), turn south, and take the Embarcadero Rd. exit. Cross the freeway and drive east on Embarcadero Rd. to the **Palo Alto Baylands Nature Preserve.** This site features 15 miles (24 km) of trails, 1,940 acres (785 h) of marsh, and viewing platforms. While compact, it's one of the region's best birding areas. It's common to see mixed waterfowl, wading birds, shorebirds, and raptors.

Palo Alto Baylands Nature Preserve
2775 Embarcadero Rd.
Palo Alto, CA 94303
(650) 463-4900
www.city.palo-alto.ca.us/community-services/pk-baylands.html

❽ U.S. Highway 1

Return north on Hwy. 101 to Hwy. 92, turn west, and drive over the coastal hills 15 miles to **Half Moon Bay** and the intersection with Hwy. 1. Turn north, drive 4 miles (6.4 km) to Prince-

ton, turn left at the small boat harbor, and drive through town to **Pillar Point.** En route check the harbor for waterfowl and seabirds, including loons, and grebes, plus brant in spring.

Walk the trail to the point, noting seabirds, gulls, and pelicans flying along the shore or roosting on the rocks.

Return to Hwy. 1, turn south, and drive approximately 40 miles (64 km) down the coast to **Santa Cruz,** a college town that marks the north boundary of Monterey Bay. Along the way, public bluffs, beaches, waysides, and coastal

Snowy **plovers** visit sea-washed **sandy margins** found near Monterey to **nest and forage** for food

streams are filled with shorebirds and wading birds, along with many types of songbirds, hawks, kites, and other soaring species.

This coastline is renowned as a scenic byway, one especially enjoyable to drive on sunny afternoons when the rocky coast and flying birds stand in silhouette against the shimmering sea.

South of Santa Cruz, Hwy. 1 dips inland behind a series of resort towns. The next destination, 26 miles (42 km) south, is **Elkhorn Slough** a National Estuarine Research Reserve and 2,500-acre (1,012-h) coastal wetland with marsh and tidal flats that hosts 346 recorded species of birds—plus many bird-watchers and kayakers.

Take Hwy. 1 past the fishing hamlet of Moss Landing to a left turn at Dolan Rd. by the power plant, drive 3.5 miles (5.6 km) to Elkhorn Rd., turn left, and drive 1.9 miles (3.1 km) to the gate and visitors center. Open 9:00 A.M. to 5 P.M. Wednesday to Sunday. Admission fee is charged,

The best way to see this area is by kayak or canoe; outfitters in Moss Landing rent equipment; others conduct guided birding tours of the refuge. The other option is to walk its many miles of shoreline trails.

Elkhorn Slough National Estuarine Research Reserve
1700 Elkhorn Rd.
Watsonville, CA 95076
(831) 728-2822
www.elkhornslough.org

Before continuing south to Monterey, return to Hwy. 1, drive 1 mile (1.6 km) north to Jetty Rd., and turn left; follow it to **Moss Landing SB.** The unit has hiking trails, sand dunes, beachfront, and bird-watching from its jetty to the Pajaro River's mouth.

CA State Parks, Monterey Dist.
2211 Garden Rd.
Monterey, CA 93940
(831) 649-2836
www.parks.ca.gov

❾ Monterey Bay

The Monterey Peninsula is heavily impacted by tourism; call well in advance of visiting for reservations. Moss Landing SB provided a sampling of the bird-watching potential of this scenic spot. With woodlands, marshes, rivers, meadows, sandy shores, and craggy coastal promontories, it's a good place to try for a birding grand slam.

Resident waterbirds include brant, cormorants, diving ducks, petrels, storm-petrels, shearwaters, and other species. Large and small wading birds are also common—egrets, herons, night-herons, black oyster-catchers—and flocks of shore-birds. In spring and fall, coastal waters fill with migratory and resident waterfowl and geese. Inland a mile or two, there are upland game birds, from California quail to band-tailed pigeons, along with hawks, Steller's jays, Hutton's vireos, falcons, swifts,

warblers, swallows, and even California condors.

Start shorebird-watching at **Point Piños** in Pacific Grove, a rocky spot with 339 recorded species. Crespi Pond, Rocky Point, and sandy beaches at low tide are good birding spots. Note that golf courses are off limits.

Just 5 miles (8 km) south on Hwy. 1 is Carmel and **Carmel River SB.** Turn right on Rio Rd., left on Santa Lucia Ave., and left again on Carmelo St., which leads to the park's day-use lot and wetland trailhead.

The marsh and sand spit is justly known for eastern warblers

during the fall, but the spot has 345 resident and migrant species notched on its belt.

Another birding spot to see south of Carmel is **Point Sur,** 19 miles (31 km) to the south on Hwy. 1. A mile (1.6 km) farther, **Andrew Molera SP** sits at the mouth of the **Big Sur River,** ending the tour. Admission fee is charged.

CA State Parks, Monterey Dist.
2211 Garden Rd.
Monterey, CA 93940
(831) 649-2836
www.parks.ca.gov

Monterey Bay is nature at its best. Here, sunbathing cormorants and a harbor seal seem to pose for the camera.

Santa Barbara, Los Angeles, and San Diego

Southern California is a setting for more than surfing and Hollywood action. Here, bird-watchers enjoy neotropical visitors and resident species in a confluence of ocean, desert, mountain, and urban habitats rarely seen elsewhere on the continent.

California's south coast differs from temperate climate zones to the north; this is an arid climate with scant rainfall. Still, winter rains bring grasslands and deserts alive with spurts of vitality, blanketing them with flowers. Avian visitors are drawn north from Mexico, and only nearby Arizona hosts more hummingbird species. Scan the skies above the coastal mountains and a life list may soon include a rare California condor, largest of all the raptors. Owls, groove-billed anis, yellow-billed cuckoos, greater roadrunners, and many other unusual sightings emerge when birders partake of the rich birding venue found on the coast between Santa Barbara in the north and San Diego to the south.

Black-necked stilts inhabit coastal lagoons and lakes throughout the Southwest. Easy identifiers are their tuxedo-like plumage and needle-shaped bills paired with distinctive, intensely red legs.

Andrée Clark Bird Refuge in Santa Barbara is a natural area sandwiched between Hwy. 1 and the city's bustling small-boat harbor.

❶ Santa Barbara

Santa Barbara nestles in a Riviera-like setting reminiscent of Mediterranean Spain or France, with the city sprinkled up the slopes of steep mountains before a vista of sparkling ocean dotted with the offshore islands of **Channel Islands NP.**

Start the tour within the city limits by visiting **Rocky Nook County Park**—from Hwy. 101, take Mission St. exit and turn north toward the hills. Turn right on Los Olivos St. (becoming Mission Canyon Rd.) at the Mountain Dr. intersection, the location of the park.

The 19-acre (7.7-h) park, with oak and sycamore trees overlooking Mission Creek, is open 8 A.M. until sunset. Follow its short trails for easy birding.

Avian residents of the riparian park include band-tailed pigeons, California thrashers, woodpeckers, Hutton's vireos, owls, and wrentits. From fall to spring, warblers, tanagers, orioles, and nuthatches migrate into the area.

Rocky Nook County Park
610 Mission Canyon Rd.
Santa Barbara, CA 93105
(805) 568-2461
www.sbparks.org

Return to Mission Canyon Rd., turn right, and drive north to the stop sign at Foothill Rd. (Hwy. 192). Turn right briefly, then left where Mission Canyon Rd. resumes, and follow the left fork onto Tunnel Rd., leading in 0.5 mile (0.8 km) to **Santa Barbara Botanic Garden.**

Admission fee charged. The garden's habitats along Mission Creek fill 78 acres (32 h) and host 123 recorded species of seasonal and resident birds with a mix of flowering plants, trees, and shrubs. Xeriscape and native plantings attract birds that feed and nest on its grounds.

Birds common on the creek include several hummingbird species, brown creepers, winter wrens, California quail, wrentits, California thrashers, and oak titmice. Follow the Garden Trail for a 1- to 3-mile (1.6- to 4.8-km) branching loop. Stop at a bench to sit quietly and watch the birds.

Andrée Clark Bird Refuge at Santa Barbara's East Beach comprises a 42-acre (17-h) saltwater marsh, enabling wild birds to mingle among its many beachgoers.

Santa Barbara Botanic Garden
1212 Mission Canyon Rd.
Santa Barbara, CA 93105
(805) 682-4726 ext. 101
www.sbbg.org

Isla Vista County Park is in the Santa Barbara suburb of Goleta. Reach it by returning to Hwy. 101, turning west, and driving 7.5 miles (12 km) to Los

69

A California quail watches over chicks as they feed

Carneros Rd. Drive south to its end at El Colegio Rd., turn left, then right on Camino Corta, which ends at the park and a series of coastal bluff trails leading west. They overlook offshore kelp beds with many seabirds, gulls, pelicans, and other wading birds and shorebirds.

Santa Barbara County Parks
610 Mission Canyon Rd.
Santa Barbara, CA 93105
(805) 568-2461
www.sbparks.org

Leaving the prior waypoint, turn right on Del Playa Dr., follow it to its end, and park on the neighborhood streets. A trail leads to the ocean and **Devereux Slough,** a brackish lagoon and sandy spit regularly visited by 290 recorded species of birds. The lagoon reserve adjoins the UC Santa Barbara (UCSB) campus.

Both the lagoon's margins and the adjacent beaches are worth a visit. Look for Caspian and least terns, curlews, plovers, and sandpipers in summer, or migratory waterfowl and wading birds in winter. Peregrine falcons and merlin regularly roost in the trees. Egrets and great blue herons stalk the shallows. Walk the 1.5-mile (2.4-km) loop that encircles the UCSB lagoon and the **More Mesa** bluff beach trails east and west of Coal Oil Point. In winter the creek may divide the sand spit and block the trails and road.

UC Santa Barbara NRS
Santa Barbara, CA 93106
(805) 893-4127
coaloilpoint.ucnrs.org/subpage1 /visitor/index.html

Retrace the outbound route to Hwy. 101 and drive east an exit to Patterson Ave. Go south 1.5 miles (2.4 km), pull off before the bridge, and park. Trails lead to the coast and **Atascadero Creek Bike Path** from the gate at the end of the road.

Walk the bike path to its end at Goleta Beach, looking for bobolinks, white-tailed kites, warblers, vireos, longspurs, lazuli and indigo buntings, blue grosbeaks, and sparrows.

Santa Barbara Conference and Visitors Bureau
1601 Anacapa St.
Santa Barbara, CA 93101
(805) 966-9222

These samplers are just a hint of Santa Barbara's rich birding possibilities. If time permits, also visit **Los Carneros Lake** in Goleta, 0.3 mile (0.5 km) north of Hwy. 101 on Los Carneros Rd. It's a good spot for raptors, kingbirds, hummingbirds, waxwings, robins, tanagers, and thrushes.

Another good spot for birdwatching is **Arroyo Burro County Beach Park,** found to the south and west of downtown; off Hwy. 101, take the Las Positas Rd. exit and follow Cliff Dr.

There's also fine shorebirding at West Beach and Palm Beach in the boat harbor, where charter boats head offshore for tours of the Channel Islands.

Finish a few blocks east at East Beach and **Andrée Clark Bird Refuge** to see dabbling and diving ducks, great blue herons, egrets, rails, and marsh wrens, as well as many small wading birds. The refuge's trails and observation platforms are open sunrise to 10 P.M. daily.

Andrée Clark Bird Refuge
1400 E. Cabrillo Blvd.
Santa Barbara, CA 93108
(805) 564-5418
www.santabarbaraca.gov/parks

❷ Channel Islands NP

Miles out in the ocean looms **Channel Islands NP,** an archipelago with more birding. Boat and catamaran tours leave from the small boat harbors in Santa

The male California quail often perches as a lookout above ground level so it can signal a warning should danger confront the covey from any direction.

Barbara and from Ventura, 29 miles (47 km) south on Hwy. 101, to visit the offshore islands of Anacapa, Santa Cruz, Santa Rosa, San Miguel, and Santa Barbara. These trips are a rare chance to see many seabirds, including Xantus's murrelets, auklets, shearwaters, jaegers, skuas, and nesting brown pelicans. On these isolated outposts many island birds have developed traits unseen elsewhere.

Channel Islands NP
1901 Spinnaker Dr.
Ventura, CA 93001
(805) 658-5730
www.nps.gov

❸ Greater Los Angeles

South on Hwy. 101 from Santa Barbara, other spots to consider for seabird and shorebird

Audubon House welcomes visitors to San Joaquin Wildlife Sanctuary in Irvine, open 8 A.M. to 4 P.M. daily.

watching include **Lookout Park,** at the Summerland exit. Also try **Carpinteria Beach SP;** exit at Casitas Pass Rd., drive to Carpinteria Ave., make a right turn at the signal, and turn left on Palm Ave. (Full services available; admission fee charged.) Just 2.2 miles (3.5 km) farther, **Rincon Beach County Park** at Bates Road is open for day use until sunset.

Then bid adieu to wide-open spaces, drive the Ventura Fwy. (Hwy. 101) south, and enter one of the largest urban multiplexes in the nation: Los Angeles. Its scores of interlocked cities extend 150 miles (241 km) south from Thousand Oaks to Orange County and beyond. For birdlife the application of water to what once was barren scrublands has transformed the L.A. basin into a subtropical habitat replete with palms, flowers, and lush shrubs.

The impact has been mixed. Many migrants winter within the area, side by side with native residents. As a result, parrots, parakeets, macaws, and other former pet birds are now endemic to the region and building thriving flocks.

Continue east on the Ventura Fwy., following the signs where it splits for Pasadena and turns into Hwy. 134, then drive past the junction with the Foothill Fwy.

(I-210), where its name changes again. About 7.5 miles (12.1 km) beyond Pasadena are the city of Arcadia and the lovingly tended grounds of **Los Angeles County Arboretum and Botanic Garden.** Open 9 A.M. to 5 P.M. daily. Admission fee is charged.

Over 230 bird species have been noted in the arboretum's 127-acre (51-h) gardens, such as hawks and other raptors, swifts, bushtits, woodpeckers, vireos, waxwings, brown creepers, owls, finches, swallows, pipits, titmice, flycatchers, nuthatches, kinglets, shrikes, and tanagers.

Arboretum of Los Angeles
301 N. Baldwin Ave.
Arcadia, CA 91007
(626) 821-3222
www.arboretum.org

About 38 miles (61 km) to the southwest across the city is **Ken Malloy Harbor Regional Park** in Harbor City. Follow Baldwin Ave. south to Huntington Dr., turn west, drive to Rosemead Blvd., turn left, and drive south to the San Bernardino Fwy. (I-10). Drive I-10 west following the Santa Monica signs to the Harbor Fwy. (I-110) junction. Last, drive 19 miles (31 km) south on I-110 to the Anaheim St. exit, turn right, and follow the street 0.7 mile (1.1 km) to the park entrance. Open 5:30 A.M. to 10:30 P.M. daily.

Unusual in the Los Angeles basin, the park has a mix of wetlands, ponds, lakes, and riparian

willows, all great bird habitats. It's a rare day here that birdwatchers count fewer than 100 species, but birds in residence peak during the winter. Several full-access trails through the park's 241 acres (98 h) link its sections.

Harbor Regional Park
25820 South Vermont Ave.
Harbor City, CA 90710
(310) 548-7728
www.laparks.org

❹ Orange County

Exit the prior waypoint, follow the outbound path to the Harbor Fwy. and turn north to its junction with the San Diego Fwy. (I-405). Drive about 34 miles (55 km) south to Jamboree Rd. exit and turn right, then left on Michelson Rd. and right on Riparian View Rd., the entrance to the Irvine Ranch Water District water-treatment plant and **San Joaquin Wildlife Sanctuary.** Follow the Audubon signs to the sanctuary, open from dawn to dusk daily.

The 300-acre (121-h) refuge set in business parks and city is a sanctuary of calm. Among its habitats are coastal freshwater wetlands, marshes, ponds, and stands of willow, alder, and cottonwood. It has 10 miles (16 km) of trails and annually hosts more than 200 bird species, such as common yellowthroats, song sparrows, marsh wrens, Anna's hummingbirds, and tree and cliff swallows, plus

 Not to Be Missed!

Mission San Juan Capistrano

Every spring around March 19 the return of the cliff swallows to Capistrano occurs practically like clockwork. This landmark mission has become world famous as a symbol of the beauty and romance of the spring migration of the far-ranging birds.

Many stories are told about why they choose the mission. The best known of these relates that a storekeeper kept sweeping down the nests and shooing them away, whereas a kindly padre at the mission welcomed all of them to nest there.

Another anecdote is taken from the Juaneno Indians, who thought the birds flew from the Holy Land and carried little twigs in their mouths to float in the ocean and give themselves a place to rest.

Scientists have since determined that the swallows migrate from Goya, Argentina, leaving there each year on February 18 and flying 7,500 miles (12,068 km) to arrive at the mission 30 days later on St. Joseph's Day. They fly at altitudes of 2,000 feet (610 m), using tailwinds to speed them on their way and stay above predators.

The festival to celebrate the end of the swallows' journey draws a large crowd. Reservations are advised.

Mission San Juan
Capistrano
26801 Ortega Hwy.
San Juan Capistrano,
CA 92675

Mission San Juan Capistrano's Sacred Garden and Bell Wall (above); one of the famous swallows that return to the mission each year on St. Joseph's Day on March 19 (far right); and an interpretive sign describing birds of the area (lower right). Look under roofs for swallows' nests.

pied-billed grebes, great blue herons, egrets, and many species of waterfowl. Also visit its Audubon House.

Sea and Sage Audubon Society
P.O. Box 5447
Irvine, CA 92616
(949) 261-7963
www.seaandsageaudubon.org

Return to Jamboree Rd. Turn left, follow Jamboree to the Pacific Coast Hwy. (Hwy. 1), then turn left and drive 5.5 miles (8.8 km). **Crescent Bay Point Park** in the northern outskirts of Laguna is found off Cliff Dr. on bluffs overlooking the Pacific Ocean. Open 6 A.M. to 10 P.M. daily.

Mainly an overlook for the rocks and waters of the marine refuge below, it's a fine place to bring a spotting scope to look at roosting seabirds and to observe hawks and gulls riding the uplifts and thermals of onshore winds as they meet the bluffs. On a calm day these are gentle breezes, but during storms the crash of waves on the shore makes the ground shudder and splashes spray far inland.

Join In

Mission San Juan Capistrano's Return of the Swallows
Held annually in March

A festival of renewal marking springtime and the conclusion of the long migration

- Traditional bell ringing
- Ethnic foods
- Docent-led guided tours
- Children's activities
- Artisans and crafts
- Music, Aztec dancers, and storytelling

Find out more at
www.missionjc.com/swallowsfest.html/

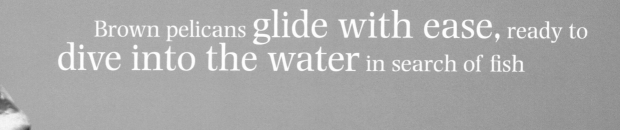

Brown pelicans **glide with ease,** ready to **dive into the water** in search of fish

Along its bluffs, Cabrillo NM offers commanding views of shorebirds and kettles of hawks, drawn by prey and effortless conditions for soaring.

Cabrillo NM commemorates the spot where seafaring Europeans first landed on the western coast of what would someday become the United States of America. Its lighthouse was built centuries later.

When the sea is calm, walk down to the cove. Gulls and shorebirds ply the strand in early morning—before the beach fills to capacity with beachcombers, surfers, sunbathers, picnickers, and skin divers.

Crescent Bay Point Park
City of Laguna Beach
505 Forest Ave.
Laguna Beach, CA 92651
(949) 497-3311
www.lagunabeachcity.net

Continue south into downtown Laguna on Hwy. 1 and Broadway St. (Hwy. 133), turn left, and drive 3 miles (4.8 km) as the road changes its name to Laguna Canyon Dr.; turn left into the parking lot of **Laguna Coast Wilderness Park.** Open weekends only for unrestricted use.

Parking fee is charged; parking hours 8 A.M. to 4 P.M. The park is closed to access for at least 72 hours following storms. When hiking park trails, take plenty of water and use sun protection in all seasons. Though near the ocean, this is a desert-dry area of chaparral and scrub brush, ideal as habitat for the cactus wren, an endangered species.

Walk fire trails into the park through canyons and rock-strewn ridges. Note wildflowers, then hummingbirds, then raptors, including rare downward views of the soaring birds from high ridges above.

County of Orange RDMD/HB&P
1 Irvine Park Rd.
Orange, CA 92869
(714) 973-6865
www.ocparks.com/lagunacoast/

❺ San Diego Area

Rejoin the San Diego Fwy. by driving east on Hwy. 133, taking the right fork onto El Toro Rd. and entering Hwy. 73 south. In about 6 miles (9.7 km) it joins I-5, hugs the Pacific coast, leaves Orange County, and heads south toward San Diego.

The first stop, about 55 miles (88 km) from the junction of Hwy. 73 and I-5, is **Torrey Pines State Reserve.** Stay on I-5 as it splits from I-805 by bearing right. Exit on Genesee Ave., turn west, then right on Torrey Pines Rd. The park's entrance is on the left. Open daily; admission fee is charged. It has a visitors center and 8 miles (12.9 km) of trails and walks.

This park, set on namesake endangered pine-studded bluffs that rise up from the beach, is

home to swifts, thrashers, crows, California towhees, woodpeckers, northern mockingbirds, bushtits, California quail, mourning doves, and wrentits, as well as hawks.

Torrey Pines Docent Society
P.O. Box 2414
Del Mar, CA 92014
(858) 755-2063
www.torreypine.org

To reach the next waypoint, **La Jolla Point,** drive south on Torrey Pines Rd. into downtown La Jolla, turn right on Prospect St., then right on Coast Blvd. This scenic street hugs the shore at Point La Jolla, site of **Ellen Scripps Browning Park** and an excellent seabird-viewing site. At the rocky north point with street parking, see shorebirds, pelagic cormorants, pelicans, gulls, and terns, especially during migration and when tides are low.

Join In

During stormy weather, the grassy field fills with gulls waiting for the wind to pass. To the south, rocky promontories shelter cusps of beach in view of offshore kelp beds, a favorite habitat for diving ducks and small wading birds, such as sandpipers. The next three waypoints and this site are all units of the San Diego Park and Recreation Dept.

SD Park and Recreation Dept.
5180 Tecolote Rd.
San Diego, CA 92110
(848) 581-9944
www.sandiego.gov/
park-and-recreation/

Marian Bear Memorial Park is nearby; head east via Prospect St. and Torrey Pines Blvd. to the split and follow La Jolla Pkwy. to I-5 and Hwy. 52. The 467-acre (189-h) park is a strip on the south side of Hwy. 52 between I-5 and I-805 with 3 miles (4.8 km) of trails into arroyos and over mesas. Exit from Hwy. 52 at Genesee Ave.

Whimbrels winter on Pacific Coast beaches.

and Regents Rd., which lead to parking areas and trailheads entering the park.

Marion Bear Park preserves the oak and riparian forests of San Clemente Canyon, a habitat rich in woodpeckers, hawks, Anna's and Costa's hummingbirds, mourning doves, wrens, wrentits, and warblers.

Return to I-5 and drive south 1.8 miles (2.9 km) to Mission Bay Dr. exit, leading to Garnet Ave. and turning west. Turn left on Noyes St. just before the junction with Grand Ave. and drive to its end at Pacific Beach Dr. Across the street are **Kendall-Frost Mission Bay Marsh Preserve** and the adjoining Northern Wildlife Preserve. Park on the street by the kiosk.

Use overlooks on Pacific Beach Rd. and Crown Point Dr. to view this remnant of the coastal salt marsh habitat and tidal estuaries. Thousands of skimmers and other shorebirds visit its waterways and mudflats.

In winter endangered light-footed clapper rails and Belding's savannah sparrow frequent the marsh. Use a spotting scope or binoculars; visitors should not enter the preserve.

Drive north on Noyes St. to Balboa Ave., turn right, follow it (it becomes Garnet Ave., then Balboa again) across I-5 to Clair-

mont Dr., and turn left. Proceed to Clairmont Mesa Blvd., turn right, then right again at Genesee Ave. Finally, turn right on Bannock Ave. and park at North Clairmont Recreation Center, the trailhead of **Tecolote Canyon Natural Park.**

Tecolote means "owl" in Spanish, and the birds are common here. Follow the 6.5-mile (10.5-km) trail along the creek, noting hawks, jays, woodpeckers, and migrating warblers as well as flammulated, northern saw-whet, and great horned owls and western screech-owls. It's a dry landscape; take lots of water and beware of rattlesnakes.

Return to I-5 by the outbound path, drive south about 3 miles (4.8 km) to Rosecrans St., and follow it southwest to Cañon St. Turn right, then left onto Catalina Blvd. The next stop, **Cabrillo NM,** is at the tip of Point Loma. Admission fee is charged.

Exhibits at the visitors center interpret the Cabrillo landing in 1542, the first European contact with the future United States's Pacific coastline.

For birders the site's 144 acres (58 h), many trails, and overlooks provide discovery of a different sort, with wrentits, towhees, western scrub-jays, soaring hawks, and Anna's, Costa's, and rufous hummingbirds; hummers are especially common sights in spring.

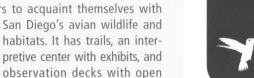

◁◁ Not to Be Missed!

Chula Vista Nature Center at Sweetwater Marsh NWR on San Diego Bay

From I-5 south of downtown San Diego, take the E St. exit in Chula Vista and go west on Gunpowder Point Dr. to the public parking lot—regularly scheduled shuttle buses service the nature center. Admission fee is charged. Open Tuesday through Sunday except major holidays, 10 A.M. to 5 P.M.

The reserve has recorded 224 species of birds and is a good starting point for visiting birders to acquaint themselves with San Diego's avian wildlife and habitats. It has trails, an interpretive center with exhibits, and observation decks with open views for bird-watching.

Chula Vista Nature Center
1000 Gunpowder Point Dr.
Chula Vista, CA 91910
(619) 409-5900
www.chulavistanature center.org

To the sea, wave after wave of brown pelicans glide by, rising and falling over glassy swells.

Cabrillo National Monument
1800 Cabrillo Memorial Dr.
San Diego, CA 92106
(619) 557-5450
www.nps.gov/cabr/

Leaving Cabrillo NM, return on Cañon St. to Rosecrans St., turn left for two blocks, and turn right on Shelter Island Dr. **Shelter Island** is ringed with bike paths, from which brown pelicans, cormorants, and—in winter—loons, grebes, surf scoters, and other waterfowl can be seen. Seabirds and ducks patrol the channel, along with seagulls.

Return to I-5 and drive south 14 miles (22.5 km) to Palm Ave.

exit (Hwy. 75) in Imperial Beach. Drive west to 7th St., at the point where Palm Ave. and Hwy. 75 diverge. Turn right on 7th St., proceed to its end, and then park. N. 7th St. and the Bayshore Bikeway parallel Silver Strand Blvd. to Coronado, with

viewing of waterfowl, shorebirds, gulls, and waders. Migrants stack up at the ponds and shallows near N. 7th St.

The last stop on the birding tour is 2,500-acre (1,012-h) **Tijuana Estuary Nature Preserve,** a few blocks away. Drive 7th St. south to Imperial Beach Blvd., turn right, turn left at 3rd St., and drive to Caspian Way. Park in the lot

at the interpretive center midway down the street. The center is open Wednesday through Sunday except major holidays, 10 A.M. to 5 P.M.

Trails totaling 4 miles (6.4 km)—some of which close after rainstorms—give visitors an opportunity to view up to 370 recorded species of birds, most of which are migratory. The habitat is intermittent saltwater marsh.

Tijuana Estuary Visitor Center
301 Caspian Way
Imperial Beach, CA 91932
(619) 575-3613
www.tijuanaestuary.com

Las Vegas and the Colorado River

Winter and spring are the times for bird-watchers to visit the California–Nevada border of the desert Southwest. Like their human counterparts, migratory birds move to the region when cold clamps down in the North. With the exception of neotropical birds that are seen for only a few days before they move on—some to Central America, others to spots as far away as Patagonia—many of the migratory waterfowl stop and stay. Take advantage of combined warm winter weather, species rarely seen during the rest of the year, birds attracted to scarce supplies of water, and a generally open landscape that makes the birds easy to spot— an invitation to enjoy a birding holiday in the desert. Start north of Las Vegas in Death Valley, then travel south to the Colorado River Valley.

From the continent's lowest elevation point in Death Valley to the immense emptiness of the high desert, the Southwest's vistas call out from scores of movie westerns. Take a fresh look at this arid land; it is filled with birds, both residents and migrants.

Henderson Bird Viewing Preserve is located at a water-treatment facility in the Las Vegas suburb of Henderson, just minutes from the Strip. Visit to see small migratory wading birds such as American avocets and white-faced ibis.

American avocets feed on crustaceans and invertebrates.

❶ Death Valley NP

Hottest. Driest. Lowest. That's how the National Park Service describes **Death Valley NP.** Drive north 117 miles (188 km) on Hwy. 95 from Las Vegas to Beatty, site of an outpost welcoming visitors. The rangers at the Beatty Information Center offer helpful, accurate information

about the park's 3 million acres (1.2 million h) of desert, 307 species of birds, and likely spots to see them in the park.

Admission fee is charged. Services in and near the park are limited; fuel up before entering. Take ample food, water, and clothing for both heat and cold; nights are chilly. Summertime

temperatures may reach 120°F (49°C) or higher. Advance reservations are strongly advised.

Locations in the park with water sources such as **Furnace Creek Ranch** and Scotty's Castle, as well as late-summer monsoon thunderstorms that fill many alkali salt pans and dry lakes with water, bring pied-billed

Mallards end their flight with Las Vegas in the distance.

13 endangered and threatened birds. At least 25 species of animals and plants are found here and nowhere else. Visit 0.3-mile (0.5-km) Crystal Springs boardwalk and interpretive trail; the trailhead is near the refuge headquarters.

Look for the refuge's resident crissal thrashers, phainopeplas, verdins, Bewick's wrens, Lucy's warblers, greater roadrunners, and Gambel's quail, along with migratory visitors that include waterfowl, shorebirds, warblers, and hummingbirds.

Ash Meadows NWR
HCR 70, Box 610Z
Amargosa Valley, NV 89020
(775) 372-5435
www.fws.gov/desertcomplex/ashmeadows

grebes, ducks, and shorebirds to the valley from nearby high elevation habitats. The highest point in the park is Telescope Peak, 11,049 feet (3,368 m), while the lowest is Badwater Basin Salt Pan, 282 feet (86 m) below sea level; they are just 15 miles (24 km) apart. Also look for year-round resident birds such as Gambel's quail, yellow-billed cuckoos, greater roadrunners, turkey vultures, hawks, kites, and owls (burrowing owls live in several park locations).

Death Valley NP
P.O. Box 579
Death Valley, CA 92328
(760) 786-3200
www.nps.gov/deva

❷ Ash Meadows NWR

Exit south from Furnace Creek Ranch in Death Valley via Hwy. 190 to join Hwy. 373, turning north. Travel 12 miles (19 km) north on Hwy. 373 to Spring Meadow Rd., turn right, and drive east 5 miles (8 km) to **Ash Meadows NWR.** Exercise caution when driving remote desert roads, take ample water, and beware of flash floods in riverbeds and dry arroyos during and after thunderstorms.

A true oasis in the desert, the refuge is 23,000 acres (9,308 h) of spring-fed wetlands and alkaline marsh. Peak times to visit are August to September and April to May, when 239 recorded bird species come to the site, including

❸ Desert NWR

Leaving the prior waypoint, head north 15 miles (24 km) on Hwy. 373, rejoin Hwy. 95, and turn south. The Corn Creek Springs Field Station of **Desert NWR** is about 60 miles (97 km) south, 5 miles (8 km) after Lee Canyon Rd., and marked by a brown sign. Turn left on Corn Creek Rd. (unpaved) and drive 4 miles (6.4 km) to the station, the best birding on the refuge's south side.

Largest of all the national wildlife refuges, it spans 1.5 million acres (607,030 h) of desert latticed with primitive roads passable only with four-wheel-drive vehicles. Desert precautions apply: Take plenty of water and food, advise the field station of an intended return time, and notify the staff upon actual return.

Habitats such as desert scrub and dry lakes at low elevations, piñon pine forests on mountain ridges, and riverine draws and canyons attract 300 recorded bird species, mostly from March to May or in winter. Bird in spring near Corn Creek Springs.

By the field station, see sage and black-throated sparrows, Le Conte's thrashers, logger-head shrikes, cactus wrens, and greater roadrunners—birds that can fly but prefer to run at astonishing 30-mile-per-hour (48-km/hr.) speeds. By the ponds and fruit trees of the historic ranch, warblers, flycatchers, and western tanagers signal the arrival of spring's many neo-tropical migratory birds.

Desert NWR
HCR 38, Box 700
Las Vegas, NV 89124
(702) 879-6110
www.fws.gov/desertcomplex/ desertrange

The boardwalk trail at Ash Meadows NWR leads through mesquite groves.

Ash Meadows NWR's artesian springs are fed by fossil water stored eons ago before the region turned to desert.

❹ Red Rock Canyon NCA and Spring Mountain Ranch SP

Return 25 miles (40 km) to Las Vegas on Hwy. 395. Once in the city, follow E. Summerlin Pkwy. from the Hwy. 95 junction to its end, turn left on Las Vegas Bltwy., then right on W. Charleston Blvd. (Hwy. 159), which becomes Blue Diamond Rd. and leads in 6 miles (9.7 km) to **Red Rock Canyon NCA.** A short way beyond is **Spring Mountain Ranch SP.** Both sites provide excellent birding opportunities with good facilities. Admission fee is charged at the state park.

Start at Calico Basin Rd., with cottonwoods growing where springs flow from the cliffs. Bird the grove and the meadow. Next, follow Red Rock Scenic Dr., a loop road that alternately clings to the steep mountains and plunges down valleys. Watch for hawks, vultures, golden eagles, and other birds of prey soaring overhead. At **Willow Springs** take the spur road to look for spotted towhees, mourning doves, quail, chukars, brown creepers, songbirds, and boreal birds.

Red Rock Canyon NCA
HCR 33, Box 5500
Las Vegas, NV 89124
(702) 515-5350
www.nv.blm.gov/redrock canyon

Next, drive south on Hwy. 153 to Spring Creek Ranch Rd., turning right and following it to Spring Mountain Ranch SP.

The facility has several trails, a nature center, meadows, a pond surrounded by mixed ash, cottonwoods, and Mojave desert scrub vegetation. The combination draws insects, which in turn attract warblers, woodpeckers, and flycatchers. Also look for predator birds: hawks and owls. In migration seasons waterfowl visit the pond. When

Birds congregate at Corn Creek Springs Field Station's ponds in Desert NWR.

desert flowers bloom in spring, check them for hummingbirds.

Spring Mountain SP
P.O. Box 124
Blue Diamond, NV 89004
(702) 875-4141
www.parks.nv.gov/smr.htm

❺ Las Vegas

The flashing signs and bustle of Nevada's largest city obscure the fact that water has created a bird-friendly island of habitat in the city and throughout its entire surrounding region.

On Las Vegas's northern edge, off Hwy. 95 at N. Durango Dr., lies 16-acre (6.5-h) **Floyd Lamb SP.** Follow Durango Dr. north past its intersection with Racel St. to Tule Springs Rd. and turn right to reach the park's entrance.

Open 7 A.M. to sunset daily. Admission fee is charged.

The park's major feature is a 7-acre (2.8-h) series of four lakes that is surrounded by lawn and trees. Despite its present appearance, the park preserves a historic wetland once known as Tule Springs. Birds return each year to visit the lakes on their twice-yearly migrations.

Ignore the resident peacocks, chickens, and domesticated ducks and concentrate on the desert birds and migrants.

Floyd Lamb SP
9200 Tule Springs Rd.
Las Vegas, NV 89131
(702) 486-5413
www.parks.nv.gov/fl.htm

Southeast of downtown in the suburban town of Henderson is

Henderson Bird Viewing Preserve, a 140-acre (57-h) site within a water-treatment facility. Drive I-515 south from Las Vegas to W. Sunset Rd. and turn east. Three blocks beyond N. Boulder Hwy., turn left on Moser Dr. The preserve is at the end of the road in the treatment plant. Open 6 A.M. to 3 P.M. daily.

The preserve and its trails may be closed during times of heightened national security.

At the site there are nine ponds surrounded by dikes and level trails. Thousands of migratory waterfowl visit the preserve in spring. Songbird visitation peaks in fall, with wood-warblers, flycatchers, thrushes, sparrows, and many other species present. Resident birds, including verdins, Abert's towhee, and crissal thrasher,

are found on the preserve all year, as are Gambel's quail.

Henderson Bird Viewing Preserve
2400 Moser Dr., Ste. B
Henderson, NV 89011
(702) 267-4180
**www.cityofhenderson.com/
parks/facilities/BVP/php/
BirdPreserve.php**

Near McCarran Airport in Las Vegas is **Sunset County Park,** a good location for desert species and migrants. From the airport terminal take E. Russell Rd. to S. Eastern Rd. and turn right. Past E. Sunset Rd., turn left onto Sunset Park Ave. Open 6 A.M. to 11 P.M. daily.

The mesquite thickets have phainopepla, black-tailed gnatcatcher, and songbirds. Examine

Desert NWR has information kiosks that describe the refuge and its birds.

The bird observation platform at upper lake, Pahranagat NWR.

Pahranagat NWR
P.O. Box 510
Alamo, NV 89001
(775) 725-3417
**www.fws.gov/desertcomplex/
pahranagat**

❼ Valley of Fire SP

Retrace the outbound route on Hwy. 93 south to Hwy. 168 and turn left. After 20 miles (32 km) the road splits; follow the left fork to I-15 and drive northwest for 3 miles (4.8 km) to Hwy. 169 (exit 75) and turn right. Along the way, stop 2 miles (3.2 km) south of Overton to visit **Overton WMA,** at the Muddy River's inlet to Lake Mead. The area has 265 recorded bird species, including 22 species of ducks; the best time to see them is fall to winter.

Valley of Fire SP is about 8 miles (12.9 km) farther on Hwy. 169, but the visitors center is about 4 miles (6.4 km) beyond. Admission fee is charged.

Optimal spots to see birds are at arroyos and washes that cross the highway and on the **Mouse's Tank Trail,** a series of sandstone potholes that gather and hold rainwater for months after storms. The trailhead is on the visitors center's spur road.

Valley of Fire SP
P.O. Box 515
Overton, NV 89040
(702) 397-2088
www.parks.nv.gov/vf.htm

❽ Lake Mead NRA

Return to the junction of Hwy. 169 and Hwy. 167 (Northshore Rd.). Turn right to follow Lake Mead. For viewing the 240 bird species in, near, and on the lake, good sites are found at the shoreline near **Stewarts Point** and by hiking along the arroyos at **Blue Point Spring** and **Rogers Spring** on Hwy. 167. (Despite their names, potable water is not available at either site.) Also check the inlets at **Echo Bay** for waterfowl. Other marinas have potential for bird-watching.

Continue south on Hwy. 167 until it ends at Lake Mead Dr. (Hwy. 564/166). Turn left, follow Hwy. 166 toward Hoover Dam and Hwy. 93, then turn right and enter Boulder City, location of the recreation area's visitors center.

Roadrunners dash after snakes at 30 miles per hour (48 km/hr.).

trees in the park for warblers, orioles, plus western and summer tanagers. During migration see dabbling and diving ducks, grebes, and herons.

Sunset County Park
2601 E. Sunset Rd.
Las Vegas, NV 89120
(702) 455-8200
**www.accessclarkcounty.com/
parks**

❻ Pahranagat NWR

Drive east about 16 miles (26 km) from Las Vegas on I-15 and turn onto Hwy. 93, traveling up an arid valley on the east edge of

Desert NWR for 85 miles (137 km) to three lakes in a marshy wetland: **Pahranagat NWR.**

Natural springs of ancient water feed the refuge, which has recorded 230 bird species, predominantly migratory birds and waterfowl. There's an observation pier on **Upper Pahranagat Lake** near the campground. Visit in spring and fall as migrations peak, or during winter when raptors visit. Look beyond the marsh and lakes at the surrounding meadows, habitat that draws western meadowlarks, mourning doves, upland game birds, shrikes, and greater roadrunners. Access roads off Hwy. 93 are the best entry points.

Before continuing south, take time at the visitors center to gain an understanding of the many species of birds that rely on the Colorado River to sustain them. Staff and docents provide information on recent bird sightings.

From Boulder City drive west on Hwy. 93 to its intersection with Hwy. 95, turning left and traveling south. Numbers of bald eagles winter in the area; check the canyon between Hoover Dam and Cottonwood Cove, the next stop.

Stop briefly at **Lake Mohave**, turning left at Searchlight where Hwy. 164 junctions with Hwy. 95. Follow Hwy. 164 to Cottonwood Cove. The lake is a resting area for thousands of migrating waterfowl and shorebirds, and shoreline vegetation attracts many species. Peregrine falcons and osprey visit Lake Mohave, both migrant birds and those on their nests.

Lake Mead NRA
601 Nevada Way
Boulder City, NV 89005
(702) 293-8990
www.nps.gov/lame

❾ Laughlin and Bullhead City

Return to Hwy. 95 south, turning left on Hwy. 163 toward Laughlin, then right on Needles Hwy. after about 12 miles (19 km). Drive 5 miles (8 km) south to **Big Bend of the Colorado SRA** in Laughlin's city limits, a mile (1.6 km) south of Casino Dr. Admission fee is charged.

The park's nearly 2 miles (3.2 km) of river shoreline and steady water supply attract many waterfowl such as ducks, coots, and herons. It's also a good spot to see hawks, owls, quail, greater roadrunners, and hummingbirds.

Big Bend of the Colorado SRA
P.O. Box 32850
Laughlin, NV 89028
(702) 298-1859
www.parks.nv.gov/bb.htm

Drive about 8.5 miles (13.7 km) south on Needles Hwy. to a left turn on A.H.A. Macav Pkwy., cross the Colorado River, and drive to Hwy. 95. Turn north; after 1.5 miles (2.4 km) turn left on Richardo Ave., leading to the **Colorado River Nature Center,** a 140-acre (57-h) site bordering the river with views of American peregrine falcons, bald eagles, and Yuma clapper rails, as well as migratory birds.

Arizona Dept. of Fish & Wildlife/Region IV
9140 E. 28th St.
Yuma, AZ 85365
(928) 342-0091
www.gf.state.az.us/outdoor_ recreation/wildlife_area_co_ river_nature.shtml

❿ The Lower Colorado River

The Lower Colorado River Valley south of Bullhead City is a beaded necklace of bird-watching sites best visited during spring and fall migrations:

- **Havasu NWR,** with 300 miles (483 km) of shore. See endangered Yuma clapper rails and willow flycatchers.
- **Lake Havasu SP,** featuring 1.5-mile (2.4-km) Mojave Sunset Trail in lowland desert and shore habitats.
- **Cattail Cove SP,** with trails, desert, and shoreline.
- **Bill Williams River NWR,** a cattail wetlands with rare stands of cottonwood-willow forest along the river. View neotropical migratory birds such as summer tanagers, yellow warblers, and vermilion flycatchers in spring and fall migrations.

Ducks in the desert follow watercourses and lakes during migration.

Visit these sites along the way...

⓱ Imperial NWR
P.O. Box 72217
Yuma, AZ 85365
(928) 783-3371
www.fws.gov/southwest/ refuges/arizona/imperial.html

From Yuma, Arizona, go north 25 miles (40 km) on Hwy. 95, turn west on Martinez Lake Rd. for 13 miles (21 km), and follow signs to the visitors center. Exhibits and native garden. Lookout points are easily accessed by car. The Painted Desert Trail has both abundant birdlife and scenic beauty.

⓲ Kofa NWR
356 1st St.
Yuma, AZ 85364
(928) 783-7861
www.fws.gov/southwest/ refuges/arizona/kofa.html

From Yuma, Arizona, take Hwy. 95 north toward Quartzite and the refuge, with 665,400 acres (269,279 h) of desert habitat. Hiking and nature observation are permitted in all areas except on patented mining claims (see staff for details). A short foot trail leads to Palm Canyon, a unique wildlife area.

⓳ Cibola NWR
66600 Cibola Lake Rd.
Cibola, AZ 85328
(928) 857-3253
www.fws.gov/southwest/ refuges/cibolanwr/

At Blythe, California, drive about 3 miles (4.8 km) west on I-10 to Neighbours Blvd. exit, turn south, and drive 12 miles (19 km) to the Cibola Bridge. Cross the bridge and drive 3.5 miles (5.6 km) south to the visitors center. Features an auto loop tour and a nature trail with an elevated observation deck.

The Rocky Mountain Region

With its lofty mountains the Continental Divide separates the western bird species from those of the East with high peaks and passes. It marks a sudden end to both the great plains of the East and the arid, baking deserts of the West.

From the prairie and mountain provinces of Canada to the Mexican border, the ridge of mountains stretches like islands in a long arc standing high above a seafloor of grass and shrubs rather than saltwater. Each elevation change creates new habitats—niches for birds of every species. Climbing the mountains has the same effect as traveling north, giving bird-watchers an opportunity to see species of the great temperate forests that stretch to the tree line. In the region's valleys and clefts, birds nest and rear their young during summer before they return to their wintering grounds in Central and South America.

Every birder should visit this mountainous land, whether the choice is Alberta, Idaho, Utah, Colorado, or the high-desert Southwest.

Edmonton to Calgary

Summer days are endless, skies are filled with flying birds, the sound of calls echo hauntingly on mirror-surfaced lakes, and birds surprise visitors with raucous territorial fights over mates, nesting spots, and efforts to protect young. Venture north to remote Lac La Biche, then travel slowly south through a rich tapestry of birds seen in breeding plumage. Along the route the Canadian Rockies rise from the fertile plains, and it's possible to see birds that are more commonly found far to the west. Still farther south are the meandering rivers and oxbow lakes of Calgary, with stands of cattails, reedy shores, and conifers in lieu of willows and aspens. Each ecosystem is filled with colorful and exciting birds to observe.

Far-ranging migratory birds end their spring migrations in the taiga forests and wetlands surrounding Edmonton, breeding grounds in the Far North. The land changes slowly with the drive south, turning to grassland prairies filled with avian wildlife.

Elk Island NP is a wetland-and-forest preserve a few minutes east of Edmonton. At Astotin Lake the Living Waters Boardwalk floats through marsh and lake, featuring views of waterfowl, wading birds, and kingfishers.

Red crossbills are found in the pines at Astotin Lake.

❶ Lac La Biche Region

Begin the birding tour by driving 137 miles (220 km) and 2.5 hours north from Edmonton to **Lac La Biche,** a vast area with 150 lakes where 230 species of birds have been recorded. To reach it, drive Hwy. 28 to Smoky Lake, turn north on Hwy. 855, east on Hwy. 663, and continue to the town of Lac La Biche. Visit from May to September to see migrants nesting.

The area surrounding the lake has been recognized as an Important Birding Area (IBA) by Birdlife International, primarily because its habitats are critical for preservation of nesting California gulls and western grebes. Besides these species, it also has large populations of nesting bald eagles, American white pelicans, long-eared owls,

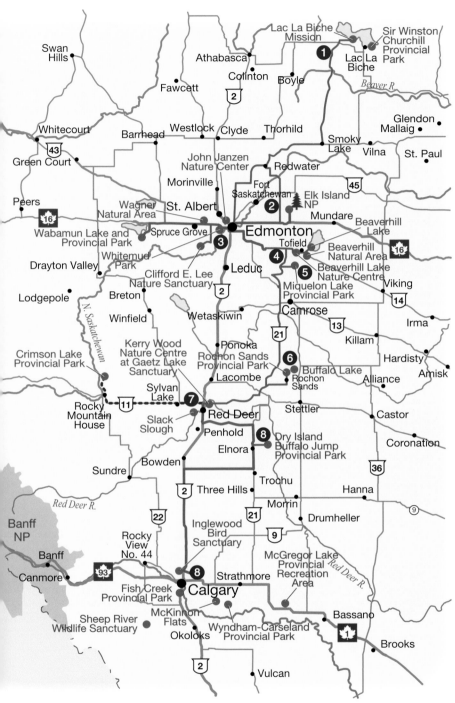

double-crested cormorants. The mixed-hardwood forest supports scores of boreal bird species.

Back through town about 10 miles (16 km) on Hwy. 55 and north on Rd. 675A is **Lac La Biche Mission,** a historic attraction with a viewing platform and a boardwalk. View gulls, terns, diving and dabbling ducks, bald eagles, ospreys, pelicans, shorebirds, and many other species of marsh birds.

Lac La Biche Region Dev. Corp.
P.O. Box 2188
Lac La Biche, AB, Canada T0A 2C0
(877) 623-9696
www.laclabicheregion.com

② Elk Island NP

Retrace the outbound route as far as Redwater, turn left on Hwy. 38, cross the N. Saskatchewan River (always a good birding site), and turn south on Hwy. 830. Drive south about 22 miles (35 km) to Hwy. 16 and turn east, entering **Elk Island NP.** Admission fee is charged.

Located just 45 minutes east of Edmonton, the park holds over 250 species of migrant and resident birds, including waterfowl, Barrow's goldeneyes, and several heron and crane species. Drive north from the entrance to the Shirley Lake trailhead. Here an 8-mile (13-km) trail wends past shallow lakes and through wetlands, making it

ideal for bird-watching. Farther north Astotin Lake's Lakeview, Amisk Wuche (Cree for "beaver hills"), and Shoreline trails and Living Waters Boardwalk are likely spots to see double-crested cormorants, black-crowned night-herons, and red-necked grebes. Large mammals and beaver are frequently sighted in addition to the avian wildlife.

Elk Island National Park
Site 4, RR #1
Fort Saskatchewan, AB,
Canada T8L 2N7
(780) 922-5790
**www.pc.gc.ca/pn-np/
ab/elkisland/index_e.asp/**

③ Edmonton

Travel west on Hwy. 16 back to Edmonton, which sprawls over an area of 264 square miles (684 km^2). Nearly 1 million Edmontonians call this northern provincial capital home. Even so, in summer many millions more birds than people are present, found in the city's many parks and open spaces.

Start by visiting **Whitemud Park** in the city's southwest corner, located just east of the spot where Fox Dr. NW crosses Hwy. 2. The park, tucked into a meandering tributary of the Saskatchewan River, is a hot spot for spotted sandpipers, ruby-crowned kinglets, belted kingfishers, Baltimore orioles, and

woodpeckers, and 20 species of warblers. Visit **Sir Winston Churchill Provincial Park,** a 7-mile (11-km) drive northeast of town across an automobile causeway leading to the island park. It is famed for its colonies of nesting Caspian terns and

Dry Island Buffalo Jump Provincial Park (top) south of Red Deer on the Red Deer River. (bottom) Inglewood Bird Sanctuary in Calgary.

northern saw-whet owls. During winter merlins pursue flocks of Bohemian waxwings in the thickets along the river.

Also visit John Janzen Nature Centre at Whitemud Dr. and Fox Dr., west of Whitemud Creek's mouth, an environmental education and nature center with birding and wildlife programs and exhibits.

Service Alberta
9920 108th St.
Edmonton, AB, Canada T5K 2M4
(780) 944-0313
www.srd.gov.ab.ca/fw/view/ edmo_wcr.html

Follow Hwy. 2 about 10 miles (16 km) north and west. It crosses the river, becomes Whitemud Dr. NW, then turns into 79th Ave. and intersects Hwy. 60. Turn left and drive 6 miles (10 km) to Woodbend Rd., turn right, and go 1 mile (1.6 km) to **Clifford E. Lee Nature Sanctuary,** a designated Alberta Special Place with a full-access boardwalk and bird-watching trails that lead to marshes through mixed pine and aspen forests and over hummocks of sand.

Spring and fall are the best times to visit to see over 100 recorded species of birds, such as red-necked grebes, American bittern, ruffed grouse, Canada geese, red-winged and yellow-headed blackbirds, marsh wrens, and black terns.

Service Alberta
9920 108th St.
Edmonton, AB, Canada T5K 2M4
(780) 987-4883
www.srd.gov.ab.ca/fw/view/ edmo_celns.html

Drive Hwy. 60 north to Hwy. 16 and turn west. Just 0.6 mile (1 km) past Hwy. 792, turn left on RR-270; to the south a gravel access road to the left leads to **Wagner Natural Area.** The site features a 0.7-mile (1.2-km) trail and boardwalk through a calcareous peat bog and spring-fed fen. Take boots and stay on the marked trail.

The fen habitat attracts least flycatchers, ruby-crowned kinglets, yellow-rumped warblers, dark-eyed juncos, and boreal chickadees. In forest areas look for pileated woodpeckers, great horned owls, and northern goshawks and other hawks.

Service Alberta
9920 108th St.
Edmonton, AB, Canada T5K 2M4
(780) 944-0313
www.srd.gov.ab.ca/fw/view/ edmo_wna.html

About 25 miles (40 km) west on Hwy. 16, **Wabamun Lake** provides a unique opportunity for winter bird-watching. Areas of water stay ice-free year-round due to heated water discharged from nearby power plants. The lake is also the site of **Wabamun Lake Provincial Park.** The park is located where highways 16 and 20 junction, just before the village. Admission fee is charged. The lake was severely impacted by an oil spill from a train derailment in 2005, but recovery has been remarkable.

The park and nearby Lake Isle host migrating, breeding, and molting waterbirds such as gulls, terns, rails, herons, loons, kingfishers, and sandpipers. Its woods have ravens, great gray owls, and gray jays that are more commonly seen in the west.

To visit the cooling ponds, follow Hwy. 20 south for 7.5 miles (12 km) to Sundance Rd. (TR-522) and turn right.

See nesting colonies of osprey, red-necked and western grebes, thousands of mallards and other waterfowl, bald eagles, and hooded mergansers.

Village of Wabamun
5217 52nd St., Box 240
Wabamun, AB, Canada T0E 2K0
(780) 892-2699
www.wabamun.ca

www.cd.gov.ab.ca/ enjoying_alberta/parks

④ Beaverhill Natural Area

Return to Edmonton and drive 31 miles (50 km) southwest on Hwy. 14 to Tofield. Stop at

In Sheep River Valley, along Hwy. 546 south of Calgary, autumn colors appear magical in the maple and aspen trees.

Crimson Lake at Crimson Lake Provincial Park has its best bird-watching in early morning or near sunset, as birds move to and from their roosting areas.

the **Beaverhill Lake Nature Centre** before passing through the village, traveling east 6.2 miles (10 km) and following Watchable Wildlife signs to **Beaverhill Natural Area**, a bird observatory southeast of Beaverhill Lake.

A total of 253 species have been recorded here, including 40 different shorebirds. Each year, beginning in March, thousands of Canada geese, greater white-fronted geese, snow geese, and tundra swans arrive, followed by birds of prey and large nesting colonies of tree swallows.

Service Alberta
9920 108th St.
Edmonton, AB, Canada T5K 2M4
(780) 944-0313
www.srd.gov.ab.ca/fw/view/ edmo_bna.html

❺ Miquelon Lake Provincial Park

Retrace the outbound route to Tofield, then drive 9.5 miles (15 km) west on Hwy. 14 to Hwy. 833 and turn left. Join Hwy. 623 after about 10.5 miles (17 km), turn left, and drive around the bottom of Lake Miquelon, following signs to **Miquelon Lake Provincial Park**. Admission fee is charged.

The park's aspen, balsam, and poplar forests and wetlands are rare remnants of once expansive native forests. They attract yellow warblers, western wood-pewees, ovenbirds, Baltimore orioles, and rose-breasted grosbeaks. Ponds are filled with grebes and soras; green-winged teals, American coots, and ruddy ducks occur in the marshlands.

Gull Island, an IBA site, is host to ring-billed and California gulls.

Service Alberta
9920 108th St.
Edmonton, AB, Canada T5K 2M4
(780) 944-0313
www.srd.gov.ab.ca/fw/view/ edmo_mlpp.html

❻ Buffalo Lake

Take Hwy. 833 south to Hwy. 617, turn left, intersect Hwy. 21 at Hay Lakes, and turn south. Drive 59 miles (95 km) south to a left turn on Hwy. 601, 8.7 miles (15 km) to a left at Hwy. 835, and 3.7 miles (6 km) to the village of Rochon Sands, **Buffalo Lake, and Rochon Sands Provincial Park**. The provincial park has

the best access for bird-watching. Admission fee is charged.

The park's potholes and wetlands support many raptors—hawks, great horned and short-eared owls, and golden and bald eagles—plus Ross's geese, ruffed grouse, and Baltimore orioles.

Service Alberta
9920 108th St.
Edmonton, AB, Canada T5K 2M4
(780) 944-0313
www.srd.gov.ab.ca/fw/view/ red_bufl.html

❼ Red Deer

From Rochon Sands follow Hwy. 601 west, cross Hwy. 12, and head south to Hwy. 11. Turn right and drive 25 miles (40 km)

Riding **atop its mother's back,** a western grebe's chick is **safe and warm,** while keeping a **watchful eye** to the rear

to the outskirts of **Red Deer.** Enter town on 55th St., turn right on 40th Ave. (which becomes 55th St. again), and turn right on 45th Ave. The avenue leads to **Kerry Wood Nature Centre at Gaetz Lake Sanctuary.**

A full-access facility with 3.1 miles (5 km) of trails, bird blinds, and viewing decks, Gaetz Lake has cattail marshes with yellow-headed and red-winged blackbirds, while its trees and understory hold boreal chickadees, red-breasted nuthatches, olive-sided flycatchers, pileated and three-toed woodpeckers, and many black-capped and white-throated sparrows.

Also visit the raised viewing platforms at **Slack Slough,** 1.9 miles (3.2 km) south of town and east of Hwy. 2 at TR-34, to see abundant migratory waterfowl from mid-spring to early fall.

If time permits, drive 47 miles (75 km) west on Hwy. 11 to Rocky Mountain House and follow the signs to **Crimson Lake Provincial Park.** Its black spruce bogs and tamarack swamps are habitats for greater yellowlegs, western tanagers, woodpeckers, sandhill cranes, and boreal and northern pygmy-owls.

Kerry Wood Nature Centre
6300 45th Ave.
Red Deer, AB, Canada T4N 3M4
(403) 346-2010
www.waskasoopark.ca

www.srd.gov.ab.ca/fw/view/ red_clpp.html

❽ Dry Island Buffalo Jump Provincial Park

Drive south from Red Deer on Hwy. 2 for 5.2 miles (8.5 km), turn left on Hwy. 42, and drive 26 miles (42 km) east to Hwy. 21. Turn right and follow Hwy. 21 to an intersection 6.2 miles (10 km) south of Hwy. 590. At the signs for **Dry Island Buffalo Jump Provincial Park,** turn left and drive to the park, on the Red Deer River. Admission fee is charged. Park facilities include observation points and hiking trails through a transition zone between moist aspen forest and dry prairie.

Over 150 bird species have been recorded at this site. They include turkey vultures, prairie falcons, golden eagles, red-tailed and Swainson's hawks, mountain bluebirds, warblers, kingfishers, great blue herons, willets, and marbled godwits.

Service Alberta
9920 108th St.
Edmonton, AB, Canada T5K 2M4
(780) 944-0313
www.srd.gov.ab.ca/fw/view/ red.html

❾ Calgary Area

Return to Hwy. 22 and turn south. At Hwy. 27, 1.7 miles (2.7 km) south of Trochu, turn right and drive 59 miles (95 km) to Hwy. 2. Turn left for Calgary, 51 miles (82 km) to the south.

This prairie city sits in the foothills of the Canadian Rocky Mountains at the confluence of the Bow and Elbow rivers. With its riparian, prairie, forest, and wetland habitats, birds come to it by the hundreds of thousands in their northern migrations.

Start birding Calgary near the city's heart, in **Inglewood Bird Sanctuary,** located at 2425 9th Ave. SE.

Despite the urban setting, along the 1.9 miles (3 km) of nature trails in a mature riparian forest near Bow River, 216 bird species have been recorded. They include bald eagles, gray partridge, ring-necked pheasants, Swainson's hawks, a number of warbler species, and nesting great horned owls. It is reputed to be the best spot in the city to see wood ducks.

City of Calgary Parks
P.O. Box 2100, Stn. M (#77)
Calgary, AB, Canada T2P 2M5
(403) 269-6688
www.calgary.ca/parks/ naturecentre

Next, stop at **Fish Creek Provincial Park.** Enter the park at the Bow Bottom Trail exit off Hwy. 2. The visitors center is open 8:15 A.M. to 4:30 P.M. on weekdays.

See Swainson's hawks; red-breasted nuthatches; pileated, hairy, and downy woodpeckers; and bald eagles year-round. Observe waterfowl, herons, and common mergansers in summer.

Service Alberta
9920 108th St.
Edmonton, AB, Canada T5K 2M4
(780) 944-0313 or (403) 297-5293
www.srd.gov.ab.ca/fw/view/ cal_fcpp.html

Other birding hot spots in southeast Calgary include:

- **Sheep River Wildlife Sanctuary,** 17 miles (27 km) south of the city; birds of prey such as golden eagles. Open May 15 to November 30.
- **McKinnon Flats,** 14 miles (23 km) east on Hwy. 22X, south on 200 St. SE; songbirds, raptors, and waterfowl.
- **Wyndham-Carseland Provincial Park,** 27 miles (43 km) east, south of Hwy. 1 on Hwy. 24; nature trail on the Bow River.
- **Lake McGregor Provincial Recreation Area,** about 62 miles (100 km) east on Hwy. 1, south at Hwy. 842; major staging area for Canada, snow, and greater white-fronted geese.

At Fish Creek a young great horned owl keeps watch.

Pocatello, Idaho, to Jackson Hole, Wyoming

The high deserts, lakes, wetlands, and forests of the lands near the Bear and Snake rivers fill each spring and fall with migratory waterfowl, neotropical migrants, boreal birds, and birds of prey in a spectacle little changed since Lewis and Clark's expedition.

Open range and alpine lakes connect the vastness between Pocatello and Grand Teton NP. The Snake River—called the river of no return—draws birds by the thousands to its banks and reservoirs. Included are vast nesting colonies of American white pelicans, cormorants, sandhill cranes, and gulls— among the largest rookeries found in North America. Nearly lost in this abundance of avian life are tiny hummingbirds and warblers, as well as a rich diversity of forest birds. At the drive's end one of North America's most scenic national parks rises in jagged majesty, inviting bird-watchers to witness its many treasures of wildlife. Whether visiting the area for a few days or a few weeks, travelers will find a bounty of exciting birds.

Grand Teton NP's glacially carved mountains are a backdrop to lush forests, rivers, fields, and lakes filled with birds. Bird checklists and recent sighting information are available from National Park Service staff at the Moose Visitors Center.

Gadwalls are often found in the company of the American wigeons.

❶ Massacre Rocks SP

Begin the birding route on I-86, traveling south from Pocatello 35 miles (56 km) to exit 28. The 1,000-acre (405-h) **Massacre Rocks SP** is on the Snake River's east bank, south of American Falls. Admission fee is charged.

Along with excellent nature and hiking trails, the park has kayaks and canoes for rent. Over 200 species of birds have been seen at the site, including bald eagles, ospreys, grebes and other diving ducks, tundra swans, American white pelicans, and great blue herons.

Massacre Rocks SP
3592 N. Park Ln.
American Falls, ID 83211
(208) 548-2672
**www.idahoparks.org/parks/
massacrerocks.aspx**

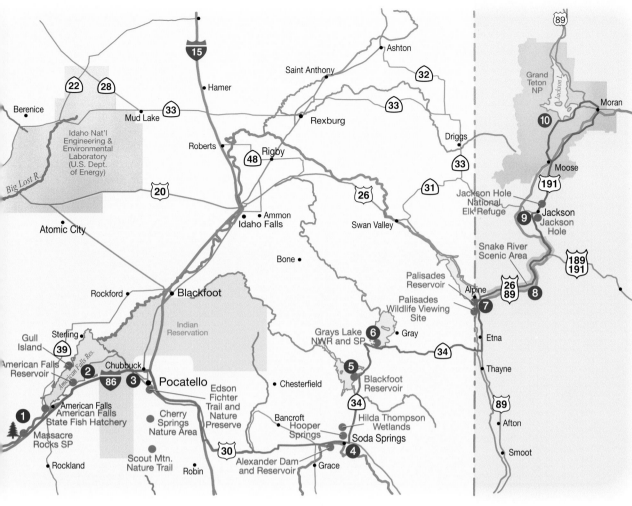

turn southeast, and follow Clark to S. Arthur Ave. Turn left, drive 3.3 miles (5.3 km) as the road becomes S. Main and N. Bannock Hwy., turn left on Cheyenne Ave., and take a right turn at the soccer field, trailhead for **Edson Fichter Trail and Nature Preserve.** Its gate is at the lot's end decorated with metal geese.

The 1-mile (1.6-km) path on the Portneuf River leads to a 40-acre (16-h) preserve with interpretive signs and a viewing deck.

Another bird-watching spot is **Cherry Springs Nature Area.** Follow S. Bannock Hwy. to W. Portneuf Rd., bearing right. Drive about 5 miles (8 km) southwest to the nature area and an amphitheater on FR-231. There are self-guided nature trails, interpretive signs, and two learning centers. Open May to September.

Over 120 bird species have been noted here, including neotropical migrants, calliope hummingbirds, and lazuli buntings.

Follow S. Bannock Hwy. 5 miles (21 km) farther south, turn left on FS-001 for 5 miles (21 km), and arrive at **Scout Mountain Nature Trail.** Its mixed forest with hiking trails hosts flammulated owls, northern pygmy-owls, and ruffed and blue grouse.

Idaho Division of Tourism Development
700 W. State St.
Boise, ID 83720
(208) 334-247
www.visitidaho.org/thingstodo

❷ American Falls Reservoir

Reach **American Falls State Fish Hatchery** by driving 7.5 miles (12 km) north on I-86 to exit 36, crossing under the highway and following S. Frontage Rd. north as it turns into Lincoln Ave. Bear right at Fort Hall Ave., turn left on Idaho St., left again at Hwy. 39, and cross the dam. Turn left on Lamb Weston Rd. and immediately left on Fish Hatchery Rd. Open 7:30 A.M. to 4 P.M. daily.

Nearby a 2-mile-long (3.2-km-long) nature trail offers a selection from more than 200 recorded bird species.

American Falls State Fish Hatchery
2974 Fish Hatchery Rd.
American Falls, ID 83211
(208) 226-2015
www.visitidaho.org/thingstodo

American Falls Reservoir is a recognized IBA, with shallow-water habitats that draw more than 5,000 shorebirds during their migrations, first in April to May, then again in September. Look for American golden, black-bellied, and snowy plovers, killdeer, black-necked stilts, both greater and lesser yellowlegs, and American avocets.

Gull Island, located southeast of Aberdeen on the west shore (follow the Sportsman's Access signs on Boat Dock Rd.), is the largest California and ring-billed gull breeding colony in Idaho.

American Falls
Chamber of Commerce
P.O. Box 207
American Falls, ID 83211
(208) 226-7214
www.americanfallschamber.org

❸ Pocatello Area

Return 22 miles (35 km) north to Pocatello via I-86 and I-15. Exit I-5 at E. Clark St., one exit south of the interstates' merge,

Marsh wrens are the songsters of the tall grasses and are heard more often than they are seen

❹ Soda Springs

Return on S. Bannock Hwy. to W. Portneuf Rd. and turn right, entering I-15E. Drive 15 miles (24 km) to exit 47, turn east, and drive 29 miles (47 km) on Hwy. 30 to Soda Point and **Alexander Dam and Reservoir,** a worthwhile stop for seeing trumpeter swans and migratory waterfowl.

Continue east on Hwy. 30 to Soda Springs, turn left on N. Main St., and park at its end. A short trail to **Hooper Springs** leads through mixed forest, creeks, and fields filled with trumpeter swans, ducks, and geese in winter.

Government Dam Rd., off Hwy. 34 north of town, leads to the 136-acre (55-h) **Hilda Thompson Wetlands.** The site is visited by trumpeter swans, ducks, great blue herons, sandhill cranes, and other shorebirds.

Soda Springs Parks Dept.
9 W. 2nd St. S
Soda Springs, ID 83276
(208) 547-2600
www.sodaspringsid.com

❺ Blackfoot Reservoir

Continue north on Hwy. 34 about 15 miles (24 km) and turn left at Henry Rd. for a view of 18,000-acre (7,284-h) **Blackfoot Reservoir,** an IBA for double-crested cormorant and American white pelican colonies.

Go 1.2 miles (1.9 km) north on Hwy. 34 to Blackfoot N. Access Rd. and turn left. The rookeries are on Gull Island, but birds also feed along the shallow shoreline.

Idaho Division of Tourism Development
700 W. State St.
Boise, ID 83720
(208) 334-247
www.visitidaho.org/thingstodo

❻ Grays Lake NWR

Drive 14 miles (23 km) north on Hwy. 34, turn left on Gray Rd., and drive 3 miles (4 km) to **Grays Lake NWR and SP,** which has both day-use and overnight camping facilities; admission fee is charged. Overlooks have good viewing spots on nearby roads that circle the reservoir. Visit from May to June or from late September to October.

Grays Lake is a shallow seasonal, high-altitude wetland, the biggest hard-stem bulrush and cattail marsh in North America. It has the largest nesting population of greater sandhill cranes in the world. In late September and early October up to 1,200 cranes stage here; 40,000 Franklin's gulls also nest at the refuge. The lake is a good spot to see eared and western grebes, terns, and peregrine falcons.

Grays Lake NWR
74 Grays Lake Rd.
Wayan, ID 83285
(208) 574-2755
www.fws.gov/pacific/refuges/ field/ID_grayslk.htm

❼ Palisades Wildlife Viewing Site

Continue east on Hwy. 34 past the Wyoming border, junction with Hwy. 89, and turn north for 9 miles (14 km). **Palisades Wildlife Viewing Site** is 1.5 miles (2.4 km) to the south of Alpine Junction.

It has a bird-viewing building as well as interpretive signs, and it is located at a wetland/mixed-forest boundary. Visit from spring to fall to see waterfowl, trumpeter swans, osprey, and bald eagles.

Wyoming Game and Fish
5400 Bishop Blvd.
Cheyenne, WY 82006
(307) 777-4600
gf.state.wy.us/services/ education/wtw/index.asp

❽ Snake River

The 37-mile (60-km) stretch of Hwy. 26/89 between Alpine Junction and Jackson follows the scenic **Snake River.** Look for blue Wyoming Wildlife signs at rest stops and waysides along the route, and stop often.

❾ Jackson Hole Area

The best birding hot spots in **Jackson Hole** are Flat Creek Ponds at the **National Elk Refuge,** just north of town, and the fields east of the airport. In spring greater sage grouse display lek mating behavior here, hooting in courtship dances.

Jackson Hole & Greater Yellowstone Visitor Center
532 North Cache Dr.
Jackson, WY 83001
(307) 733-3316
www.fws.gov

❿ Grand Teton NP

Just north of Jackson Hole, enter **Grand Teton NP,** a place of scenic views with abundant birdlife. Admission fee is charged. Stop for information at Moose Visitors Center, 8 miles (12 km) beyond the park boundary sign.

Don't miss these sites in the park, abundant with birdlife:

- **Blacktail Ponds Overlook,** for goldeneye, teal, and other waterfowl.
- **Willow Flats,** for woodpeckers, hummingbirds, songbirds, and shorebirds.
- **Two Ocean Lake,** for grebes, swans, and loons.
- **Grand View Point,** with mixed boreal and upland game birds.
- **Christian Pond,** for ruddy, ring-necked, and other ducks.
- **Swan Lake,** for trumpeter swans.
- **Phelps Lake Overlook,** for flickers, buntings, warblers, and kinglets.
- **Hiking trails,** for dippers, woodpeckers, and raptors.

Grand Teton NP
P.O. Drawer 170
Moose, WY 83012
(307) 739-3300
www.nps.gov/grte/

Salt Lake City Area

This natural remnant of a once-vast inland salt sea is also a wonderfully diverse place to observe an ever-changing parade of migratory waterfowl and shorebirds. Nearby arid rangeland and deserts host a variety of other bird species.

Great Salt Lake is a one-of-a-kind natural wonder, a vestige of what was once a 20,000-square-mile body of water called Lake Bonneville that started drying up 18,000 years ago. It lacks an outlet, so water can exit the lake only by evaporating. In the process it leaves behind mineral salts. No fish live in the lake proper, but it produces millions of tons of protein annually in the form of crustaceans and other invertebrates—food that birds need to lay their eggs and molt. For bird-watchers Salt Lake City and its surroundings are richly rewarding places to watch shorebirds and waterfowl in a continually changing array; the outlying deserts and rangelands host many other bird species.

White-faced ibis and Franklin's gulls take flight at Bear River Migratory Bird Refuge.

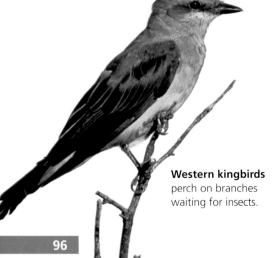

Western kingbirds perch on branches waiting for insects.

❶ Cutler Marsh

From Salt Lake City drive 81 miles (130 km) north to Logan on I-15 and Hwy. 89. Once on Main St., turn left on 200 St. N (Hwy. 30), drive 3.3 miles (5.3 km) west to Water Trough Rd., and turn north. At the junction with W. 3000 N Rd., turn left. Drive

to **Benson Marina** and the trail-head for a 2.5-mile (4-km) loop path into **Cutler Marsh.**

A year-round raptor viewing spot, the marsh in spring and summer fills with many song-birds, American bitterns, Clark's and western grebes, egrets, white-faced ibis, and herons; in fall sandhill cranes arrive.

The best viewing spots are at bridges that cross the marsh.

Utah Office of Tourism
P.O. Box 147420
Salt Lake City, UT 84114
(801) 538-1030
**www.utah.com/wildlife/
bird_watching.htm**

➋ Wellsville HawkWatch Site

Return to Hwy. 30, turn west, and drive 3.5 miles (5.6 km) to Hwy. 23. Turn south, enter the town of Mendon, turn west on W. 300 N St., and drive to the road's end and trailhead. Take a strenuous 3.5-mile (5.6-km) hike and 3,000-foot (914-m) climb into the Wellsville Mountains. There are no facilities; bring water and layered clothing.

During migration, from late summer to early fall, raptors pass by in the thousands, riding the updrafts from the ridge and preserving energy for their journey.

HawkWatch International
1800 S.W. Temple St., Ste. 226
Salt Lake City, UT 84115
(801) 484-6808
www.hawkwatch.org

➌ Salt Creek WMA

Return to Hwy. 30. Turn west, junction with I-15 after about 13 miles (21 km), and go south on I-5 about 9 miles (14.5 km) and one exit past the junction with I-84. Exit on 9600 Rd. N, turn right, then turn right immediately on the frontage road, then west on 9600 Rd. N Two access roads lead south to parking and the trailheads to **Salt Creek WMA.**

Bring a spotting scope and a tripod or binoculars to view birds from the dike trails in the ponds, marshes, and lakes. Several bird festivals, including Utah Bald Eagle Days (February) and Tundra Swans Day (March), are held at the site.

Locations in the unit bear the names of the birds that frequent them: Swan Bay; Ibis, Stilt, Snipe, Egret, Wren, Willet, and Heron ponds; and Gadwall, Redhead, Canvasback, Mallard, Teal, and Goose lakes. Many species of waterfowl and wading birds will be found at Salt Creek.

Utah Div. of Wildlife Resources
P.O. Box 146301
Salt Lake City, UT 84114
(801) 538-4700
www.wildlife.utah.gov

Join In

Great Salt Lake Bird Festival

Mid- to late May. The festival attracts birders from across the United States and Canada.

- **Workshops**—teaching the hows, whys, and whens of bird-watching.
- **Booths**—featuring live animals, artists, vendors, and food.
- **Banquet**—enjoying the essence of good food.
- **Keynote speakers**—sharing experiences and tips.

Knowledgeable Guides

- Tours of lands normally closed to the public and held privately or by conservation groups.
- Half and all-day tours, some at sunrise, others lasting into the night, including: ducks—amphibious open-air vehicles—and kayaks, horseback tours, walks, and hikes.
- Youth activities both educational and fun, with crafts and live-bird presentations.

For details, visit
www.greatsaltlakebirdfest.com

➍ Bear River Migratory Bird Refuge

Return to I-15 and drive south to the W. Forest St. exit in Brigham City, either turning west for one block and entering the

Fowl-in-Focus

WILSON'S PHALAROPE
Phalaropus tricolor

Length 8 in.–10 in.
(20–25 cm)

What to look for
Long, slender neck; thin bill; female with black-and-red stripe on neck; male paler, less reddish; gray backs and wing tops on nonbreeding birds.

Habitat Areas with pools of shallow water, including marshes and tidal flats. Phalaropes are remarkable birds in several respects. Although technically shorebirds, they spend much time swimming in open water. When they breed, the females do the courting and the drab males build the nests, incubate the eggs, and raise the young. Wilson's phalarope is the phalarope most likely to be seen, for it is mainly a freshwater species. It feeds in the middle of shallow prairie lakes and ponds, spinning in tight circles and dabbling for floating food with its long, slender bill. The red and northern phalaropes (*Phalaropus fucilaria* and *P. lobatus*) are more marine.

Wildlife Education Center for **Bear River Migratory Bird Refuge,** or following the road 15 miles (24 km) farther to the old refuge headquarters. The education center is open sunrise to sunset daily and is equipped with full-access facilities.

Visitors may drive, walk, or bicycle a 12-mile (19.3-km) loop road that encircles the dikes of a large water impoundment teeming with waterfowl, marsh birds, and waterbirds. Viewing decks and photography blinds are strategically placed to aid bird-watchers.

The Bear River delta has long been considered one of the most valuable freshwater wetlands in the Intermountain West. Set on the eastern edge of the Pacific Flyway and the western edge of the Central Flyway, it is a vital resting, feeding, and nesting area for migratory birds.

The refuge manages and protects over 41,000 acres (16,592 h) of freshwater wetlands in the delta ecosystem. A series of 25 impoundments capture fresh water from the river and maintain water levels to ensure aquatic habitat is avail-

able for feeding and breeding birds, including American avocets, black-necked stilts, and snowy plovers, as well as tundra swans, Wilson's phalaropes, and northern pintails.

The refuge is a staging area in fall for migratory waterfowl. Ducks number over 500,000, 85,000 Canada geese are present, and almost 75 percent of the western tundra swan population use the refuge. All five bays of Great Salt Lake will soon be designated by the National Audubon Society as IBAs of global importance.

Bear River Migratory Bird Refuge
2155 W. Forest St.
Brigham City, UT 84302
(435) 723-5887
www.fws.gov/bearriver/

❺ Ogden

Situated by the fresh water of the Bear River and the brine of Great Salt Lake, Ogden boasts a remarkable variety of birdlife, both residents and migrants.

Tour **Ogden Nature Center** with over 1.5 miles (2.4 km) of trails in an urban 152-acre (62-h) wildlife sanctuary. Take the 12th St. exit and head east for about 0.5 mile (0.8 km); The center is on the left. Open 9 A.M. to 5 P.M. daily except Sundays and major holidays. Stop by the visitors center.

Possible sightings include spotted towhees, several spar-

row species, evening grosbeaks, goldfinches, and black-capped chickadees, along with hawks, owls, falcons, and eagles.

Ogden Nature Center
966 W. 12th St.
Ogden, UT 84404
(801) 621-7595
www.ogdennaturecenter.org

Another birding hot spot is the **Ogden Cemetery,** set in a conifer forest two blocks east of Washington Blvd. on 20th St. Please bird-watch from the roads only. This site provides shelter in winter for red crossbills, rosy-finches, hairy woodpeckers, mountain chickadees, red-breasted nuthatches, and both the bohemian and cedar waxwings.

Just east of I-5 on the Weber River off W. 24th St. is **Fort Buenaventura SP,** with both shoreline and lakeside trails. Admission fee is charged. Canoe rentals are available.

The male yellow warbler's reddish breast streaks stand out on its otherwise all-yellow body.

The James V. Hansen Wildlife Education Center was designed to mimic a bird in flight.

◀◀ Not to Be Missed!

James V. Hansen Wildlife Education Center at Bear River Migratory Bird Refuge

The interactive exhibits at the James V. Hansen Wildlife Education Center educate visitors about the Great Salt Lake, habitats found in the vicinity, and its birds and animals.

The building, which has lots of pointed rather than square corners, is designed to be evocative of a bird in flight, with a roof that slopes on top, its points mimicking wings. Another interesting feature is its brown hood: The building is concave on the marsh side and wraps around part of the wetland, and the centrally placed hood is parabolic in shape, amplifying bird sounds so they're more easily heard by visitors standing on the large observation deck. And it works!

The center opened in April 2006. It has a 3,500-square-foot (235-m²) exhibit hall, a 200-seat auditorium, classrooms, a research lab, and a gift shop. Trestle wood salvaged from the bottom of the lake was used to construct the exhibit hall's upper deck.

Take Wilson Ln. exit, go east to Wall Ave., turn right, drive to Martin Luther King Ave., turn right, and take a left on A Ave., which leads to the park entrance. In this wooded riparian area, look for Bullock's orioles, red-tailed hawks, northern flickers, ospreys, western tanagers, and California quail.

Ft. Buenaventura State Park
2450 A Ave.
Ogden, UT 84401
(801) 399-8099
www.utah.com/stateparks/buenaventura.htm

❻ Ogden Bay WMA

Return to I-15S, drive 5.6 miles (9 km) to exit on W. 5600 S St. (Hwy. 97) in Roy, and head west. (Hwy. 97 curves north to become W. 5500 S St.) Approximately 5 miles (8 km) west of I-5, follow the signs to the entrance and headquarters of **Ogden Bay WMA**, a 20,000-acre (8,094-h) wetland with birds such as grebes, herons, geese, sandpipers, ducks, and gulls. More than 15,000 ducks are born in the unit each year. Within its boundaries, find year-round opportunities to view waterfowl from its dike roads or auto loop.

Ogden Bay WMA
4786 S. 7500 W
Hooper, UT 84315
(801) 985-1398
www.publiclands.org

❼ Antelope Island SP

Return to I-15, drive south for 6 miles (9.6 km), take exit 332 west on Antelope Dr. to the Davis County Causeway (toll required), and enter **Antelope Island SP**, situated far offshore on Great Salt Lake's largest island. Admission fee is charged. Stop at the park visitors center for trail information and a bird checklist.

The best bird-watching in the park takes place from late fall to early winter, when eared grebes and Wilson's phalaropes use the lake to stage. In summer look for owls, thrashers, horned larks, and Say's phoebes. The grasslands and shores with wetlands provide varied bird habitats.

Antelope Island SP
4528 W. 1700 S
Syracuse, UT 84075
(801) 652-2043
www.stateparks.utah.gov

❽ Great Salt Lake Shorelands Preserve

Returning to the mainland over the causeway, turn right from W. Antelope Dr. on N. 3200 W St., and drive south to its end (it is unpaved after Gentile St.).

Formerly called Layton Wetlands Preserve and now named **Great Salt Lake Shorelands Preserve** by the Nature Conservancy, these saltwater and

Pelicans are **social and gregarious,** and they **congregate** in large flocks for much of the year

freshwater marshes attract large gatherings of birds to migratory feeding grounds. The visitors center, an open-air pavilion, a 30-foot (9.1-m) observation tower, and a 1-mile (1.6-km) boardwalk offer views of the lake and wetlands. Open April to September, 7 A.M. to 8 P.M. daily; October to March, 8 A.M. to 5 P.M.

The preserve is the lake's largest nesting area for white-faced ibis, and its shorelines on the salt flats and in bulrush marshes are important nesting sites for snowy plovers, black-necked stilts, and American avocets. Also look for redhead ducks, cinnamon teal, mallards, and gadwalls on the lake's shores.

The Nature Conservancy
Field Office
559 E. South Temple St.
Salt Lake City, UT 84102
(801) 531-0999
www.nature.org/where
wework/northamerica/states/
utah/preserves/art5834.html/

❾ Farmington Bay WMA

Return to I-15 by Gentile St., turning right on S. Main St. and taking the on-ramp. Travel two exits south to Park Ln., turn left and cross over I-15 and Hwy. 89, and turn right at N. Main St. Follow it south, turn right at W. State St. and right on S. 2nd W Ave., avoiding the on-ramps and continuing on a frontage road to W. Glover Ln. Turn west. The main entry to **Farmington Bay WMA** is straight ahead. Open 8 A.M. to 5 P.M. daily.

The best time to visit is late February to August, as birds arrive, mate, build nests, and rear young. The lake attracts different birds as the season progresses, including American white pelicans, black terns, red-headed ducks, soras, Wilson's phalaropes, burrowing owls, white-faced ibis, black-necked stilts, and American avocets, as well as geese, swans, and ducks.

Farmington Bay WMA
1325 W. Glover Ln.
Farmington, UT 84025
(801) 451-7386
www.wildlife.utah.gov/
habitat/farmington_bay.php/

❿ Salt Lake City Area

Spilling down the mountains to the shore of the lake, Salt Lake City's location on both the Pacific and Central flyways is like a siren call to bird-watchers and birds alike.

City Creek Canyon, within walking distance of downtown, is the first stop and is one of the state's best songbird areas. Head east from State St. on N. Temple St. and turn left on B St. Go uphill, then enter the canyon; park near the hairpin turn. Paved trails skirt the stream north (into the mountains) and south (to Memory Grove Park and the downtown's edge). Visit the streamside woods during

spring and summer; they are accessed from the bike paths.

Located in the southeast city 3.4 miles (5.5 km) east of 3800 S and Wasatch Blvd., the steep-walled canyon and stream in **Mill Creek Canyon** and the Desolation Trail (trailhead just past Millcreek Inn) attract a wide variety of birds, from fly-catchers to thrushes and nut-crackers to grouse. Visit at night to hear and see great horned, flammulated, and saw-whet owls and northern pygmy-owls.

Big Cottonwood Canyon is east of Salt Lake City in the Wasatch Mountains. From I-215 south, follow the signs to the Brighton Ski Area. This is a great place to see streamside songbirds and high-elevation birds, plus summer wildflowers.

Wasatch Audubon Society
P.O. Box 3211
Ogden, UT 84409
(801) 621-7595
www.wasatchaudubon.org

Western meadowlarks have brighter markings than the eastern species.

Visit these sites along the way...

⓫ Jordan River Parkway
SLC County Parks & Recreation
2001 S. State St., Ste. S4400
Salt Lake City, UT 84190
(801) 468-2299
www.recreation.slco.org/parks/
html/jordan.html

I-15S to W. 7200 S in West Jordan, west to Triumph Ln. Restored willow and cottonwood riparian habitat attracts songbirds and other perching birds in spring and fall migration. Trails extend north and south along the river for several miles.

⓬ Lake Mount Raptor Loop
Wasatch Audubon Society
P.O. Box 3211
Ogden, UT 84409
(801) 621-7595
www.wasatchaudubon.org

Rush/Cedar Valley, west of Provo on Utah Lake in an area bounded by highways 73, 68, 36, and 6, is home to such exciting species as ferruginous, Swainson's, and red-tailed hawks and prairie falcons. In winter see bald eagles, rough-legged hawks, and merlins.

⓭ Provo Bay
Wasatch Audubon Society
P.O. Box 3211
Ogden, UT 84409
(801) 621-7595
www.wasatchaudubon.org

A recognized IBA on Provo Bay west of Springville at Utah Lake, with three locations: on Hwy. 77 north of Spanish Fork River bridge; on the north frontage road at exit 265 of I-15; or on the dikes near Provo's airport. Large numbers of freshwater marsh birds.

Fort Collins, Denver, and Colorado Springs

Start birding mile-high and climb to the roof of the Rockies with migratory birds winging north and south on the Central Flyway. Then enjoy the expanse and rich birdlife found on the great western prairie grasslands with a tour of Colorado.

The Rocky Mountains dominate the terrain in a great wall extending from Canada in the north to New Mexico in the south. Along its spine, waterfowl pass neotropical birds in their twice-annual rituals of migration. To the east a sea of grass and scrub brush broken by meandering streams and pothole lakes offers habitat and home to hundreds of species of songbirds, shorebirds, and the birds of prey that soar above the plains. Drive north from Denver to Fort Collins, head east and west, then tour along the mountains back to Boulder. Finish the drive with a thrust to the south and Colorado Springs, ending the drive atop the soaring pinnacle of Pikes Peak.

Say's phoebe in Red Rocks Park, near Denver's urban core.

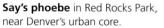

Bluff Lake Nature Center, at the site of Denver's old Stapleton Airport, has observation decks constructed with bird-watching in mind. The walk and platforms nestle in the marsh grass, concealing birders from view.

❶ Fort Collins Area

For birders Fort Collins has a remarkable 43 natural areas along the Rocky Mountain foothills, Fossil Creek, and the Poudre River. Start the birding tour by driving 65 miles (105 km) north on I-25 from Denver to **Fort Collins**. Exit on Prospect Rd. and turn west for about 0.3 mile (0.4 km). A sign on the south side of the road announces the **Environmental Learning Center,** or ELC, and a Welcome Center managed by Colorado State University's Warner College of Natural Resources. It has 212 acres (86 h), with 2.5 miles (4 km) of interpretive trails, and is host to the Rocky Mountain Raptor Program, a treatment center for birds of prey; here, see birds held in captivity that cannot be returned to the wild.

Also at the Welcome Center are a short interpretive trail along Boxelder Creek and a trail entering **Running Deer NA,** an open space to the south.

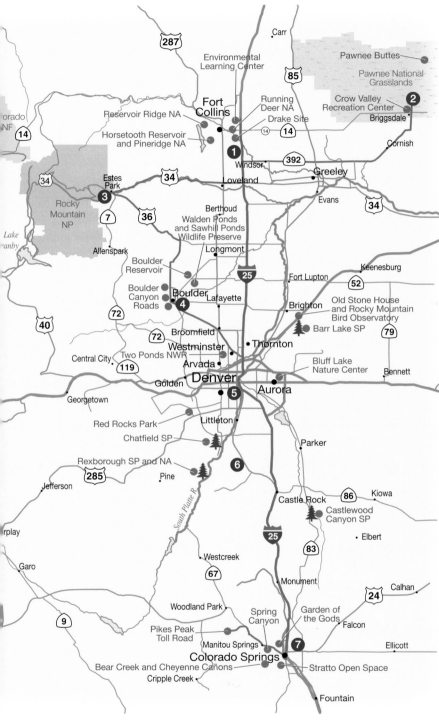

Yellow-rumped warblers are often sighted along woodland trails.

and yellow-headed blackbirds, egrets, killdeers, American white pelicans, woodpeckers, owls, and warblers in wetland areas and kingbirds in the groves. The trail has boardwalk sections and features many interpretive signs.

Next, drive west on Prospect Rd. to Timberline Rd., turn left, proceed to Drake Rd., and turn right. Turn left on Environment Dr., cross a one-lane bridge, turn left on the gravel road, cross the railroad tracks, and note the entrance sign to ELC's **Drake Site.** It has a picnic pavilion and a self-guided nature trail, the site of the raptor program. The city's Poudre River Trail ends nearby and can also be entered at this location.

Colorado State University, Warner College Environmental Learning Center
3745 Prospect Rd.
Fort Collins, CO 80525
(970) 491-1661
www.warnercnr.colostate.edu/ elc/sitewelcome.html

To reach natural areas on Fort Collins's west side, drive west on Drake Rd. to Overland Trail, turn right, and drive 0.3 mile (0.5 km) to a left turn at Co. Rd. 42C. Descend to the **Horsetooth Reservoir** and **Pineridge NA** and park at Co. Rd. 42C and Horsetooth Rd.

The natural area has 3 miles (4.8 km) of marked trails and is also the south access to the 5.8-mile-long (9.3-km) Foothills Trail. Near the trail's other end is **Reservoir Ridge NA**, known for its raptors, including falcons, eagles, and hawks.

Other important Fort Collins's natural areas worth birding:

- **Cathy Fromme Prairie NA**, Seneca St. and Harmony Rd.; see ground-nesting birds, bald eagles, and hawks, plus a raptor observation building and Fossil Creek Trail access.
- **Fossil Creek Reservoir NA**, on Carpenter Rd., just east of I-25; waterfowl, shorebirds, and perching birds.

Fort Collins Natural Areas
P.O. Box 580
Fort Collins, CO 80522
(970) 416-2815
www.fcgov.com/naturalareas/

❷ Pawnee NG and Pawnee Buttes

Drive east on Carpenter Rd. from Fossil Creek Reservoir as it becomes Hwy. 392. Proceed east about 43 miles (69 km) beyond

Just west of the ELC site on Prospect Rd., Prospect Ponds NA and Cottonwood Hollow NA are entry points to the 10.2-mile (16.4-km) Poudre River Trail, which links 16 natural areas along the river. Walk the trail to see shorebirds, red-winged

I-25 to Hwy. 14, continuing straight. Turn left 0.2 mile (0.3 km) past Hwy. 14 at Co. Rd. 77 and enter Crow Valley Recreation Area. Ask at the recreation area for a Pawnee auto bird-tour map with details of 193,060-acre (78,129-h) **Pawnee NG** and the **Pawnee Buttes.** Both are recognized IBA raptor hot spots, best visited during migration. The Pawnee Buttes are a nesting spot for hawks and swallows; they are closed to the public from

The distinctive rock formations in Red Rocks Park are well suited to roosting raptors. Songbirds favor the scrub brush habitats.

March to June to protect nesting birds. To see the lark bunting, Colorado's state bird, a better season to visit prairie areas is spring to early summer. In most areas of the grasslands, also look for chestnut-collared longspurs, eastern and western kingbirds, Swainson's and ferruginous hawks, burrowing owls, northern harriers, blackbirds, orioles, and long-billed curlews. Near Murphy's Pasture mountain plovers are common.

U.S. Forest Service, Pawnee National Grasslands
150 Centre Ave., Bldg. E
Fort Collins, CO 80526
(970) 295-6600
www.fs.fed.us/r2/arnf/

❸ Estes Park and Rocky Mountain NP

Return to Fort Collins and I-25, drive south to Hwy. 34, and turn west for about 42 miles (68 km). The town of **Estes Park** is one gateway to **Rocky Mountain NP,** a designated global IBA and home to 280 reported species of birds. Admission fee is charged. There is a visitors center in Estes Park where highways 34 and 36 divide. NPS visitors centers are found on Hwy. 34 and on Hwy. 36, as well as at the south end of the park. Obtain a bird checklist and learn about recent sightings before proceeding into the park. In summer check out the hummingbirds to be

seen at the many bird feeders in Estes Park.

The best times to visit are from snowmelt to late summer. For truly alpine birds, such as white-tailed ptarmigan, check out the tundra above tree line. They are easiest to see in spring before their plumage changes from snow white to mottled brown, making them well camouflaged amid the rocks and grasses.

Birds seem to funnel through the valley as they migrate in spring and fall. It's a prime spot to see large flocks of Cassin's finches and all three species of rosy-finches traveling together in migration. Because of its habitats and foliage conditions, the park is also a good viewing spot for blue grouse; gray jays; Clark's nutcrackers; red crossbills; three-toed woodpeckers; Williamson's sapsuckers; Townsend's solitares; black swifts; mountain chickadees; Wilson's, MacGillivray's and Virginia's warblers; pine grosbeaks; American dippers; pygmy nuthatches; western tanagers; brown-capped rosy-finches; numerous species of owls; and northern pygmy-owls; as well as eagles, harriers, hawks, kites, vultures, and other predatory birds.

Rocky Mountain NP
1000 Hwy. 36
Estes Park, CO 80517
(970) 586-1206
www.estesparkcvb.com

❹ Boulder Area

Return to Estes Park and follow Hwy. 36 southeast 38 miles (61 km) to the university town of **Boulder.** Located where the expansive prairie ends abruptly at the soaring Rocky Mountains, the city has abundant birdlife.

Start birding by driving into the canyons on Flagstaff Rd., Boulder Canyon Dr., or Sunshine Dr. Each has paths and hiking trails ideal for seeing the boreal and riverine birds of the area.

About 3 miles (4.8 km) north of town on Jay Rd. and 51st St., off Diagonal Hwy./Hwy. 119, **Boulder Reservoir** attracts waterfowl, gulls, and shorebirds in summer and short-eared owls in winter. The area is closed mid-spring to protect nesting ospreys. Admission fee is charged.

Next, drive east on Jay Rd. to E. 75th St. and turn right. Just 0.5 mile (0.8 km) south on Walden Pond Rd. is **Walden Ponds,** a cottonwood marsh with waterfowl, ibis, swallows, and yellow-headed blackbirds, all easily seen from its 550-foot (168-m) full-access boardwalk. Paths also lead from the pond to **Sawhill Ponds Wildlife Preserve,** a series of 20 ponds dotted along Boulder Creek.

City of Boulder Parks and Recreation Dept.
5565 51st St.
Boulder, CO 80301
(303) 413-7200
www.bouldercolorado.gov

Red Rocks Park (above) is located in suburban Morrison. It has numerous trails from which to see pink-sided dark-eyed juncos (top right) and downy woodpeckers (bottom right). The nearby ridges attract migrating ferruginous hawks by the thousands and are the site of one of only three HawkWatch locations in Colorado.

❺ Denver Area

Take Hwy. 36 for 29 miles (47 km) to Denver, closing the outbound loop. Despite its urban persona, the mile-high city is a rich area for birding, especially during spring and fall migrations, when birds rest in its parks, lakes, and open spaces before venturing farther to their summer nesting grounds or winter feeding areas.

Bird around the city beginning at **Barr Lake SP,** located about 15 miles (24 km) northeast of Denver and home to the **Rocky Mountain Bird Observatory** at the Old Stone House. To get to the state park, drive I-76 northeast 15 miles (24 km) to exit 22, turn east on E. Bromley Ln. (152nd St.), and turn south on Picadilly Rd. to reach the park. Admission fee is charged.

Almost 330 species of birds have been seen here, including a pair of nesting bald eagles in spring. A permanent spotting scope is mounted at the lakeside gazebo, or watch from the park trails. Kayaks and canoes are welcome on the lake.

It's a likely place to see herons, double-crested cormorants, and white pelicans, along with wading birds, waterfowl, neotropical migrants, and a large number of perching birds drawn to the park's trees and shrubs.

Barr Lake SP
13401 Picadilly Rd.
Brighton, CO 80603
(303) 659-6005
www.parks.state.co.us

Old Stone House at the **Rocky Mountain Bird Observatory** is open Monday through Friday, 9 A.M. to 5 P.M. Retrace north on Picadilly Rd. to E. Bromley Ln. (152nd. Ave), turn left, then left again on the first road before the railroad tracks. Follow the gravel road to the Rocky Montain Bird Observatory headquarters.

The observatory welcomes visitors. It has an education program to impart an understanding of wild birds, the habitats they need to survive, and their intriguing habits.

Rocky Mountain Bird Observatory
14500 Lark Bunting Ln.
Brighton, CO 80603
(303) 659-4348
www.rmbo.org

Travel back south on I-76 to Hwy. 470 (a tollway), head

east, exit westbound at Pena Blvd., and merge into I-70 west. In 4 miles (6.4 km) exit south at Havana Blvd. **Bluff Lake Nature Center** is located on the former site of Denver Stapleton Airport. Today its 123 acres (50 h) of restored habitat is a wildlife refuge along Sand Creek. It attracts over 130 species of birds. Three trails meander through wetland, shortgrass prairie, and riparian forest. There are blinds, overlooks, a boardwalk, and an amphitheater for music performances.

Bluff Lake Nature Center
7350 E. 29th Ave., Ste. 300
Denver, CO 80238
(303) 468-3240
www.blufflakenaturecenter.org

Cross the city to Denver's west side and visit **Two Ponds NWR,** the smallest urban refuge. Take I-76 west to Hwy. 36, exit at Hwy. 287, and go north. Turn left on 80th Ave. and continue 3 miles (4.8 km); the refuge is on the left side of the road. It supports 113 bird species, including 22 that breed here. Also note Bullock's orioles's pouchlike nests hanging in the trees. Open daily from dawn to sunset; a kiosk at the refuge has current information on trails, closures, and other information useful to visitors.

Two Ponds NWR
9210 W. 80th Ave.
Arvada, CO 80005
(303) 289-0930
www.fws.gov/twoponds/

A final stop in southwest Denver is **Red Rocks Park.** Return to I-70 and drive west to exit 259 at Morrison, turn left at the bottom of the exit ramp, and follow Hwy. 29 south about 1.5 miles (2.4 km). It leads to the park entrance. Admission fee is charged.

A 1.4-mile (2.3-km) hike on Trading Post Loop passes through rough terrain with drop-offs and steep grades and requires strenuous effort. Rosy-finches are often seen here in the winter months, while mountain bluebirds and golden-crowned sparrows are common in spring.

The park closes early on days when concerts are held in the amphitheater. Plan to stay for a night of music under the stars.

Garden of the Gods has both fascinating rock formations and birding opportunities. The visitors center hosts educational programs and dining, with views of the park from the center's Cafe at the Garden.

Red Rocks Park & Amphitheater
18300 W. Alameda Pkwy.
Morrison, CO 80465
(303) 295-4444
www.redrocksonline.com

Before leaving, note that many more bird-watching parks are located near Red Rocks Park, including Matthews Winters Open Space Park, Morrison Park, and Dinosaur Ridge HawkWatch, the latter with numerous ferruginous hawks.

❻ South of Denver

Next, from Morrison, enter Hwy. 470 (toll) and drive 10.5 miles (17 km) south to Wadsworth Blvd. (Hwy. 121), turn south, drive 0.6 mile (1 km), and turn into **Chatfield SP.** Admission fee is charged.

From March to September the park has a heronry for great blue herons on its south side. It also has miles of hiking trails along the lake, good for seeing least flycatchers and American redstarts. View migrating flocks of warblers along the South Platte River.

Chatfield SP
11500 N. Roxborough Park Rd.
Littleton, CO 80125
(303) 791-7275
www.parks.state.co.us

Drive south on Hwy. 121, turn left on W. Waterton Rd., then right on N. Rampart Range Rd.

It leads to **Roxborough SP and NA,** an IBA known for breeding MacGillivray's warblers and prairie falcons. Admission fee is charged.

The best birding is found on the Fountain Valley and South Rim Loop trails. The Carpenter Peak trail is steep and strenuous.

Roxborough SP
4751 Roxborough Drive
Littleton, CO 80125
(303) 973-3959
www.parks.state.co.us

Return to Hwy. 470 (toll), drive east to I-25, and turn south. At Castle Rock exit 182, and turn east on Hwy. 86 for about 6 miles (10 km). Turn south on S. Parker Rd. (Hwy. 83) and drive 5 miles (8 km) to **Castlewood Canyon SP**'s entrance. Admission fee is charged.

Another IBA for breeding prairie falcons, Cordilleran flycatchers, western tanagers, and Virginia's warblers, the park has 13 miles (21 km) of trails and a visitors center.

Follow the Canyon Rim, Cherry Creek, and Lake Gulch trails to see violet-green swallows, warblers, wrens, and gnatcatchers. Check the open fields for bobolinks and dickcissels.

Castlewood Canyon SP
2989 S. State Hwy. 83
Franktown, CO 80116
(303) 688-5242
www.parks.state.co.us

Red-breasted nuthatches are found in conifer and mixed hardwood forests.

❼ Colorado Springs Area

Like Boulder, Colorado Springs is nestled against the rising peaks of the Rocky Mountains, with creeks spilling down to the city. It's another bird-rich area.

From I-25S, take exit 146, Garden of the Gods Rd., and head west for 2.5 miles (4 km). Turn left on 30th St.; about 1 mile (1.6 km) beyond, the visitors center for **Garden of the Gods** is on the road's left side. This city park is a registered National Natural Landmark, and entry is free to the public.

These 1,400 acres (567 h) of sandstone formations and scrub brush habitat have 15 miles (24 km) of trails to explore; several are easy to moderate. The visitors center has maps of all the trails. Open 5 A.M. to 11 P.M. daily in summer and 5 A.M. to 9 P.M. in winter, it is a perfect spot for dawn and sunset bird-watching.

See canyon wrens, violet-green swallows, rock pigeons,

prairie falcons, and several species of hummingbirds as white-throated swifts soar amid erosion-carved rocky spires.

Garden of the Gods
1805 N. 30th St.
Colorado Springs, CO 80904
(719) 634-6666
www.gardenofgods.com

Other nearby locales worth birding are **Spring Canyon** off Hwy. 24 in the west city and **Bear Creek Cañon** and **N. Cheyenne Cañon** parks, just south off Cresta Rd.

Next, drive west on Hwy. 24 for about 9.5 miles (15 km) to Pikes Peak Toll Rd. exit. Follow the signs to **Pikes Peak.**

The 14,110-foot (4,301-m) summit is open year-round except for weather closures, and its birding attraction is raptors. While technically not a hot spot, the remarkable view from the top and the chance to glimpse rosy-finches near the peak make it a worthwhile place to end a birding tour of Colorado.

Flagstaff, Phoenix, and Tucson

This birding tour captures the spirit of the region's sophisticated cities and its frontier past, traversing Arizona's high volcanic plateaus near Flagstaff, the Gila and Salt rivers lowlands of Phoenix, the tall mountains and saguaro-filled deserts of Tucson, and the borderlands near Mexico. Visit in winter or early spring or come to Arizona in late autumn, when north-migrating species return to their winter resting grounds to avoid the extreme heat of summer. This is a historic and colorful land with much to see beyond its wildlife. View birds that migrate north from Central and South America, making the trip here a once-in-a-lifetime experience to remember.

The crested caracara is often seen feeding with vultures, but it is actually a large falconlike raptor.

The birding attractions of the desert Southwest include many rarely seen species that seldom find their way this far north on the continent. The combination of vast space, sparse vegetation, and rare habitats spells unmatched opportunities for bird-watchers.

Predators stay far away from nests built amid the protective spines of cacti in the Desert Botanical Garden in Phoenix.

Wupatki NM, is 18 miles (29 km) to the north and is on the same road, which loops back to Hwy. 89. Admission fees are charged at all NPS units; one seven-day pass is good for all. Visitors centers are open 9 A.M. to 5 P.M. daily except Christmas.

The road between the two moves from ponderosa pine forest at Sunset Crater to piñon pine and juniper woodland, to high-desert scrub brush, and to grasslands at Wupatki. For each change in landscape or season, equal variation can be seen in the birds that fill these habitats. A word to the wise: Use patience and a keen eye to spot birds in such vast spaces. Start by looking for Steller's and pinyon jays, hawks, eagles, white-breasted nuthatches, and roadrunners.

Flagstaff Area NMs
6400 N. Hwy. 89
Flagstaff, AZ 86004

Sunset Crater Visitors Center
(928) 526-0502
www.nps.gov/sucr/

Wupatki Visitors Center
(928) 679 2365
www.nps.gov/wupa/

❶ Wupatki NM and Sunset Crater NM

Start the birding route in Flagstaff, 144 miles (232 km) north of Phoenix via I-17. From Flagstaff drive 12 miles (19 km) north on Hwy. 89 and turn right at Sunset Crater–Wupatki Loop Rd. (NF-545). **Sunset Crater NM** is 2 miles (3.2 km) east of the junction. Sunset's sister park,

At Montezuma Castle ancient inhabitants were cliff dwellers.

❷ Flagstaff

Return to **Flagstaff** to visit more birding locales.

Start with the **Arboretum at Flagstaff,** so much more than just a garden. Take historic Rte. 66 west to Woody Mountain Rd., turn left, and drive 3.8 miles (6.1 km) south. (The last section, while unpaved, is easily traveled.) Admission fee is charged. Open 9 A.M. to 5 P.M. daily, April through October.

Over 100 bird species have been recorded at the arboretum, including pygmy nuthatches. It has several miles of beautiful trails, Saturday morning bird walks (7:30 A.M.), and live birds-of-prey displays on weekends.

The Arboretum at Flagstaff
4001 Woody Mountain Rd.
Flagstaff, AZ 86001
(928) 774-1442
www.thearb.org

Next, travel 7.5 miles (12 km) east of Flagstaff on I-40, turn south at exit 204, and drive 3 miles (4.8 km), arriving at **Walnut Canyon NM.** Towed vehicles not advised. Admission fee is charged. Open 9 A.M. to 5 P.M. daily, November to April except Christmas; 8 A.M. to 5 P.M., May to October.

The unit has a visitors center, museum, and two trails: The 0.9-mile (1.4-km) Island Trail is a strenuous hike, but 0.7-mile (1.1-km) Rim Trail is easy to walk.

Because of its varied exposures, elevation, and water, the area is a birding hot spot that has recorded 121 species. They include red-tailed, Cooper's, and sharp-shinned hawks, plus falcons and eagles. It also has raptors rarely seen in the Southwest, such as Mexican spotted owls, peregrine falcons, and northern groshawks.

Flagstaff Area NMs
6400 N. Hwy. 89
Flagstaff, AZ 86004

Walnut Canyon Visitors Center
(928) 526 3367
www.nps.gov/waca

❸ Upper Oak Creek Canyon

Drive 2.3 miles (3.7 km) south of Flagstaff on I-17, turn left at Hwy. 83, and enter **Oak Creek Canyon.** The upper canyon has a year-round stream and is quite different from the high volcanic plateau around Flagstaff. The lower canyon opens to red-rock

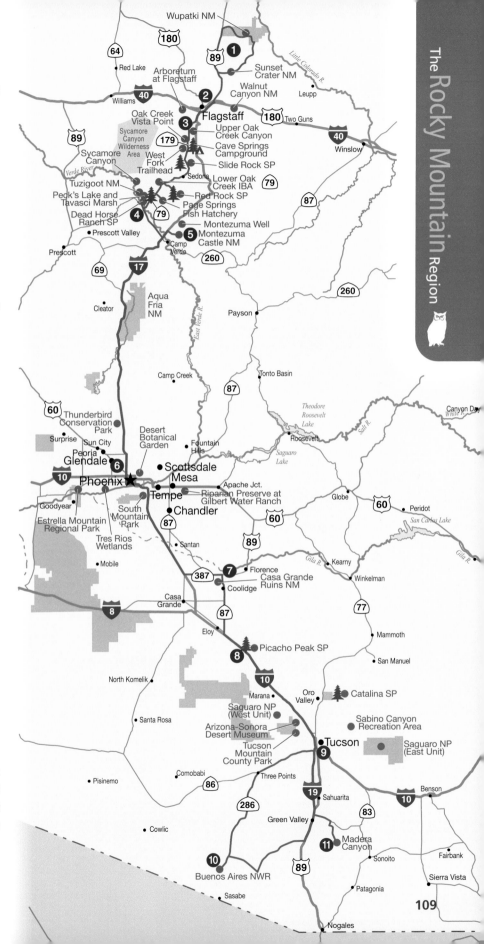

Phoenix's Thunderbird Park offers a birding observation spot with a concealed view of the water (above), where sparrows line up to take a drink (right).

formations and open countryside. Take advantage of the changes to sample birding spots along the route, noting how species change with the miles.

The first stop is **Oak Creek Vista Point**, 9 miles (14.5 km) south of the I-17 turnoff. From its lofty perch, look off the edge of the vast Mogollon Rim, which winds for miles through Arizona. Birds seen from here include black-hawks, white-throated swifts, peregrine falcons, and Townsend's solitaires.

Beyond, the road descends in a series of hairpin turns to enter a pine forest. Stop at **Cave Springs Campground**, 3 miles (4.8 km) below the switchbacks, to look for warbling vireos, painted red-starts, hepatic tanagers, and Lucy's, Grace's, and red-faced warblers along the cliffs.

Coconino NF
1824 S. Thompson St.
Flagstaff, AZ 86001
(928) 527-3600
www.fs.fed.us

Continue south on Hwy. 89 as the ponderosa pine forest becomes mixed with hardwoods. A mile (1.6 km) south of Cave Springs is **West Fork Trailhead,** which leads up a good birding canyon.

The last stop in the upper canyon is **Slide Rock SP**, 3 miles (4.8 km) south. Admission fee is charged. Here, join others for the thrill of plunging down a mossy chute in the river or scanning the creek for American dippers and trees for woodpeckers.

Slide Rock SP
6871 N. Hwy. 89A
Sedona, AZ 86336
(928) 282-3034
www.pr.state.az.us

❹ Sedona and Lower Oak Creek IBA

The resort town of **Sedona** is renowned for its striking scenic setting, a geological garden of colorful buttes and mesas set in the Coconino NF.

Turn left and southeast at Hwy. 179 in north Sedona, then take the next left at Schnelby Hill Rd. It winds for more than 6 miles (9.6 km) through Bear Wallow Canyon to its crest at a vista point, all with boreal birds.

In Sedona take advantage of the city's many trails, bike paths, open spaces, and parks suitable for birding.

Sedona Visitor Info. Svcs.
331 Forest Rd.
Sedona, AZ 86339
(800) 288-7336
www.visitsedona.com

From Sedona, drive south on Hwy. 79 for 0.5 mile (0.8 km), turn left on Lower Red Rock Loop Rd., and follow the signs to the entry to **Red Rock SP.** Admission fee is charged.

A 5-mile (8-km) network of looping trails winds along Oak Creek and through rock spires. Again, songbirds and boreal birds are commonly seen.

Red Rock SP
4050 Red Rock Loop Rd.
Sedona, AZ 86336
(928) 282-6907
www.pr.state.az.us

South of Sedona on Hwy. 79, the Audubon Society has recognized the entire **Lower Oak Creek** area as an IBA; it provides rare chances to see unusual Mexican migrants, including common black-hawks, greater pewees, painted redstarts, and magnificent hummingbirds, plus neotropical migrants that nest along the creek.

Next, turn left off Hwy. 79 at Page Springs Rd. and drive about 2.5 miles (4 km) southeast until it meets Oak Creek and **Page Springs Fish Hatchery,** open 8 A.M. to 4 P.M. daily, with a creekside nature trail. Migrants pass through or nest here in spring and fall. In winter juncos, marsh wrens, sparrows, and waterfowl fill the area. Look up to see ferruginous hawks, harriers, martins, and bald eagles. Also see yellow-billed cuckoos near their range's western boundary.

Arizona Game and Fish Dept.
Page Springs Fish Hatchery
500 S. Lake Mary Rd.
Flagstaff, AZ 86001
(928) 774-5045
www.azgfd.gov

Return to Hwy. 79, drive 5 miles (8 km) south to Cottonwood, follow S. Main St. north at the split, then west as its name changes, and right on 5th St. to **Dead Horse Ranch SP.** Open daily. Admission fee is charged.

More than 200 species have been counted in the park and surrounding area. Located in riparian willows and cotton-woods, the 430-acre (174-h) park teems with birds. Ten trails, including one leading to nearby **Tavasci Marsh** and **Pecks Lake,** and others to raptor viewing areas, are a paradise for bird-watching during spring and fall migrations. Even in winter waterfowl and shorebirds fill the park, drawn to its unique habitat. Counts of ducks climb to over 1,000 birds. Also look for wood ducks and herons along the river, marshes, and lakes.

Desert Botanical Garden bird sightings might include a pyrrhuloxia (top right) or its relative, the brightly colored northern cardinal (bottom right).

The Riparian Preserve at Gilbert Water Ranch attracts birds with running water and native plantings.

which meanders northwest into Sycamore Canyon Wilderness Area. Birds found on Sycamore Creek are similar to those on the Verde River.

❺ Montezuma Castle NM

Retrace the outbound path on Hwy. 260 to Cottonwood. Follow it 14 miles (23 km) southwest to Camp Verde and I-17. Turn north on I-17 for 3.2 miles (5.1 km), turn at the blinking light, and enter **Montezuma Castle NM,** an 826-acre (334-h) preserve of riparian mixed-forest habitat on Beaver Creek. Open 8 A.M. to 6 P.M. daily during summer, 8 A.M. to 5 P.M. Labor Day to Memorial Day. Admission fee is charged. The monument has a visitors center and trails leading to a five-story Sinagua cliff dwelling.

Despite their historic appeal, the monument's second unit is the prime attraction for birders.

Dead Horse Ranch SP
675 Dead Horse Ranch Rd.
Cottonwood, AZ 86326
(928) 634-5283
www.pr.state.az.us

Nearby is **Tuzigoot NM,** with 228 known bird species, including 60 species that nest there. Reach it by continuing north on 5th St., which becomes Tuzigoot Rd. Admission fee is charged.

The visitors center is open 8 A.M. to 6 P.M. daily during summer, 8 A.M. to 5 P.M. Labor Day to Memorial Day.

Visible on its hilltop perch long in advance, this pueblo was abandoned in A.D. 1400 by people of the Sinagua culture.

The best bird-watching at Tuzigoot is at Tavasci Marsh and nearby Peck's Lake, though birds frequently forage on the slopes below the ruins. In spring and summer the neotropical migrants dominate; in winter the population changes to waterfowl and shorebirds. Year-round, resident Arizona species visit the park, including hawks, falcons, harriers, brown-headed cowbirds, black-throated sparrows, and Bewick's wrens.

Tuzigoot NM
P. O. Box 219
Camp Verde, AZ 86322
(928) 634-5564
www.nps.gov/tuzi/

A last stop on the Verde River is **Sycamore Canyon.** Follow Tuzigoot Rd. west to Sycamore Canyon Rd. and turn right. The road ends in 11 miles (18 km) at a trailhead for Parson's Trail,

Gilbert Water Ranch boasts large wading birds, shorebirds, and waterfowl. This great egret glides along just above the water's surface.

Drive north on I-17 to exit 293, turn right on Beaver Creek Rd., and follow it about 11 miles (18 km) to **Montezuma Well.**

In this broad limestone sinkhole that formed when the roof of an underground cavern collapsed, a spring-fed pond attracts over 200 bird species, including neotropical migrants and eight hummingbird species; four of them nest nearby.

Montezuma Castle NM
P.O. Box 219
Camp Verde, AZ 86322
(928) 567-3322
www.nps.gov/moca/

❻ Phoenix Area

Arizona's largest city is part low desert, part oasis. It has many sites of interest to birders.

South Mountain Park, in the south city, is convenient to I-10 off Baseline Rd. at Central Ave. or Elliot Rd. Open 8 A.M. to 2 P.M. Wednesday to Saturday, 8 A.M. to 1 P.M. Sunday. The visitors center has trail maps and birding information.

The park's trails range in length from short and easy to long and strenuous. They are the best places in the area to see representative desert bird species, such as Gambel's quail, phainopeplas, black-throated sparrows, gilded flickers, and cactus wrens, along with woodpeckers, hummingbirds, hawks, falcons, and shrikes.

South Mountain Park
10409 S. Central Ave.
Phoenix, AZ 85042
(602) 534-6324
phoenix.gov/PARKS/smeec.html

For **Tres Rios Wetlands** on the Salt River, return to Baseline Rd., turn west, drive to 91st Ave., turn right, and cross the river; just before the water-treatment plant on the other side, note a yellow gate east of the road. Turn, drive east to another yellow gate, and park. Riparian trails start here. (In winter, when rains may close the river crossing, reach 91st Ave. from I-10 at exit 134, driving south 5 miles (8 km) to the wetlands.)

Sometimes, at dawn, so many birds are present here that they seem to darken the sky. There is also a heron rookery.

Tres Rios Wetlands
200 W. Washington St., 9th Fl.
Phoenix, AZ 85007
(602) 495-7927
phoenix.gov/tresrios/

The 19,000-acre (7,689-h) **Estrella Mountain Regional Park,** located west in Goodyear near the meeting of the Salt and Agua Fria rivers, is latticed with 33 miles (53 km) of trails. It also has a large wetland birding area.

To reach the park, go west on I-10 to S. Estrella Pkwy., turn south, and follow the road to W. Vineyard Ave. Turn left, then right, and enter the park.

Most of the park is a pristine desert preserve. On its trails see gray flycatchers, cactus wrens, killdeer, greater roadrunners, ruby-crowned kinglets, curved-billed thrashers, and falcons.

Estrella Mountain Regional Park
14805 W. Vineyard Ave.
Goodyear, AZ 85338
(623) 932-3811
www.maricopa.gov/parks/estrella

Thunderbird Conservation Park is located northwest in suburban Glendale between Deer Valley Rd. and Pinnacle Peak Rd. on 59th Ave. Open sunrise to sunset daily.

It has four viewing blinds, 20 miles (32 km) of trails, and full-access paths. Visit the lake just north of Deer Valley Rd. and 59th Ave. to view wading birds and waterfowl. Desert areas to the north have quail, greater roadrunners, owls, and woodpeckers, plus hummingbirds.

Glendale Parks and Recreation
5850 W. Glendale Ave.
Glendale, AZ 85301
(623) 930-282
www.ci.glendale.az.us/parksandrecreation/

The **Riparian Preserve at Gilbert Water Ranch** at 2757 E. Guadalupe Rd. in Gilbert, east of Greenfield Rd., is open dawn to dusk daily, year-round. Admission fee is charged.

At this water reclamation facility over 120 species of birds have been noted. During migration it's common to see 50 or more species of waterfowl, shorebirds, and migrants per day. More than 4.5 miles (7.2 km) of boardwalk and trails wind through wetlands, on dikes, and into typical desert upland vegetation and shrubs.

The Riparian Institute
50 E. Civic Center Dr.
Gilbert, AZ 85296
(480) 503-6744
www.riparianinstitute.org

Make a last stop in Phoenix at McDowell Rd. and Galvin Pkwy., site of the **Desert Botanical Garden.** Open 8 A.M. to 8 P.M. daily except on major holidays, October to April; 7 A.M. to 8 P.M., May to September. Admission fee is charged.

Pick up bird checklists at the admission booth, and reserve a guided tour with an expert birder.

Desert Botanical Garden
1201 N. Galvin Pkwy.
Phoenix, AZ 85008
(480) 941-1225
www.dbg.org

Killdeer

Barn owls **love the nightlife**— though they
are usually solitary, **flying on silent wings**

Not to Be Missed!

Raptor Free Flight Demonstration
Arizona-Sonora Desert Museum in Tucson

Raptor Free Flight is a unique demonstration where birds are the focus of the program. Learn lifestyle and behavioral facts about the resident raptors. Watch barn owls glide low and effortlessly across the desert. See Harris's hawks or prairie falcons dive from the sky or soar overhead.

From the end of October until mid-April, this popular program is held at 10:30 A.M. and 1:30 P.M. daily. Allow about 30 minutes to walk from the museum entrance to the Raptor Free Flight viewing area, just off Desert Loop Trail. Be sure to pick up the self-guiding tour map at the entrance.

Also stop by the walk-in aviary, featuring over 40 species of Arizona native birds.

Watching hummingbirds? There are seven species in the Hummingbird Aviary. Walk in, look closely, and admire the antics of these aerial acrobats.

Arizona-Sonora Desert Museum has experienced handlers with highly warranted respect for the predator birds that perform at their museum.

❼ Casa Grande Ruins NM

Driving 36 miles (58 km) south from Phoenix on I-10, turn east on Hwy. 387, travel about 7 miles (11 km) to Hwy. 87, and turn southeast. In 6 miles (9.6 km) on the right, see **Casa Grande Ruins NM.** Open 8 A.M. to 5 P.M. daily except Christmas. Admission fee is charged.

The 700-year-old four-story edifice was called Casa Grande—Spanish for great house—by a padre in 1694.

Daytime summer temperatures regularly exceed 100°F (37.7°C), and most birds are active from evening to morning. See rare Gila woodpeckers, found only in the Sonoran Desert. Others dwell here too: northern cardinals, quail, doves, greater roadrunners, hummingbirds, and owls.

Casa Grande Ruins NM
1100 W. Ruins Dr.
Coolidge, AZ 85228
(520) 723-3172
www.nps.gov/cagr/

❽ Picacho Peak SP

Return to I-10 by driving Hwy. 87 south from Coolidge, turn southeast, and take exit 219 after 7 miles (11 km) to enter **Picacho Peak SP.** The visitors center is open 8 A.M. to 10 P.M. daily; no food or supplies are available in the park. Admission fee is charged.

Make a strenuous climb to the top of Picacho Peak on the 2-mile (3.2-km) Hunter Trail or the 3.1-mile (5-km) Sunset Vista Trail; Calloway Trail is easier and leads to an overlook, and the Nature Trail is also an easy walk. Regardless of choice, note the

Gambel's quail, cactus wrens, greater roadrunners, burrowing owls, and prairie falcons.

Picacho Peak State Park
P.O. Box 275
Picacho, AZ 85241
(520) 466-3183
www.pr.state.az.us/

❾ Tucson

Drive south 40 miles (64 km) and enter Tucson. Exit on W. Grant Rd., follow the frontage road 1 mile (1.6 km), turn left on Speedway Blvd., and drive west to the 20,000-acre (8,094-h)

Saguaro NP visitors center (above) is the best starting point for planning a birding outing in the park. Two units, located on either side of Tucson, preserve the giant cactus and protect their wildlife.

A magic time comes at dusk (upper right), when the sun sets and the air rapidly cools. Listen at sunset for the calls of nocturnal birds coming out of their diurnal slumber as those that were active during the day begin to roost and prepare to sleep. In fall and late winter, if the moon is full, choose a comfortable vantage point and watch its face with binoculars or a spotting scope for the silhouetted forms of migrating songbirds, waterfowl, shorebirds, and other fowl in flight.

Raised viewing platforms and fixed binocular telescopes (bottom right) at Saguaro NP raise visitors high enough to see birds over smokebush and mesquite. Full-access paths lead between observation points.

Tucson Mountain County Park. Open 7 A.M. to 10 P.M. daily. Admission fee is charged.

The higher elevations here add species such as curve-billed thrashers, vermilion flycatchers, and warblers; traveling south increases the likelihood of finding birds that are rare elsewhere.

Pima Co. Natural Resources, Parks, and Recreation
3500 West River Rd.
Tucson, AZ 85741
(520) 877-6000
www.pima.gov/nrpr/index.htm

Arizona-Sonora Desert Museum is also within the park's boundaries, with a renowned zoo, arboretum, and natural history museum. Open 7:30 A.M. to 5 P.M. daily March to September; 8:30 A.M. to 5:00 P.M. October to February. Admission fee is charged.

Look for Gila woodpeckers, thrashers, and cactus wrens along 2 miles (3.2 km) of paths. Take in the captive bird aviaries as well as the Raptor Free Flight Demonstration.

Arizona-Sonora Desert Museum
2021 N. Kinney Rd.
Tucson, AZ 85743
(520) 883-2702
www.desertmuseum.org

Nearby, **Saguaro NP** has its west unit—the park's east unit is 30 miles (48 km) southwest across the city of Tucson—with looming giant saguaros. These huge cacti are nesting sites for

Gila woodpeckers and gilded flickers, which bore holes in cactus limbs, often moving on before they finish. Leftover holes provide nesting spots for American kestrels, elf and screech-owls, Lucy's warblers, and cactus wrens.

Red Hills Visitors Center is in the west unit, on Kinney Rd. The east unit's visitors center is on Old Spanish Trail just north of Escalante Rd. Both drives and trails loop from the visitors centers; ask for bird checklists.

Saguaro NP
3693 S. Old Spanish Trail
Tucson, AZ 85730
(520) 733-5158
www.nps.gov/sagu/

Other birding sites worth a visit in Tucson:

- **Catalina SP,** 9 miles (14 km) northwest of Tucson on Hwy. 77; 170 species reside in a park with many trails and outstanding bird-watching.
- **Sabino Canyon Recreation Area,** 12 miles (19 km) east of town; flowing year-round creek draws many birds; especially good in winter.

❿ Buenos Aires NWR

Drive almost to the international border and **Buenos Aires NWR** by heading about 18 miles (29 km) west on Hwy. 86 to Three Points, then south 38 miles (61 km) on Hwy. 286 to milepost

7.5 and the refuge headquarters. The visitors center is open 7:30 A.M. to 4 P.M. daily except major holidays and weekends between June 1 and August 15.

An elevation of 1,000 feet (305 m) above the surrounding desert creates an arid grassland habitat with vernal marshes, meadows, and groves along Arivaca Creek and Arivaca Cienega. They sustain 330 bird species, including flame-colored, hepatic, summer, and western tanagers; vermilion flycatchers; black-bellied whistling ducks; tropical kingbirds; rose-throated becards; rare hummingbirds; and, even rarer, masked bobwhite.

Buenos Aires NWR
P.O. Box 109
Sansabe, AZ 85633
(520) 823-4247
www.fws.gov

⓫ Madera Canyon

Drive north on Hwy. 286 to its intersection with Arivaca-Sasabe Rd. and turn east. In about 35 miles (56 km) it intersects I-19

at Arivaca. Turn north on I-17 and drive to Green Valley. Turn east on Continental Rd., transition to White House Canyon Rd., and drive 5.7 miles (9.2 km) to Madera Canyon Rd. About 3 miles (4.8 km) farther the road enters **Madera Canyon.** Parking fee is charged.

The canyon is a nexus for a 1,100-mile (1,770-km) trail system through Coronado NF, named the Sky Islands for its lofty peaks. Mountains rise to over 10,000 feet (3048 m) with changing climate and vegetation.

Some 175 threatened or endangered species are found here, from Mexican gray wolves and ferruginous pygmy-owls to Pima pineapple cacti. More than 200 recorded bird species occur in the canyon. The spot is especially prized for its broad-billed, blue-throated, violet-crowned, and white-eared hummingbirds.

Coronado National Forest
300 W. Congress St.
Tucson, AZ, 85701
(520) 388-8300
www.fs.fed.us/r3/coronado/

Buenos Aires NWR is Arizona's southernmost outpost of the NWR system.

Santa Fe to Albuquerque

With more than 500 avian species documented in New Mexico, birding the Land of Enchantment is a treat to repeat again and again. Migratory birds from South and Central America wing north in spring to nest within the state. Their travels bring them within view of ancient pueblos and modern cities, never far from the sophisticated resorts, great restaurants, cultural events, and Native American art for which the state is famous. Plan to visit in fall or spring, when temperatures are moderate and birds are plentiful. The route travels from piñon and ponderosa pine forests and peaks soaring above 7,000 feet (2,134 m) to end in the expansive desert cut by the Rio Grande River Valley.

Diverse birdlife, scenic grandeur, and ancient cultures make New Mexico a prized travel destination. Straddling high country from the southern Rockies to the Sierra Madre Orientale Mountains, it is a land filled with both familiar and rare birds.

Water and riparian groves attract many species of birds to Rio Grande Nature Center SP. The pond fills with migrating dabbling and diving ducks and geese in winter, while its shoreline attracts wading birds and gathers flocks of songbirds in its trees. Overhead, birds in flight dot the enormous cerulean-blue bowl of the Southwest's sky.

Rufous
hummingbird

❶ Storrie Lake SP

Begin the birding route by driving 121 miles (195 km) northeast from Albuquerque on I-70 to Las Vegas, enter town, and turn left on 7th St. (Hwy. 518). Travel north 4 miles (6.4 km) to **Storrie Lake SP.** Open 6 A.M.

to sunset April to September, 7 A.M. to sunset October to March. Admission fee is charged.

Fall and spring migrations of geese and ducks produce large numbers of waterfowl at the lake, making it a must-see birding destination. The park also has

neotropical migrants; scan the trees, cattails, and shrubs.

Both trails and access roads nearly circle the lake. Take Hwy. 518 north for 1.3 miles (2.1 km) and turn left on Lakeview Dr. to access shoreline trails near the lake's inlet.

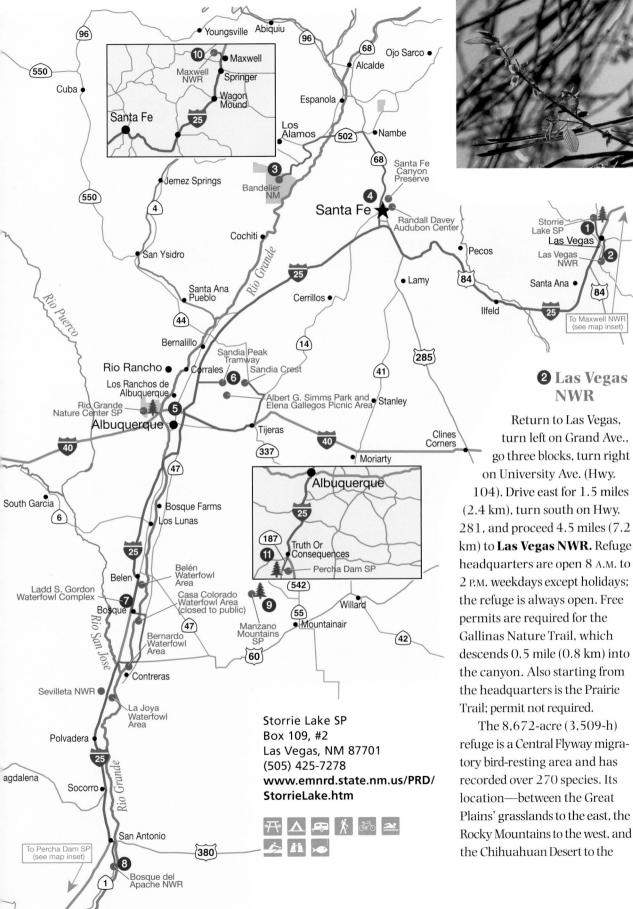

Scissor-tailed flycatcher

south—has grassland meadows, streams, canyons, ponds, tilled fields, and marshes that provide both feeding and breeding habitats for many species of birds.

An 8-mile (12.8-km) auto loop passes through the heart of the refuge. Make a stop at Fred Quintana Overlook with an extended observation deck overlooking Crane Lake and a permanently mounted spotting scope.

Over 80 different birds nest at the refuge; 50 of them are neotropical species.

Las Vegas NWR
Rte. 1, Box 399
Las Vegas, NM 87701
(505) 425-3581
www.fws.gov

❸ Bandelier NM

Return to I-25, drive south 62 miles (100 km) to exit 284 (Hwy. 466), and turn north toward Santa Fe. After 500 feet (160 m) the road becomes Old Pecos Trail. Continue through Santa Fe, turning left on Alameda St. and right on Guadalupe St., which becomes Hwy. 84. Drive 14 miles (23 km) north, exit on Hwy. 502 to Los Alamos, head west

❷ Las Vegas NWR

Return to Las Vegas, turn left on Grand Ave., go three blocks, turn right on University Ave. (Hwy. 104). Drive east for 1.5 miles (2.4 km), turn south on Hwy. 281, and proceed 4.5 miles (7.2 km) to **Las Vegas NWR.** Refuge headquarters are open 8 A.M. to 2 P.M. weekdays except holidays; the refuge is always open. Free permits are required for the Gallinas Nature Trail, which descends 0.5 mile (0.8 km) into the canyon. Also starting from the headquarters is the Prairie Trail; permit not required.

The 8,672-acre (3,509-h) refuge is a Central Flyway migratory bird-resting area and has recorded over 270 species. Its location—between the Great Plains' grasslands to the east, the Rocky Mountains to the west, and the Chihuahuan Desert to the

Storrie Lake SP
Box 109, #2
Las Vegas, NM 87701
(505) 425-7278
www.emnrd.state.nm.us/PRD/StorrieLake.htm

119

Sandia Peak Tramway in Albuquerque is a ride to remember.

for 11.5 miles (18.5 km), and merge south onto Hwy. 4. The entrance road to **Bandelier NM** is clearly marked. Hours vary by season; only campers with permits can remain overnight. Admission fee is charged.

On the site of this ancestral home to Native American predecessors of the modern Pueblo people, ruins date back to the twelfth century. A 2-mile (3.2-km) trail to the ancient dwellings starts at Frijoles Canyon visitors center. Along the way, see canyon wrens, plumbeous and warbling vireos, Hammond's and dusty flycatchers, tanagers, hawks, warblers, nuthatches, mourning doves, and grosbeaks.

There's a good chance of seeing three-toed woodpeckers on the left fork of the trail to White Rock Canyon, which leads to Upper and Lower Frijoles Falls. It enters a side canyon where the birds are frequently active.

These walks just scratch the surface of the monument's more than 70 miles (113 km) of trails and over 200 species of birds, including white-throated swifts, broad-tailed hummingbirds, violet-green swallows, and many other avian species.

Bandelier NM
15 Entrance Rd.
Los Alamos, NM 87544
(505) 672-3861
www.nps.gov/band/

④ Santa Fe

Returning to Santa Fe, the Nature Conservancy's 190-acre (77-h) **Santa Fe Canyon Preserve** and the **Randall Davey Audubon Center** are both found off Upper Canyon Rd. Turn left on Gordo Canyon Rd. after 1 mile (1.6 km), then make an immediate left into the preserve's parking lot.

The unit preserves upper Sonoran piñon pine and juniper trees, mixed forests of ponderosa pines and fir trees, and riparian habitat along the Santa Fe River. It is also a trailhead for the 20-mile (32-km) Dale Ball Foothill Trail, which accommodates both hikers and bicyclists; only foot traffic is allowed in the preserve.

Pick up a bird list at Randall Davey Center and begin birding on Dale Ball, 0.5-mile (0.8-km) El Temporal, 1-mile (1.6-km) Bear Canyon, or the 1.5-mile (2.4-km) interpretive trails.

Over 140 species of birds have been recorded at the preserve. Bluebirds, bushtits, spotted and canyon towhees, and vireos are a few of the common birds found in Santa Fe Canyon. Before continuing the route, consider driving a bit farther along Upper Canyon Rd. It passes two reservoirs before dead-ending at a third. All are good sites to see wading birds, waterfowl, and neotropical migrant songbirds.

Randall Davey Audubon Center
P.O. Box 9314
Santa Fe, NM 87504-9314
www.audubon.org/chapter/nm/nm/rdac/audubon_center/center.html

⑤ Albuquerque

Divided near its center by the waters of the Rio Grande River, this bird-friendly town has

Join In

Festival of the Cranes

Held in November

Help to celebrate the sandhill cranes' return:

- **Tours**—Birding tours from dawn to dusk of Bosque del Apache NWR, with facilities and operations tours of the wildlife refuge. Raptor flight demonstrations.

- **Exhibits**—Live exhibits from animal rescue groups are on display, along with a variety of art and learning exhibits.

- **Workshops**—Learn topics from wildlife photography to bird identification in classes and lectures.

Find out more at www.friendsofthebosque.org/crane

numerous open spaces and parks worthy of bird-watching.

Begin at **Rio Grande Nature Center SP,** with riverside groves and meadows with a 3-acre (1.2-h) pond in the Rio

Grande's migratory bird flyway. From I-25 take exit 227 (Frontage Rd.) and turn right on Candelaria Rd. Park is open 8 A.M. to 5 P.M. daily; visitors center is open 10 A.M. to 5 P.M. Admission fee is charged.

Sandhill cranes are the local favorite of the 260 species of birds that have been recorded here. On the site are 2 miles (3.2 km) of nature trails and 21 self-guided interpretive exhibits, many of which feature birds of the Rio Grande Valley.

At the nature center a viewing port gives an underwater look into the pond; speakers share the sounds of ducks and birds in the aviary. Staff-guided nature walks are held Saturday mornings; advance reservations are advised.

Rio Grande Nature Center SP
2901 Candelaria Rd. NW
Albuquerque, NM 87107
(505) 344-7240
**www.emnrd.state.nm.us/PRD/
RGNC.htm**

In northeast Albuquerque, from I-25, take exit 234 (Tramway Rd.), head east and south for about 6 miles (9.7 km), and turn left on Simms Park Rd. Signs lead to **Albert G. Simms Park.** Open 7 A.M. to 9 P.M. summer; 7 A.M. to 7 P.M. winter. Admission fee is charged.

The highlight of this city park is 640-acre (259-h) **Elena Gallegos Picnic Area,** a wilderness of grasslands, junipers, and pines in an urban setting under the soaring Sandia Mountains.

There are trails for every level of fitness and ability, along with a bird-watching blind that overlooks a pond. Remain alert; both rattlesnakes and Gila monsters, a venomous lizard, are common in rocky areas near trails.

The park and picnic area are home to numerous raptors, such as American kestrels, prairie falcons, and sharp-shinned, red-tailed, and Cooper's hawks.

Other year-round residents include greater roadrunners, Gambel's quail, meadowlarks, bluebirds, towhees, vultures, and Bewick's wrens. With the changing seasons come migrant birds. Visit in early fall and in early spring to see warblers, vireos, sparrows, juncos, jays, and colorful tanagers. along with other songbirds.

Albert G. Simms Park
P.O. Box 1293
Albuquerque, NM 87103
(505) 452-5210
**www.cabq.gov/openspace/
elenagallegos.html**

❻ Sandia Crest

A visit to the high country of the Sandia Mountains above Albuquerque can be either a short trip or a long ride.

The quick way is to ride the **Sandia Peak Tramway** to the top of Sandia Peak, a 2.7-mile (4.4-km) trip on high-wire cars above canyons and forests to Crest House. From the junction of Tramway Rd. and Tramway Blvd., turn east on Sandia Peak Tramway Loop. Open 9 A.M. to 9 P.M. daily Memorial Day to Labor Day, otherwise 9 A.M. to 8 P.M. daily. Closed Tuesdays.

An alternate is to drive 14 miles (22.5 km) east on I-40 from the I-25/I-40 junction, turn left at Hwy. 14, proceed 6.9 miles (11.1 km) to Sandia Crest Rd., and turn left. A twisty but scenic road leads to mountain forest habitat that attracts all three rosy-finch species—and many outdoors lovers. Remember the altitude here reaches 10,678 feet (3,255 m)—acclimatization is advised for a safe visit.

Watch along the way in trees and shrubs for dark-eyed juncos, white-throated swifts, hermit thrushes, red-naped sapsuckers, curve-billed thrashers, saw-whet owls, northern pygmy-owls, and violet-green swallows.

Bosque del Apache NWR is an annual migration stopover for colorful flocks of red-winged blackbirds.

Meadowlarks are **melodic masters;** eastern and western species can be **distinguished** only by their **songs**

Bosque del Apache NWR preserves wetlands along the Rio Grande River that are important to migrating songbirds.

Sandia Crest Visitors Center
Cibola National Forest
2113 Osuna Rd. NE, Ste. A
Albuquerque, NM 87113
(505) 248-0190
**www.fs.fed.us/r3/cibola/
districts/sandia.shtml**

www.sandiapeak.com

❼ Ladd S. Gordon Waterfowl Complex

Follow I-25 south 35 miles (56 km) from Albuquerque to Belen, site of the **Ladd S. Gordon**

Waterfowl Complex, an IBA of refuges and preserves run by the state of New Mexico. All are adjacent to I-25, the Rio Grande River, and adjacent state highways.

Visit from late fall to early spring, when wintering birds peak. The complex includes:

- **Belén Waterfowl Area**, 1.3 miles (2 km) south of Belen on Hwy. 109; trail with over 300 observed species of birds.
- **Casa Colorado Waterfowl Area,** closed to the public except for seasonal waterfowl hunting.

- **Bernardo Waterfowl Area,** intersection of I-25 and Hwy. 60 at Bernardo; trails and viewing tower; cranes, upland birds, and waterfowl.
- **La Joya Waterfowl Area,** exit 169 off I-25 just north of Socorro; trail; doves, songbirds, and waterfowl.

Located across I-25 from La Joya is **Sevilleta NWR,** a NFS research facility. The unit is usually closed to the public. Staff may accommodate bird-watching visits if contacted in advance.

New Mexico Game and Fish
3841 Midway Pl. NE
Albuquerque, NM 87109
(505) 222-4700
**www.wildlife.state.nm.us/
conservation/wildlife_
management_areas**

Sevilleta NWR
P.O. Box 1248
Socorro, NM 87801
(505) 864-4021
www.fws.gov

❽ Bosque del Apache NWR

Drive 15 miles (24 km) south of Socorro on I-25 to reach **Bosque del Apache NWR** (in Spanish "the woods of the Apache"). When tribal hunters visit today, they still find over 340 species and thousands of birds resting here each winter. Visitors center open 7:30 A.M. to 4 P.M. weekdays, 8 A.M. to 4:30 P.M. weekends. Admission fee is charged.

Take a 15-mile (24-km) auto tour for bird viewing using cars as a blind. See sandhill cranes, snow and Canada geese, and many varieties of ducks, raptors, and songbirds.

Bosque del Apache NWR
P.O. Box 1246
Socorro, NM 87801
(505) 835-1828
**www.fws.gov/southwest/
refuges/newmex/bosque**

Visit These Sites Along the Way...

❾ Manzano Mountains SP
HC-66, Box 202
Mountainair, NM 87036
(505) 847-2820, (505) 344-7240
**www.emnrd.state.nm.us/PRD/
Manzano.htm**

From I-25 take Hwy. 60 east to Mountainair, Hwy. 55 north to Manzano, and Hwy. 131 south to park; located in a raptor flyway where up to 7,000 raptors of 18 species migrate. Open April to October. Trails, camping, picnicking. Admission fee is charged.

❿ Maxwell NWR
P.O. Box 276
Maxwell, NM 87728
(505) 375-2331
**www.fws.gov/southwest/refug
es/newmex/maxwell**

I-25 east from Las Vegas to exit 426 at Maxwell, Hwy. 445 north to Hwy. 505, west to refuge; a wintering waterfowl migratory area with short-grass prairie, playa lakes, and wetlands. Over 219 species; 70 nest. Nearly 7 miles of roads provide numerous viewing opportunities.

⓫ Percha Dam SP
P.O. Box 32
Caballo, NM 87931
(505) 743-3942
**www.emnrd.state.nm.us/PRD/
Percha.htm**

I-25 south from Bocha des Apaches NWR to exit 59, Hwy. 187 to park; among the top birding sites in New Mexico; ducks, American white pelicans, trumpeter swans, herons, cranes, and eagles. Trails, camping, picnicking, fishing. Admission fee is charged.

A prairie chicken struts for a mate.

The Central Region

In the North, this land lay claim to mighty rivers and vast, numerous lakes, with prairie grasslands waving in an unceasing wind. To the south, the land becomes gentler and hardwood forests appear, changing its semblance yet again as it turns to surf and sand on the Gulf of Mexico. It is the land of the Central Flyway, where myriad waterfowl brush wingtips with both common birds and exquisitely rare whooping cranes. It is a place for migratory song-birds to pass, find a mate, and rear their young. It is the North Woods, the Great Prairie, the heartland, the Lone Star state, and Cajun Country.

Perhaps no region so typifies the birdlife of the continent as does the Central. Whether one's love is of giant raptors, the pulse-pounding drum of grouse, or tiny hummingbirds, this is a must-see, must-experience locale.

Winnipeg Area

Carved by glaciers from the Canadian shield into plains during the last ice age, the province of Manitoba is a grassy wetland filled during the summer months with northern migrants: geese, swans, and ducks, but also neotropical and long-distance migrants such as plovers and terns. All are drawn to the abundance of food, the spacious habitat, and the long daylight hours. With their arrival they bring an opportunity for birders to see all types of species in colorful plumage exhibiting courtship and territorial behaviors—mating, nesting, and rearing their chicks, ducklings, and goslings. Start the tour in Manitoba's capital and largest city, Winnipeg, ending it among the nesting birds of Lake Winnipeg's Hecla Island, a portion of magnificent Hecla/Grindstone Provincial Park.

When birds migrate north in spring, they arrive in the Red River Valley surrounding the Manitoba provincial capital. Take advantage of long summer days to see hundreds of thousands of birds of all species in mating colors and with young.

Oak Hammock Marsh Interpretive Centre is stylistically harmonious with the Important Breeding Area, or IBA, that surrounds it. The marsh is known worldwide for its vast population of birds, including rare short-billed dowitchers.

Male northern shoveler

❶ Winnipeg

The prairie city of Winnipeg, Manitoba, is situated on the Red River on both the Atlantic and Mississippi migratory flyways. As a result, more than 380 bird species have been recorded in and around the urban area and its surrounding countryside.

Winnipeg's many parks make it a great place to start birding before venturing to the north.

On the south bank of the Assiniboine River in the city's east side is **Assiniboine Park,** an 1,100-acre (445-h) area with walking trails through meadows, forest, and riverine habitats. Hours vary by season; check

the park's website for information. Admission fee is charged.

Walk the forest at the river's edge to see migratory waterfowl, wading birds, and boreal species. Along the north section of the park is a footbridge that crosses the river to another park section. Just to the west of the bridge in the main park is a

Farther south, just east of Kenaston Blvd. on Macgillivray Rd., is **Fort Whyte Nature Centre.** Open 9 A.M. to 5 P.M. daily weekdays; 10 A.M. to 5 P.M. weekends and holidays. Admission is charged.

The facility preserves 600 acres (243 h) of prairie, lake, forest, and wetland. It has 3.1 miles (5 km) of interpretive trails and floating boardwalks good for bird-watching. Check out feeding stations for birds found throughout the preserve. The Interpretive Centre has exhibits and a waterfowl viewing room.

FortWhyte Alive
1961 McCreary Rd.
Winnipeg, MB Canada R3P 2K9
(204) 989-8355
www.fortwhyte.org

large duck pond, a good spot to view waterfowl of all species as well as small and large waders.

To see the perching species, such as finches, warblers, and other small songbirds, also visit **Assiniboine Forest,** just south of the park. It is a large urban nature park, and in late spring to summer it fills with birds. In autumn, especially at sunset, watch geese and ducks fly to the river. It's also a good spot to look for hawks, owls, and woodpeckers. The Sagimay Trail, a 1-mile (1.6-km) paved loop, leads to Eve Werier Memorial Pond for more waterbird viewing. It intersects with another 3.1 miles (5 km) of wood-chip paths.

Winnipeg Community Services
395 Main St., 2nd Fl.
Winnipeg, MB Canada R3B 3N8
(204) 986-3441
www.winnipeg.ca/cms/

Assiniboine Park
2355 Corydon Ave.
(204) 986-7275

Assiniboine Forest
Chalfont St. and Grant Ave.
(204) 832-0167

Fowl-in-Focus

NORTHERN SHOVELER
Anas clypeata

Length 8˝–10˝ (20–25 cm)

What to Look For Long, wide, spoon-shaped bill; female, mottled buff to brown with orange bill and legs (right); male, green head, white breast, reddish brown sides and belly, with black bill (see male plumage, opposite page).

Habitat Marsh and shallow ponds. Breeds in the prairie provinces of Canada, Alaska, and north-central United States. Winters in southern United States and Central America. Birds use their wide bills and fine teeth to strain small aquatic invertebrates, seeds, and vegetation from water. Feed in small groups.

Canada geese number in the hundred thousands at Oak Hammock Marsh during migration.

East and south, follow the Perimeter Hwy. to Waverley St., turn right, then drive south 3.3 miles (5.3 km) and make a left turn into **La Barriere Park.** It is set on the banks of the La Salle River with groves of ash, elm, and oak trees, and it has a robust system of several trails good for bird-watching both riverine birds and waterfowl.

La Barriere Park
Waverley St.
(204) 986-3441

To reach **Kings Park,** drive north to Perimeter Hwy., east to Pembina Hwy. (Hwy. 42), and north to a right turn at Dalhousie Dr., followed by a left on Silverstone Ave. and a right on Kings Dr., which leads to the park.

An oxbow surrounded on three sides by the Red River, this city park has three waterfalls to view from its many pathways along the river, by its pond, and through its various meadows and marshes. As a diversion from birding, there's also a Chinese garden and pagoda in its center.

Visit in spring and summer to see nesting migrants of every species; from autumn to winter the park's resident owls, ravens, and magpies are its dominant avian attractions.

Kings Park
Kings Dr.
(204) 986-3441

Finish birding Winnipeg at three parks in the north end of the city noted as prime bird-watching sites with good facilities:

- **Rotary Prairie Nature Park,** Regent Ave. and Bradley St.; 20 acres (8.1 h) of tallgrass prairie with walking trails and interpretive signs.
- **Kildonan Park,** Main St. (Hwy. 52) and McKay Dr.; trails along the Red River and through urban forest.

- **Little Mountain Park,** Klimpke Rd. northwest of Hwy. 90 and Inkster Blvd.; hiking trails and naturalist guided tours; reservations: (204) 832-0167.

❷ Oak Hammock Marsh WMA

Every birder who visits Winnipeg should see **Oak Hammock Marsh WMA.** From Perimeter Hwy. take Hwy. 8 north for 11 miles (17.7 km) to Hwy. 67, turn left, and follow signs to the site. Open 10 A.M. to 8 P.M. daily May to August; 10 A.M. to dusk September to October; 10 A.M. to 4:30 P.M. November to April. Admission fee is charged.

The 8.9-acre (3.6-h) birding hot spot is vital habitat for 296 bird species, including short-billed dowitchers, black and Forster's terns, Hudsonian godwits, black-crowned night-herons, white-rumped sandpipers, Franklin's gulls, and both species of yellow-legs. It is a recognized Ramsar site and an IBA. During migration over 400,000 waterfowl may be present at the site, including up to 200,000 each of Canada and lesser snow geese. Ducks are also plentiful.

The Interpretive Centre is a tasteful addition to the site's facilities, blending into its setting. It offers displays, a rooftop observation deck, educational programs, and an extensive boardwalk and trail system.

Oak Hammock Marsh WMA
1 Snow Goose Bay/Hwy. 220
Oak Hammock Marsh, MB
Canada R0C 2Z0
(204) 467-3300
www.ducks.ca/ohmic/

❸ Birds Hill Provincial Park

Birds Hill Provincial Park was named after the Birds, a family who once owned the land,

Oak Hammock Marsh offers canoes for rent in season.

starting early in the 1800s. It's still occupied by birds today, of the feathered variety.

To reach the park, follow Hwy. 67 east 8.5 miles (13.7 km) until it dead-ends at Main St., turn right, enter Lockport, turn left on Hwy. 44, and cross the Red River. At Hwy. 59 turn right; the park entrance is 5 miles (8 km) south on the left.

The park preserves 8,704 acres (3,522 h) of prairie and wetlands. Open for year-round use. Admission fee is charged.

The Cedar Bog trail is 2.2 miles (3.5 km) long and passes through grasslands, aspen and oak forests, and a unique white-cedar bog. Look for pine grosbeaks, woodpeckers, yellow-bellied sapsuckers, warblers, flickers, and ruffed grouse.

Manitoba Conservation Dept.
Birds Hill District Office
Box 183, R.R. #2
Dugald, MB Canada R0E 0K0
(204) 654-6730
www.gov.mb.ca/conservation/
parks/popular_parks/birds_hill
/info

❹ Kenosewun Interpretive Centre

Return by the outbound route to the bridge over the Red River. Located on Hwy. 44 on the east side of the bridge is **Kenosewun Interpretive Centre.** Open 9 A.M. to 5 P.M. daily May to September. An interpretive trail on the riverbank gives a good view of many American white pelicans near the fish ladder.

Kenosewun Interpretive Centre
1 Keystone Dr.
Selkirk, MB Canada R1A 2H5
(204) 785-5080
www.gov.mb.ca/conservation/
parks/education/centres/
lockport

❺ Selkirk Park

Cross the river, turn right on Hwy. 9A, and drive about 4 miles (6.4 km) to Selkirk. **Selkirk Park** is at the town's northeast end on Eveline St., a block southeast of Hwy. 9A. Open 6 A.M. to 11 P.M. daily, late May to October. Admission fee is charged.

Set on the Red River, the park includes a 22-acre (8.9-h) wetland bird sanctuary with an observation deck. Four separate trails total 4.5 miles (7.2 km). Avian migrants visit the sanctuary en route to and from Lake Winnipeg, a few miles north.

Selkirk Chamber of Commerce
P.O. Box 89
Selkirk, MB Canada R1A 2B1
www.selkirkchamber.com

❻ Netley-Libau Marsh

Follow Hwy. 9 from Selkirk north 13 miles (21 km) to Petersfield. To the east beyond the town is **Netley-Libau Marsh.**

A broad lake, river, stream, and marsh complex, it is a recognized IBA for nesting Forster's terns. Franklin's gulls and black-crowned night-herons also raise broods in the marsh, and migration brings yellow-headed and red-winged blackbirds, swallows, and waterfowl. Altogether, 114 species are resident, and annual migrants add more than 100 additional bird species.

A tower at the end of Main Street by the boat launch gives a good view of Goldeneye Lake, Netley Creek and Lake, and the Red River.

Netley Marsh Waterfowl Foundation Inc.
383 Eveline St.
Selkirk, MB Canada MB R1A 1N4
lssd.ca/netleymarsh

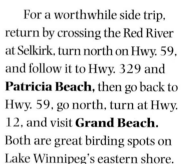

❼ Riverton and Hecla/Grindstone Provincial Park

Drive 12 miles (20 km) north on Hwy. 9 to Gimli, skirting Lake Winnipeg's west shore. At the town turn left and connect with Hwy. 8, turn right and proceed 25 miles (40 km) to Riverton, gateway to **Hecla/Grindstone Provincial Park** and site of **Riverton Sandy Bar,** an IBA recognized for its ring-billed gulls and common terns. Myriad shorebirds and waterfowl congregate on the peninsula and spit. Reach the Riverton Bar by turning right at Hwy. 329 on the south end of Riverton and driving to its end.

If time permits, continue to **Hecla Island,** one island in the group that make up the park. Driving over the causeway to the island allows an excellent view of the marshes and lakeshore where grebes, pelicans, ducks, and geese often appear.

Manitoba Conservation
Box 70, Riverton, MB Canada
R0C 2R0
(204) 378-2261
www.gov.mb.ca/conservation/
parks/popular_parks/hecla_
grindstone/info

For a worthwhile side trip, return by crossing the Red River at Selkirk, turn north on Hwy. 59, and follow it to Hwy. 329 and **Patricia Beach,** then go back to Hwy. 59, go north, turn at Hwy. 12, and visit **Grand Beach.** Both are great birding spots on Lake Winnipeg's eastern shore.

A Canada goose family takes a morning swim.

Minneapolis/St. Paul attracts birds primarily due to the Mississippi River, which winds gracefully through the urbanized countryside to its rendezvous with the Minnesota River.

Twin Cities and Upper Mississippi River

Minneapolis/St. Paul is a gathering place for birds that ply its many rivers and lakes. Twice a year migrants sweep through in passage between their wintering and breeding grounds, filling the cities and nearby areas with hundreds of species.

Yellow-headed blackbirds are attracted to marshes with cattails.

Follow the North Star to the land of lakes and find a bird-watching paradise well worth visiting in spring, summer, and fall. Bring a life list and sharp eyes. Begin the birding tour in the heart of Minneapolis, a lake-studded city of open greenspace parks, rivers, and forests appealing to birds that range from tundra and trumpeter swans and geese to the smallest of warblers. Circle the urban area before embarking on a trip down the mother river—the vast Mississippi—for a journey that leads across the state border into Wisconsin before returning to Minnesota and heading upriver to the starting point. On the way, see eagles, falcons, and kettles of hawks soaring over swans, geese, and wading birds.

❶ Minneapolis/St. Paul

This amazing urban area for bird-watching has, within its metropolitan area alone, 950 lakes. It is located on the Central Flyway but also gathers tundra-nesting birds that turn east to the Atlantic shores.

Start birding at **Elm Creek Park Preserve** in the northwest suburb of Osseo. From central Minneapolis take I-94 north to I-394, turn west, and drive 5 miles (8 km) to Hwy. 169. Turn north and drive to Co. Rd. 81, right on Fernbrook Ln., and right on Territorial Rd. and follow it to reach the entrance of Elm Creek Park Preserve, or continue on Fernbrook to Elm Creek Rd., turn right, and follow the signs to **Eastman Nature Center.** The park is open 5 A.M. to sunset daily; nature center, 9 A.M. to 5 P.M. daily except Sunday. Parking fee is charged.

Interpretive trails total 4.5 miles (7.2 km), and the center has a wildlife viewing room with floor-to-ceiling windows. See nesting waterfowl, upland game birds, green and great

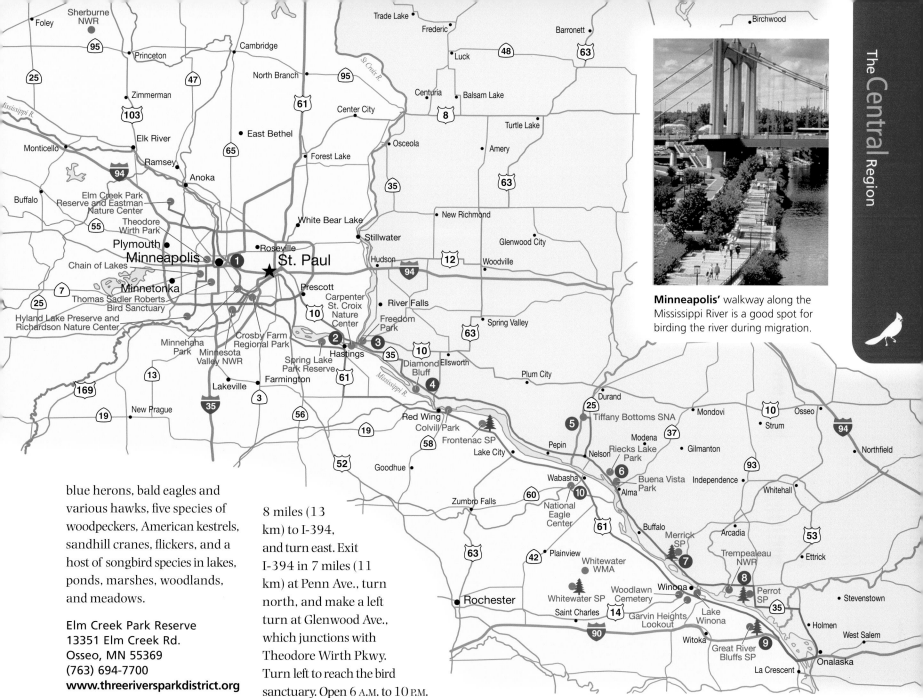

Minneapolis' walkway along the Mississippi River is a good spot for birding the river during migration.

blue herons, bald eagles and various hawks, five species of woodpeckers, American kestrels, sandhill cranes, flickers, and a host of songbird species in lakes, ponds, marshes, woodlands, and meadows.

Elm Creek Park Reserve
13351 Elm Creek Rd.
Osseo, MN 55369
(763) 694-7700
www.threeriversparkdistrict.org

Next, stop at Eloise Butler Wildflower Garden and Bird Sanctuary in **Theodore Wirth Park.** Follow Fernbrook Ln. south to 93rd Ave., turn west, and junction with I-94 east. In 3 miles (4.8 km) take I-494 south, drive about

8 miles (13 km) to I-394, and turn east. Exit I-394 in 7 miles (11 km) at Penn Ave., turn north, and make a left turn at Glenwood Ave., which junctions with Theodore Wirth Pkwy. Turn left to reach the bird sanctuary. Open 6 A.M. to 10 P.M. daily April to October 15; park as marked to avoid fines.

The sanctuary includes a 0.6-mile (1-km) natural garden trail through woodland, wetland, and prairie habitats with wildflowers and birds to enjoy.

Another stop, across the parkway opposite Birch Pond, is

Quaking Bog. Hike the switchbacks of its up-and-down trail leading to a floating boardwalk with good views of shorebirdsm wading birds, and waterfowl. Other locations in the park for waterfowl include Bassett's Creek and Wirth Lake.

Minneapolis Parks and Recreation Board
Theodore Wirth Park
1339 Theodore Wirth Pkwy.
Minneapolis, MN 55411
(612) 230-6400
www.minneapolisparks.org

Distinctively marked male wood ducks and the more subtle females perch on tree limbs and nest in tree cavities

Just to the south via Theodore Wirth Pkwy. across I-394 is **Chain of Lakes,** with over 50 miles (80 km) of pathways. Made up of linked parks at Brownie, Cedar, and Harriet Lakes, Lake of the Isles, and Lake Calhoun, it is also the home of **Thomas Sadler Roberts Bird Sanctuary,** a block east of Lake Harriet Pkwy. Open 7:30 A.M. to 10 P.M. daily year-round.

Chain of Lakes and Thomas Sadler Roberts Bird Sanctuary
4124 Lake Harriet Pkwy.
Minneapolis, MN 55409
(612) 230-6400
www.minneapolisparks.org

Gather information about the city's birding hot spots at **Minnesota Valley NWR** visitors center, off I-494 at the 34th Ave. E exit. Turn south, then left on American Blvd. E, and drive 0.3 miles (0.4 km) to the refuge entrance.

Ask at the information desk for a Songbird Trail Pack. Open 9 A.M. to 5 P.M. Tuesday to Sunday. A short loop trail leads to an observation platform overlooking Long Meadow Lake.

Minnesota Valley NWR
3815 American Blvd.
Bloomington, MN 55425
(952) 854-5900
www.fws.gov

Minneapolis/St. Paul has many other bird-watching parks, open spaces, and refuges. Here are other perennial favorites of local bird-watchers:

- **Hyland Lake Preserve,** Normandale Blvd. at 84th St. in south city; Richardson Nature Center, 1,000 acres (405 h) of lakes, ponds, mature forest, and prairie. Hawks, woodpeckers, bluebirds, ducks, and geese.
- **Minnehaha Park,** Minnehaha Pkwy. and Hiawatha Ave. at the West River Pkwy.; 193 acres (78 h) with striking waterfall, owls, and waterfowl in sight of high-rises.
- **Crosby Farm Regional Park,** I-35 to Shepard Rd. at Crosby Rd.; 6.7 miles (10.8 km) of paved trails in woods and floodplain of the Mississippi River, plus wetlands of Crosby Upper Lake.

❷ Carpenter St. Croix Valley Nature Center

Cross the Mississippi River on I-494 E, turn south on Hwy. 10, and drive toward Prescott. Just before the St. Croix River, turn left onto St. Croix Trail (Co. Rd. 21) for 1 mile (1.6 km). **Carpenter St. Croix Valley Nature Center** is on the right. Open 8 A.M. to 4:30 P.M. daily except holidays.

The facility, which spans both Minnesota and Wisconsin, has an interpretive center with exhibits and live animals and over 10 miles (16 km) of trails through mixed forest, prairie, ravine, and riverine habitats.

Carpenter St. Croix Valley Nature Center
12805 St. Croix Trail
Hastings, MN 55033
(651) 437-4359
www.carpenternaturecenter.org

❸ Freedom Park

Return to Hwy. 10, cross the St. Croix River and the state border, drive through Prescott, and turn right on Broad St. (Hwy. 35). In 0.5 mile (0.8 km) note a visitors center sign for **Freedom Park** and turn right on Monroe St. The park's perch above the Mississippi and St. Croix rivers' confluence often gives fall and winter views of bald eagles soaring overhead.

Freedom Park
200 Monroe St.
Prescott, WI 54021
(715) 262-0104
www.prescottwi.org/parks.html

❹ Diamond Bluff

Continue south 18 miles (29 km) on Hwy. 35 to **Diamond Bluff,** opposite Red Wing, Minnesota. Stop at the riverbank to look for waterfowl and shorebirds. Eagles and other raptors are common at this location.

Pierce Co. Partners in Tourism
P.O. Box 53
Ellsworth, WI 54011
(800) 474-3723
www.travelpiercecounty.com

❺ Tiffany Bottoms SNA

Continue south 33 miles (52 km) to Nelson. Turn north on Hwy. 25, drive 7 miles (11.3 km) to a signed parking area, and walk a trail and cross Buffalo Slough to reach the **Tiffany Bottoms SNA.** The site, an extensive river delta, is undeveloped. It attracts red-shouldered hawks, egrets, herons, whip-poor-wills, gnatcatchers, and cerulean and prothonotary warblers.

Tiffany Bottoms SNA
Wisconsin Dept. of Natural Resources
P.O. Box 4001
Eau Claire, WI 54702
(715) 839-3700
dnr.wi.gov/org/land/er/sna/sna30.htm/

❻ Riecks Lake Park and Buena Vista Park

About 6 miles (10 km) south of Nelson on Hwy. 35, **Riecks Lake Park** is on the east side of the road at the junction with Hwy. 37. In October and November it

Riverboats ply the Mississippi River, a great platform for bird-watching.

is a spot where thousands of tundra swans rest on their migration south. An observation platform provides great viewing.

Riecks Lake Park
Wisconsin State Rd. 35
Alma, WI 54610
(608) 685-3330
www.almaswanwatch.org

Just minutes south, off Hwy. 35 in Alma, turn left from S. Main St. onto Alma Dugway Rd. (Co. Rd. E), then left after 0.8 mile (1.3 km) on Buena Vista Rd. to enter **Buena Vista Park.**

A panoramic view 500 feet (152 m) above the Mississippi River awaits; a trail descends to town. In spring migrating red-tailed and broad-winged hawks and peregrine falcons transit the river. In fall see these hawks and falcons, plus American kestrels and Cooper's hawks, along with songbirds in the woods. Before continuing, also stop at Alma's locks beginning in late October to see tundra swans and other waterfowl.

Buena Vista Park
P.O. Box 277
Alma, WI 54610
(608) 685-3330
www.buffalocounty.com

❼ Merrick SP

Drive 17 miles (27 km) south on Hwy. 35 to **Merrick SP,** minutes north of Fountain City, on a cut-off channel of the river with wetland habitat and views of Fountain City Bay. Open with full services Memorial Day to Labor Day, then limited staffing until October 15. Admission fee is charged.

The park is home to egrets, herons, shorebirds, and waterbirds. Best time to visit is early fall, during peak flyway activity. The park features hiking trails, a canoe trail, and a nature center.

Merrick SP
P.O. Box 127
Fountain City, WI 54629
(608) 687-4936
www.dnr.wi.gov

❽ Trempealeau NWR and Perrot SP

As Hwy. 35 passes Winona on the opposite bank, 7 miles (11 km) south of Fountain City, it combines with Hwy. 54 and briefly sweeps inland. Drive 5.7 miles (9.2 km) farther to W. Prairie Rd., turn right, and continue about 1 mile (1.6 km). Turn left on Refuge Rd., which leads to **Trempealeau NWR.** Refuge open dawn to dusk year-round; office open 7:30 A.M. to 4 P.M. weekdays.

This 6,200-acre (2,509-h) refuge, inhabited by waterfowl and marsh birds, is cut off from the Mississippi and Trempealeau rivers. It has a 4.5-mile (7.2-km) drive and the 0.5-mile (0.8-km) Prairie View Trail. Woods Trail is another short hike, leading to an observation deck. See nesting black terns, herons, wood ducks, bald eagles, and osprey. Major attractions are flocks of hundreds of American white pelicans and tundra swans.

Trempealeau NWR
W28488 Refuge Rd.
Trempealeau, WI 54661
(608) 539-2311
midwest.fws.gov

Just a short distance southeast via W. Prairie Rd. is **Perrot SP77** Follow it to Lehmann Rd., turn right, and enter the park. Open with full services Memorial Day to Labor Day, then limited staffing until October 15. Admission fee is charged.

The Trempealeau River meets the Mississippi at this 1,400-acre (567-h) park beneath 460-foot (140-m) bluffs. Several trails skirt wetlands with such diverse birds as scarlet tanagers, orchard orioles, waterfowl, and bald eagles.

Perrot SP
P.O. Box 407
Trempealeau, WI 54661
(608) 534-6409
www.dnr.wi.gov

❾ Great River Bluffs SP

Exit on Park Rd., head east, and enter the town of Trempealeau. Turn right on Main St. and left on 3rd St. (Hwy. 35), which first intersects Hwy. 53, then I-90.

Trumpeter swans make floating cattail hummocks a place to rear young.

Drive west on I-90, cross the river back into Minnesota, take exit 266, and follow the signs to **Great River Bluffs SP.**

Of the two major trails, take the 6.5-mile (10.5-km) trail to King's and Queen's Bluffs Scientific Area, with scenic overlooks for viewing waterfowl, hawks, and eagles traveling the river flyway. Also note ruffed grouse, wild turkeys, and the many songbirds.

Great River Bluffs SP
43605 Kipp Dr.
Winona, MN 55987-9427
(507) 643-6849
www.dnr.state.mn.us

⑩ Winona and the Mississippi's West Bank

Following the western shore of the Mississippi River from Great Bluffs SP north on Hwy. 61 and through Winona, Kellogg,

Wabasha, Lake City, Red Wing, and Hastings is a route filled with habitats and birdlife similar to those seen west of the river.

The high bluffs overlooking wetland flood plains make for ideal waterfowl and songird habitats. The best time to visit is from April to June and from September to October, when migrations peak. Make stops to bird-watch along the way:

- **Winona,** 280 recorded bird species; visit Lake Winona (Gillmore St.), Woodlawn Cemetery (W. Lake Blvd.), and Garvin Heights Lookout (Riverview Dr.).
www.visitwinona.com

- **National Eagle Center,** Wabasha (Hwy. 60 west to Pembroke Ave.), Tuesday to Saturday; observation deck, eagle feeding program daily.
www.nationaleaglecenter.org

- **Frontenac SP,** Lake City (Co. Rd. 2); over 260 recorded bird species on Lake Pepin, good views of migrating birds.
www.dnr.state.mn.us

- **Colvill Park,** Red Wing (Hwy. 292 frontage); watch wintering bald eagles. See migrating waterfowl, wading birds, and songbirds.
www.exploreminnesota.com/attractions/15149

- **Spring Lake Park Reserve,** Hastings (Hwy. 55 to Mississippi Trail, Idell Ave.); trail to Shaar's Bluff through woodlands and along the river bluffs, excellent for seeing migrating hawks, osprey, peregrine falcons, and bald eagles, as well as boreal birds.
www.co.dakota.mn.us/parks/spring.htm/

◀◀ Not to Be Missed!

Sherburne NWR
17076 293rd Ave.
Zimmerman, MN 55398
(763) 389 3323
www.fws.gov/midwest/sherburne/

To reach the refuge, drive 22 miles (35 km) northwest of Minneapolis on I-94, exit at Rogers (Hwy. 101), drive 24 miles (38 km) north to 293rd Ave. (Co. Rd. 169) past Zimmerman, turn west, and drive 5 miles (8 km) to the refuge headquarters. Open 8 A.M. to 4:30 P.M. weekdays. Visit during daylight hours from April through October, or check the refuge website for other seasons.

Oak savanna, wetlands, and upland woodlands make up the 30,700-acre (12,424-h) Sherburne refuge, only parts of which are open to the public. There are three popular ways for birders to view members of the 233 recorded bird species found here:

- **Tour by auto:** Follow the 7.3-mile (11.7-km) Prairie's Edge Wildlife Loop, with three observation decks.
- **Hike:** Walk 2.7-mile (4.3 km) Mahnomen Loop, 4.4-mile (7.1-km) Blue Hill Loop, 0.3-mile (0.4-km) Oak Savanna, 0.5-mile (0.8-km) Prairie, or 0.5-mile (0.8-km) Wetlands trails. These pass through woodlands and grasslands populated with boreal birds and songbirds.
- **Canoe:** Follow the St. Francis River canoe route for a close look at wetland, marsh, pond, and river birds and waterfowl, especially in spring and fall.

Sioux Falls, South Dakota, to Omaha, Nebraska

Follow the Central Flyway south from Sioux Falls down the Missouri River Valley, first to Sioux City, then to Omaha and Council Bluffs. This land was scoured by glaciers millennia ago, leaving a pothole landscape of lake-filled tallgrass plains, rolling hills, and meandering rivers. Where forests grow, they form green bands along the rivers and creeks. These are lush habitats for migrating songbirds, neotropical migrants enduring their long flights from Central America to near the Arctic Circle, and waterfowl of all species. The best time to visit is in spring; avoid the days of midsummer and return from October to December when the migration south peaks.

Meriwether Lewis and William Clark blazed the first western trails through the heartland states of South Dakota, Iowa, and Nebraska, marveling at their abundant birdlife. Today, cross their path and view both scenic grandeur and a wealth of avian beauty.

Green-winged teal males are small ducks, up to about 14 inches long. They are distinctively marked with reddish brown heads, iridescent green bands above their eyes, and black-and-white-patterned wing feathers.

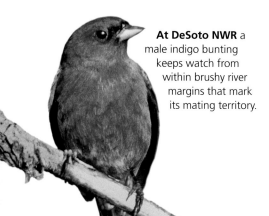

At DeSoto NWR a male indigo bunting keeps watch from within brushy river margins that mark its mating territory.

❶ Sioux Falls Area

Sioux Falls, on the meanders of the Big Sioux River in southeast North Dakota, is the start of a birding route that winds down the Missouri River, first to Sioux City, Iowa, then south to Omaha, Nebraska.

Of Sioux Falls's more than 70 public parks, **Falls Park** is its best known. It is also a worthwhile stop for bird-watchers. Near the center of the city, it is at Weber Ave. and Falls Park Dr.

In the park the Sioux Falls River cascades over a series of rocky shelves. Pools and shores near the river draw wading birds and migratory waterfowl. The park also has meadows and forest habitats for perching songbirds.

Joining many of the parks and roughly encircling the city is a 14.3-mile (23-km) bike and nature trail. Following the trail, it's possible to bird from park to park, moving northwest to **Elmwood Park** (southwest of W. Russell St. and N. Kiwanis Ave.). This spot, also along the river, is probably the best downtown locale for birding. Orioles, warblers, eastern bluebirds, sandpipers, and grosbeaks are common here in summer.

Next, take I-29 south, exit at W. 41st St., turn east, drive to Louise Ave., turn south, continue to W. 49th St., turn left, and make a final right turn on Oxbow Ave., entering **Sertoma Park,** also site of the Outdoor Campus. Open 8 A.M. to 10 A.M. daily, year-round.

Sioux Falls City Parks and Recreation Dept.
100 E. 6th St.
Sioux Falls, SD 57104
(605) 367-8222
www.siouxfallsparks.org

With 100 acres (40 h) of tallgrass prairie and riparian woodlands, the Outdoor Campus is a good spot to start birding. Visit a series of oxbow lakes on 2 miles (3.2 km) of pedestrian-only trails. Look for magnolia and Nashville warblers, Swainson's and hermit thrushes, eastern screech-owls, and ruby-crowned kinglets from spring to summer. In early spring and again in October, see waterfowl and other migrants in large numbers.

The Outdoor Campus
4500 S. Oxbow Ave.
Sioux Falls, SD 57106
(605) 362-2777
www.outdoorcampus.org

Return to Louise Ave., turn south, enter I-229, and head

east to E. 26th St. exit, drive east about 2 miles (3.2 km), turn right on S. River Bluff Rd., and enter **Arrowhead Park,** a 130-acre (53-h) nature park of birding trails along water-filled quarries. Open 5 A.M. to 10 A.M. daily.

Perry Nature Area is a 23-acre (9.3-h) satellite unit across Hwy. 42 at the park's north border. Plans exist to connect the parks with a path. View birds near the quarries, such as belted kingfishers, yellow-bellied sapsuckers, cedar waxwings, northern flickers, and downy woodpeckers.

Next, visit **Great Bear Recreation Park.** Return to I-229, head north to exit at E. Rice St., and drive 2 miles (3.2 km) east. The park is a mixed-use facility; avoid the target and archery range areas.

Bird along Ralph and Doris Wallin Nature trails; most are 1 mile (1.6 km) or shorter, offering a range from easy walking to strenuous hikes.

Nearby **Big Sioux Recreation Area,** on the banks of the Big Sioux River, has woods, tallgrass prairie, and bluffs that make for good raptor and boreal bird viewing. Turn right on E. Rice St., which becomes W. Holly Blvd. at Brandon. At the first right after the city limits, turn south on S. Sioux Blvd. and right on W. Park St. to enter the park.

The landscape of this park was sculpted by the ice of

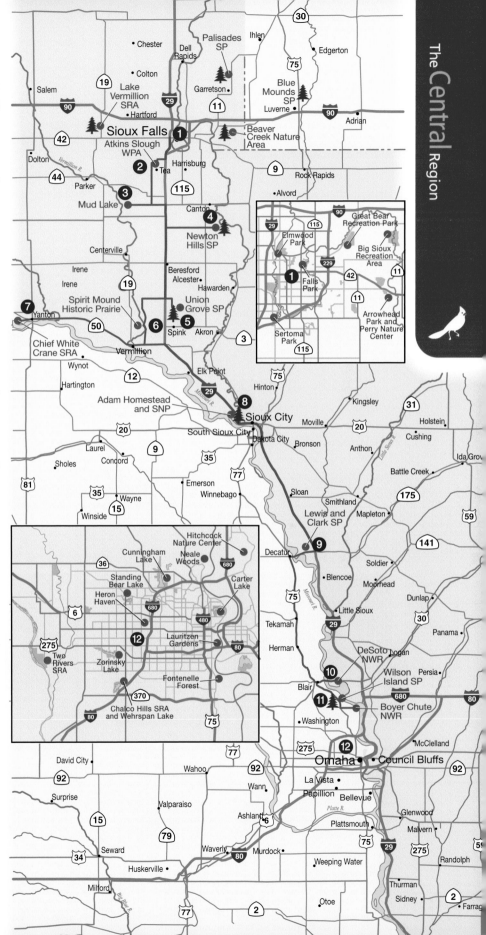

retreating glaciers thousands of years ago. Bike on a marked path or walk the Prairie Vista and Valley of the Giants trails. Either option travels along the river, bringing chances to see waterfowl, shore and river birds, and larger wading birds.

Big Sioux Recreation Area
SD Dept. of Parks and Recreation
410 Park Ave.
Brandon, SD 57005
(605) 582-7243
www.sdgfp.info/parks/regions/heartland/bigsioux.htm

To reach the next stop, return by Park St. to S. Sioux Blvd., turn south, join Splitrock Blvd. (Hwy. 11), and drive 0.7 mile (1.2 km) to 264th St. Turn left; **Beaver Creek Nature Area** has 1.5 miles (2.4 km) of trails. The short Homestead Loop at the log cabin

connects to the longer Homesteader Nature Trail that follows Beaver Creek through forests, marshes, and prairie. Bird species change along with the vegetation. In the north a shelter belt and arboretum is a good place to find owls and woodpeckers.

Beaver Creek Nature Area
25495 485th Ave.
Garretson, SD 57030-6117
(605) 594-3824
www.sdgfp.info/parks/regions/heartland/beavercreek.htm

If time allows, make two other birding stops in Sioux Falls:

- **Palisades SP,** I-90 east of Brandon at 486th Ave., then north; raptors soar above sheer quartzite bluffs that plunge to Split Rock Creek, often filled with waterfowl.

- **Lake Vermillion SRA,** I-90 west to Canistota exit 374, then south; from March to September, egrets, flycatchers, and waterfowl are visible from Otter Stream Trail.

❷ Atkins Slough WPA

Just 2.4 miles (4 km) south of the I-29/I-229 junction, near the town of Tea, is **Atkins Slough WPA,** a 160-acre (65-h) wetland. Take exit 73 (271st St.) west to 469th Ave. and turn south. At 1st St. turn east, drive through town, and turn north on 468th Ave. Signs mark the parking area and trailhead.

An interpretive trail leads through cattail marshes, grasslands, and cottonwood forests. Bufflehead and ring-necked ducks, sparrows, wrens, yellow-headed blackbirds, and least

bitterns frequent the site. In fall waterfowl are also present.

U.S. Fish and Wildlife Service/
Lake Andes W.M. Dist.
420 S. Garfield Ave., Ste. 400
Pierre, SD 57501
(605) 487-7603
southdakotafieldoffice.fws.gov

❸ Mud Lake

The next stop is a prairie pothole lake within Schaeffer Geographic Protection Area (GPA). From the prior waypoint, return to 272nd St., turn south, drive 6 miles (9.7 km) to 282nd St., and turn west to reach **Mud Lake.** The site has marshes, sloughs, and mixed-hardwood and cedar forests, and it offers chances to see birds such as black-crowned night-herons, marsh wrens, egrets, and bitterns; use a kayak or canoe for best viewing.

S.D. Game, Fish, and Parks/
Wildlife Division
500 S. Oxbow Ave.
Sioux Falls, SD 57106
(605) 362-2700
www.sdgfp.info/wildlife

❹ Newton Hills SP

Follow 282nd St. back to I-29, turn south, and exit on 288th St. Head east about 10 miles (16 km) and continue; the road leads straight into **Newton Hills SP.** Open year-round. Admission fee is charged.

Gaggles of snow geese at DeSoto NWR always have room for one more.

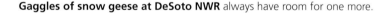

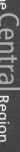

Habitats range from open grasslands to dense oak and basswood forest. The Arboretum Trail observation tower is one spot to look for some of the more than 200 recorded species of birds that reside in or visit the park. They include eastern bluebirds, wild turkeys, northern goshawks, eastern phoebes, and many species of warblers and vireos. Another birding location is the 6-mile (10-km) Woodland Trail.

Newton Hills SP
28771 482nd Ave.
Canton, SD 57013
(605) 987-2263
www.sdgfp.info/parks/regions /heartland/newtonhills.htm

❺ Union Grove SP

Return to I-29, drive south for approximately 18 miles (29 km) to exit 38 (306th St.), go east to 471st St., and drive south 2.2 miles (3.5 km) to enter 150-acre (61-h) **Union Grove SP.** Open year-round. Admission fee is charged.

The park's habitat consists primarily of rolling hills with mixed vegetation along Brulle Creek. Its trails make two loops, one to the northern park, the other to the south; both are shared with horseback riders, hikers, and bikers.

The best time to visit is in spring when neotropical migratory birds pass through the

Birds blanket DeSoto NWR at sunset as mists rise into the cooling air over the Missouri River.

park in large numbers. Look for a mix of perching bird and songbird species, concentrating on the northern loop trail near where the track parallels the creek.

Union Grove SP
28771 482nd Ave.
Canton, SD 57013
(605) 987-2263
www.sdgfp.info/parks/regions/ heartland/uniongrove.htm

❻ Spirit Mound Historic Prairie

Return to 306th St., drive past I-29 west 8.5 miles (13.7 km) to Hwy. 19, and turn south. In 5 miles (8 km), just beyond 311th St., is **Spirit Mound Historic Prairie.** Visited by Lewis and Clark in 1804, the mound is considered by Native Americans a sacred site and

is a restored tallgrass prairie. Open year-round.

An interpretive trail leads 0.6 mile (1.2 km) to the summit of the mound. Birds are attracted to the promontory; look for ring-necked pheasants, mourning doves, barn swallows, savannah and grasshopper sparrows, bobolinks, dickcissels, western meadow larks, and red-winged blackbirds, as well as warblers.

Spirit Mound Historic Prairie
28771 482nd Ave.
Canton, SD 57013
(605) 987-2263
www.sdgfp.info/parks/regions/ heartland/spiritmound.htm

❼ Chief White Crane SRA

To see impressive numbers of bald eagles, drive south 5 miles (8 km) on Hwy. 19 to Vermillion,

turn west on Hwy. 50, drive to Yankton, and turn left 1.8 miles (2.9 km) past town on S. Deer Blvd. to arrive at **Chief White Crane SRA.** Open year-round. Admission fee is charged. Motor vehicles are prohibited November to March to avoid disturbing nesting areas of the bald eagles found in the reserve.

Eagles often perch near the riverbank; look for them in cottonwood trees along the water at early morning, when they are most active and fly to nearby dams to feed on fish. They return in late afternoon to perch in the trees.

Chief White Crane SRA
43349 S. D. Hwy. 52
Yankton, SD 57078
(605) 668-2985
www.sdgfp.info/parks/regions/ lewisclark/chiefwhitecrane.htm

Lauritzen Gardens in downtown Omaha has many nesting songbirds.

⑧ Adam Homestead and SNP

Return to I-29 and drive south about 22 miles (35 km) to exit 4 (Northshore Dr.). Head east, then turn left at Westshore Dr., which leads to **Adams Homestead and SNP.** Open year-round. Call visitors center for hours of operation.

The preserve has over 10 miles (16 km) of trails that follow the Missouri River and lead to cottonwoods, prairie, and forest. Top birding picks are Lake Loop and River Loop, with blinds.

Of its more than 100 recorded bird species, most common are least flycatchers and northern bobwhites in open areas, least terns and Bell's vireos along the river, and cuckoos, woodpeckers, and eastern wood-pewees in woods. Also view the many exhibits in the visitors center.

Adams Homestead and SNP
272 Westshore Dr.
McCook Lake, SD 57049
(605) 232-0873
**www.sdgfp.info/parks/regions/
heartland/adamshomestead.htm**

⑨ Lewis and Clark SP

Rejoin I-29, head south about 45 miles (72 km), crossing the Iowa border, and exit at Hwy. 175, turning west. **Lewis and Clark SP** is just north of the road at Blue Lake on Hwy. 324. An interpretive center was under construction as this book went to print; check the park for current information. Admission fee is charged.

The main attractions here are migratory waterfowl and songbirds. A self-guided nature trail and several hiking trails provide good opportunities to see birds.

Lewis and Clark SP
21914 Park Loop
Onawa, IA 51040
(712) 423-2829
**www.iowadnr.com/parks/
state_park_list/lewis_clark.html**

⑩ DeSoto NWR

Follow Hwy. 175 west to Decatur, turn south on Hwy. 75, drive 35 miles (56 km) to Blair, and turn east on Hwy. 30 (Washington St. becoming W. Erie St.). At DeSoto Ave. turn right and make a quick turn onto 316th Ln., arriving at **DeSoto NWR** visitors center. Open 30 minutes before sunrise and after sunset, daily except major holidays; visitors center, 9 A.M. to 4:30 P.M. daily. Admission fee is charged.

The 7,823-acre (3,166-h) refuge comprises both a cutoff oxbow lake and tilled fields. It has over 250 recorded species of birds. During migration more than 500,000 snow geese feed and rest at the site. Besides several species of geese, its other birds include ducks, songbirds, warblers, raptors, and bald eagles.

See the refuge by using cars as blinds or hike one or more of its three nature trails. The visitors center has exhibits, bird checklists, and maps.

DeSoto NWR
1434 316th Ln.
Missouri Valley, IA 51555
(712) 642-4121
www.fws.gov/refuges

⑪ Boyer Chute NWR

Return to Hwy. 75 in Blair and turn south. Drive 9 miles (14 km) to Fort Calhoun, turn left on Madison St., then right on 7th St. (Hwy. 34); 3,350-acre (1,356-h) **Boyer Chute NWR** is about 3 miles (4.8 km) ahead (look for its sign). Open sunrise to sunset daily except major holidays; office, 8 A.M. to 4:30 P.M. weekdays only.

The refuge has restored tallgrass prairie, floodplain, woodland, and wetland habitats. A 2.3-mile (3.7-km) auto route and three trails are available for birders. Watch for orioles, wrens, swallows, bluebirds, geese, and bald eagles, just a few of its 259 recorded birds.

Boyer Chute NWR
3720 Rivers Way
Ft. Calhoun, NE 68023
(402) 468-4313
www.fws.gov/refuges

Fontenelle Forest's boardwalk trails beckon birders of all ages.

⑫ Omaha and Council Bluffs Area

Between them, **Omaha** and **Council Bluffs** have over 102 miles (164 km) of paved trails and 220 parks, many on the Missouri River. The northern metropolitan area is rich with places to go bird-watching.

On weekends start just south of the last waypoint at **Neale Woods.** From Hwy. 75 make a series of four left turns on Ponca Rd., N. River Dr., White Deer Ln., and Edith Marie Ave., leading to the woods and its nature center. Open 8 A.M. to 5 P.M. Saturdays, 12 to 5 P.M. Sundays. Admission fee is charged.

Its 20 trails traverse woods and the river. Combined with **Fontenelle Forest,** its sister facility (Hwy. 75 to Chandler Rd., east to Bellevue Blvd. and south), it is one of the city's best birding areas. Over 250 bird species visit annually, and 35 species of warblers have been recorded.

Fontenelle Nature Association
1111 N. Bellevue Blvd.
Bellevue, NE 68005
(402) 731-3140
www.fontenelleforest.org

While still in the north metropolitan area, try these other top bird-watching spots:

- **Hitchcock Nature Center,** I-29 and I-680 intersection, east on Old Mormon Bridge Rd. to Old Lincoln Hwy. and north; from September to December, over 16,000 raptors of 20 species have been recorded at the site.
- **Carter Lake,** just west of Eppley Airfield; waterfowl and wading birds on an oxbow lake in the city.
- **Cunningham Lake,** Hwy. 75 to I-680 west, turn on 72nd St. and drive to Rainwood Rd.; see ducks, geese, gulls, bald eagles, American woodcocks, and owls.
- **Standing Bear Lake,** I-680 to 72nd St., south to State St., west to Military Rd., and south to 132nd St.; visit the nature area northwest of the lake where migrating waterfowl gather.
- **Heron Haven,** 132nd St. south to W. Maple Rd., east to 120th St., and north to Old Maple Rd.; an Audubon nature center with a viewing deck and boardwalk trails on Papillion Creek. See herons, egrets, and wading birds.

In southern Omaha and Council Bluffs, first take in all the habitats at Fontenelle Forest, then try **Zorinsky Lake,** to the west. Take I-80 to Hwy. 275, drive east to S. 156th St., and head south to this expansive lake.

Open 5 A.M. to 11 P.M. daily. Admission fee is charged.

Omaha Parks, Recreation, and Public Property
1819 Farnam St., Ste. 701
Omaha, NE 68183
(402) 444-5900
www.ci.omaha.ne.us/parks/

Travel east on I-80, exit at 13th St., head north to Bancroft St., then east to **Lauritzen Gardens** and Oberman Bird Sanctuary. Open 9 A.M. to 5 P.M. daily. Admission fee is charged.

Feeders and nesting boxes throughout this 4-acre (1.6-h) botanical garden offer good views of nesting songbirds.

Lauritzen Gardens
100 Bancroft St.
Omaha, NE 68108
(402) 346-4002
www.omahabotanicalgardens.org

To the east and south of the city, also check two of the several nearby state recreation areas:

- **Two Rivers SRA,** Hwy. 275 west to 264th St., south to F St.; waterfowl, shorebirds, and songbirds.
- **Chalco Hills SRA** at **Wehrspan Lake,** Hwy. 275 east to Hwy. 6, south to Hwy. 370 at Gretna; migrants, waterfowl, and shorebirds.

Wood duck females possess distinctive white eye rings.

Milwaukee, Wisconsin, to Chicago, Illinois

From Northwoods natural to Midwest urban, bird-watching the shores of Lake Michigan and the states of Wisconsin, Illinois, and Indiana brings the opportunity to enjoy a region recognized for its preservation of the habitats that birds need for nesting.

Long summer days shorten as autumn approaches, bringing the southward migration of birds down the shore of Lake Michigan. These travelers follow the lake's coast, giving birders a chance to see again the birds they watched earlier in the year. Begin the route north of Milwaukee at Horicon Marsh, head south, and view birds in the countryside; enter Illinois, explore Chicago's parks, and finish the drive far to the south in the scenic wonder that is Indiana Dunes National Lakeshore. Along the way linger to see waterfowl of every description, and some rare birds—even whooping cranes—to add to life lists, plus shorebirds, waders, raptors, and perching birds.

Schlitz Audubon Nature Center in Milwaukee has many trails and observation points that allow bird-watchers time to pause and reflect on the scenic beauty of Lake Michigan.

Northern cardinal males are among the most colorful birds found near Great Lake waters and woods.

❶ Milwaukee North

Start the birding tour at the **Schlitz Audubon Nature Center** on the shores of Lake Michigan. From Milwaukee take I-43 north 10 miles (16 km) to Brown Deer Rd., turn east, and drive 1 mile (1.6 km) to the center. Open 9 A.M. to 5 P.M. daily except holidays. Admission fee is charged.

Birding may be foremost on your mind, but take a moment to admire the architecture of this beautifully built center. It is a tribute to the green building construction philosophy.

There are 6 miles (9.7 km) of trails, boardwalks, an obser-vation tower, and viewing decks. Center staff also offers worth-while guided tours, available by advance reservation.

"Raptor Saturday" and other programs offer demonstrations with live bald eagles, owls, hawks, and falcons. The performing birds were injured and remain in cap-tivity for their health and safety.

Schlitz Audubon Nature Center
1111 E. Brown Deer Rd.
Bayside, WI 53217
(414) 352-2880
www.schlitzaudubon
center.com

Make your way back to I-43 heading south and take W. Silver Spring Dr. exit, go west for 2.4 miles (3.9 km), and turn north on N. 43rd St., which turns into N. Sherman Blvd. Turn left on W. Douglas Ave. to enter **Havenwoods State Forest.** Open from 6 A.M. to 8 P.M.

A 237-acre (96-h) natural area with grasslands, forests, wetlands, creeks, and an environmental center with 6 miles (9.7 km) of trails, the forest has birds such as great blue herons, fly-catchers, American kestrels, and other boreal birds, river birds, and songbirds found on the central flyway.

It is also an access point for Oak Leaf Trail, 100 miles (160 km) of paved trails linking the major parks in the Milwaukee metropolitan area. Pick up a map at the center.

Havenwoods State Forest
6141 N. Hopkins St.
Milwaukee, WI 53209
(414) 527-0232
www.dnr.state.wi.us

Return to I-43 south, exit at W. Locust St., and drive east to N. Oakland Ave. Turn right, then right again at E. Park Pl. to enter the Urban Ecology Center at **Riverside Park.** Open 9 A.M. to 7 P.M. Monday through Thursday, 9 A.M. to 5 P.M. Friday and Saturday. Climb the tower for a great overlook of the city, take a look at the exhibits, or access the Oak Leaf Trail.

Riverside Park
1500 E. Park Pl.
Milwaukee, WI 53211
(414) 964-8505
www.county.milwaukee.gov

Join In

Bald Eagle Watching Days Celebration at Ferry Bluff

Ferry Bluff Eagle Council
Sauk Prairie, Wisconsin

—

10 A.M. Saturdays, early January to mid-February
Call (800) 683-2453
for reservations

A grassroots, not-for-profit conservation organization

• Maintains the Ferry Bluff eagle-viewing overlook and trail.

• Preserves habitat for 100 to 200 wintering, feeding, and nesting bald eagles.

• Provides public education about these birds.

Celebration

• Held annually in January: two days of fun, eagle-viewing, and educational exhibits at River Arts Center.

Guided bus tours for viewing

Find out more at

Ferry Bluff Eagle Council
P.O. Box 532
Sauk City, WI 53583

www.ferrybluffeaglecouncil.org

Return to I-43, drive south, and just after I-894 turns east, take the S. 108th St. exit. Drive south, cross W. Forest Home Ave., and turn left at College Ave. It leads to Wehr Nature Center in **Whitnall Park.** Center open 8:30 A.M. to 4 P.M. daily except holidays. Parking fee charged.

There are seven short trails that traverse restored prairie, wetlands, and 150-year-old oak trees, the homes of nuthatches, black-capped chickadees, wood thrushes, jays, screech-owls, and pheasants.

Whitnall Park
9701 W. College Ave.
Franklin, WI 53132
(414) 425-8550
www.co.milwaukee.wi.us

❷ Racine Area

Depart Milwaukee west on I-43, turn south on I-94, and exit at 7 Mile Rd. Drive east past Douglas Ave., turn right on Michna Rd., and enter **Cliffside Park.**

The 233-acre (94-h) park offers panoramic views of Lake Michigan and both waterfowl and raptors during migration.

Cliffside Park
7375 Michna Rd.
Racine, WI 53406
(262) 884-8440
racine.wi.net/parks1.html

A short drive away is the village of **Wind Point.** Return to Douglas Ave. (Hwy. 32), turn south, drive to 4 Mile Rd., then turn east, and arrive at Wind Point Lighthouse. Open sunrise to 11 P.M. daily.

From this promontory rising above Lake Michigan, see birds such as sanderlings, Franklin's and ring-billed gulls, along with many ducks, including buffleheads, mallards, blue-winged teal, and common goldeneyes.

Schlitz Audubon Nature Center. Choose from a vantage point on the tower above the trees or walk the boardwalks for easy-access birding.

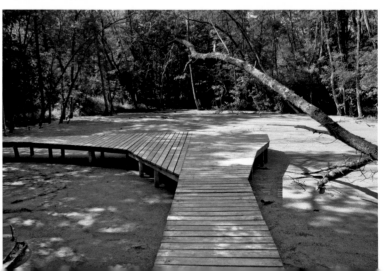

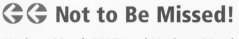 **Not to Be Missed!**

Horicon Marsh NWR and Horicon Marsh SWA

At 32,000 acres (12,950 h), Horicon is a designated Wetland of International Significance and a Globally Important Bird Area. It is also the largest freshwater cattail marsh in the United States. Horicon NWR forms the northern section, with Horicon Marsh SWA to its south. Over 265 species fill the marsh in spring and fall, including endangered whooping cranes, egrets, other waterfowl, and marsh bird.

Also look for great horned and barred owls, yellow-headed blackbirds, and pelicans. Some upland areas have bobolinks, eastern meadowlarks, warblers, and willow flycatchers.

The site has auto tours, hiking trails, floating boardwalks, observation decks, and photo blinds for easy access to birding sites.

Public education programs and information for the entire marsh are readily available at both facilities. The Horicon Marsh Bird Festival is a combined effort, held annually on the second weekend of May.

Horicon Marsh NWR: (920) 387-2658
www.fws.gov/midwest/horicon

Horicon Marsh SWA: (920) 387-7860
www.dnr.state.wi.us/org/land/wildlife/reclands/horicon

One of many boardwalks at Horicon Marsh WMA (above). The endangered whooping crane (right), found here, is the tallest North American bird.

Wind Point
4739 Lighthouse Dr.
Racine, WI 53402
windpointwi.us

Follow Lighthouse Dr. southwest to N. Main St., turn left, and drive south to 4th St. Turn east on 4th St. (Christopher Columbus Causeway), which leads to **Racine Harbor Park.** Both the breakwater and the opposite jetty are good spots to see greater scaups, red-breasted mergansers, snowy owls, and assorted gulls and shorebirds, as well as herons and cranes.

Racine Harbor Park
1 Christopher Columbus Cswy.
Racine, WI 53403
(262) 636-9131
racine.wi.net/parks1.html

If time permits, visit two other Racine birding sites:

- **Colonial Park,** Main St. north to State St., right on Northwestern Ave., and left on W. High St.; hike along the Root River Pathway to look for warblers, indigo buntings, vireos, and northern cardinals.
- **YWCA River Bend Nature Center,** drive northwest on Northwestern Ave., right at

Rapids Dr., and left at Green Bay Rd.; 80 acres (32 h) and river trails.

❸ Richard Bong SRA

To leave Racine, return to Green Bay Rd., drive southwest past Northwestern Ave. to Washington Ave., and turn west. After 5 miles (8 km) cross under and enter I-94 south, drive 7 miles (11 km) to exit at Burlington Rd., and follow it west 7.5 miles (12 km) to **Richard Bong SRA.**

Once intended as a jet fighter base, today it is an IBA recognized

for its grassland birds, including eastern meadowlarks, bobolinks, and Henslow, field, and savannah sparrows. Peak birding takes place in May. Shrub areas attract flycatchers, towhees, and warblers, while wetlands support bitterns, great blue and green herons, and sedge and marsh wrens. Terns are also present in the spring, and northern harriers appear in winter.

There are two self-guided nature trails, one with a boardwalk and views of Wolf Lake; the other passes through a hardwood forest. Also try 4.4-mile (7-km) Yellow Trail with

Wild turkey hens cluck
to their broods, giving orders
to stay close

wetlands, woodlands, and grasslands; 8.3-mile (13.4-km) Red Trail for bluebirds; and 1.8-mile (2.9-km) Green Trail with a boardwalk and two ponds. Climb the viewing platform that overlooks the refuge.

Richard Bong SRA
26313 Burlington Rd.
Kansasville, WI 53139
(262) 878-5600
**www.dnr.state.wi.us/org/
land/parks/specific/bong/**

Ring-billed gulls (top) gather on the pier at historic Wind Point Lighthouse (right), near Racine, Wisconsin.

❹ Big Foot Beach SP

Turn right from Burlington Rd. onto 256th Ave. and drive south about 5 miles (8 km) to Hwy. 50. Turn west and continue to Lake Geneva, turn south on S. Lake Shore Dr., and drive 2 miles (3.2 km) to enter **Big Foot Beach SP** on the lakeshore. Admission fee is charged.

Visit during spring and fall migration when Lake Geneva is filled with wading birds, cranes, and waterfowl, including common mergansers, buffleheads, and ring-necked, ruddy, and common goldeneye ducks.

The park has a 5.5-mile (8.8-km) self-guided nature trail in meadows and forests.

Big Foot Beach SP
1452 Hwy. H
Lake Geneva, WI 53147
(262) 248-2528
**www.dnr.state.wi.us/org/
land/parks/specific/bigfoot/**

❺ Chain O' Lakes SP

Take Wells St. north to N. Bloomfield Ave. and turn right. Drive 2 miles (3.2 km) east, turn southeast on Hwy. 12, crossing the Illinois border and driving about 9 miles (14.5 km). Where Hwy. 12 splits, follow N. Main St. south, turn left on Kenosha St. (Hwy. 173), and drive east to a right turn at Wilmot Rd. and the entrance to 2,793-acre (1,130-h) **Chain O' Lakes SP** and its neighboring conservation area. Open 6 A.M. to 9 P.M. daily April to October; otherwise 8 A.M. to sunset. Admission fee is charged.

The chain consists of three natural and seven man-made lakes along the Fox River. With 488 miles (785 km) of shoreline, the park has recorded over 200 bird species. Recent sighting information and a checklist are available from the staff at the park office.

The park has four trail systems, including 2.3-mile (3.6-km) Nature's Way Trail at Oak Grove picnic area and 0.25-mile (0.4-km) full-access Pike Marsh Trail at North Picnic Area. There are 6 miles (9.7 km) of other mixed-use trails and 8 miles (12.9 km) of horse paths.

Also within the park and worth visiting is Turner Lake Nature Preserve, with 80 acres (32 h) of marsh and bog habitats standing over deep layers of peat. These acidic bogs are the right spot to see many small and large wading birds, cranes, egrets, and waterfowl. Visit the oak and hickory forests to view woodpeckers and owls.

Chain O' Lakes
8916 Wilmot Rd.
Spring Grove, IL 60081
(847) 587-5512
dnr.state.il.us/lands/landmgt/
parks/r2/chaino.htm

❻ Illinois Beach SP

Return to Hwy. 173, drive east about 14 miles (22 km) to Hwy. 137, and either head south to a left turn at W. 17th St. at 4,160-acre (1,683-h) **Illinois Beach SP** or north to Main St. and

Richard Bong SRA's observation platform overlooks wetlands and prairie.

Spring Bluff Forest Preserve.
Open sunrise to 8 P.M. Memorial Day to Labor Day; dawn to sunset otherwise. The park office is staffed from 8 A.M. to 4 P.M. daily. Admission fee is charged.

Besides the beach on Lake Michigan, there are marshes, woods, and grasslands with many boreal birds and perching birds. The many trails provide good access to all these birding sites. An interpretive center with natural history exhibits and displays is located in the preserve.

Birds of the spring and fall migration have a large showing along the bluffs. Songbirds and great horned owls can be heard at night, and red-tailed hawks are common overhead during the days.

Illinois Beach SP
Zion, IL 60099
(847) 662-4811
dnr.state.il.us/lands/landmgt/
parks/r2/ilbeach.htm

❼ Chicago Area

Follow Hwy. 173 back to I-94, head south toward Chicago, follow the Eden Expressway at the I-294 split, then exit on Hwy. 14 headed east. Straight ahead are Evanston, Lakeshore Dr., and the Lake Michigan shoreline. Lakeshore Dr. connects many parks and gives access to great bird-watching spots. Turn south and let the urban birding begin.

The first stop is Lincoln Park, west of Lakeshore Dr. Six major lakefront bird sanctuaries in Chicago provide lakefront habitat for birds to visit during their spring and fall migrations. Three are in Lincoln Park:

- **Montrose Point Bird Sanctuary,** 440 N. Montrose Ave.; this 15-acre (6-h) sanctuary is an IBA. Visit Magic Hedge, a belt of shrubs and trees renowned for attracting migratory songbirds, including purple martins, warblers, thrushes, and sparrows; over 300 species stop at the sanctuary.

- **Bill Jarvis Migratory Bird Sanctuary,** 3600 Addison St. at Lakeshore Dr.; closed to the public. Use a viewing platform recently built on the east side to see 150 species, including hawks, hummingbirds, 18 different sparrows, and 34 species of warblers.
- **North Pond,** Fullerton Pkwy. between Cannon Dr. and Stockton Dr.; up to 100,000 birds visit daily in May during migration, and a total of 160 species have been recorded at the site.

Lincoln Park
2045 Lincoln Park W.
Chicago, IL 60610
(312) 742-7726
www.chicagoparkdistrict.com

Follow Lakeshore Dr. south past the Field Museum and turn left at E. McFetridge Dr. Turn left at E. Solidarity Dr., then right at S. Lynn White Dr., and enter **Northerly Island Park,** a 91-acre (37-h) public preserve with wide, grassy fields and many migrant shorebirds and songbirds. It is especially full of sparrows in spring. Also see night-herons and American kestrels.

Northerly Island Park
1400 S. Lynn White Dr.
Chicago, IL 60605
(312) 745-2910
www.chicagoparkdistrict.com

The Chicago Museum of Science and Industry is a background to the peaceful setting of Osaka Japanese Garden on Wooded Island in Jackson Park.

About 1.8 miles (2.8 km) south on Lakeshore Dr., park on 31st St. or at McCormick Place to access 6-acre (2.4-h) **McCormick Place Bird Sanctuary** at **Burnham Park.**

Two prairies, shrubs, and woodlands make up this nature park, built in 2003. It is filled with birds, including carnivores that feed on prairie-plant insects. Keep an eye toward the meadow margins in early morning, then work the prairie sections. Birds often seen include juncos, eastern towhees, brown thrashers, gold-crowned and ruby-crowned kinglets, rose-breasted grosbeaks, hermit thrushes, indigo buntings, and warbler and sparrow species.

Burnham Park
425 E. McFetridge Dr.
Chicago, IL 60605
(773) 256-0949
www.chicagoparkdistrict.com

Paul H. Douglas Nature Sanctuary on Wooded Island in **Jackson Park** is at Science Dr. and Lakeshore Dr., south of the Museum of Science and Industry. It shares the island and its bridge access with Osaka Japanese Garden. The sanctuary has recorded over 250 species, including 48 that nest there.

Just to the south in the park, on the peninsula west of East Lagoon, is **Bobolink Meadow Nature Sanctuary.** Despite its name, bobolinks are not a likely site at this transformed former missile site, now a meadow. However, monk parakeets have nested near the tennis court on the north end, and American goldfinches come to feed in the fall. They are joined by several hundred other bird species. East Lagoon also fills with waterfowl and shorebirds from fall to early winter and again in late spring.

Jackson Park
6401 S. Stony Island Ave.
Chicago, IL 60637
(773) 256-0903
www.chicagoparkdistrict.com

❽ **Indiana Dunes**

Take S. Jeffrey Blvd. south 1.7 miles (2.7 km), cross under I-90, turn left on S. Anthony Ave., and enter the Interstate. Travel south about 18 miles (29 km) total, crossing the border, proceeding east to Gary, Indiana, and exiting at exit 14B (Hwy. 53). Turn right on Broadway, left on E. 5th

Cedar waxwings **socialize** within their flocks, sometimes **singing a chorus** or even **sharing food**

Ave. (Hwy. 12), and follow the north split onto E. Dunes Hwy. A final left turn on S. Lake St. leads north to the first of many sites in **Indiana Dunes National Lakeshore.** Open daily except major holidays. Admission fee is charged.

Pick up park information at the kiosk. The 1-mile (1.6-km) Miller Woods trail leads over a pedestrian bridge, across a boardwalk, to a marsh and overlook.

At the park's dunes, shorelines, and beaches, see bank swallows, gulls, doves, terns, prairie warblers, semipalmated plovers, sanderlings, least sandpipers, American woodcocks, and sparrows. Near water and in forest areas are pied-billed grebes, owls, green herons, mute swans, American black ducks, and wood ducks.

There are many birding sites within Indiana Dunes:

- **West Beach,** Hwy. 12E, left on N. County Line Rd.; 3.6 miles (15.8 km) of trails and boardwalks.
- **Inland Marsh Overlook,** Hwy. 12E; a turnout on the south side of the highway with good views of Inland Marsh. Trailhead for 3-mile (4.8-km) Inland Marsh Trail.
- **Chelberg Farm,** Hwy. 12, right on W. Oak Hill Rd., right on Howe Rd.; 3.7 miles (6 km) of trails and boardwalks.
- **Cowles Bog,** Hwy. 12, left on Mineral Springs Rd.; trailhead for 4.6-mile (7.4-km) Cowles Bog Trail.
- **Dorothy Buell Visitors Center,** Hwy. 20 and Hwy. 49; main NPS visitors center.
- **Indiana Dunes SP,** Hwy. 12, left on Waverly Rd., right on State Park Rd.; nature center and hiking in 2,102 acres (851 h) of woods and shore. **www.in.gov/dnr/parklake/ properties/park_dunes.html**
- **Calumet Dunes,** Hwy. 12, south on Kemil Rd.; 0.8-mile (1.2-km) Calumet Dune Trail and 8-mile (13-km) Ly-co-ki-we Horse and Hiking Trail.
- **Kemil, Dunbar, Lake View, and Central Beaches,** Kemil Rd., north on Beverly Dr.; shorebirds on beach and dunes, waterfowl offshore in Lake Michigan.
- **Heron Rookery,** Hwy. 12, south on Brown Rd. 500 E, east on 1400 North Rd., south on 600 East Rd.; up to 100 nesting great blue herons roost in the trees during the summer months.

Indiana Dunes Natl. Lakeshore
1100 N. Mineral Springs Rd.
Porter, Indiana 46304
(219) 926-7561
www.nps.gov/indu/

The **Indiana Dunes West Beach Bath House** (left) and Cowles Bog Trail (right) reveal the highly varied habitats of Indiana Dunes and National Lakeshore. More than 200 species of birds are attracted to these natural areas.

Visit these sites along the way...

❾ Warren Dunes SP
12032 Red Arrow Hwy.
Sawyer, MI 49125
(269) 426-4013
www.dnr.state.mi.us

A 1,952-acre (790-h) park designated by Michigan as a Watchable Wildlife Site, with trails through dunes up to 260 feet (80 m) high. Open daily year-round. Fee.

❿ Grand Mere SP
Thornton Dr.
Stevensville, MI 49127
(269) 426-4013
www.michigan.gov/dnr

Trails through a natural area with dunes and coastal lagoons that attract many species of birds, plus 1 mile (1.6 km) of shoreline. Open 8 A.M. to 10 P.M. year-round. Fee.

St. Louis Area

Drive west to see the Missouri River's meanders and marvel at its large population of bald eagles, then follow the Big Muddy east to where it mingles with the waters of the Illinois and Mississippi rivers. Next, circle St. Louis, a place rich in history where millions of migrating birds flock each spring and fall. Finally, explore scenic byways in the south to visit a place held sacred by the Cherokees, and see pristine country preserved from the loggers' axes and the farmers' plows. From north to south, it's a land filled with majestic and beautiful birds.

Red-tailed hawks often roost in dead snags.

Gather in quiet contemplation and follow the example of three great rivers, witnessing in silence the annual migration spectacle of hundreds of thousands of birds as they travel past the bluffs and sandy bars of St. Louis's shore.

Eagle Bluffs Conservation Area has a viewing deck that sits on a 300-foot-high (91-m-high) perch overlooking the Missouri River. It affords good views of bald eagles, hawks, and other raptors that fly along the river.

❶ Eagle Bluffs Conservation Area

Begin the tour with a visit west of St. Louis. Drive I-70 west 83 miles (134 km) to Columbia, go south about 13 miles (21 km) on Hwy. 163 (Providence Rd., which becomes Rte. K), and continue west 0.8 mile (1.3 km) past McBaine to a left turn at

Star School Rd., which leads to the 4,269-acre (1,728-h) **Eagle Bluffs Conservation Area.** Open 4 A.M. to 10 P.M. daily.

The bluffs preserve an area that once was a main channel of the Missouri River, but in the mid-1800s the river moved west, leaving an area that was developed into 13 ponds encircled by 16 miles (26 km) of dikes.

A 1-mile (1.6-km) hiking trail leads to a bluff-top viewing deck. Its 300-foot (91-m) perch provides sweeping views of the Missouri River and its floodplains. During early fall, egrets, herons, waterfowl, and other migrants fill the area's forests, wetlands, and rivers. Following them are bald eagles and other raptors trailing behind the flocks. Nesting

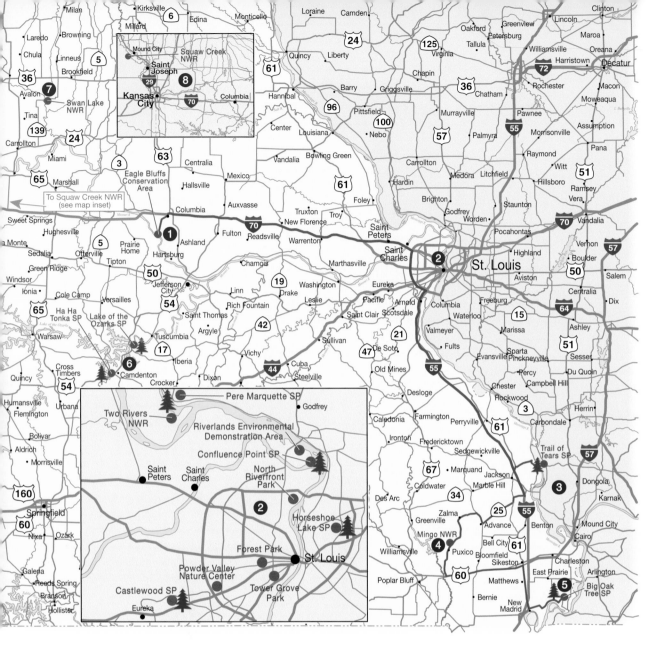

named **Confluence Point SP,** which lies northeast of downtown where the Big Muddy joins the mighty Mississippi. Drive northeast on I-270 from I-70 for 11 miles (18 km), take Hwy. 67 north about 9 miles (14.5 km), and exit south on Riverlands Way. The 1,118-acre (452-h) park is at the end of the road. Open sunrise to sunset daily.

Watch from a vantage point between the rivers as millions of raptors, waterfowl, shorebirds, wading birds, and songbirds migrate past the park each spring and fall. The park was formally opened in 2004. Plans are in place to restore the natural floodplain with native trees and marsh plants, enhancing it for bird and wildlife habitat.

Confluence Point SP
1000 Riverlands Way
West Alton, MO 63386
(636) 899-1135
www.mostateparks.com/ confluence.htm

Riverlands Environmental Demonstration Area is also on Riverlands Way, near the Hwy. 67 turnoff. Boy Scouts performing public service have

Eagle Bluffs has still waters at day's end.

wood ducks are also common here. Most of these migrants eventually move on, but the bald eagles remain behind to feed and overwinter in the area.

Eagle Bluffs Conservation Area
6700 W. Rte. K
Columbia, MO 65203
(573) 445 3882
www.mdc.mo.gov

While in the area, consider traveling south to **Lake of the Ozarks SP** and **Ha Ha Tonka SP,** about 75 miles (121 km) via Jefferson City, or heading north to **Swan Lake NWR,** then west to **Squaw Creek NWR,** about 230 miles (368 km) distant (see page 155). All four areas are excellent spots for bird-watching, with numerous geese, ducks, wading birds, and neotropical migrants.

❷ St. Louis Area

Return to St. Louis by I-70. This western gateway city was built at a site where the Missouri and Illinois rivers merge with the Mississippi River. It is also on the Mississippi Flyway; millions of birds migrate along the three rivers each spring and fall.

Where better to start a city birding tour than at the aptly

Mingo NWR is one of the last unbroken remnants of original hardwood river bottomland (left). It has been a migration destination since prehistory, attracting wading birds such as the great blue heron (right).

built trails and an observation deck with mounted binoculars, and they have placed interpretive signage on the site, which is adjacent to the Melvin Price Lock and Dam. Use these facilities to see both migrating and resident birdlife, especially waterfowl and shorebirds.

Rivers Project, USACE
301 Riverlands Way
West Alton, MO 63386
(314) 899-2600
**www.greatriverroad.com/
Cities/wAlton/Riverlands.htm**

Join Hwy. 67 north, cross the Mississippi into Illinois, immediately turn left on Landmarks Blvd., and drive to W. Broadway St. Turn left and head upriver, noting that the route becomes Great River Rd. at Grafton, and drive 2.5 miles (4 km). Next fol-

low the signs on Graham Hollow Rd. to 8,000-acre (3,237-h) **Pere Marquette SP** on the Illinois River. Camping fees are charged. Bird checklists are available at the visitors center.

Over 230 bird species have been recorded here. It is well known as a bald eagle wintering ground (eagle tours are conducted from late December to February).

With 12 miles (19 km) of mixed-use trails, the best birding spots to visit are Stump Lake, McAdams Peak, the river floodplain, and the overlooks.

Pere Marquette SP
Rte. 100, P.O. Box 158
Grafton, IL 62037
(618) 786-3323
**dnr.state.il.us/lands/landmgt/
parks/r4/peremarq.htm**

Return to Great River Rd., turn left, drive 1 mile (1.6 km), and catch the Brussels Ferry, crossing the Illinois River. (The ferry operates 24 hours daily.)

Take Illinois River Rd. south and west to Deer Plain Rd., turn right, and follow the signs to **Two Rivers NWR,** one of five wildlife refuges that make up the Mark Twain NWR Complex. Open sunrise to sunset daily January to mid-October; visitors center open 8 A.M. to 4 P.M. weekdays.

From October to November and March to April, over 200 species of birds visit this 8,000-acre (3,237-h) refuge; see up to 5 million ducks and 50,000 geese just during fall migration. In winter bald eagles may number a thousand individuals or more. Visit in May for shorebirds and warblers, and return in summer for herons and egrets.

Two Rivers NWR
H.C.R. 82, Box 107
Brussels, IL 62013
(618) 883-2524
**www.fws.gov/midwest/
tworivers/**

Take the ferry back to Great River Rd., drive south, and take Berm Hwy. 143 south at Alton for 4 miles (6.4 km). Follow the highway past Hwy. 3, transition to Hwy. 255, and drive south 10 miles (16 km) to exit at Horseshoe Lake Rd., which leads to **Horseshoe Lake SP.**

The park's centerpiece is a shallow 2,400-acre (971-h) oxbow lake only minutes from downtown, encircled by trails through bald cypress, tupelo gum, and swamp cottonwood forest. Look for great blue herons and black-crowned nightherons, snowy egrets, bald eagles, and other waterfowl.

Horseshoe Lake SP
P.O. Box 85
Miller City, IL 62962
(618) 776-5689
**dnr.state.il.us/lands/landmgt/
parks/r5/horshu.htm**

Sweep through central St. Louis to visit its key city parks:

- **North Riverfront Park,** I-270 to Riverview Dr. south; the 11-mile Riverfront Trail near Chain of Rocks bridge. Bald eagles, raptors, and river birds. Open pre-sunrise to sunset daily.

- **Tower Grove Park,** I-40 south on Grand Blvd. to Arsenal St.; over 200 birds species recorded, a favorite for migrating warblers and thrushes.
- **Forest Park,** Arsenal St. to Hampton Ave. and north; site of Kennedy Forest, woods that attract migrant birds in spring and fall.

St. Louis Dept. of Parks, Recreation and Forestry
5600 Clayton Rd.
St. Louis, MO 63110
www.stlouis.missouri.org/citygov/parks/parks_div/

Take I-44 west to Hwy. 141, turn north to Big Bend Rd., west to Ries Rd., and left to 1,802-acre (729-h) **Castlewood SP** and World Bird Sanctuary. Park open 7 A.M. to sunset daily; sanctuary open weekends only.

Walk Grotpeter and River trails to see warblers and other songbirds, along with formerly wild raptors. The sanctuary houses captive birds of prey and displays them to visitors.

Castlewood SP
1401 Kiefer Creek Rd.
Ballwin, MO 63021
(636) 227-4433
www.mostateparks.com/castlewood.htm/

❸ Trail of Tears SP

Take I-55 south 102 miles (164 km) to exit 105 (Hwy. 61), turn north, then go east at Hwy. 177 and drive 9.5 miles (15 km) to 3,415-acre (5495-h) **Trail of Tears SP.** Open 7 A.M. to 10 P.M. April to October; call otherwise.

Once the site of a tragic Native American historical event, it is now a beautiful place to see birds on the Mississippi River. There are 14.5 miles (23 km) of trails. Neotropical songbirds nest in the deciduous forest. Raptors and waterfowl are abundant.

Trail of Tears SP
429 Moccasin Springs
Jackson, MO 63755
(573) 334-1711
www.mostateparks.com/trailoftears.htm

❹ Mingo NWR

Return to Hwy. 61, drive southwest to Jackson, and exit town on Hwy. 25. Drive southwest 27 miles (43 km) to Advance, turn west on Hwy. 91, go south on Hwy. 51, and note signs for **Mingo NWR.** Open one hour before sunrise to one hour after sunset daily; center hours vary by season. Admission fee is charged.

Preserving 21,676 acres (8,772 h) of hardwood bottomland, the refuge is a waterfowl migration rest stop and wintering area. See ducks, geese, herons, nesting bald eagles, and many neotropical migrants. There is a 12-mile (19-km) auto tour, along with four observation decks and a boardwalk.

Mingo NWR
24279 State Hwy 51
Puxico, MO 63960
www.fws.gov/refuges

❺ Big Oak Tree SP

Follow Hwy. 51 south to Hwy. 60. Turn west, drive to Hwy. 61, and go south to New Madrid. Turn right at Dawson Rd., follow Co. Rd. WW south, and take Co. Rd. 520 east. Turn north at Hwy. 102 to enter **Big Oak Tree SP.** Open 6 A.M. to 10 P.M. daily.

Tall trees sheltering thickets and wetlands are home to more than 150 bird species. A boardwalk gives easy access.

Big Oak Tree SP
13640 S. Hwy. 102
East Prairie, MO 63845
(573) 649-3149
www.mostateparks.com/bigoak.htm

Visit these sites along the way...

❻ Lake of the Ozarks SP
P.O. Box 160
Kaiser, MO 65047
(573) 348-2694
www.mostateparks.com

Lake of the Ozarks SP (near Hwy. 54 and Hwy. 42) and **Ha Ha Tonka SP** (Hwy. 54 and Hwy. 5) both offer many lakeside trails. With easy access and a wide variety of birds—neotropical migrants to bald eagles—this is an area rich with avian life in large numbers.

❼ Swan Lake NWR
16194 Swan Lake Ave.
Sumner, MO 64681
(660) 856-3323
www.fws.gov/midwest/swanlake

I-70 to Hwy. 65 north to Hwy. 24 east to Hwy. 139, and north. Visitors center, exhibits, trails, and auto tours. Visit in October and November when waterfowl migration is at its peak. Nesting and resting grounds for 150,000 snow geese and tens of thousands of ducks.

❽ Squaw Creek NWR
P.O. Box 158
Mound City, MO 64470
(660) 442-3187
www.fws.gov/midwest/squawcreek

South of Mound City off I-29 at exit 79, 3 miles (5 km) west. A self-guided auto loop plus 1.5-mile (2.4-km) Eagle Overlook trail; Loess Bluff trail climbs 200 feet (61 m) to scenic views. Broad spectrum of birdlife, from migrants to residents.

A common moorhen at Squaw Creek NWR, with feet that are adapted for walking on floating vegetation.

Dallas and Fort Worth Area

Texas and southern Oklahoma are transition areas for birding. A scan of the range maps in any birding field guide shows an invisible line drawn at the states' shared border. It marks the northernmost extent of many southern birds, and the farthest southern travels of many more northerly species. Add to these the many neotropical migratory birds and waterfowl, and the area becomes a birding hot spot where dozens of species can be seen each day. The countryside is as varied as the birds that reside or visit it. Prairie grasslands, scrublands, riverine belts of woodlands, lakes, and mixed forest filled with many different kinds of vegetation all beckon birds to feed, nest, and rear young. Come to bird-watch and stay to see the Lone Star state's natural spectacle.

Texas is the most diverse bird-watching destination in North America, with its number of recorded birds standing at over 600. Thrill to the avian abundance by visiting Big D, exploring the nearby lakes and woods of two states, and returning to see Fort Worth.

River Legacy Parks are clustered midway between Dallas and Fort Worth. The complex has numerous and extensive hiking trails. Given its large area and many habitats, rarely seen birds are frequently observed in Texas parks.

Male house finches become brightly colored during spring mating season. By summer their plumage fades, leaving just a hint of pink near their eyes and under their beaks.

❶ Dallas Area

The Dallas urban core and its suburbs are dotted with creeks, wooded parks, greenbelts, and lakes that attract birds of many species. It is also favored by its geography; birds migrating the shoreline of the Gulf of Mexico instinctively turn north as the Gulf sweeps east, a route that takes their flight path over Dallas or Fort Worth.

Before exploring the Texas countryside outside the cities, on a birding tour that pokes a bit into Oklahoma to the north and the Hill Country to the south, exhaust the rich bird-watching hot spots nearby. Start with **White Rock Lake,** a nearby favorite of local birders.

Take I-30 east to Grand Ave., turn northwest for 1.5 miles

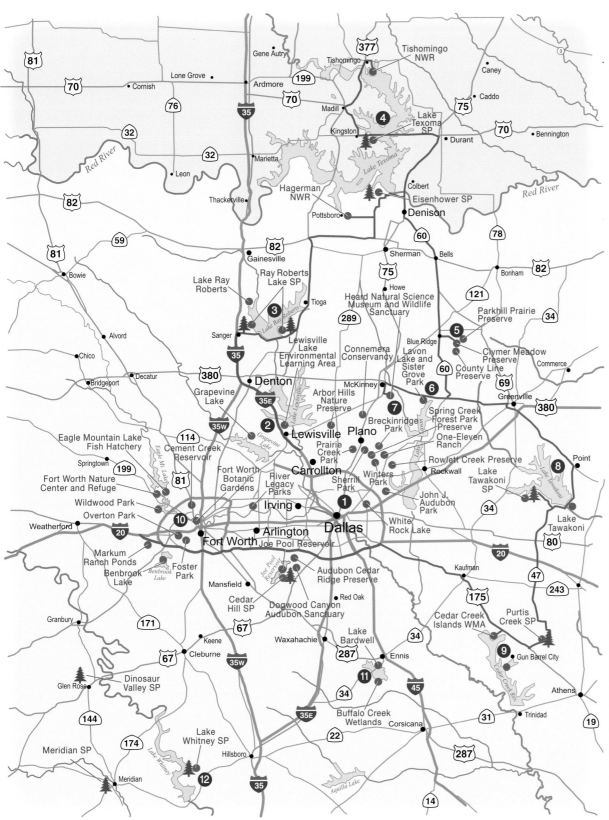

(2.4 km) to Winstead Dr., and turn left. A right on White Rock Rd. and a left on W. Lawther Dr. begins a loop around this park-encircled lake. Pull off to bird-watch; the marshes at the north end are the best choice for seeing shorebirds, though during migration rafts of ducks, scaups, coots, and American white pelicans cover the lake under the watchful overhead gaze of ring-billed gulls.

Dallas Parks and Recreation Dept.
830 E. Lawther Dr.
Dallas, TX 75218
(214) 670-8281
www.dallasparks.org

The summer range of little blue herons is confined to a crescent of states bordering the Gulf of Mexico and north as far as Oklahoma.

Red-shouldered hawks are usually seen in meadow margins near wooded areas. They roost in trees, watching the fields for the movements of their prey.

A short way east via I-30, with an exit at Northwest Dr., a turn northwest, and a right on Oates Dr. is **John J. Audubon Park** in Garland. The park gives access to the 3.1-mile (5-km) Duck Creek Greenbelt and six linked city parks and, in spring, is also a good spot to see boreal songbirds and perching birds, including Swainson's thrushes, warblers, blue-headed vireos, northern waterthrushes, and indigo buntings. Mulberry and pecan trees attract both fruit-eating and nut-eating birds.

Garland Parks and
Recreation Dept.
634 Apollo Rd.
Garland, TX 75040
(972) 205-3991
www.ci.garland.tx.us

If one were to name a birding hot spot northeast of Dallas, it would have to be each side of President George Bush Turnpike (Hwy. 190), from Garland and Rowlett to Richardson and Plano. Plan to spend lots of time birding these clustered sites:

- **Rowlett Creek Preserve,** E. Centerville Rd. and Castle Dr., Rowlett; a year-round bird magnet with mixed habitats. See sparrows, hawks, juncos, towhees, warblers, vireos, and owls. **www.ci.rowlett.tx.us**
- **One-Eleven Ranch,** on E. Brand Rd. next to Firewheel Golf Park, Garland; creekside park with brush understory. Visit spring and fall for northern parulas, American redstarts, blue-headed vireos, gnatcatchers and flycatchers. **www.ci.garland.tx.us**
- **Breckinridge Park,** on E. Brand Rd. at Park Vista Rd., Richardson; a large suburban park that attracts sandpipers, warblers, indigo buntings, and sparrows in spring, and finches, creepers, meadowlarks, juncos, and sapsuckers throughout winter. The lake has waterfowl in migration.
- **Winters Park,** Arapaho Rd. and N. Garland Dr., Garland; bird the wooded area behind the soccer field for sparrows, kinglets, sapsuckers, finches, waxwings, and woodpeckers.
- **Spring Creek Forest Park Preserve,** Holford Rd. between Arapaho Rd. and Hwy. 190, Garland; over 150 recorded bird species, best in spring and fall. Birds include soras, Carolina chickadees, kinglets, bobwhites, woodpeckers, and buntings.
- **Sherrill Park,** E. Lookout Dr., Richardson; creekside habitat with kingfishers, snowy egrets, herons, shorebirds, orioles, tanagers, swallows (nest under bridge), flycatchers, and hawks. **www.cor.net/parks/ homepage.html**
- **Prairie Creek Park,** N. Collins Blvd. and Campbell Rd., Richardson; favored by local bird-watchers as the best warbler spot, with over 24 recorded warbler species attracted to larvae on pecan trees. Visit April to May and in September.

Just a bit farther north are two more worthwhile stops:

- **Arbor Hills Nature Preserve,** north of W. Parker Rd., just west of Dallas North Tollway, Plano; walkways, trails, and paths through hilly prairie and scrub brush habitats. See passerines and neotropical migrant birds. **www.plano.gov**

River Legacy Parks has full-access trails in its mixed-forest areas, which allow everyone to enjoy its birdlife and natural setting.

- **Connemara Conservancy,** east of Alma Dr. on Hedgecoxe Rd., Allen; 72 acres (29 h) of prairie and creekside habitat with nesting dickcissels, blue grosbeaks, and painted and indigo buntings in spring. **www.cityofallen.org**

Across metropolitan Dallas to the southwest is **Joe Pool Reservoir.** The fastest route to reach it is by taking the Lyndon B. Johnson Fwy. (I-635 south becoming I-20 west) to S. Belt Line Rd., turning south for 3.2 miles (5.1 km) and entering 1,810-acre (732-h) **Cedar Hill SP.** Open 8 A.M. to 10 P.M. daily. Admission fee is charged.

Escarpments of limestone jut from remnant patches of native prairie and scattered cedars, providing a last habitat for rare golden-cheeked warblers and now-extinct Eskimo curlews. It still provides refuge to many neotropical migrants in spring and fall as they travel through the region. Painted buntings, Chuck-will's widows (a nightjar), and yellow-billed cuckoos are commonly seen here.

Cedar Hill SP
1570 FTM Rd. 1382
Cedar Hill, TX 75104
(972) 291-3900
www.tpwd.state.tx.us/spdest/ findadest/parks/cedar_hill

If time permits, also visit the trails of Lynn Creek Park on the south shore of the reservoir.

Dogwood Canyon Audubon Sanctuary is nearby, 0.5 mile (0.8 km) southeast of the park entrance on S. Belt Line Rd. Open sunrise to sunset daily.

Rare and endangered birds as well as threatened plants are preserved here. See black-chinned and ruby-throated hummingbirds, golden-cheeked warblers, ladder-backed woodpeckers, scissor-tailed flycatchers, eastern and western kingbirds, and white-eyed vireos.

Audubon Dallas
7171 Mountain Creek Pkwy.
Dallas, TX 75249
(972) 293-5150
www.audubondallas.org

Return north via S. Belt Line Rd. to Eagle Ford Dr., turn right, drive 0.7 mile (1.1 km), turn right again on Mountain Creek Pkwy., and follow it 0.8 mile (1.3 km) to **Audubon Cedar Ridge Preserve.** Open sunrise to sunset daily, Tuesday to Sunday.

With Dogwood Canyon this second facility, operated by Audubon Dallas, is a 633-acre (256-h) preserve with 10 miles (16 km) of hiking trails, including full-access Little Bluestem Trail. It also features a butterfly garden and up to 200 recorded bird species. The best bird-watching is on the Cattail Pond, Fossil Valley, and Cedar Brake trails. There's also a birding observation tower at Cattail Pond. Visit in October to see rare black-capped vireos.

The Living Science Center at River Legacy Parks in Dallas's suburb of Arlington has natural-history exhibits and features an exhibit hall with a high-definition simulation of a canoe ride down the nearby Trinity River.

Audubon Dallas
7171 Mountain Creek Pkwy.
Dallas, TX 75249
(972) 293-5150
www.audubondallas.org

A final stop, midway on I-30 between Dallas and Fort Worth, is **River Legacy Parks.** Take Fielder Rd. exit in Arlington, turn north, drive 1.3 miles (2.1 km), and turn east on Green Oaks Blvd., which leads to the parks' entrance and Living Science Center. Parks open sunrise to sunset daily; center open 9 A.M. to 5 P.M. Tuesday to Saturday.

This complex of multiple parks has 28 miles (45 km) of trails, including 20 miles (32 km) of unpaved foot-traffic-only hiking trails ideal for birding. Many rarely seen birds, such as hooded and golden-cheeked warblers, are among the 25 warbler species known to visit the site. Also look for summer tanagers, crested caracaras, great crested flycatchers, lazuli buntings, and other uncommon and resident birds.

Arlington Parks and Recreation Dept.
717 W. Main St.
Arlington, TX 76013
(817) 459-5474
www.ci.arlington.tx.us

❷ Lewisville Lake

Take the Lyndon B. Johnson Fwy. to I-35, turn north, and drive about 13 miles (21 km) to Valley Ridge Blvd., turning east. At Mill St. turn left, drive to Jones St., and drive east to the **Lewisville Lake Environmental Learning Area**

Parkhill Prairie Preserve is a place to savor a remnant of the prairie that once stretched in an unbroken belt from Texas to Canada.

below the dam. Open Fridays and weekends 7 A.M. to 7 P.M. March to October; 7 A.M. to 5 P.M. otherwise. Admission fee is charged.

The 2,000-acre (809-h) area on the Elm Fork of the Trinity River is at the boundary of prairie and bottomland forests, an ideal setting for birds. Look for waterfowl, wood ducks, wading birds, wild turkeys, and painted buntings on its three trails overlooking the bottomlands and river below the dam.

Lewisville Lake Environmental Learning Area
Jones and Kealy Sts.
Lewisville, TX 75057
(972) 219-7980 (Friday to Sunday)
www.ias.unt.edu/llela/main

Return to Mill St., turn north, and drive 1.1 mile (1.8 km) to its end at 682-acre (276-h) Lake Park. Walk the tree-covered spit, scanning the shoreline and trees for woodpeckers, kingfishers, shorebirds, and waterfowl. During migration also see neotropical migrants. The park receives heavy recreational use during the day; visit in the early morning for best results.

Lewisville Parks and Recreation
151 W. Church St.
Lewisville, TX 75057
(972) 219-3400

Just past the bridge on I-35 north are two other parks to see on Lake Lewisville: Westlake Park, to the east of the interstate,

and Hickory Creek Park, to the west. When lake levels are high, the eastern edge of Westlake Park becomes a wetland, ideal for bird-watching. The two bays and many inlets in Hickory Creek Park provide waterfowl with shelter from winds.

❸ Ray Roberts Lake SP and Lake Ray Roberts

Return to I-35, drive about 18 miles (29 km) north to Sanger, turn right on FM 455, and look for a sign to the Sanger unit of **Ray Roberts Lake SP,** one of a complex of six parks around 30,000-acre (12,141-h) **Lake Ray Roberts.** Open 24 hours daily. Admission fee is charged.

This unit is a marina and boat launch with rental facilities, an excellent way to view aquatic birds on the reservoir.

For terrestrial bird-watching continue east on FM 455 just past Sam Garrett Memorial Overlook Park (another good place for birding). The entrance to the park's Isle du Bois unit is on the left.

Here, the Elm Fork and Jordan Park trails are the best bird-watching sites. The first trail follows the Trinity River's Elm Fork through hardwood forest with huge trees. In summer the woods echo with the calls of black-and-white and prothonotary warblers, northern parulas, white-breasted

Heard Wildlife Sanctuary boasts tree-shaded ponds with shorebirds.

Heard Natural Science Museum and Wildlife Sanctuary features full-access boardwalks that traverse open forest marshes and wetlands filled with boreal birds, woodpeckers, and owls.

nuthatches, summer tanagers, and both white-eyed and red-eyed vireos. The second trail heads north of the camping area into prairie and woodland margins, another good place to look for woodpeckers and hawks.

Ray Roberts SP
100 PW 4137
Pilot Point, TX 76258
(940) 686-2148
www.tpwd.state.tx.us

❹ Lake Texoma

Return to FM 455, turn east, drive to Hwy. 377, and head 21 miles (34 km) north to Whitesboro. Turn east on Hwy. 82 for

about 11 miles (18 km) to Old Southmayd Rd. and follow the signs to **Hagerman NWR** on the south shore of the Big Mineral arm of **Lake Texoma.** Open dawn to dusk daily.

Take the 4-mile (6.4-km) self-guided auto tour, ply the lake's waters by boat or canoe (April to September only), or hike Crow Hill Trail through prairie habitat. The best time to visit is in fall or winter.

This is Red River country, home to nesting neotropical songbirds, quail, doves, and upland gamebirds. During the migration in fall, the refuge fills with geese, ducks, cranes, swans, egrets, and pelicans. Also look for huge flocks of scissor-tailed flycatchers and blackbirds.

Hagerman NWR
6465 Refuge Rd.
Sherman, TX 75092
(903) 786-2826
www.fws.gov/refuges

To reach the next stop, **Eisenhower SP,** follow Refuge Rd. east to FM 996, turn north, jog west at Pottsboro, continue north on Hwy. 120, and turn right at Hwy. 406. Follow Eisenhower Rd. where the highway splits from Texoma Dr. (Hwy. 84). It leads to the park entrance.

The 423-acre (171-h) park named for President Dwight D. Eisenhower preserves tallgrass prairie leading to rocky bluffs at the lake shoreline. The forest is very diverse and attracts an

equally wide range of bird species. In winter bald eagles, pelicans, loons, and waterfowl fill the area. Trails loop the park, with best boreal birding along the west boundary of the park. For waterbirds and shorebirds follow the lakeshore or rent a boat at the marina.

Eisenhower State Park
50 Park Rd. 20
Denison, TX 75020
(903) 465-1956
www.tpwd.state.tx.us

Follow Eisenhower Rd. east to Hwy. 91, turn left and cross the Oklahoma border, drive to Hwy. 75 at Colbert, turn north again, and drive 15 miles (24 km) to Durant. At Durant turn west on Hwy. 70, cross Lake Texoma, and turn into **Lake Texoma SP.**

The best locations for birding are near the heel of the boot-shaped peninsula on the southeast end of the park. Shallows near the island fill with wading shorebirds and migratory waterfowl in fall. Also scan the sky for hawks, eagles, and other raptors that follow the ducks and geese south.

Lake Texoma State Park
Hwy. 70 E
Kingston, OK 73439
(800) 528-0593
www.oklahomaparks.com

Fort Worth Nature Center and Refuge is on the shore of Lake Worth, an excellent birding location near town.

turn left, and drive 1.7 miles (2.7 km) on FM 668 to remote **Parkhill Prairie Preserve.** The site is a rare native tallgrass prairie within a 436-acre (176-h) county preserve. Look for dick-cissels, orchard orioles, grass-hopper and lark sparrows, bobwhites, and meadowlarks.

Take a moment to savor the silence of the open prairie and look overhead for hawks.

The special nature of the spot may be the reason that **Clymer Meadow Preserve** is just 3 miles (4.8 km) north and **County Line Preserve** is 1 mile (1.6 km) south. Visit all three; they are a rare treat for bird-watchers.

Collin County Special Projects
825 N. McDonald St., Ste. 145
McKinney, TX 75069
(972) 424-1460, ext. 3744
www.co.collin.tx.us/parks/ parkhill_prairie.jsp/

Drive west on Hwy. 70. At Kingston the highway turns north; follow it to Madill, then turn northeast on Hwy. 377 and go to Tishomingo. Turn east on Hwy. 78, drive to the edge of town, and turn south on Refuge Rd. for 3 miles (4.8 km) to reach **Tishomingo NWR.**

Because access to the refuge is restricted from October to February, the best time to visit is March to April and again in September.

At those times follow Craven Nature Trail to Dick's Pond, or climb the observation tower east of Big Sandy Creek and Jemison's Lookout at Nida Point for views of Cumberland Pond. More than 100,000 ducks and 45,000 geese frequent the refuge. Especially common are snow geese mixed with greater white-fronted and Canada geese.

In summer look for members of the 250 recorded species of woodland birds and shorebirds.

Tishomingo NWR
12000 S. Refuge Rd.
Tishomingo, OK 73460
(580) 371-2402
www.fws.gov/refuges

❺ Parkhill Prairie Preserve

Tishomingo is the most northern waypoint on the route. Return by the outbound roads to Durant, turn south for 16 miles (26 km) on Hwy. 75 to Denison, and turn southeast on Hwy. 69. Travel 35 miles (56 km), passing through Bells and Whitewright, where the road divides, and take Hwy. 60 south to Blue Ridge. Just south of town where Bus. Hwy. 78 rejoins Hwy. 78, turn left on FM 825, drive 3 miles (4.8 km), turn right, proceed 1 mile (1.6 km),

❻ Lavon Lake

Return to Hwy. 78, turn south, and drive 10.5 miles (17 km) to Farmersville. Turn left on Hwy. 380 and travel the causeway over **Lavon Lake,** turning right midway across the lake. This road leads north to the lake's two arms and, on a left spur, **Sister Grove Park.** Follow its day-use-only biking trail to see waterfowl on the lake, boreal birds in the mixed-hardwood forest, and wading birds in the marshes and wet-lands inland from the lake.

See long-billed dowitchers, Wilson's snipes, greater yellowlegs, ring-billed and herring gulls, and pectoral sandpipers, as well as ducks and geese.

Collin County Special Projects
825 N. McDonald St., Ste. 145
McKinney, TX 75069
(972) 424-1460, ext. 3744
www.co.collin.tx.us/parks/ sister_grove.jsp/

❼ Heard Natural Science Museum and Wildlife Sanctuary

Return to Hwy. 380, turn west, and drive 10 miles (16 km) to McKinney. Turn at S. McDonald St. (Hwy. 5) and drive south through town. Follow Greenfield Rd. left from Hwy. 5, turn left on Country Club Rd. (FM 1378), and drive 1 mile (1.6 km) to **Heard Natural Science Museum and Wildlife Sanctuary.** Open 9 A.M. to 5 P.M. Monday to Saturday, 1 P.M. to 5 P.M. Sunday. Admission fee is charged.

This 289-acre (117-h) sanctuary has trails through both prairie and bottomland hardwood forest and is a recognized IBA. Follow Hootowl, Bluestem, or Sycamore trails to see birds of the prairie and woodlands, or take Hilltop trail to look for hawks. Owls are common on the site, and the curators guide night walks; advance reservations are recommended.

Heard Natural Science Museum and Wildlife Sanctuary
1 Nature Pl.
McKinney, TX 75069
(972) 562- 5566
www.heardmuseum.org

❽ Lake Tawakoni

Retrace the outbound path past Lavon Lake to Farmersville, go east 15 miles (24 km) on Hwy. 380 to Greenville, and follow

Hwy. 69 southeast 21 miles (34 km) to Point. Turn south on FM 47, which leads to the dam at **Lake Tawakoni.** The wetlands below the dam are a favorite weekend birding site for Dallas residents.

In winter see Smith's and Lapland longspurs around the grass airstrip to the north of the marshes as bald eagles soar by to fish the reservoir.

Next, drive FM 47 west, dip south to Wills Point, then turn

American kestrels are open-grassland hunters that perch and scan for prey.

north on Tawakoni Dr. In about 4 miles (6.4 km) the entrance to **Lake Tawakoni SP** is on the right. Open 7 A.M. to 10 P.M. daily. Admission fee is charged.

This 376-acre (152-h) park with 5 miles (8 km) of shoreline consists mainly of regrowth forest and a bit of prairie. It's a fine spot to see Mexican spotted, burrowing, and elf owls, eastern screech-owls, American peregrine and arctic falcons, and several species of woodpeckers. At the shore look for waterbirds and shorebirds. Bald eagles fish the reservoir waters and winter in the area.

Lake Tawakoni SP
10822 FM 2475
Wills Point, TX 75169
(903) 560-7123
www.tpwd.state.tx.us/spdest/ findadest/parks/lake_tawakoni/

❾ Purtis Creek SP and Cedar Creek Islands WMA

Return to FM 47, turn southwest, drive through Wills Point, cross I-20, and continue south to Hwy. 198, about 25 miles (40 km). Turn left on Hwy. 198, drive 2 miles (3.2 km), turn right on FM 316, and follow it south 3.5 miles (5.6 km) to 1,582-acre (640-h) **Purtis Creek SP.** Open 24 hours daily year-round; heavy visitation March to November. Admission fee is charged.

Cape May warblers savor the sweet nectar found in the blossoms of flowering trees

Bird-watch the weedy margins at the lake's northeast end. Besides the usual waterfowl, see white-faced ibis and herons. Trees near the campground have eastern bluebirds and painted buntings. In spring and fall note neotropical migratory passerines that visit the park.

Purtis Creek State Park
14225 FM 316
Eustace, TX 75124
(903) 425-2332
www.tpwd.state.tx.us/spdest/findadest/parks/purtis_creek/

Cedar Creek Islands WMA is just to the west. Travel FM 316 south, turn west at Co. Rd. 2938, go northwest at Hwy. 175, and drive 6.8 miles (11 km) to a left turn at Old Hwy. 40 Rd. The road ends in a marshy area adjacent to the wildlife management area offshore about 0.5 mile (0.8 km).

Refuge visitation is restricted to protect the rookeries; view egrets, herons, and cormorants from the shore or by boat. Small-boat rentals are available locally.

Cedar Creek Islands WMA
1670 FM 488
Streetman, TX 75859
(903) 389-7080
www.tpwd.state.tx.us/hunt wild/hunt/wma

Also consider a visit to Lake Bardwell and Lake Whitney, just a short distance west.

❿ Fort Worth Area

Drive 41 miles (66 km) via Hwy. 175 to I-20, turn west, and drive 50 miles (80 km) to Fort Worth. Exit at 429B and take Winscott Rd. south to **Benbrook Lake,** ringed by six county parks. Best for birding are Memorial Oak Park, Holiday Park, and Rocky Creek Park. Look for migrant birds in spring and fall, raptors and owls in winter, and waterbirds on the lake itself.

U.S. Army Corps of Engineers
Benbrook Project Office
P.O. Box 26619
Fort Worth, TX 76126
(817) 292-2400
www.swf-wc.usace.army.mil/benbrook/main.htm

With this introduction to Fort Worth birding, explore these other top birding sites:

- **Markum Ranch Ponds,** west from I-820 to I-20, exit Markum Ranch Rd. south, go east on Aledo Rd.; ranch ponds attract mute swans, shorebirds, and other waterfowl. Also look for owls in the open fields.

- **Fort Worth Nature Center and Refuge,** north from I-820 for 2 miles (3.2 km) on Hwy. 199; 3,412 acres (1,381-h) with 20 miles (32 km) of trails in varied habitat. Black-chinned and ruby-throated hummingbirds, wild turkeys, yellow-throated and prothonotary warblers, plus many other migrant songbirds. Also visit **Wildwood Park** on Silver Creek Rd. on the west shore of the lake. www.fwnaturecenter.org

- **Eagle Mountain Lake Fish Hatchery,** west from I-820 on Azle Ave., north on FM 1220, west on Ten Mile Bridge Rd. to Eagle Mountain Cir.; see hawks, falcons, and eagles from the hills and shorebirds such as tricolored herons, roseate spoonbills, and white ibis by the reservoir.

Call (817) 237-8585 for access to the locked gate. www.tpwd.state.tx.us/fishboat/fish/recreational/lakes/eagle_mountain/

- **Cement Creek Reservoir,** south from I-820 on Hwy. 287 for 0.3 mile (0.5 km), turn west at the airfield fence; reed-and-cattail-filled lake with least bitterns, rails, least terns, sparrows, and longspurs, as well as many waterfowl species.

- **Fort Worth Botanic Gardens,** University Dr. and I-30; trees near the zoo fill with neotropical migrants in April to May and October. www.fwbg.org

Also visit the Fort Worth Audubon Society website for information about recent sightings, upcoming guided field trips, and current local hot spots: www.fwas.org

Visit these sites along the way...

⓫ Lake Bardwell
4000 Observation Dr.
Ennis, TX 75119
www.swf-wc.usace.army.mil/bardwell/

Three types of wetlands are found in the Buffalo Creek Wetlands of Lake Bardwell: flooded fields, sloughs, and bottomland marshes. Multiple trails enter each habitat. See great egrets, killdeer, dowitchers, herons, and numerous ducks, geese, and mergansers. Sky sightings include bald eagles and hawks.

⓬ Lake Whitney SP
P.O. Box 1175
Whitney, TX 76692
(254) 694-3793
www.tpwd.state.tx.us/

This park on the east lakeshore has trails and a bird observation blind for viewing waterbirds and shorebirds on the reservoir. This is a fly-in park; also bird the runway areas for songbirds, hawks, peregrine falcons, and occasional bald eagles. Open 8 A.M. to 10 P.M. daily. Admission fee is charged.

A northern cardinal's plumage is brightest after it molts in the fall.

Houston, Corpus Christi, and Brownsville

Allow a week or longer to travel the 400-mile-long (644-km-long) Texas gulf coast, from Galveston Bay to the Rio Grande, and enjoy some of the most exciting bird-watching in North America. This crescent of shore is the meeting ground for migratory birds of both the equatorial region and the Arctic. Acting almost like a natural funnel, the Texas coast collects birds crossing the Gulf of Mexico and those flying along the Central American coast, their numbers reaching several million in April and May, with 623 recorded species. They meet wintering birds that nest during summer in the far-northern reaches of Canada and Alaska, mingling and creating a paradise for birders.

Take a drive to the wild side of Texas, join the other 6.8 million area bird-watchers, and enjoy the spring, fall, and winter spectacle of both subtropical and temperate-climate birds teeming along the coastal bend from Galveston to Brownsville.

Chenier Plain NWR Complex, east of Galveston, comprises four refuges that feed, nurture, and house many flocks of birds, some that number 100,000 or more. Included are many subtropical species, such as these roseate spoonbills.

Reddish egrets are rare coastal visitors from south of the border. See them in wetlands from south of Corpus Christi to Brownsville.

❶ Galveston Bay

Begin the birding route with a circle tour of Galveston Bay and its Texas Chenier Plain NWR Complex—**Moody NWR, Anahuac NWR, McFaddin NWR,** and **Texas Point NWR**—which stretches on the bay's east side from the Bolivar Peninsula to Sabine Lake at Port Arthur.

These are legendary birding grounds with reputations known around the world, and the tour samples their very best. Start in Houston, drive I-10 east to exit 812 (Hwy. 61), and turn south 3.8 miles (6.1 km). Note that the road changes to Hwy. 562. Continue 8.5 miles (13.7 km) to FM 1985, a left fork; Anahuac NWR is 4 miles (6.4 km) beyond. Follow the signs to the refuge visitors information station.

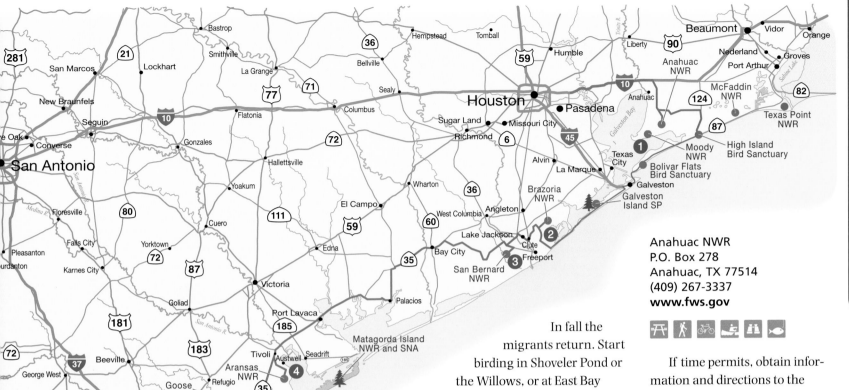

Anahuac NWR
P.O. Box 278
Anahuac, TX 77514
(409) 267-3337
www.fws.gov

Open daily; visitors station open 8 a.m. to 4 p.m. daily in April, otherwise only on weekends. Anahuac is an ancient Aztec word meaning watery plain. Bayous on the 34,000-acre (13,759-h) refuge cut in ancient river floodplains, creating wetland marshes filled with wildlife and birds.

In spring migrant warblers, orioles, tanagers, and songbirds fill the refuge, joined by over 27 species of ducks, geese, swans, other waterfowl, and myriad shorebirds.

Throughout summer see roseate spoonbills, great egrets, white-faced ibis, and yellow rails on the ponds and marshes.

In fall the migrants return. Start birding in Shoveler Pond or the Willows, or at East Bay bayou (with a canoe trail).

The auto tour at Shoveler Pond yields good views of purple gallinules, American bitterns, and marsh wrens, and there is a 750-foot (229-m) boardwalk. Stay alert; American alligators are also present here.

After strong north winds in spring, the Willows may experience a "fallout," a phenomenon in which migrant songbirds crossing the gulf from Central America to the refuge become exhausted and collect in large numbers—15 or more species have been sighted perched in a single tree at the Willows at such times.

From the East Bay Bayou overlook and trail, located 7 miles (11.3 km) east of the main refuge, see seemingly countless waterfowl, hummingbirds, and perching songbirds.

If time permits, obtain information and directions to the other refuges in the complex. Otherwise, return to FM 1985, turn east, follow it to Hwy. 124, then turn south for 7 miles (11.3 km) to reach **High Island Bird Sanctuary.** Open dawn to sunset daily March 15 to May 15; call for other times.

Houston Audubon Society maintains four sanctuaries here: S. E. Gast Red Bay, Eubanks Woods, Boy Scout Woods, and Smith Oaks, which also contains Clay Bottom Pond rookery, a neotropic cormorant, little blue and tricolored heron, roseate spoonbill, snowy and cattle egret, and white ibis nesting site.

Next, drive south from High Island to Hwy. 87, turn west, and drive about 25 miles (40 km) to a left turn at Retillon Rd. and **Bolivar Flats Bird Sanctuary,** another Houston Audubon facility and both an IBA and a recognized Audubon top 100 birding site.

Nearly 150,000 birds of 37 shorebird species feed and roost on this beach and nearby mudflats, including gulls, rails, terns, killdeers, snipes, plovers, ibis, egrets, and sandpipers. Also seen are endangered brown pelicans and peregrine falcons. Marshes have willets, Wilson's and black-bellied plovers, and sanderlings.

Houston Audubon Society
440 Wilchester Blvd.
Houston, TX 77079
(713) 932-1639
www.houstonaudubon.org

Next, drive Hwy. 87 west and cross Galveston Bay on the Bolivar ferry (free). Take note of the brown pelicans and magnificent frigatebirds en route.

Take Ferry Rd. south a few blocks to Seawall Blvd. and turn southwest. Drive just over 5 miles (8 km) beyond Galveston on FM 3005 to 2,013-acre (815-h) **Galveston Island SP,** another top 100 birding site. Open daily except in late-summer hurricane periods. Admission fee is charged.

A checklist item here is the reddish egret, Galveston's official city bird, which nests only in Texas, Louisiana, and Florida.

These striking birds may be hard to spot among the more than 500 other species that reside at, winter in, or migrate through the park.

The park has beach, bayou, and dune trails with observation platforms, plus a visitors center where there are bird checklists and staff to advise on recent bird sightings and hot spots.

Galveston Island SP
14901 – FM 3005
Galveston, TX 77554
(409) 737-1222
**www.tpwd.state.tx.us/spdest/
findadest/parks/galveston**

❷ Brazoria NWR

Continue southwest 10 miles (16 km) on FM 3005, cross the toll bridge from Galveston Island to Follets Island, note the road number change to FM 257, and drive 11 miles (18 km) more before turning inland on Hwy. 332. En route across Drum Bay from Follets Island is **Brazoria NWR,** the next stop.

Chenier Plain NWR Complex has outstanding bird-watching facilities, such as blinds (top), full-access paths and trails in many areas (above), and piers and boardwalks (left). Use them to observe unusual bird species seen only in coastal Texas and other Gulf of Mexico states.

Follow Hwy. 322 northwest 3 miles (4.8 km) to a right turn on FM 523, drive 4.5 miles (7.2 km) north, turn right on Hoskins Mound Rd. (Co. Rd. 227), and drive 1.7 miles (2.7 km) to the refuge boundary. The refuge office is 3 miles (4.8 km) farther. It is, with **San Bernard NWR** and Big Boggy NWR, part of the Texas Midcoast NWR Complex.

The season to visit this place of freshwater sloughs traversing saltwater marshes is winter, as more than 100,000 waterfowl—Canada and snow geese and dabbling and diving ducks—plus sandhill cranes, herons, egrets, and over 200 species of shorebirds and songbirds make the refuge their home.

In summer see nesting birds, including clapper rails, horned larks, black skimmers, mottled ducks, white-tailed kites, and scissor-tailed flycatchers.

The 7.5-mile (12-km) Big Slough auto-tour route travels to the heart of the refuge, passes Olney, Teal, and Rogers ponds, and winds along Big Slough, making it a good place to sample the refuge. Early mornings and evenings are the best time to visit, when geese and ducks rise and settle on Teal Pond. A full-access observation deck with viewing scopes and interpretive panels make Teal Pond a good first stop. A boardwalk at Big Slough is an ideal spot to photograph birds in the marshes. Five other trails provide more birding opportunities. Always exer-

cise caution, however; alligators are present in large numbers.

Brazoria NWR
1212 N. Velasco Rd., Ste. 200
Angelton, TX 77515
(979) 849-7771
www.fws.gov

❸ San Bernard NWR

Return to FM 523, turn north, then turn southwest on Clute–Stratton Ridge Rd. and drive about 5 miles (8 km) to Clute. Pass through town on Main St. to Hwy. 332 and turn northwest again for about 4 miles (6.4 km). Turn left on FM 2004, drive 7 miles (11.3 km), and note as the road number changes to FM 2611. Turn south on FM 2918 for 1 mile (1.6 km), then turn west on Co. Rd. 306, which leads to San Bernard NWR. Open dawn to sunset daily.

Take Cocklebur Slough and Moccasin Pond auto tours for a total of 6 miles (10 km) of easy birding. Bobcat Woods Trail and boardwalk gives full access to a forest area, while Scissor-tail Trail passes through the scrub brush habitat favored by perching birds and songbirds. Cowtrap Trail crosses a wetland on a levee.

Look for clapper and king rails and listen intently for their seldom-seen cousins, black rails. Trees in the refuge shelter barred owls. In spring when prairie wildflowers bloom, look for hummingbirds, orioles, and other

The visitors information station and pond at Anahuac NWR. The refuge's easy access from Houston and Galveston makes it popular for weekend outings.

nectar-loving birds. In wetland areas see ibis, herons, and egrets near the shore as rafts of snow geese feed in deeper marsh.

The refuge also has several boat-launching ramps for kayaking and canoeing its waterways.

San Bernard NWR
1212 N. Velasco Rd., Ste. 200
Angelton, TX 77515
(979) 849-7771
www.fws.gov

❹ Aransas NWR and Goose Island SP

Return to FM 2611, turn left, drive about 8 miles (13 km) to FM 457, turn right, and drive northwest about 18 miles to Bay City and Hwy. 35.

Follow Hwy. 35 southwest for 90 miles (145 km), making

stops at promising birding sites; this bountiful area is filled with avian life. Offshore from Port Lavaca, remote **Matagorda Island NWR** and Texas State Natural Area, for example, is a great barrier birding island accessible only by boat. No motorized vehicles are allowed. It is primitive, with no services, managed jointly by Texas and the U.S. Fish and Wildlife Service.

The next waypoint is 59,000-acre (23,877-h) **Aransas NWR.** Drive Hwy. 35 to 1 mile (1.6 km) south of Tivoli and FM 239, turn left, drive to Austwell Bypass Rd., turn right, and then left on Cemetery Rd. (FM 2040).

The refuge is straight ahead about 6 miles (9.7 km) on the right. Register at the visitors center. Open 8:30 A.M. to 4:30 P.M. daily except major holidays. Admission fee is charged.

High Island Bird Sanctuary roseate spoonbill rookery, a group nesting site for the spoonbills and other birds, offers once-in-a-lifetime experiences of seeing courtship behaviors.

fall migration are Jones and Hogs lakes.

For pulse-pounding excitement, however, visit the refuge mid-October through March, when strident unmistakable whoops and clarion bugles echo over the marsh: the calls of wintering whooping cranes.

Of exquisite rarity, yet still nearly the best known of all endangered birds, these cranes fly from their summer grounds in Wood Buffalo NP in Canada's Northwest Territory to Aransas NWR in Texas each year. They are huge, distinctly marked, and stand 5 feet (152 cm) tall, with wingspans of 7 feet (213 cm). In the refuge upward of 200 birds share companionship with sandhill cranes. Pairs and families are usually seen near the observation tower.

But whooping cranes are not the only attraction. Look for hawks, pelicans, herons, roseate spoonbills, reddish egrets, and a host of other waterfowl and shorebirds. In total, 390 different bird species have been counted among the avian visitors to Aransas NWR.

**Aransas NWR
P.O. Box 100
Austwell, TX 77950
(361) 286-3559
www.fws.gov/southwest/
refuges/texas/aransas**

The refuge features a 16-mile (26-km) auto tour over gravel roads, seven walking trails in a variety of habitats, three bird-viewing decks, an observation tower, photography blinds, a boardwalk, and an American alligator viewing area. Favorite viewing sites during spring and

Retrace the outbound path back to Hwy. 35, turn south, drive 22 miles (35 km), and turn left on Main St. (PR 13) in Lamar just before the Copano Bay Bridge. The entrance to **Goose Island SP** is 2 miles (3.2 km) east. Open daily year-round. Admission fee is charged.

The park consists of a bluff overlooking the Gulf of Mexico and an island connected to the mainland by a bridge and road. The shoreline around the island has mudflats and marshes that attract wading birds, and offshore seabirds raft in the open water within easy view.

Even better bird-watching occurs on the fishing pier that extends east from the island to approach a sandy bar and shallows a short distance away.

❺ Mustang Island and Padre Island National Seashore

Stretching not far to the south is the urban area of Corpus Christi. Before visiting the city and its bay, drive south on Hwy. 35 to Aransas Pass, a seaside town that is gateway to the offshore barrier island domain of **Mustang Island and Padre Island National Seashore** and **North Padre Island.**

Start birding in Aransas Pass at Newberry Park, home to Texas's largest hummingbird garden; ruby-throated, black-chinned, buff-bellied, and rufous are likely sightings in winter. Next, look for seabirds at the Intercoastal Channel and at the nearby ship harbor.

Kayaks available for hire on the waterfront increase the odds of seeing waterfowl and seabirds at close distances. Paddle over to Lighthouse Lakes Park, a fleet of small islands permanently moored in the channel between Mustang Island and the mainland. The black mangroves at this park host birds rarely seen in other areas, and their branches sometimes hold magnificent frigatebirds.

When finished, take the free ferry across the channel to Port Aransas and Mustang Island.

Aransas Pass Chamber of Commerce
130 W. Goodnight Ave.
Aransas Pass, TX 78336
(361) 758-2750
www.aransaspass.org

Of the country's 800 species of birds, nearly 500 have been recorded in the Coastal Bend region centered at Port Aransas. All times of the year are good for birding here: 100 species nest in the area during summer; fall brings kettles of hawks and flocks of hummingbirds; winter lures cranes, egrets, and herons to the shore; and flights of neotropical migrant songbirds peak in spring.

Visit four key areas in Port Aransas of interest to birders:

- **Lynn Gavit Memorial Bird Habitat,** at Port Aransas Civic Center; 15 bird species exhibited in a natural habitat.
- **Leonabell Turnbull Birding Center,** south end of Ross Avenue; boardwalk, observation tower, and butterfly and native plant gardens. (Also see the resident alligators, Boots and Bags.)
- **Port Aransas Wetland Park,** just west of Hwy. 361; a full-access tidal flat with boardwalk and an observation deck. See wading birds and shorebirds.
- **Scott and Joan Holt Paradise Pond Birding Habitat,** Cut Off Rd.; a willow-ringed freshwater pond noted for its warblers and other passing migrants, with boardwalks, observation decks, and a butterfly garden.

City of Port Aransas
710 W. Ave. A
Port Aransas, TX 78373
(361) 749-4111
www.cityofportaransas.org

Black-necked stilts frequent the coastal waterways, bayous, and beaches of coastal Texas.

171

Drive south on Hwy. 361 for 14 miles (23 km) to **Mustang Island SP.** Open daily except in hurricane watches in late summer. Admission fee is charged.

Like Matagorda, Mustang Island is a barrier island with constantly shifting sand dunes. Dunes with vegetation sometimes reach 35 feet (10.6 m) in height, and they provide shelter and habitats for birds.

Hawks often hunt the dunes for mice, pocket gophers, and ground squirrels. Calm waters of Corpus Christi Bay provide fish to peregrine falcons, gulls, and other birds, while waterfowl work its shallows for vegeta-tion, mollusks, and crusta-ceans. The gulf waters hold an estimated 600 fish species, and birds feed at the surf and shore.

Watch for Wilson's, piping, and snowy plovers; red knots; terns; and glaucous gulls; lesser black-backed gulls are sometimes seen in winter. On grassy dunes see sedge wrens, horned larks, and Le Conte's sparrows.

Mustang Island SP
P.O. Box 326
Port Aransas, TX 78373
(361) 749-5246
**www.tpwd.state.tx.us/spdest/
findadest/parks/mustang_island/**

Laguna Atascosa NWR hosts flocks of great-tailed grackles.

Continue south on Hwy. 361, cross over Corpus Christi Pass onto Padre Island, join PR 22, and drive south 10 miles (16 km) to 130,434-acre **Padre Island National Seashore.** Open daily; visitors center open 8:30 A.M. to 6 P.M. summers, 8:30 A.M. to 4:30 P.M. winters except major holidays. Admission fee is charged.

Over 350 bird species have been noted at the seashore; the number seen includes rare and accidental birds blown off course during tropical storms. At least nine threatened or endangered birds are found at Padre Island: peregrine falcons, brown pelicans, reddish egrets, white-tailed hawks, least terns, ospreys, and Wilson's, piping, and snowy plovers. It also has the usual assortment of migratory songbirds and waterfowl seen elsewhere along the Texas coast.

With so many avian riches, make the first stop the visitors center to receive a bird checklist and hear of recent hot spots. The paved park road continues for 5 miles (8 km) before becoming a four-wheel-drive-only sandy trace. Bird from automobiles on the paved section of Bird Basin Rd., 2.6 miles (4.2 km) north of the visitors center.

Pay special attention to the wide variety of raptors found in Padre Island's open country, including white-tailed kites; ferruginous, Harris's, and white-tailed hawks; northern harriers; and American kestrels.

Songbirding Tip
Small perching songbirds are often hard to spot in scrub brush and on tree branches. Bird-watch with ears as well as eyes. Listen closely to identify the direction of the sound and learn the calls of birds to help identify and locate them for viewing.

Among all of the shorebirds, waterfowl, and cranes, remember to look for Padre's grassland birds: northern bobwhites, eastern meadowlarks, Sprague's pipits, loggerhead shrikes, killdeer, horned larks, and kingfishers, as well as songbirds.

Padre Island National Seashore
P.O. Box 181300
Corpus Christi, TX 78480
(361) 949-8068
www.nps.gov/pais

❻ Corpus Christi Area

Drive back north to Hwy. 358, turn west, and cross the JFK Cswy. to Corpus Christi. This compact city on its bay has three sites to bird before continuing south to the Brownsville area:

- **Held/Moran Nature Preserve,** Hwy. 358 to Waldron Dr., south to Caribbean Dr., east to Jamaica Dr., park on Mediterranean; 90 acres (36 h) of coastal oaks and ponds good for seeing migrant perching birds in spring and fall, waterfowl in winter.

- **Fred Jones Nature Sanctuary,** I-37 to Hwy. 35 north to Moore Ave. (Hwy. 893) exit, east 6.5 miles (10.5 km) to Koonce Loop Rd.; open fields attract warblers, vireos, and other migrants in spring.

- **Hazel Bazemore County Park,** I-37 east to Hwy. 77 south, exit Northwest Blvd., west to Hazel Bazemore Pkwy. Over a million hawks transit this park in fall, and it's routine to see kettles of over 10,000 birds, such as Mississippi kites, Swainson's and broad-winged hawks, and other raptors. Also see anhingas, wood storks, and other aquatic and wading birds and waterfowl.

Coastal Bend Audubon Society
P.O. Box 3604
Corpus Christi, TX 78463
(361) 885-6203
www.corpuschristi-tx-cvb.org

❼ Kingsville Area

Return to the I-35/Hwy. 77 intersection. The historic **King Ranch** is 29 miles (46 km) south off Hwy. 77; exit at King Ave. (Hwy. 141), turning west. In 3.5 miles (5.6 km) note the entrance on the left to the Santa Gertrudis division of King Ranch. Guided birding and nature tours are offered by advance reservation

only. A tour fee is charged. The cattle ranch, near the Mexican border and larger than Rhode Island, embraces bird-friendly ecology principles and visitation. Its Running W brand, which looks like a sidewinder rattlesnake, is a trademark recognized around the world.

The ranch has many birds seldom seen farther north. It's a place to spot rare ferruginous pygmy-owls, northern parulas— even such oddities as northern beardless-tyrannulets, aplomado falcons, and Botteri's sparrows.

King Ranch Visitors Center
P.O. Box 1090
Kingsville, TX 78364
(361) 592-8055
www.king-ranch.com

While in Kingsville, also visit **Dick Kleberg Park** and **Santa Gertrudis Creek Bird Sanctuary.** Kleberg Park is at the south end of town on Hwy. Bus. 77 at Escondido Rd. Walk its trails in winter to see vermilion flycatchers and lark sparrows, or visit in summer to see cave swallow nesting. Also common are great kiskadees and curve-billed thrashers.

To reach Santa Gertrudis Creek, turn east on Escondido Rd., turn left on Brahma Blvd. (S. 14th St.), then right on FM 1717. Park in the turnout just west of Santa Gertrudis Creek Bridge and walk the dike along the creek overlooking the ponds.

Nearly 130 species of birds reside at the sanctuary's cattail marsh, including Lincoln's and swamp sparrows, sedge wrens, green jays, black-crowned and yellow-crowned night-herons, green-backed and tricolored herons, thrashers, great kiskadees, and cave swallows.

Kingsville Convention and Visitors Bureau
501 Hwy. 77
Kingsville, TX 78363
(800) 333-5032
www.kingsvilletexas.com

❽ Sarita Area

Return to Hwy. 77, turn south, and drive 14 miles (22.5 km) nearly to Riviera, the home of **Louise Trant Bird Sanctuary.** Operated by the Audubon Outdoor Club of Corpus Christi, it is located 0.1 mile (0.2 km) north of town on the east side of the highway and has a 2-acre (0.8-h) site with a cattail marsh and an occasional pond.

The tiny habitat is known locally as the spot to see sora, yellow-headed blackbirds, neotropic cormorants, egrets, and herons. It has also logged some true rarities; among them are masked ducks, red-billed pigeons, and neotropical birds at the northern end of their ranges.

Continue on Hwy. 77 to **Las Olmas Creek,** which crosses under the highway 1.3 miles (2.1 km) south of Riviera.

Join In

The Great Texas Birding Classic

Held annually in April

A weeklong celebration during peak migration

- **Tournaments:** Participate in all-adult, roughwings, outta-site songbirder, or big-sit bird counts.

- **Gulf Coast Bird Observatory Staff:** Ask questions and puzzle over birds with expert ornithologists.

- **Conservation Project Prizes and Awards:** Learn about prizewinning ecological and conservation projects that span the entire Texas Gulf Coast.

- **Exhibits and Demonstrations:** See birds, birding merchandise, techniques, and displays.

Find out more at www.gcbo.org/gtbc.html

Note that the countryside has changed. This creek marks the boundary of the coastal grasslands dotted with a few oak clusters. South of the creek, birds appear that are considered rarities everywhere except along the Rio Grande River and south into Mexico.

See Harris's and white-tailed hawks mingling near crested caracaras. The best times to visit are during migration and

The painted bunting's song is melodious and nearly as beautiful as the male's colorful plumage

in winter. Besides waterfowl and wading birds in large numbers, see least grebes, green jays, vermilion flycatchers, painted buntings, soras, and anhingas.

South 3 miles (4.8 km) on Hwy. 77 are **Sarita** and **Kenedy Ranch,** which sprawls all the way to Harlingen. Sarita has seasonal wetlands; a boardwalk and picnic area are planned for use by birders.

During migration these brush-cloaked ephemeral ponds fill with painted buntings, kingbirds, and many other species of colorful songbirds.

Make a short stop at **Sarita Rest Area** 6 miles (9.7 km) farther south, especially in late spring. It is a frequent nesting spot for tropical parulas. Also to be seen are scissor-tailed and brown-crested flycatchers, hooded orioles, and Couch's kingbirds. A sharp eye might even spot a buff-bellied hummingbird on its nest; look in the foliage of the wild olive trees.

Kingsville Convention and Visitors Bureau
501 Hwy. 77
Kingsville, TX 78363
(800) 333-5032
www.kingsvilletexas.com

❾ Santa Monica Wetlands

Drive about 40 miles (64 km) south through spacious country —in the 2000 census Kenedy County had just 414 souls. In years with scant rainfall, this poorly drained wetland bakes dry, but in wet periods it fills with all manner of shorebirds and waterfowl, from wood storks and roseate spoonbills to white-faced ibis, warblers, and vireos.

At Raymondville turn east on Red Fish Bay Rd. (Hwy. 186). Just past the San Perlita turnoff, turn south on FM 1420, stopping en route at willow-shrouded ponds and intersecting Levee Rd. (FM 101). Turn east and drive 1 mile (1.6 km) to the **Santa Monica Wetlands.**

Before turning attention to the marsh, scan the sky for raptors and look at birds perched on fenceposts in the grasslands; released aplomado falcons from nearby Laguna Atacosa NWR visit these open fields. Look for their distinctive dark fan tail, red belly, and white chin and breast as they soar overhead.

The full import of birding so far south should now be apparent in the birds to be seen: little blue, green, and tricolored herons, crested caracaras, kingbirds,

Vermilion flycatchers perch, waiting for their meal of flying insects.

reddish egrets, neotropic and double-crested cormorants, parulas, and purple gallinules. Astoundingly, bird-watching continues to improve to the south.

Port Mansfield Chamber of Commerce
P.O. Box 75
Port Mansfield, TX 78598
(956) 944-2354
www.port-mansfield.com/ chamber.htm

❿ Laguna Atascosa NWR

Drive south about 10 miles (16 km) on FM 1420 to FM 50, continue south of Rio Honda, and turn left on Colorado Ave., which becomes General Grant Rd. Proceed 14 miles (22.5 km) to a T intersection, turn left, and drive 3 miles (4.8 km) to

Santa Ana NWR on the lower Rio Grande River is home to the bright-colored altamira orioles that claim a small tip of southeastern Texas in their range.

the visitors center at **Laguna Atascosa NWR.** Open dawn to dusk daily; center open 10 A.M. to 4 P.M. daily October to April, 10 A.M. to 4 P.M. weekends in May; closed otherwise. Admission fee is charged.

Graded 15-mile (24-km) Bayside Drive loop auto trail passes through thorn trees, scrub brush, and prairie, then on to Laguna Madre. There are blinds, observation points, and turnouts along the way. Another, shorter auto tour, Lakeside Drive, goes to Atascosa Lake; en route, Osprey Overlook has two fixed spotting scopes for viewing.

Six trails, ranging from very short walks to a 3-mile (4.8-km) hike, are in various locations near the visitors center. Cameron County maintains a boat ramp, campground, and fishing piers at Arroyo Colorado.

Mild winters make the site a wintering ground for migratory waterfowl, cranes, and egrets. They cross paths with southern species at the northernmost extent of their ranges. The result is a setting where nearly 400 bird species have been recorded.

Look for aplomado falcons that are being reintroduced to their native range. Also stay alert when a large blackbird appears; it could be a groove-billed ani. Likely sightings include white-tipped doves, summer tanagers, great kiskadees, olive sparrows, and plain chachalacas, plus sandhill cranes, American golden-plovers, and upland sandpipers.

Laguna Atascosa NWR
P.O. Box 450
Rio Hondo, TX 78583
(956) 748-3607
www.fws.gov

⓫ Brownsville Area

Return inland on General Grant Rd. to Olmito North Rd. (FM 803) and turn south for 3.3 miles (5.3 km). Pause at Stevens, Cross, and two Sweeny lakes for a look at birdlife in their shallows before continuing south 10 miles (16.4 km) to Hwy. 77. Turn southeast and drive 11.5 miles (18.5 km) to **Brownsville.**

International in flavor with regard to more than its culture and food, Brownsville is birding country, with over 500 recorded bird species. By coincidence it is also butterfly country, with over 300 different kinds of the colorful insects drawn to 800 flowering trees and flowers that thrive here.

Each April to May the town swells with bird-watchers. For two months birds are on everyone's mind. After a quiet summer the spectacle repeats in fall and winter, when binoculars and field guides again become fashion accessories downtown. It all culminates in February, with the Brownsville International Birding Festival, a two-day-long blowout worth a year's planning to attend.

Visit these birding hot spots in Brownsville:

- **Texas Coastal Fisheries Field Station,** Hwy. 77 and Stillman Rd.; 20 ponds with whistling ducks, anhingas, bitterns, green kingfishers, and Couch's kingbirds.
- **Resaca de la Palma SP,** Military Rd. (Hwy. 281) west to Carmen Ave. north; 1,700 semitropical acres (688 h) and a World Birding Center site. Renowned as a place for neotropical and nearctic migrants to meet.

Brownsville Convention and Visitors Bureau
650 Ruben M. Torress Blvd.
Brownsville, TX 78520
(800) 626-2639
www.brownsville.org

⓬ South Padre Island

Just offshore of the mouth of the Rio Grande River and stretching north over 100 miles (161 km) is **South Padre Island.** This coastal barrier island shelters from the gulf's waves the equally long and narrow lagoon, Laguna Madre.

The strip of ever-shifting dunes and beach vegetation also harbors, houses, and feeds over 300 bird species, ranging from subtropical seabirds to tiny hummingbirds.

Fowl-in-Focus

SEMIPALMATED PLOVER
Charadrius semipalamatus

Length: 7.25″–19″ (18.4–48.3 cm)

What to Look for: darker than other plovers; orange bill with black tip; bill dark on non-breeding bird; legs orange to yellow; female slightly larger.

Habitat: shores and tide flats. Summers in the Arctic and winters in coastal North America into South America. Forages alone but roosts and flies in flocks. One of the few plovers whose numbers are increasing due in part to its expanded habitat and food selections. Surprisingly, the semipalmated plover does occasionally swim short distances during foraging while migrating. Even the chicks will swim to reach islets.

Drive east 23 miles (37 km) from Brownsville to Port Isabel on Hwy. 48, cross the Queen Isabella Cswy. (PR 100) to the island, and turn south on Padre Blvd., which leads to **Isla Blanca Park.** Open daily. Admission fee is charged.

In spring trees just outside the park entrance fill with neotropical migrants, such as warblers, orioles, tanagers, and buntings. The jetty and surrounding warm gulf waters are good places to see such oceanic wanderers as northern gannets, bridled terns, Cory's shearwaters, and magnificent frigatebirds. Also scan the shoreline for wading birds.

Make a second stop 5 miles (8 km) north at Padre Blvd. and Orca Circle, where the World Birding Center's 1,500-foot (457-m) Nature Trail Boardwalk, which features over 4 acres (1.6 h) of wetland marsh, faces **Andy Bowie Park,** another birding hot spot.

Water-treatment effluent is the secret to this location; the cattails and bulrushes transition from freshwater to cordgrass in the brackish shallows. View shorebirds such as rails, herons, egrets, roseate spoonbills, sandhill cranes, and snowy and piping plovers.

South Padre Island Chamber
of Commerce
600 Padre Blvd.
South Padre Island, TX 78597
(956) 761-4412
www.spichamber.com

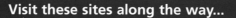

Visit these sites along the way...

⓭ The Lower Rio Grande Valley

Extend a visit to the Brownsville area by exploring the Rio Grande border area.

Mouth of the Rio Grande

The principal reason many birdwatchers visit the tip of south Texas is to see the remarkable lower valley of the Rio Grande, a place filled with birds both uncommon in the north and exciting to view because they are so plentiful.

Start the trip by driving from Hwy. 77 in Brownsville east 1.5 miles (2.4 km) on Boca Chica Blvd., where it becomes Hwy. 4; proceed east 15 miles (24 km) to an information kiosk for **Boca Chica Beach.**

This beach, simultaneously a state park, the largest unit of **Lower Rio Grande NWR** and a WMA, is open only to foot traffic dawn to dusk daily. See aplomado and peregrine falcons and merlins during migration; other sightings include red knots, horned larks, Tamaulipas crows, Chihuahuan ravens, and various other shorebirds. Also look for seabirds, including rare brown boobies and piping plovers.

Sabal Palm Grove

Return to International Blvd. in Brownsville, turn east, drive 0.8 mile (1.3 km), and turn right on Southmost Rd. Drive 6 miles (9.7 km) to **Sable Palm Audubon Center**. Open 7 A.M. to 5 P.M. daily except holidays; visitors center open 9 A.M. to 5 P.M. daily. Admission fee is charged.

The 527-acre (213-h) sanctuary preserves riparian sabal palm grove habitat unique to the Rio Grande. See green jays, olive sparrows, buff-bellied and other hummingbirds, and plain chachalacas along the sanctuary trails, along with green kingfishers, altamira orioles, and black-bellied whistling ducks. Rare animals, including jaguarundi, are also present.

Los Ebanos Preserve

Return to Hwy. 77, drive north 16 miles (26 km) to Hwy. 100, and turn right. The 82-acre (33-h) **Los Ebanos Preserve** is a bit farther, on the left. Open daily October to May and by appointment. Fee.

The ebony thorn trees and river habitat hosts hooded orioles, great kiskadees, green jays, and northern beardless-tyrannulets, as well as golden-fronted woodpeckers and several hummingbird species.

Up the Rio Grande

Travel upriver to see these other well-known birding hot spots:

• **Las Palomas WMA,** Hwy. 281 to FM 1479, go north 2.7 miles (4.3 km), turn on unmarked gravel road; woodlands with an observation platform for viewing an oxbow rasaca lake with least grebes, Couch's kingbirds, and other waterfowl, waterbirds, and shorebirds. On nearby FM 675, also visit Vieh's Bed and Breakfast in a 15-acre (6-h) palm forest bordering a lake.

• **Estero Llano Grande,** Hwy. 281 west 12.5 miles (20.1 km) to Progresso, north 2 miles (3.2 km); day use only, shorebirds and waterfowl on a World Birding Organization site.

• **Welasco,** Hwy. 281 west 2.2 miles (3.5 km) to FM 88, north 5 miles (8 km) to Welasco; Welasco Wetlands, Fontera Audubon Park, and Valley Nature Center. See red-crowned parrots, green parakeets, plain chachalacas, neotropical migrants, hummingbirds, and unusual butterflies.

• **Santa Ana NWR,** Hwy. 281 west to Military Hwy.; 2,088-acre (845-h) refuge with walking trails and an auto route through thorn forest habitat with 400 species of birds.

Green jays are an exciting sight to those only familiar with Steller's and blue jays. They're among the unusual birds to be seen in the Rio Grande Valley.

New Orleans and Lower Mississippi River

A recovered coast and untouched inland regions await bird-watchers who visit the wetlands of Louisiana's southern coast and the Atchafalaya Basin, traveling through the Acadian countryside from historic New Orleans to the heart of Cajun country.

Fall and spring are the best seasons to travel into the heart of Louisiana's birding country. Avian travelers arrive from the North, bid adieu to their migratory companions destined for Central America and points farther south, and settle in for the winter. Waterways fill with rafts of birds—American white and brown pelicans, ducks, geese, mergansers, cormorants, and others—and the shoreline becomes packed with tall and small waders. Then, in spring, the migrant songbirds reappear. They drop in flocks from the sky, exhausted from their flights across the Gulf of Mexico. Trees fill with perching birds, waves of waterfowl begin to lift off, and the great northern migration leaves for the nesting grounds.

Wood storks, though rare, nest high in cypress trees.

Cajun Coast bald cypresses mingle with tupelo gums in the swamps of south-central Louisiana. These humid wetlands are divided by ridges of mixed hardwood forest, creating habitats that support hundreds of resident and transient birds.

❶ New Orleans Area

New Orleans sits in a bowl surrounded by now infamous levees guarding against the waters of the Mississippi River, Lake Pontchartrain, and the Gulf, barriers that in some places tower two stories over-head. Like its residences, the metropolitan area's parks, preserves, and sanctuaries suffered in 2005 from hurricanes—in part from wind but mainly from saltwater intrusion into freshwater bayous and marshes. Still, nature weaves its magic; the land drains, falling rain dilutes salt, limbs regrow, and across the area, habitats recover. With effort structures and facilities will also be rebuilt.

At time of publication, the impact of these storms was fresh, and bird-watching spots visited in the past required renewed evaluations before they could be recommended as destinations to visit.

Here, then, are places in the city and its suburbs that birding experts on the ground agree are still worth visiting and can only improve as years pass:

From I-10, drive south 1.9 miles (3.1 km) on I-310 to exit 2 (Hwy. 61), turn west, go 4.5 miles (7.2 km) to Prospect Ave., turn south, drive to River Rd., and turn west for 1.9 miles (3.1 km) to reach **Bonnet Carre Spillway,** an 8,000-acre (3,237-h) complex of swamps, marshes, meadows, and hardwood forests.

The best time to visit the area is in late fall to early spring. See anhingas; great blue, little blue, tricolored, and green herons; black-crowned night-herons; roseate spoonbills; white, white-faced, and glossy ibis; plus many thousands of waterfowl and other shorebirds. In summer least and American bitterns nest in the area.

U.S. Army Corps of Engineers New Orleans District Public Affairs Office
7400 Leake Ave.
New Orleans, LA 70160
(504) 862-2201
www.mvn.usace.army.mil

Follow River Rd. east to I-310, turn south and cross the river, take exit 7 (Hwy 18), drive east 3.1 miles (5 km) to Barton Ave., and turn right. At Hwy. 90 turn east and drive 10 miles (16 km), turn right on Westbank Expy., and go 1.9 miles (3.1 km) to the entrance of **Bayou Segnette SP.** Open year-round. Admission fee is charged.

Several species of raptors visit the park, including red-shouldered and red-tailed hawks, Mississippi kites, American kestrels, and bald eagles. Also see pileated woodpeckers; northern flickers;

barred owls; ruby-crowned kinglets; great and snowy egrets; anhingas; tricolored, little blue, and green herons; and yellow-crowned night-herons; plus many seabirds, wading birds, and shorebirds.

Bayou Segnette SP
7777 Westbank Expy.
Westwego, LA 70094
(888) 677-2296
www.crt.state.la.us/parks

The **Barataria Preserve** of **Jean Lafitte NHP** is nearby to the south. Leave the prior waypoint heading east on Lapaico Blvd. for 4 miles (6.4 km). Turn right on

Brownell Memorial Park and its Carillon Tower, north of Morgan City.

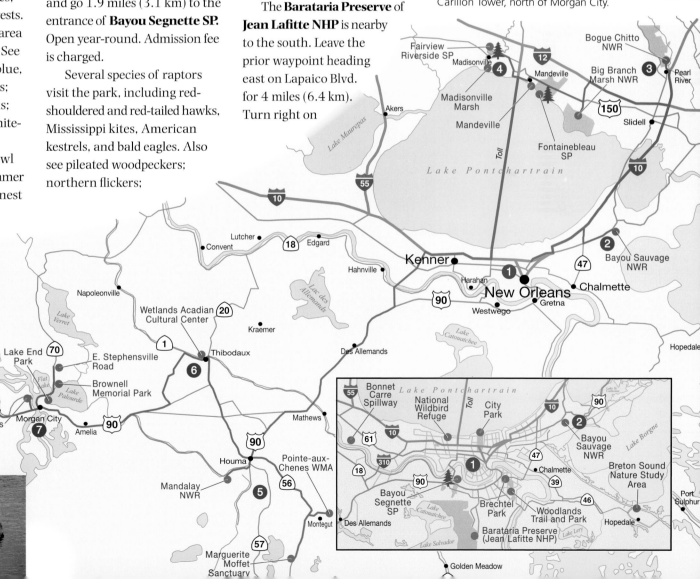

Snowy egrets look stylish in white plumage, black leggings, and golden spats

Barataria Blvd., go 8 miles (13 km) south, enter Jean Lafitte NHP, and 20,000-acre (8,094-h) Barataria Preserve. Open 9 a.m. to 5 p.m. daily except December 25 and Mardi Gras. Admission fee is charged. An environmental education center has bird checklists and sighting reports.

Over 300 recorded species of birds visit the bayous, swamps, forests, and wetlands of the preserve. Make a visit that is both convenient and rewarding in terms of birds seen by taking full advantage of this site's many walking trails, boardwalks, and canoe trails. There are full-access paths with observation decks and towers, and blinds to add to the experience of this totally natural setting in a Louisiana marsh.

Barataria Preserve Unit
Jean Lafitte NHP
6588 Barataria Blvd.
Marrero, LA 70072
(504) 589-2330, ext. 10
www.nps.gov/jela

The 2005 hurricanes severely damaged New Orleans's southeast quadrant, which previously were home to top birding areas. Check local sources before visiting:

• **Brechtel Park,** in Algiers, I-90 to General DeGaulle Dr., east to Lennox Blvd.; 14-acre (5.7-h) lagoon surrounded by mixed hardwood forest. See wood ducks; tree swallows; red-bellied, downy, hairy, and pileated wood-peckers; owls; and screech-owls. In spring see warbler, kinglet, and sparrow species.

• **Woodlands Trail and Park,** in Algiers, General DeGaulle Dr. east to Woodland Hwy.; 609-acre (246-h) site with Acadian and great crested flycatchers, tufted titmice, yellow-breasted chats, blue-gray gnatcatchers, and white-eyed and red-eyed vireos.

• **Breton Sound Nature Study Area,** from Chalmette, Hwy. 39 southeast to Florissant Hwy. (Hwy. 46), east to end of road; 200-acre (81-h) barrier island–like site with gulf seabirds, pelicans, common loons, cormorants, gadwalls, and nesting neotropical migrant birds.

To the north on Lake Pontchartrain's southern shore, bird-watchers visiting in spring will find nearly 200,000 purple martins at **National Wildbird Refuge,** adjacent to the west anchor of Lake Pontchartrain Cswy. The birds stage on the bridge understructure before continuing their migration north. The best time to visit is in evening.

From I-10 take exit 228 (N. Causeway Blvd.) north 1.4 miles (2.3 km) and park as designated on the right side of the highway. Observe safety rules when going to and from the viewing area.

While purple martins may be the chief draw, large numbers of other birds are seen at the site throughout the year. They include ring-billed, laughing, and other gulls; brown pelicans; eared and horned grebes; and royal, Forster's, and Caspian terns. Many shorebirds and wading birds are also present, such as roseate spoonbills and egrets.

National Wildbird Refuge, Inc.
P.O. Box 7066
Metairie, LA 70010
(504) 888-5510
www.gnofn.org/~swallow

Return on Causeway Blvd. to W. Esplanade Ave. S, turn east for 1.8 miles (2.9 km), left on Carrollton Ave. for 0.5 mile (0.8 km), right on Hammond Hwy. (which becomes Robert E. Lee Blvd.), and drive 1.6 miles (2.6 km) east to **City Park.** Open daily year-round.

The best spots to bird in the park are the Couterie Forest, at Marconi Blvd. and Filmore Ave., and wooded areas around the lagoon at the park's heart.

During spring and fall migration see owls, hawks, songbirds, boreal birds, flycatchers, wrens, warblers, and vireos. Many species of perching birds remain in the park through the summer to nest and rear young.

New Orleans City Park
1 Palm Dr.
New Orleans, LA 70124
(504) 482-4888
www.neworleanscitypark.com

Jean Lafitte NHP and Barataria Preserve feature a viewing deck and bridge on the Bayou Coquille Trail to Lower Kenta Canal.

❷ Bayou Sauvage NWR

Drive I-10 east to exit 246A (I-510), drive south 3.2 miles (5.1 km), exit on Hwy. 90 E, turn left, and drive 3.4 miles (5.5 km) to the entrance of 23,000-acre (9,308-h) **Bayou Sauvage NWR** and the Learning Lab. Open dawn to dusk daily except holidays.

The refuge has noted over 340 recorded bird species, a total that reflects both its location at the southern end of the Central Flyway and its many distinct habitats: bayous, beaches, chenieres (former beaches), hardwood forests, and brackish and freshwater marshes.

Take a short walk on Ridge Trail or hike along more than 26 miles (42 km) of trails on levees, bike the 9-mile (14.5-km) Bayou Sauvage bike trail (obtain a map at the office), or follow one of three canoe trails.

Visit during May to July to see nesting mottled and wood ducks, or come in winter when many species of dabbling and diving ducks arrive from the north, accompanied by hawks, bald eagles, herons, and other waterfowl and shorebirds. In brushy and forest areas note the smaller songbirds in spring and fall.

Bayou Sauvage NWR
61389 Hwy. 434
Lacombe, LA 70445
(985) 882-2000
www.fws.gov/bayousauvage

❸ Bogue Chitto NWR

Return to I-10, turn east, and drive 21 miles (33 km) across Lake Pontchartrain to Slidell, merge left onto I-59, and go 5 miles (8 km) to exit 11 (Pearl

Hurricane Aftermath

The storm surge that accompanied hurricane Katrina pushed seawater over the freshwater marshes and rivers of southern Louisiana. Mass vegetation death affected everything from grass to mature trees; wind damage impacted mainly large, established trees. It is widely believed, however, that much habitat will soon begin to recover. What will remain unchanged for decades is the appearance of mature forest areas. Fortunately, the swath of the storms, while heavily damaging in their impact for humans, left broad areas unscathed. The importance of having redundant preserves and refuge habitats in every wildland area was underscored by this hurricane season with its millennium storms.

River). Cross under the interstate and follow River Rd. (Old Hwy. 11) as it loops to Holmes Bayou Trail and 36,000-acre (14,569-h) **Bogue Chitto NWR.** Open dawn to dusk daily. Foot access is limited; boat launches give access to canoes, kayaks, and boats.

The refuge is a critical habitat for the threatened swallow-tailed kite, whose habitat needs for river bottomland hardwood forests closely match the landscape found along the Pearl and Bogue Chitto rivers and various creeks.

Hike the trail along Holmes Bayou to the Pearl River. Among the birds likely to be seen out of the several hundred recorded at the site are yellow-billed cuckoos, white-eyed vireos, woodcocks, wild turkeys, wood ducks, hawks, and owls. In spring migratory songbirds fill the trees around the river, while in winter waterfowl are abundant, as are raptors.

Bogue Chitto NWR
1010 Grause Blvd., Bldg. 936
Slidell, LA 70458
(504) 646-7555
www.fws.gov/boguechitto

❹ Lake Pontchartrain's Northern Shore

Like southeast New Orleans, the area along the northern shore of Lake Pontchartrain was heavily impacted by the hurricane of 2005. Most structures and facilities were destroyed, trees were broken off, and saltwater flooded the shore during the storms.

Nature quickly heals, however, so plan visits to these key birding areas:

- **Big Branch Marsh NWR,** I-59 south to I-12, west to Hwy. 434, south to Lacombe, follow the signs to the refuge's entrance; a 15,000-acre (6,070-h) refuge composed of pine flats, ridges of oak forest, and coastal freshwater marsh. Endangered red-cockaded woodpeckers, brown pelicans, and bald eagles nest here. In winter waterfowl and wading birds frequent the refuge. In April to May, songbirds and perching birds arrive, migrating north. They pass through again on their flight south in September to October. Hike or bike 4.5-mile (7.2-km) Boy Scout Trail, walk the marsh boardwalk, or canoe or kayak Cane Bayou. Fee. **www.fws.gov/bigbranch-marsh**

- **Fontainebleau SP,** Hwy. 190 west from Lacombe to park entrance on Hwy. 1089; this 2,800-acre (1,133-h) former sugar plantation has mixed hardwood forest, brackish and freshwater marsh, beach, and grassy meadow habitats. See pileated and downy woodpeckers, spotted sandpipers, royal and Forster's terns, brown pelicans, and boat-tailed grackles. In spring nearctic and neotropical waterfowl, shorebirds, wading birds, warblers, wrens, yellowthroats, purple martins, and yellow-shafted flickers are common. Fee. **www.crt.state.la.us/parks/ifontaine.aspx**

- **Mandeville,** Hwy. 190 west to city, left on Jackson St. to Lakeshore Dr.; in winter ducks, geese, mergansers, grebes, and other waterfowl flock in bobbing rafts offshore. Also look for hawks, ospreys, merlins, kestrels, and eagles in the trees across the creek from Jackson St. In spring and summer songbirds nest in the same trees. **www.ci.mandeville.la.us**

- **Fairview Riverside SP,** west on Monroe St. in Mandeville to W. Causeway Blvd., north to Hwy. 22, west 3 miles (4.8 km); 99-acre (40-h) park on the Tchefuncte River has bald cypress–tupelo gum swamp and pine and hardwood bottomland forest. See blue-gray gnatcatchers, scissor-tailed flycatchers, tufted titmice, ruby-crowned and golden-crowned kinglets, and various warblers in spring and fall. Fee. **www.crt.state.la.us/parks/ifairview.aspx**

- **Madisonville Marsh,** west across the Tchefuncte River, south on Main St. in Madisonville, east on the

Fairview Riverside SP on the Tchefuncte River north of Lake Pontchartrain has many migrant songbirds in spring.

second Mable Dr., and park; Main St. continues as a 1.4-mile (2.3-km) unpaved road that parallels the Tchefuncte River. It leads through cattail marsh and bald cypress–tupelo gum swamp to Lake Pontchartrain. See gulls, brown pelicans, terns, snowy egrets, and raptors.

St. Tammany Parish Tourist and Convention Commission
68099 Hwy. 59
Mandeville, LA 70471
(800) 634-9443
**www.neworleansnorth
shore.com**

❺ Houma Area

Start exploring the Atchafalaya Basin—the largest swamp/river complex in the country—by returning via Lake Pontchartrain Cswy. (Hwy. 190) to New Orleans. At I-10 turn west, then southwest on I-310, and follow it to its end at Hwy. 90. Turn west and drive 22 miles (35 km) to the turnoff to Houma, Bus. Hwy. 90. Turn southwest, go 7.5 miles (12 km), and enter the town of **Houma.** There are three great birding sites nearby:

- **Mandalay NWR,** from Main St. and Barrow St. in Houma, drive south 1.7 miles (2.7 km), turn right following Bus. Hwy. 90, and drive 3.6 miles (5.8 km) to the refuge headquarters; 4,200 acres (1,670 h) of freshwater marsh and bald cypress–tupelo gum swamp. Access to the refuge is mostly limited to watercraft; tours and rental craft are available in Houma. Call ahead to the headquarters office at (985) 853-1078 for directions and a key to the 0.5-mile (0.8-km) nature trail located on Service Rd., 0.7 mile (1.1 km) west of the headquarters on Bus. Hwy. 90, to see wood ducks; barred owls; downy, red-bellied, and pileated woodpeckers; and many wrens, chickadees, and other songbirds. Trees hold nesting bald eagles from October to May, and the eagles hunt open water and marsh areas. Open daily sunrise to sunset. **www.fws.gov/southeast/mandalay**

- **Marguerite Moffet Sanctuary,** follow Main St. (Hwy. 56) in Houma southeast for 17.8 miles (28.6 km) from Hwy. 24; the Orleans Audubon Society's 86-acre (35-h) sanctuary consists of a wooded ridge surrounded by brackish marsh, with a 600-foot (183-m) board-walk and a viewing platform. See many wading birds, such as roseate spoonbills; clapper rails; great blue, little blue, and green herons; black-necked stilts; greater yellow-legs; and sandpipers. In winter waterfowl are abundant, as are gulls, Caspian, and Forster's terns, double-crested cormorants, and American white and brown pelicans. During spring migration also see eastern phoebes, orange-crowned warblers, swamp sparrows, marsh wrens, and other neotropical migrant songbirds and perching birds. **www.jjaudubon.net**

- **Pointe-aux-Chenes WMA,** retrace the outbound route 7.5 miles (12 km) to Hwy. 58 in Sarah Plantation, turn east, drive 1.5 miles (2.4 km) to Hwy. 56, turn left, followed by a quick right on Dolphin St. The headquarters is behind Montegut Middle School on Point Farm Rd.; 29,000-acre (11,736-h) site is brackish wetlands divided by ridges cloaked in hard-wood forests. Obtain directions to the Montegut trail at the headquarters. In summer see ruby-throated hummingbirds, white-eyed vireos, yellow-billed cuckoos, indigo and painted buntings, brown thrashers, Carolina wrens,

Fontainebleau SP gives a picturesque sampling of the mixed-hardwood forests and wetlands habitats that attract hundreds of species of birds to the Lake Pontchartrain area north of New Orleans each year from fall to spring.

and a variety of small raptors. In fall and winter see yellow-bellied sapsuckers, ruby-crowned kinglets, orioles, warblers, and larger birds of prey.

www.wlf.louisiana.gov/ hunting/wmas

Houma-Terrebonne Chamber of Commerce 6133 Hwy. 311 Houma, LA 70360 (985) 876-5600 **www.houmachamber.com**

❻ Thibodaux Area and Wetlands Acadian Cultural Center

Drive Hwy. 24 north 16 miles (26 km) to Thibodaux, entering town on Jackson St. Continue north to Bayou Lafourche, turn

left on St. Mary St., and arrive at **Wetlands Acadian Cultural Center,** another unit of Jean Lafitte NHP. Open 9 A.M. daily except December 25 and Mardi Gras; closing hours vary by day. Admission fee is charged.

The park celebrates historic Cajun—Acadian—culture with exhibits, interpretive talks, walks, and festivals. For bird-watchers two attractions are worthwhile: a boat tour of Bayou Laforche, the so-called "longest street in the world" and Louisiana's first highway, and a boardwalk overlooking the bayou from which riverine birds are seen.

Also walk or bike First St. east along the bayou's edge. It provides ample opportunities to see waterfowl, kingfishers, shorebirds, and raptors soaring along the waterway in their continual hunt for food.

Wetlands Acadian Cultural Center of Jean Lafitte NHP 314 Saint Mary St. Thibodaux, LA 70301 (985) 448-1375 **www.nps.gov/jela**

❼ Morgan City Area

Depart Thibodaux on Hwy. 1, travel west 3 miles (4.8 km) to Hwy. 309, turn south, drive 9 miles (14 km) to Hwy. 90, and turn west for 19 miles (31 km) to **Morgan City.**

Exit on Brashear Ave., turn right on Ninth Ave., drive 1 mile (1.6 km), turn right on Marguerite St. (Hwy. 70), and drive 1.1 miles (1.8 km). Turn right into **Lake End Park,** a trailhead for Morgan City Walking Trail.

From October to April, the park and trail on Lake Palourde are especially good for birding. Southern bald eagles, double-crested cormorants, and American white pelicans throng the lake, joining boat-tailed grackles, neotropic cormorants, gulls, and Forster's, royal, and Caspian terns and creating a grand show for bird-watchers.

Next, turn right on Marguerite St., right on Hwy. 70, and cross the causeway, driving 3 miles (4.8 km) and making a right turn into **Brownell Memorial Park.** Set in nearly virgin bald cypress and tupelo gum wetlands, it also has a carillon tower from which birders can scope the lake for birds.

Expect wading birds, including great blue herons and great egrets, but also note in spring the large number of songbirds, such as yellow-rumped warblers, northern cardinals, Carolina wrens, and Carolina chickadees. In fall yellow warblers stage for their flights south in the park as the skies fill with waterfowl.

Louisiana Dept. of Tourism 1051 N. 3rd St. Baton Rouge, LA 70802 (225) 342-8100 **www.louisianatravel.com**

If time permits, visit these nearby bird-watching sites:

- **E. Stephensville Rd.,** 1.9 miles (3.1 km) north on Hwy. 70, right on Hwy. 901, cross the bridge, turn north; a scenic rural route into the heart of the Atchafalaya Basin. See swampland birds along the last 7 miles (11 km) of the road. It is especially good in spring, with snowy egrets, wood ducks, ruby-throated hummingbirds, northern parulas, three species of herons and two of night-herons, and many species of warblers and other songbirds.

- **Berwick Walking Trails,** return to Hwy. 90 in Morgan City, turn west, cross the bridge, and turn north on Hwy. 182 to Gillmore Dr.; the trailhead leads to a 1.5-mile (2.4-km) path along the

Lacassine NWR is a worthwhile side trip for viewing western Louisiana's birds.

Atchafalaya River levee. See yellow-billed cuckoos, loggerhead shrikes, and various gnatcatchers, fly-catchers, and other song-birds in migration.

❽ Bayou Teche NWR

Return to Hwy. 90, drive west 16 miles (26 km) to exit on Alice C Rd. south of Franklin, go north 1.4 miles (2.3 km), and turn right on Hwy. 182,

which leads to an information center for 9,028-acre (3,654-h) **Bayou Teche NWR.** Managed by Mandalay NWR in Houma, the information kiosk contains maps and brochures about the refuge, including directions to boat ramps and auto-tour access roads that provide bird-watching opportunities.

The refuge consists of multiple management units south of Hwy. 90. It has several habitats, including bottomland bald cypress–tupelo gum forest, swamps, marshes, and grassy meadows. All are critical habitat for threatened Louisiana black bears and avian wildlife.

Good bottomland birding is possible from Yorkely Canal Rd., a loop south of Franklin. The canal has numerous wading birds and shorebirds, and the forest east of the road fills with migratory songbirds in spring. Among the species seen are Acadian flycatchers, white-

eyed and red-eyed vireos, and yellow-throated, hooded, and prothonotary warblers. Also see mourning doves, Carolina chickadees, and a variety of woodpeckers. They include the largest American woodpecker— the pileated, a colorfully marked bird with wings that span 29 inches (74 cm) or more. Other woodpeckers common in Bayou Teche are downy, red-bellied, and hairy. Formal counts have yet to be established for the refuge, but it certainly will total more than 300 species.

Bayou Teche NWR
10816A Hwy. 182 E
Franklin, LA 70538
(337) 828-0092
www.fws.gov/bayouteche

The wander west from New Orleans gives only a sampling of Louisiana's great birding. If time permits, also visit its other nearby wildlife refuges.

Two new chicks, with faces only a snowy egret mother could love.

Visit these sites along the way...

Sabine NWR
3000 Holly Beach Hwy.
Hackberry, LA 70645
(337) 762-3816
www.fws.gov

Tucked south 8 miles (13 km) on Hwy. 28 from Hackberry in Louisiana's far southwest corner, this is an area rich in birds of prey, waterfowl, wading birds, and migratory perching birds and songbirds. The best time to visit is late winter to mid-spring, then again in fall.

Lacassine NWR
209 Nature Rd.
Lake Arthur, LA 70549
(337) 774-5923
www.fws.gov

Located in southwest Louisiana, south of I-10 at the end of Hwy. 3056; 30 miles (48 km) of levee trails access most of the refuge. Here, forest, swamp, marsh, broad rivers, and lakes provide riches to birders in search of rare subtropical birds and Gulf Coast waders.

Delta NWR
61389 Hwy. 434
Lacombe, LA 70445
(985) 882-2000
www.fws.gov

Follow Hwy. 23 south for 75 miles (121 km) from New Orleans; while severely impacted by hurricanes in 2006, the Mississippi Delta lowlands are a meeting place for land-dwelling birds and seabirds and are expected to recover. Bird along the route; only boats have access to the refuge.

The Eastern Region

How can one sum up a region with so many different faces? Which would describe it best: the great Canadian cities of Toronto on the shores of Lake Ontario and Montreal; an island metropolis in the St. Lawrence River; the New York countryside carved by glaciers into lakes and wetlands; the Adirondacks' lofty forests; or the Northeast's rocky shores? Perhaps Chesapeake Bay; South Carolina's barrier islands and estuaries; the crest of Tennessee's Appalachian Mountains; or the palm-studded white-coral beaches of Florida? In truth, the East is all these things to bird-watchers.

The diversity of habitats found in these locales gives rise to equally large variety in the birds that have adapted to their features: shorebirds, large and small wading birds, birds of prey, birds of the open water, songbirds, and birds of the forest; all are here in the East to see, hear, and enjoy.

Toronto, Ontario, to Buffalo, New York

Take a ferry to one of Toronto's several island parks, hop from point to point along Lake Ontario's shore, hike woodlands and wetlands filled with nesting birds; all are options to be found in the heart of one of Canada's most vibrant cities. Linger to see waterfowl mix with small and large wading birds, then meander south to Hamilton and St. Catharines, experience the surprising abundance of birdlife along the Niagara River, and sample a bit of Lake Erie's shore as a finishing touch. At its core it's a hospitable land filled with birds great and small. For best birdwatching, plan to visit in April and May or in September, when birds move between their winter and summer grounds.

Cosmopolitan Toronto, with its many parks and wooded areas, is a gateway to the Lake Ontario countryside filled with migrating birds. Visit its birding hot spots and scenic wonders before traveling south to see the birds of Niagara Falls and Lake Erie.

Toronto Island Park, where no cars are allowed, is a popular Toronto destination for recreation. Hike, bike, or paddle the shore to see birds on Lake Ontario. In spring and fall migrating waterfowl, shorebirds, and perching birds fill the area.

Red-breasted nuthatches, while common, are a challenge to see in their preferred habitat of coniferous forests mixed with hardwoods. Listen for their rising call: *yna, yna, ynaeen.*

❶ Toronto Area

Toronto's setting on the north shore of Lake Ontario makes it a natural collection point when birds begin to migrate south for the winter in fall.

The birding tour begins in northwest Toronto at **Boyd Conservation Area** on the Humber River. Take Hwy. 400 north to Hwy. 407, turn west, exit at Pine Valley Dr., and go north 4.6 miles (7.4 km). Turn left on Hwy. 72, right on Islington Ave. (Hwy. 17), and note the preserve's entrance on the right. Open 9 A.M.; closing times vary with season and day of week. Admission fee is charged.

Boyd has 4.4 miles (7 km) of hiking trails on its north and east sides. The north trail weaves through historic apple orchards, woods, and meadows, good for seeing boreal birds such as nuthatches, orioles, and warblers. The east trail follows the Humber River in fairly open country; see wading birds, wood ducks, and waterfowl, especially in spring and fall.

A short distance north on the Humber River is 800-acre (324 h) **Kortright Centre for Conservation.** Take Islington Ave. northwest 0.8 mile (1.3 km) to Rutherford Rd. and turn right, then left on Pine Valley Rd.; the center is 0.6 mile (1 km) farther, on the left. Open 9 A.M. to 4 P.M. daily except December 24 to 31, during Sugarbush Maple Syrup Festival, held March 5 to April 9. Admission fee is charged.

About 200 species of birds have been recorded on the site, including ospreys, wood ducks, black-capped chickadees, herons, spotted sandpipers, warblers, indigo buntings, bobolinks, bluebirds, Bohemian waxwings, and meadowlarks. Ask staff for a bird checklist and trail guide.

The Raptor Centre is one of the facility's educational programs, with live birds-of-prey demonstrations. There are also 10.6 miles (17 km) of trails, from cattail marsh with boardwalks to woodlands and meadows with a viewing tower, ideal for bird-watching.

Drive north 0.7 mile (1.1 km) on Pine Valley Rd., turn right on Major MacKenzie Rd., continue 12.7 miles (20.4 km), and turn left on Warden Ave. for 3.3 miles (5.3 km) to reach the entrance of **Bruce's Mill Conservation Area.** Open 9 A.M. daily April to October; closing times vary by season and

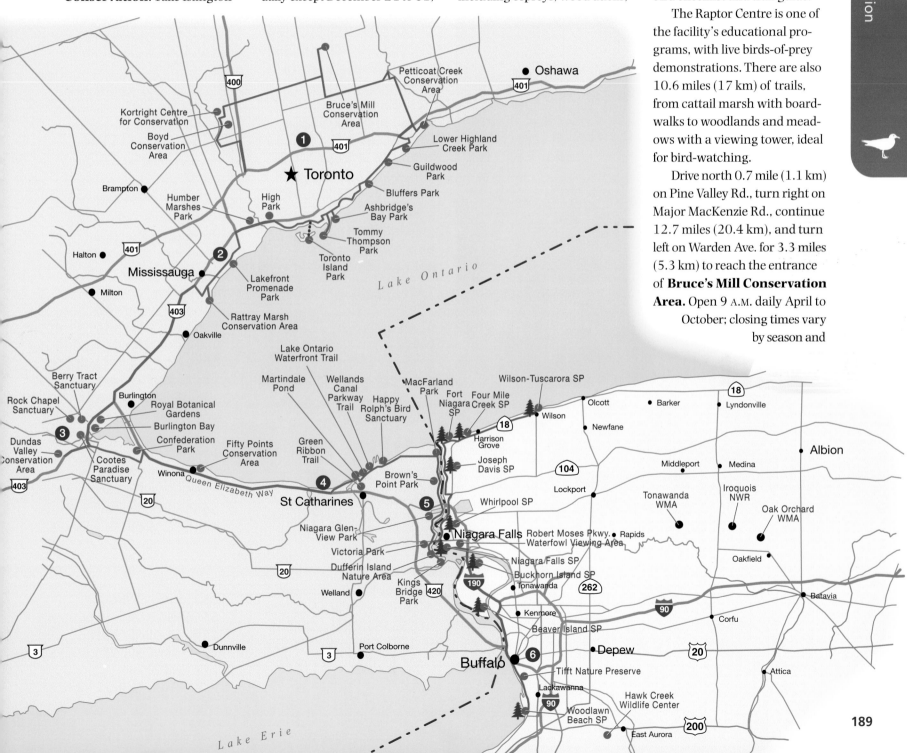

189

Dundas Valley Mills Waterfall is scenic and has a large variety of birds that make it a worthwhile birding spot. It is located in Hamilton between Toronto and Niagara Falls.

day of the week; consult the facility before going. Admission fee is charged.

Over 50 bird species reside at the site. It has 6.2 miles (10 km) of hiking trails winding through wetlands, woods, and grass areas.

In addition to forest birds, look for hawks and other raptors overhead, especially in spring, when they follow waterfowl and other migrants through the area on their flights to their nesting sites in the north.

Next, visit southeast Toronto. Travel 6.5 miles (10.6 km) south on Warden Ave. to Hwy. 407. Go east 8 miles (12.7 km) to exit 98 (York Rd.), go south, take the first left, and turn right on Altona Rd. Go south 5 miles (8 km) to Dyson Rd., turn left, then right on Rodd Ave. and enter **Petticoat Creek Conservation Area** on the shores of Lake Ontario. Open 9 A.M. daily, mid-May to early September; closing times vary by season. Admission fee is charged.

The end of Rodd Ave. is an entry point to the Waterfront Trail that passes in and out of groves of trees along the coastal bluffs before forking inland to follow Petticoat Creek. See hawks, peregrine falcons, northern cardinals, yellow warblers, and blue jays.

Toronto Regional Conservation Authority
5 Shoreham Dr.
Downsview, ON Canada M3N 1S4
General: (416) 661-6600
Kortright: (416) 667-6295
www.trca.on.ca

Four more shoreline parks with good bird-watching potential are strung along the northeastern shore of Lake Ontario. Most parks are open dawn to dusk daily. Plan to visit:

- **Lower Highland Creek Park,** Hwy. 401 west to Port Union Rd., south to Lawrence Ave. E, west to Beechgrove Dr., north and right at the left bend to enter the park;

61-acre (24.7-h) reserve with creekside hiking trails that cross Stevenson Swamp, a wetland of cattails on a floodplain, en route to the creek's mouth at Lake Ontario.

- **Guildwood Park,** Beechgrove Dr. south to Copperfield Rd., west to Manse Rd., north to Coronation Dr., west to Galloway Rd, south to park; best birding is on the park's south edge from the bluffs to the fence. Good for warblers; also see wrens, gnatcatchers, and northern shrikes. Forest paths west of Guild Inn hold migrant songbirds in spring.

- **Bluffers Park,** Galloway Rd. north to Kingston Rd., west to Brimley Rd., south to park; 474-acre (192-h) site at base of Scarborough Bluffs. Bird both the top of the bluffs and the lakeshore; Bluffers Park is one of only a few that permit close approach to the shoreline. Resident birds include trumpeter and mute swans, gulls, ducks, and geese. Best in early morning. Check wooded areas along Brimley Rd. for songbirds.

- **Ashbridge's Bay Park,** Brimley Rd. north to Kingston Rd., west to Woodbine Ave., south to park on Lake Shore Blvd. E; strand and trails on grassy bluffs overlooking marshlands and a small-boat harbor. Best in early morning; see loons, gulls, ducks, geese, and swans.

Tourism Toronto
P.O. Box 126
207 Queens Quay W
Toronto, ON Canada M5J 1A7
(800) 363-1990
www.toronto.ca/visitors

Toronto's downtown area and the northwestern shore of Lake Ontario also have excellent birding sites:

- **Tommy Thompson Park,** Lake Shore Blvd. E, west to Leslie St., south to the park; extends 3.1 miles (5 km) into Lake Ontario at the mouth of the Don River. Meadows, forest, wetlands, and mud-flats host over 290 recorded bird species. Large nesting colonies of black-crowned night-herons, double-crested cormorants, and ring-billed gulls. During migration see raptors, songbirds, shorebirds, owls, terns, and waterfowl. A recognized IBA of Global Significance. Two trails provide easy access: Martin Goodman and Waterfront.

- **Toronto Island Park,** west on Gardiner Expy., exit at Yonge St., south to Queens Quay E and the passenger ferry docks (fee); several sand-dune barrier islands with mixed habitats and many trails and bike paths that provide access for birders.

- **High Park,** Lake Shore Blvd. W to Parkside Dr. (Sundays from May 1 to October 1, enter only on Bloor St.); the oak savannahs are the fourth-largest stand globally. Hike Spring Creek Trail for orioles, flycatchers, cedar waxwings, northern cardinals, vireos, goldfinches, and downy woodpeckers. At Grenadier Pond see swans, wood ducks, egrets, herons, and migratory waterfowl.

- **Humber Marshes Park,** the Queensway west to Park Lawn Rd., south to Lake Shore Blvd. W; two parks on spits of land east and west of Mimico Creek, with mixed meadow and lake cove habitats, offer good birding. A good spot is a restored wetland in the east unit, where wading birds are common. Also look in the Carolinian forest for songbirds, woodland birds, and perching birds.

Access Toronto
100 Queen St. W
Toronto, ON Canada M5H 2N2
(416) 338-0338
www.toronto.ca/accesstoronto

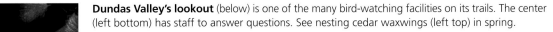

Dundas Valley's lookout (below) is one of the many bird-watching facilities on its trails. The center (left bottom) has staff to answer questions. See nesting cedar waxwings (left top) in spring.

The Canadian side of Niagara Falls has a large park downstream. Birds roost in the trees overlooking the Niagara River.

waterfowl shelter in migration. The forest area on the northwest edge is also good for perching birds in spring and early fall.

In the shallows on the west margin of the park where the creek enters to create Cawthra Creek Wetlands, look for ducks, geese, swans, egrets, herons, and killdeer and other shorebirds.

Lakefront Promenade Park
300 City Centre Dr.
Mississauga, ON Canada L5B 3C1
(905) 615-4100
**www.mississauga.ca/portal/
discover/parksandgardens**

Continue southwest on Lakeshore Rd. W, turn left on Bexhill Rd. just beyond Jack Darling Memorial Park, and drive to the end of the road and trailhead for **Rattray Marsh Conservation Area.** Open daily dawn to dusk. Admission fee is charged.

Excellent bird-watching is possible from the interpretive boardwalk, hiking trails, viewing platforms, and nature trail.

Depending on the season, see black-crowned night-herons, great blue herons, eastern kingbirds, wood-warblers, tree swallows, and spotted sandpipers, plus migratory visitors.

Credit Valley Conservation
1255 Old Derry Rd.
Mississauga, ON Canada L5N 6R4
(905) 670-1615
**www.creditvalleycons.com/
recandleisure/rattray.htm**

❷ Mississauga area

Drive west 1.2 miles (1.9 km) from Toronto on Lakeshore Rd. W to Mississauga and turn south on Lakefront Promenade to visit **Lakefront Promenade Park,** an access for the Waterfront Trail. Open dawn to dusk daily.

Ignore the small-boat harbor and concentrate on the inlet to the west side of the park, where large rafts of ducks and other

❸ Burlington and Hamilton area

Drive south on Lakeshore Blvd. W and join Hwy. 403, driving 17 miles (27 km) to exit at Hwy. 6 in Burlington. Turn right on Plains Rd. W and cross back under Hwy. 403. Follow the signs to **Royal Botanical Gardens.** Open 10 A.M. to dusk daily except January 1 and December 25; Nature Interpretive Centre open 10 A.M. to 4 P.M. Admission fee is charged.

The gardens administer the arboretum, Interpretive Nature Centre, and four wildlife sanctuaries: Hendrie Valley, Rock Chapel, Berry Tract, and Cootes Paradise. Obtain recent sighting reports and directions to each sanctuary at the visitors center.

The **Cootes Paradise Sanctuary** is a 2,075-acre (840-h) site designated a Provincially Significant Class 1 Wetlands, an Area of Natural and Scientific Interest, and an Environmentally Sensitive Area. It is considered one of the most important waterfowl staging habitats on the lower Great Lakes. Between the three sanctuaries, there are 19 miles (30 km) of walking trails.

Royal Botanical Gardens
680 Plains Rd. W
Burlington, ON Canada L7T 4H4
(905) 527-1158
www.rbg.ca

From the Interpretive Nature Centre at the last way point, drive York Rd. southeast to Cootes Dr., turn left, go to Dundas St., turn left, and follow it 2.6 miles (4.2 km) to **Dundas Valley Conservation Area** trailhead. The site is recognized as an IBA hooded warbler nesting area, Acadian flycatchers, cerulean warblers, and Louisiana waterthrushes and a World Biosphere Reserve by UNESCO. Open 8 A.M. to sunset daily. Admission fee is charged.

Over 100 bird species are known to nest in the 2,965-acre (1,200-h) marsh, forest, and its streamside habitats. There are 25 miles (40 km) of trails from which to bird-watch.

See eastern bluebirds, nuthatches, chickadees, and warblers, and be ready for surprises, such as the cave swallows noted during the fall 2005 bird count. Tree and northern rough-winged swallows are also found here.

Hamilton Conservation Authority
P.O. Box 7099
Ancaster, ON Canada L9G 3L3
(905) 627-1233
**www.conservationhamilton.ca
/parks/visit/dundas_valley.asp**

If time permits, also visit Van Wagner's Beach at **Confederation Park,** just northeast of the Queen Elizabeth Way at Centennial Pkwy. N.

❹ Hamilton to St. Catharines

Follow Queen Elizabeth Way east 6.5 miles (10.5 km) to Winona, exit at 50 Rd., cross the highway, and turn right on N. Service Rd. to Base Line Rd. and the entrance of **Fifty Points Conservation Area**. Open 7 A.M. to sunset weekdays, 6 A.M. to sunset weekends. Admission fee is charged.

The 200-acre (81-h) site has a promontory jutting into Lake Ontario and has recorded more than 200 bird species. Over 65 nest, including Caspian terns, great black-backed gulls, and long-tailed ducks. At Garehouse pick up the Birds at Fifty checklist and recent sightings.

Fifty Points Conservation Area
1479 Base Line Rd.
Winona, ON Canada L8E 5G4
(905) 525-2187 or
(905) 643-2103
**www.conservationhamilton.ca
/parks/visit/fifty_point.asp**

Drive 16.5 miles (27 km) east on Queen Elizabeth Way to exit 51 (Lakeshore Rd. W), turn northeast, and drive to **Martindale Pond** in St. Catharines. This wetland lagoon is a junction spot for the **Green Ribbon,**

Red-winged blackbirds are common in the cattail marshes of Martindale Pond.

Lake Ontario Waterfront, and **Welland Canals Parkway** trails. Each has excellent shorebird and waterfowl viewing. The wooded trails shelter nesting boreal birds in spring and summer, including northern cardinals and migratory birds such as warblers and vireos.

Continue northeast as Lakeshore Rd. W becomes Main St., follow it to Lakeport Rd., turn right, drive to Lakeshore Rd., and turn left. Drive 3.4 miles (5.5 km) to Read Rd., turn left, and follow the signs to **Happy Rolph's Bird Sanctuary,** a 15-acre (6-h) municipal park with full-access trails adjacent to a pond and woods filled with small perching birds and songbirds. Open 7 A.M. to dusk daily, May to October. Admission fee is charged.

Visit the pond adjacent to the park to see hundreds of geese, swans, ducks, and other waterfowl. Smaller birds are found at the many feeders placed on the facility's grounds. The sanctuary also has a small-animal petting zoo for children, exotic birds on view, and striking views of Lake Ontario.

St. Catharines Parks and Trails
50 Church St.
St. Catharines, ON Canada
L2R 7C2
(905) 688-5600
www.stcatharines.ca

❺ Niagara Falls

Bird both the Canadian and the American sides of the 35-mile (56-km) Niagara River, a migratory feeding area with ice-free water in winter and a recognized IBA of Global Significance. Follow Niagara Pkwy. along the river to see ducks, geese, swans, and other waterfowl.

Numerous parks along the Canadian side provide good stops for bird-watching. From north to south along the river, visit **MacFarland Park, Browns Point Park, Niagara Glen-View Park, Victoria Park,** and **Kings Bridge Park.**

Dufferin Island Nature Area, just above the falls on Dufferin Isle Rd. and Niagara Pkwy., has trails with bird feeding stations and bird boxes. It is open daily year-round.

At Horseshoe Falls, Sabine's Bonaparte's, and Franklin's gulls become the focus; over 100,000 have been counted in the area, including some rare bird sightings.

Next, cross the Peace Bridge to the United States and explore the New York state parks along the other bank of the river and visit Buffalo, New York.

Niagara Parks Commission
P.O. Box 150
Niagara Falls, ON Canada L2E 6T2
(905) 357-2400
www.niagaraparks.com

Drive south on Rainbow Blvd., turn right at 1st St., cross the American Rapids Bridge to Goat Island, and enter **Niagara Falls SP.** Open year-round. Admission fee is charged.

This park is the first of several New York state parks adjacent to the Niagara River. Like the Canadian parks, it's another good spot for gull-watching.

Follow the Robert Moses Pkwy. north and downriver. Stop after 3.5 miles (5.6 km) at **Whirlpool SP** to overlook the gorge and thrill to the sight of peregrine falcons nesting. In the excitement of the rushing water, also note the nuthatches, chickadees, and kingfishers in the trees.

Other state parks downstream include **Joseph Davis SP,** off Lower River Rd., with nature trails, ponds, and woodlands; **Fort Niagara SP,** at the Niagara River mouth flowing into Lake Ontario, with wood-

Iroquois NWR is northeast of Niagara Falls, a short distance north of I-90. It is worth a side trip during migration season.

Red-tailed hawks have keen eyesight and superb flying skills.

⮈⮈ Not to Be Missed!

Hawk Creek Wildlife Center

The center is an accredited wildlife sanctuary in the Association of Sanctuaries and is home to over 80 resident raptors that, because of permanent injury or human imprinting, cannot be released into their natural habitat. Neither a zoo nor a shelter, the facility isn't open to the public but hosts several opportunities each year to see hawks and other birds of prey.

In past years four events have been scheduled each year:

- Earth Day Celebration in April
- The Wildlife and Renaissance Festival in July
- Enrichment Days in August
- Here Be Dragons in October

Check the center's website for these and other irregularly scheduled events; call for additional information. The center exhibits at the nearby Walden Galleria Mall.

For more information:
(716) 652-8646 or **www.hawkcreek.org**

land hiking and nature trails. A bit to the east via W. Lake Rd. is **Four Mile Creek SP.** This park is a very worthwhile birding stop. On Four Mile Creek, it features a marsh with great blue herons and other marsh and shorebirds plus trails through bluffs clothed in a bower of forest.

Still farther east on W. Lake Rd. is **Wilson-Tuscarora SP,** a narrow strip of land that divides the Tuscarora Bay from Lake Ontario. The 395-acre (160-h) park has woods, meadows, and marshes, with 4 miles (6.4 km) of nature trails.

Return along the Niagara River south toward Buffalo. At the city of Niagara Falls, return to the Robert Moses Pkwy., travel south 2 miles (3.2 km), and exit at the **Robert Moses Pkwy. Waterfowl Viewing Area**. During migration, see as many as 10,000 waterfowl, including canvasback and redhead ducks, geese, mergansers, and scaup.

Follow Robert Moses Pkwy. east to I-190, turn south, cross the bridge, and take the first exit heading east to **Buckhorn Island SP,** an 895-acre (350-h) marsh, meadow, and woodland area along the Niagara River.

Here, find eagles and hawks, which concentrate in the area during spring. The hawks "kettle" in large, ever-soaring groups.

Also visit **Beaver Island SP** at Grand Island's southerly end, a good viewing area for marsh and wading birds. It has a boat and canoe launch.

NY State Office of Parks
P.O. Box 1132
Niagara Falls, NY 14303
(716) 278-1796
nysparks.state.ny.us/parks/

❻ Buffalo, NY, Area

Drive south on I-190, cross the bridge, and continue 10.5 miles (16.9 km) south of Buffalo; take exit 7 (Hwy. 5) and drive 6.5 miles (10.5 km) to **Woodlawn Beach SP** off Lake Shore Rd. Open dawn to dusk year-round. Admission fee is charged.

The park has a 1-mile 1.6-km sandy beach and boardwalk trails in wooded wetlands on the Lake Erie shore, with shorebirds, gulls, and terns in the fall.

Follow Hwy. 5 north 2.2 miles (3.5 km), take the Tifft St. exit, turn left at the underpass, then left on Ohio St. to reach **Tifft Nature Preserve.** Hours vary by day and season; check website. Donations appreciated.

An IBA urban nature sanctuary with 264 acres (107 h), the refuge has 75 acres (30 h) of freshwater cattail marsh, with over 260 recorded bird species, including 66 that nest on the site. The preserve offers a quality viewing experience for birding, with 5 miles (8 km) of nature trails, three boardwalks, and viewing blinds. It is located on a primary migration route for perching birds and warblers.

Tifft Nature Preserve
Buffalo Museum of Science
1020 Humboldt Pkwy.
Buffalo, NY 14211
(716) 896-5200
**www.sciencebuff.org/tifft_nat
ure_preserve_visitor_info.php**

Montreal, Quebec, to Lake Champlain

A modern Canadian city firmly rooted in French traditions is also an enchanted place for bird-watching. Hop from park to park and island to island, finding hot spots for shorebirds, waterfowl, songbirds, and birds of the forest at every stop. Whether birding atop Mount Royal—from which Montreal gained its name—or in the carefully groomed grounds of McGill University's Morgan Arboretum, hundreds of bird species are to be seen, heard, and enjoyed. Next, trek south to Lake Champlain and trace the path birds fly, stop where they stop, and see the scenic grandeur of the lake and its inlet streams and rivers. This is high-intensity birding compacted into a few weeks of spring and fall, a journey that will provide memories to share for generations.

From its island on the St. Lawrence River, Montreal—the largest city in Quebec—attracts the birds of the Atlantic Flyway. Just to its south in New York and Vermont is Lake Champlain, with waterways, forests, and marshes that are important nesting grounds.

Mount Royal Park in urban Montreal is nature's reminder of the treasures in store for bird-watchers in the city's parks, forests, and waterways. A quick break or after-work stroll as the seasons change often turns up unusual bird sightings.

Hermit thrushes are the only thrush likely to reside all through the winter.

❶ Montreal Area

Take Hwy. 40 to the northeast tip of the island and to Blvd. Henri-Bourassa E, follow it to Rue Sherbrooke E, merge, and note the blue signs to **Pointe-aux-Prairies Nature Park.** Park open year-round; reception center open 9:30 A.M. to 4:30 P.M. daily, May to October. Parking fee is charged.

Visit the park reception center for tips on recent bird sightings in the mature maple forest areas west of the center, filled with boreal birds and migrant perching birds such as warblers, or follow Rue Sherbrooke to Blvd. Gouin E, turn left, and follow the shoreline to Marshland Pavilion. There, visit a chain of wetlands with green herons and other wading birds, great horned owls, mergansers, ducks, swans, geese, and 176 other recorded species of birds.

Pointe-aux-Prairies Nature Park
14905 Rue Sherbrooke E
Montréal, QC Canada H1A 3X1
(514) 280-6691
ville.montreal.qc.ca/portal/
page?_pageid=175,1722262
&_dad=portal&_schema=portal

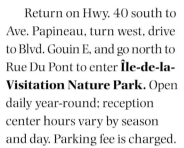

Return on Hwy. 40 south to Ave. Papineau, turn west, drive to Blvd. Gouin E, and go north to Rue Du Pont to enter **Île-de-la-Visitation Nature Park.** Open daily year-round; reception center hours vary by season and day. Parking fee is charged.

The historic park overlooking the Des Prairies River has hiking trails with good views of shorebirds, waterfowl, and raptors. Take the trail south from the dam to view the river, then loop back along Bassin des Moulins or walk the shoreline trail north on the main island along the east side of Bassin du Pêcheur through wooded areas.

Île-de-la-Visitation Nature Park
2425 Blvd. Gouin E
Montréal, QC Canada H2B 1X7
(514) 280-6733
ville.montreal.qc.ca/portal/
page?_pageid=175,1722245
&_dad=portal&_schema=portal

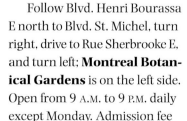

Follow Blvd. Henri Bourassa E north to Blvd. St. Michel, turn right, drive to Rue Sherbrooke E, and turn left; **Montreal Botanical Gardens** is on the left side. Open from 9 A.M. to 9 P.M. daily except Monday. Admission fee is charged.

In spring and fall migrating songbirds drop by to enjoy the gardens; in winter check the many feeding stations that attract hungry resident birds, including raptors and owls. The manicured grounds are a welcome break from more rustic birding sites.

Montreal Botanical Gardens
4101 Rue Sherbrooke E
Montréal, QC Canada H1X 2B2
(514) 872-1400
www.ville.montreal.qc/jardin/
en/propos/propos.htm

Go north on Rue Sherbrooke E, turn east on exit 89 (Hwy. 25), traverse the tunnel, and emerge midriver at 33-acre (8.1-h) **Îles-de-Boucherville Park,** five islands with 12.5 miles (20 km) of mixed-use trails, interpretative signs, and a viewing tower. Open 8 A.M. to sunset daily. Admission fee is charged.

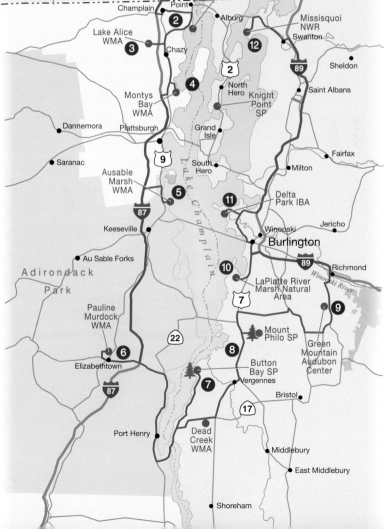

Great gray owls usually hunt boggy marsh areas in forests. Mostly nocturnal, they sometimes seek prey on winter days.

Parc du Mont-Royal
1260 Chemin Remembrance
Montréal, QC Canada H3H 1A2
(514) 843-8225
www.lemontroyal.qc.ca/
en_courriel/index.html

Exit the park, turn east on Chemin de la Côte-des-Neiges, bear right as it becomes Chemin McDougall, and turn right on Ave. Atwater. Follow the avenue to Hwy. 15, head east, take exit 57 to **Île des Soeurs.** Follow Blvd. de l'Île-des-Soeurs to its end at **Adrien d'Archambault Park** and the park's forest, or turn right at Blvd. Marguerite-Bourgeois and left at Blvd. de la Forêt for open grassy meadows.

The site's large lake has red-throated loons, pied-billed grebes, and resident and migratory waterfowl and shorebirds. See owls, woodpeckers, jays, and other woodland birds in a boreal remnant of the mixed hardwood forests that once blanketed the region. The park is home to a dozen known birds of prey, including nesting short-eared owls and eastern screech-owls, as well as more than 280 other bird species.

The Saint Lawrence River wends around the park's islands, which are linked by wooden bridges. Canoes and kayaks are a popular way to explore this watery world and its birds. Look for ospreys, northern harriers, great blue and other herons, swans, and various ducks.

Îles-de-Boucherville Park
P.O. Box 310
Boucherville, QC Canada J4B 5J6
(450) 928-5088
www.sepaq.com/pq/bou/en

If time permits, take Hwy. 25 east, turn south on Hwy. 20, and follow the river 2.8 miles (4.5 km) and make a stop at **Marie-Victorin Park.** Paths and lookouts along the shoreline have a variety of river birds and shorebirds plus raptors.

Once back on the island, take Blvd. Rene-Levesque E south to Rue de Bleury, and turn west as its name changes to Avenue du Parc and leads to 469-acre (190-h) **Mount Royal Park,** a bit of nature atop the mountain that is the heart of Montreal. Open daily year-round.

In spring migrants visit the park and adjacent **Mount Royal Cemetery.** Nesting hawks and owls provide year-round birding. Hike the 4-mile (6.5-km) Summit Loop Trail bird-feeder circuit on Chemin Olmsted from November to April, and visit the lookouts at Crags' Trail and Voie Camillien-Houde. Forest areas of the park are good in spring and fall for seeing songbirds such as indigo buntings, eastern blue-birds, and olive-sided flycatchers.

If time permits, take Chemin Remembrance, turn left at Chemin de la Côte-des-Neiges, right at Chemin Belvedere, and right again at Summit Circle, leading to **Summit Park.** Open daily year-round.

In May this locally popular birding site harbors 33 different species of warblers.

Borough of Verdun
4555 Rue de Verdun
Verdun, QC Canada H4G 1M4
(514) 765-7150
ville.montreal.qc.ca/portal/page?
_pageid=2480,3229567&_dad=
portal&_schema=PORTAL

Return to Hwy. 15, drive west, turn south on Hwy. 40, take exit 60 at Blvd. Henri-Bourassa, drive north, and immediately turn left on Rue Douglas-B.-Floreani, the entry road to 393-acre (159-h) **Bois-de-Liesse Nature Park.** Open daily year-round. Parking fee is charged.

Liesse forest is a large hardwood woodland along Bertrand Brook. Focus on the park's west section to see over 128 recorded forest bird species, or go to the brook's mouth for river birds, waterfowl, and shorebirds. The park plays an important role for migratory birds that travel along the Des Prairies and St. Lawrence river corridors. Hiking and bike trails connect the park's two main sections.

Bois-de-Liesse Nature Park
3555 Rue Douglas-B.-Floreani
Saint-Laurent, QC Canada H4S 1Y6
(514) 280-6678
**ville.montreal.qc.ca/portal/
page?_pageid=175,1722196
&_dad=portal&_schema=portal**

Follow Blvd. Gouin W. south from the park to Blvd. Jacques-Bizard, turn north, cross the bridge, and follow the blue signs to **Bois-de-l'Île-Bizard Nature Park.** Open 10 A.M. daily May to October; closing times vary by day and season. Parking fee is charged.

The 497-acre (201-h) site overlooking Deux Montagnes Lake has swamp, marsh, and

maple and cedar woodlands. It has hiking paths and a 0.3-mile (0.5-km) boardwalk that crosses the swamp, affording views of tree swallows, ducks, herons, and great horned owls.

Bois-de-l'Île-Bizard Nature Park
2115 Chemin du Bord-du-Lac
L'Ile-Bizard, QC Canada H9C 1P3
(514) 280-8517
**ville.montrealqc.ca/portal/
page/_pageid=175,1722213
&_dad=portal&_schema=portal**

 **Fowl-in-Focus**

SNOW BUNTING
Plectrophenax nivalis

Length 6.75 in. (17.1 cm)

What to Look for White wing patches show in flight. Female breeding (top): black with whitish edgings on back and white head and chest. Male breeding: black back and larger, more distinct white wing patch, white head, and white underside. Non-breeding

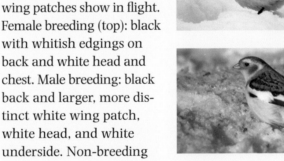

males and females (bottom right): marked with a dusting of cinnamon; females have a prominent breast band, while the males' bands are less distinct.

Habitat Nesting in the arctic tundra and wintering in parts of northern United States and southern Canada. Frequently found in open fields and beaches during winter. Flocks in flight sweep close to the ground. Sings a melodious though monotonous song plus whistles and calls.

A final stop on this sampler of Montreal bird-watching sites is at the far west end of the island. Return to the main island, turn west on Blvd. Pierrefonds, drive to Blvd. Saint-Charles, and turn south. Enter Hwy. 40, drive west, take exit 41 (Chemin Ste.-Marie), drive northeast, and turn north on Chemin des Pins. The road leads to **Morgan Arboretum.** Open 9 A.M. to 4 P.M. daily year-round. Admission fee is charged. Ask for a bird checklist at the information desk and consult staff on current hot spots.

The 605-acre (245-h) arboretum is an excellent birding location in every season and has numerous sites within it for seeing birds. Chickadees may feed on seeds held in a patient hand, but the park also has a full array of wild birds.

Spring migrants include warblers, summer is rich with forest nesters, fall is a good time to see migrating hawks, and winter brings pine grosbeaks, crossbills, woodpeckers, and owls. See barred owls, red-shouldered hawks, scarlet tanagers, and ovenbirds. Local birders say that more species are found in the arboretum than at any other site in Montreal.

Morgan Arboretum
McGill Macdonald Campus
Ste.-Anne-de-Bellevue, QC
Canada H9X 3V9
(514) 398-7811
www.morganarboretum.org

❷ Kings Bay WMA

Take Chemin Ste.-Marie south to Hwy. 40, turn northeast, and drive 15 miles (24 km) to exit 66 (Hwy. 15). Turn southeast, cross the Saint Lawrence, and continue south on Hwy. 15 for 38 miles (61 km) to the international border, where the road becomes I-87 south.

Take exit 42 onto Hwy. 11 south of the border and drive east to a T-intersection with Hwy. 9B. Drive south to a left turn on

Point au Fer Rd. and enter 421-acre (170-h) **Kings Bay WMA.** Open dawn to dusk year-round. (Two other roads with separate parking lots service the site: Stony Point Rd. and Camey Rd.)

The site has swamp, cattail marsh, and pasture habitats. There is a 0.5-mile (0.8 km) trail to Catfish Bay, a reed-and-cattail inlet. Wood duck nesting boxes are scattered along the trails. During migration wood ducks, black ducks, mallards, teal, and Canada geese offer the main attractions, but rare black terns also nest here, as do pied-billed grebes, northern harriers, and black-crowned night-herons.

Kings Bay WMA/NYS DEC Reg. 5
P.O. Box 296
Ray Brook, NY 12977
(518) 897-1291
www.dec.state.ny.us/website/ reg5/wmamaps

❸ Lake Alice WMA

Follow Hwy. 9B south to Hwy. 9, turn left, drive to Miner Farm Rd., turn west, and drive to Ridge Rd., which enters **Lake Alice WMA.** Turn south, pass Macadam Rd., and park across from the lake. Open dawn to dusk year-round.

The 1,468-acre (594-h) area supports many species of waterfowl, shorebirds, and wading birds. The trailhead leads to footpaths that ring the lake and join Old Railroad Grade Trail. The hardwood forest along the site's east edge harbors ruffed grouse, which nest on the site. These woods are also a good site to see pileated woodpeckers and owls.

Lake Alice WMA/NYS DEC Reg. 5
P.O. Box 296
Ray Brook, NY 12977
(518) 897-1291
www.dec.state.ny.us/website/ reg5/wmamaps

❹ Montys Bay WMA

Return via Ridge and Miner Farm roads to Hwy. 9, turn south for 4.7 miles (7.6 km) to Dunn Rd., turn left, and drive to Lake Shore Rd. **Montys Bay WMA** parking lot is 1.9 miles (3.1 km) south, on the west side of the road. Open dawn to dusk year-round.

The site has units to the east and west of the road. The east side is a swamp and marshy area at the south end of Montys Bay, good for viewing waterfowl, marsh birds, and wading birds. The west side is agricultural fields along a creek where snow and Canada geese frequently graze during migration in spring and fall. The floodplain has one of the oldest stands of old-growth hardwood forests with hollow nesting cavities for wood ducks, woodpeckers, and many cavity-dwelling species of songbirds. Also look up for raptors; many hawks migrate here.

Montys Bay WMA/NYS DEC Reg. 5
P.O. Box 296
Ray Brook, NY 12977
(518) 897-1291
www.dec.state.ny.us/website/ reg5/wmamaps

❺ Ausable Marsh WMA

Return via Lake Shore Rd. and Dunn Rd. to Hwy. 9, turn south, drive to Spellman Rd., turn right, and enter I-87 south. Drive 15.5 miles (25 km) to exit 35 (Bear Swamp Rd.), head east to Hwy. 9, turn left, then right on Ausable Point Rd. and enter **Ausable Marsh WMA.** Open dawn to dusk year-round.

The 580-acre (235-h) site encompasses most of the delta of the Ausable River. Diked empoundments make ideal waterfowl resting and feeding areas. View the ponds directly from Ausable Point Rd., or backtrack on Hwy. 9 to Bear Swamp Rd. A short distance south on the road's east side is the trailhead for a 1-mile (1.6-km) path along the dike. Walk this trail to see habitats from river and marsh to bottomland forest.

Ausable is a great site to see waterfowl, including common goldeneye, wood ducks, black ducks, mergansers, and teal.

Visit Missisquoi NWR headquarters as a good place to start a birding visit. Look at the exhibits and gather the current sighting information.

Also look for tundra swans and Canada geese. Two osprey nesting platforms have successfully been used by mating pairs to raise young; in spring these large birds of prey are visible over the wetlands and lake.

Ausable WMA/NYS DEC Reg. 5
P.O. Box 296
Ray Brook, NY 12977
(518) 897-1291
www.dec.state.ny.us/website/ reg5/wmamaps

❻ Pauline Murdock WMA

Return to I-87, drive south 26.5 miles (42.6 km) to Westport, turn west on Hwy. 9N to Elizabethtown. From River St. turn north on Maple St. and bear right at Elizabethtown–Wadhams Rd., arriving at **Pauline Murdock WMA,** just past High Meadows Ln. The parking lot and trail are on the east side of the road. Open dawn to dusk daily.

The 69-acre (27.7-h) refuge is a floodplain and hillside site, adjacent to the Boquet River, with successional vegetation that gradually is changing from cleared farmland to mixed hardwood forest.

It has a 0.4-mile (0.6-km) trail that fills with songbirds in spring migration and nesting birds through the summer, including eastern bluebirds, tanagers, vireos, swallows, and cedar waxwings.

Pauline Murdock WMA/NYS DEC Reg. 5
P.O. Box 296
Ray Brook, NY 12977
(518) 897-1291
www.dec.state.ny.us/website/ reg5/wmamaps

❼ Button Bay SP

Return to Hwy. 9N, turn west, drive to Westport, turn south on Main St. (Hwy. 22) for 14.5 miles (23.3 km), and east on Bridge Rd. (Hwy. 903).

Pass through Crown Point SHP, over Lake Champlain, and enter Vermont. Continue north on Lake St. (Hwy. 17), bearing left at Arnold Bay Rd. and again at Button Bay Rd., which leads to **Button Bay SP.** Open late May to early October. Admission fee is charged. Visit the Nature Center to obtain a bird checklist and consult staff for recent bird sightings.

Follow the hiking trail from the Nature Center to the point to view the shorebirds and waterfowl on Button Island. The park's western edge is a stand of hardwoods, excellent for seeing ospreys and hawks as they perch.

Button Bay SP
5 Button Bay State Park Rd.
Vergennes, VT 05491
(802) 475-2377
www.vtstateparks.com/htm/ buttonbay.cfm

Missisquoi NWR is Vermont's only black tern nesting site, with over 100 pairs.

❽ Dead Creek WMA and Mount Philo SP

Return to Hwy. 17 on Button Bay Rd. and turn east. If time permits, stop at the viewing overlook just past the bridge over Dead Creek. Over 200 bird species have been recorded here at **Dead Creek WMA,** recognized as an IBA for its raptors. It is also a bald-eagle release site. Very large flocks of snow geese collect at the lake during late fall and early spring. The refuge is closed to the public.

Continue east on Hwy. 17 to Main St. (Hwy. 22A), turn left, then north on Hwy. 7. Drive 6.8 miles (11 km) north to State Park Rd., turn east, and enter 168-acre (68-h) **Mount Philo SP** on a narrow steep road (towed vehicles not advised). Open late May to mid-October. Admission fee is charged.

During early fall the park's lofty perch is ideal for viewing raptors. Kettles of hawks soar past the site, following the migrating songbirds and waterfowl south. In early morning and again at dusk, the birds settle onto roosts for the night.

Mount Philo SP
5425 Mount. Philo Rd.
Charlotte, VT 054454
(802) 425-2390
www.vtstateparks.com/htm/ philo.cfm

❾ Green Mountain Audubon Center

Getting to **Green Mountain Audubon Center** takes less time to drive than to describe. Head north on Hwy. 7 to Churchill Rd. and turn east. Churchill becomes Hinesburg Rd., doglegs north as Baldwin Rd., then east again as Charlotte Rd. to meet Hwy. 116. Turn right, drive 3.7 miles (6 km) to a left turn at Hollow Rd., a left at Main Rd. for 2.7 miles (4.3 km), and left on Sherman Hollow Rd. In all, the trip is just

21 miles (34 km). Open 8:30 A.M. to 5 P.M. weekdays; noon to 3 P.M. Saturday; the preserve's trails are open dawn to dusk.

The site is a wonderful slice of the most beautiful and natural areas of Vermont, with 5 miles (8 km) of trails through forest, swamp, and Huntington River bottomland. Over 100 species of birds either nest or winter here, including red-eyed vireos, rose-breasted grosbeaks, and Blackburnian warblers.

The center also has interactive displays and a butterfly garden—hummingbirds stop in summer to visit blooming flowers—along with staff to suggest sites and help identify birds.

Green Mountain Audubon Center
255 Sherman Hollow Rd.
Huntington, VT 05462
(802) 434-3068
vt.audubon.org/centers.html

⑩ LaPlatte River Marsh Natural Area

Drive north on Sherman Hollow Rd., turn right on Bridge St., left on W. Main St., and enter I-89 west. Drive 9.5 miles (15.3 km), take exit 13 to I-189, and go to Hwy. 7, turning south. Drive 3 miles (4.8 km), turn west on Bay Rd. for 1 mile (1.6 km), and park at Shelburne Bay Fish and Wildlife access adjacent to **LaPlatte River Marsh Natural Area,** a Nature Conservancy preserve.

McCabe's Brook joins the LaPlatte River at Shelburne Bay, creating an important migratory waterfowl habitat. The site noted 13 pairs of nesting bald eagles in spring. Black-crowned night-herons, common yellow-throats, woodcocks, and ruffed grouse are also seen in the marsh.

LaPlatte River Marsh Natural Area/The Nature Conservancy
27 State St.
Montpelier, VT 05602
(802) 229-4425
www.nature.org/wherewework/ northamerica/states/vermont

⑪ Delta Park IBA

Follow Hwy. 7 north to Burlington, turn west on Pearl St., north on Hwy. 127, and drive 5 miles (8 km) to Porters Point Rd. Turn west, go to Colchester Point Rd., turn left, then left and south on Windemere Way, which leads to **Delta Park IBA,** with trails to a marsh-and-swamp habitat and bottomland hardwood forest at the meandering Winooski River.

The site is another wintering site for bald eagles and ospreys, often seen fishing the lake and river. It was recognized as an IBA, however, because it is a critical habitat of migrating gulls, shorebirds, waterfowl, songbirds, and several tern species.

See least and pectoral sandpipers, dunlins, and Wilson's snipes; songbirds include great crested flycatchers, American

Ospreys soar over rivers and lake between April and late September. See them near Lake Champlain from LaPlatte River Marsh to Delta Park.

redstarts, ruby-crowned kinglets, northern parulas, and warblers.

Delta Park IBA/Audubon Vermont
255 Sherman Hollow Rd.
Huntington, VT 05462
(802) 434-3068
vt.audubon.org/IBADelta.html

⑫ Missisquoi NWR

If time permits en route to the next stop, visit **Knight Point SP** on North Hero Island via Hwy. 2; the west shoreline is a Vermont Natural Area with trails good for birding; open late May to early September.

Return to Hwy. 127, turn north, and follow it to I-89 north. Drive 25.5 miles (41 km) to exit 21 (Hwy. 78), turn west, pass through Swanton, and drive 5.7 miles (9.1 km) to Tabor Rd., a

left turn. Note the signs to the headquarters of **Missisquoi NWR,** on the left. Refuge open dawn to dusk daily; headquarters open 8 A.M. to 4:30 P.M. weekdays.

The 6,642-acre (2,688-h) refuge is another critical rest stop for songbirds and waterfowl flying the Atlantic Flyway.

Maquam Creek and Black Creek interpretive trails lead through 1.5 miles of floodplain forests and fields. Other trails sample the refuge habitats, and there is an 11-mile (17.7-km) canoe or kayak loop.

Missisquoi NWR
29 Tabor Rd.
Swanton, VT 05488
(802) 868-4781
www.fws.gov/northeast/ missisquoi

Boston to Cape Cod

Situated on the Eastern Flyway, Massachusetts draws birds from as far north as the Arctic Circle to its many beaches, wetlands, dunes, and forests. Spring and fall are replete, with wave after wave of waterfowl, pelicans, egrets, swans, and smaller songbirds passing through as they migrate from nesting to wintering ranges and back. The birding tour swings north as far as Salisbury, then winds south through Boston's park reservations before sampling the south shore of Scituate and curving onto Cape Cod. Allow time to savor the region's avian riches, its unparalleled scenery, and its colorful avian denizens.

Atlantic puffins are seabirds of the rocky shores. Their range extends north from Parker River.

Take a birding trek north of Boston to see rare and unusual coastal birds and visit the city's nearby state preserves and sanctuaries before traveling south to Cape Cod. It's birding in a compact, relaxed setting as easy as 1–2–3.

The beaches of Massachusetts are visited by many different species of shorebirds. Early morning hours are most productive for bird-watching along the shore, since the birds actively feed for a few hours after sunrise.

❶ Boston North

Begin the birding tour by driving 7.5 miles (12 km) north from Logan Airport on Hwy. 1A to Lynn. Turn right on Lynnway, exit the traffic circle on Nahant Rd., and drive south 3.2 miles (5.1 km) to Wharf St. Turn right, go left on Walton Rd., and make a final right on Furbush Rd., which leads to **Nahant Thicket Wildlife Sanctuary.** Open daily dawn to dusk.

This Mass Audubon facility is a 4-acre (1.6-h) red maple swamp with limited trails and recognized as an IBA. It fills with neotropical migrants in spring and fall, such as magnolia warblers, scarlet tanagers, and ruby-throated hummingbirds. Uncommon visitors include mourning warblers and white-eyed vireos.

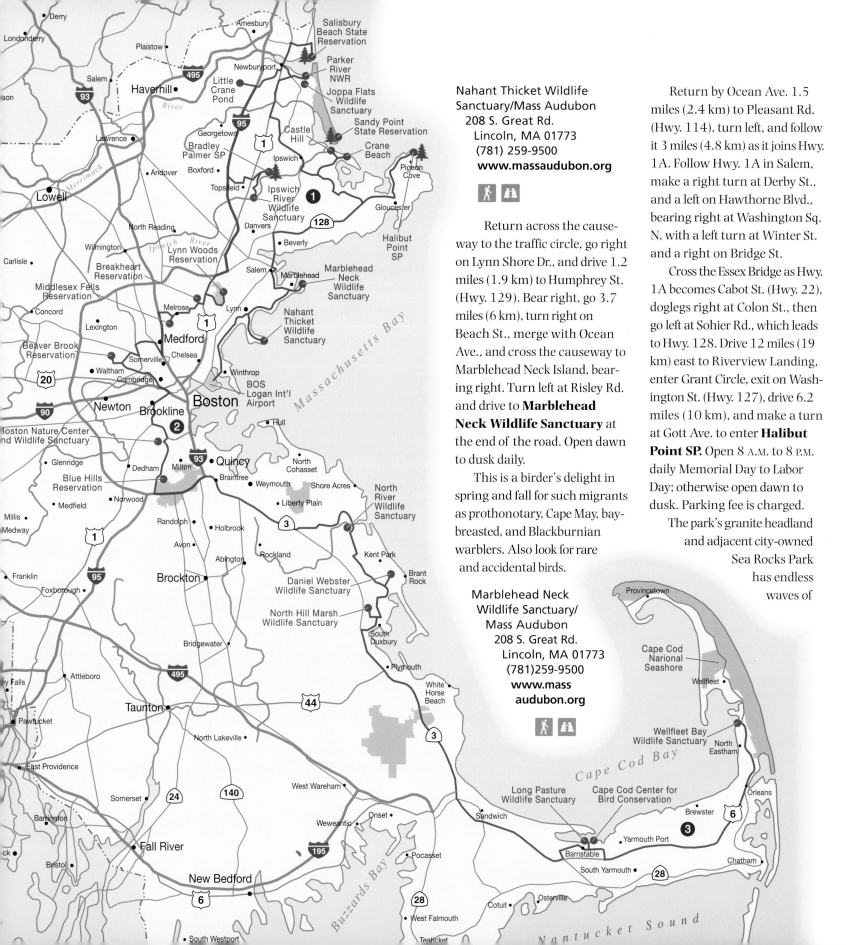

**Nahant Thicket Wildlife
Sanctuary/Mass Audubon
208 S. Great Rd.
Lincoln, MA 01773
(781) 259-9500
www.massaudubon.org**

Return across the causeway to the traffic circle, go right on Lynn Shore Dr., and drive 1.2 miles (1.9 km) to Humphrey St. (Hwy. 129). Bear right, go 3.7 miles (6 km), turn right on Beach St., merge with Ocean Ave., and cross the causeway to Marblehead Neck Island, bearing right. Turn left at Risley Rd. and drive to **Marblehead Neck Wildlife Sanctuary** at the end of the road. Open dawn to dusk daily.

This is a birder's delight in spring and fall for such migrants as prothonotary, Cape May, bay-breasted, and Blackburnian warblers. Also look for rare and accidental birds.

**Marblehead Neck
Wildlife Sanctuary/
Mass Audubon
208 S. Great Rd.
Lincoln, MA 01773
(781)259-9500
www.mass
audubon.org**

Return by Ocean Ave. 1.5 miles (2.4 km) to Pleasant Rd. (Hwy. 114), turn left, and follow it 3 miles (4.8 km) as it joins Hwy. 1A. Follow Hwy. 1A in Salem, make a right turn at Derby St., and a left on Hawthorne Blvd., bearing right at Washington Sq. N, with a left turn at Winter St. and a right on Bridge St.

Cross the Essex Bridge as Hwy. 1A becomes Cabot St. (Hwy. 22), doglegs right at Colon St., then go left at Sohier Rd., which leads to Hwy. 128. Drive 12 miles (19 km) east to Riverview Landing, enter Grant Circle, exit on Washington St. (Hwy. 127), drive 6.2 miles (10 km), and make a turn at Gott Ave. to enter **Halibut Point SP.** Open 8 A.M. to 8 P.M. daily Memorial Day to Labor Day; otherwise open dawn to dusk. Parking fee is charged.

The park's granite headland and adjacent city-owned Sea Rocks Park has endless waves of

Parker River NWR marshes near Newburyport are visited by 300 bird species.

seabirds, such as loons and grebes. Ascend its 60-ft. (18.3-m) observation tower and view seabirds from Massachusetts to Maine, such as kittiwakes, terns, pelicans, and harlequin ducks. Don't miss the quarry pond, a good place for migratory waterfowl, and follow its many paths with small perching birds and songbirds.

Halibut Point SP
Gott Ave.
Rockport, MA 01966
(978) 546-2997
**www.mass.gov/dcr/parks/
northeast/halb.htm**

Retrace the outbound path 6.1 miles (9.8 km) to Hwy. 128, turn east for 2.4 miles (3.9 km) to Hwy. 133, turn north, and go 6.2 miles (10 km) through several name changes to a right turn at Northgate Rd. Go north, bear right on Argilla Rd., and follow it to its end at 1,200-acre

(486-h) **Crane Beach.** Open 8 A.M. to sunset daily.

The site is one of the world's most important dune nesting areas for threatened piping plovers; least terns and bank swallows also nest here. Elevated boardwalks lead to 5.5 miles (8.8 km) of marked trails and viewing platforms. Both biting flies and Lyme disease–bearing ticks are present; use repellents and wear protective clothing.

Castle Hill, a neighboring site east on Argilla Rd., has another 4 miles (6.4 km) of trails. Also nearby is Crane Wildlife Refuge, accessible only by private boat or by guided tours. Cross the Castle Neck River to see sharp-shinned hawks and golden-crowned kinglets.

Crane Beach and Castle Hill
Argilla Rd.
Ipswich, MA 01938
(978) 356-4354
www.thetrustees.org

Follow Argilla Rd. west 4.1 miles (6.6 km) to Hwy. 1A, pass through Ipswich, drive 4.1 miles (6.6 km) to a left turn at Central St., and turn northeast at Hwy. 1 (Newburyport Tpke.). Drive 3.7 miles (2.1 km) to Hanover St., turn right, continue as it becomes Rolfes Ln., and arrive at the headquarters of **Parker River NWR.** Open sunrise to sunset daily; subject to temporary closures during nesting. Admission fee is charged.

This 4,662-acre (1,887-h) refuge has over 350 recorded bird species, and its roads have turnouts, and facilities such as viewing platforms and many trails; it also has a boat launch for canoes and kayaks. Roads and trails give access to Plum Island for fine marsh and water birding. Obtain a bird checklist and trail guide at the headquarters. Separate **Sandy Point State Reservation** is at its far tip.

Each season the birds to view vary. In spring see purple martins, piping plovers, osprey, and mating woodcocks. In summer songbird migration finishes, but shorebirds and tree swallows gather. Peregrine falcons, hawks, and waterfowl appear in fall. In winter watch loons, scoters, and grebes raft on refuge waters.

Parker River NWR
6 Plum Island Tpke.
Newburyport, MA 01950
(978) 465-5753
**www.fws.gov/northeast/
parkerriver**

Follow Plum Island Tpke. back northwest to **Joppa Flats Wildlife Sanctuary.** Open 8:30 A.M. to 4 P.M. Tuesday to Sunday and holiday Mondays. Donations are appreciated.

The visitors center has both indoor and outdoor observation areas overlooking the Merrimack River, and staff have recorded over 300 bird species, including bald eagles, warblers, snowy owls, geese, ducks, grebes, and many species of shorebirds.

Joppa Flats Wildlife Sanctuary
1 Plum Island Tpke.
Newburyport, MA 01950
(978) 462-9998
**www.massaudubon.org/
joppaflats**

Follow Plum Island Tpke. northwest as it becomes Water St. and Merrimac St., turn right on Hwy. 1, drive 2 miles (3.2 km), turn right on Beach Rd. (Hwy. 1A), turn right on State Reservation Rd., and follow the signs to 521-acre (211-h) **Salisbury Beach State Reservation,** with 4 miles (6.4 km) of shore. Office open 8 A.M. to 10 P.M. daily. Admission fee is charged.

Combined beach, dune, river, and salt-marsh habitats make the reservation a good spot to see birds such as waterfowl, scoters, eiders, horned larks, and snow buntings in winter and migrating songbirds, shorebirds, and wading birds in spring and fall. Raptors include snowy, long-eared, and short-eared owls.

Salisbury Beach State
Reservation
Beach Rd., Rte 1A
Salisbury, MA 01952
(978) 462-4481
**www.mass.gov/dcr/parks/
northeast/salb.htm**

Return on Beach Rd. to Hwy. 1, turn south, drive 2.3 miles (3.7 km) to Low St. in Newburyport, turn right, go left on Parker St., and follow it 3.9 miles (6.2 km) and through several name changes to make a right turn on Moulton St., leading to **Little Crane Pond,** a city reservoir.

The pond is encircled by roads with good views of waterfowl. Spotting scopes or binoculars are helpful. Pull completely off the pavement to observe birds.

Return to I-95, drive south to exit 52 (Topsfield Rd.), turn east, take a left turn on Washington St., go left on Main St., bear right on Ipswich Rd., and turn right on Asbury St. Follow the signs to **Bradley Palmer SP,** a Massachusetts IBA. Open sunrise to sunset daily. Admission fee is charged.

The park has mixed hardwood and red maple forest with wetland swamps. It is a reliable place to see great horned owls, red-bellied woodpeckers, eastern towhees, and Cooper's hawks. In migration see brown creepers, eastern wood-peewees, rose-breasted grosbeaks, and a mix of vireos, warblers, gnatcatchers,

and flycatchers. Also view wading birds and waterfowl.

Bradley Palmer SP
Asbury St.
Topsfield, MA 01983
(978) 887-5931
**www.mass.gov/dcr/parks/
northeast/brad.htm**

If time permits, also visit the **Ipswich River Wildlife Sanctuary.** Take Asbury St. to Ipswich Rd., go left to Perkins Row, which leads to the sanctuary. It has an observation tower, a visitors center, 10 miles (16 km) of wetland, shrub-covered swamp, and woodland trails, plus 8 miles (13 km) of canoe trails on the Ipswich River. Open dawn to dusk Tuesday to Sunday and holiday Mondays. Admission fee is charged.

Ipswich River Wildlife Sanctuary
87 Perkins Row
Topsfield, MA 01983
(978) 887-9264
**www.massaudubon.org/
ipswichriver**

❷ Boston Area

Return to Boston on I-95 south, take exit 46 (Newburyport Tpke./ Hwy. 1), drive 4.5 miles (7.2 km) as its name changes to Newbury St. and Broadway, and turn right at Walnut St. Drive east 1.9 miles (3.1 km), turn left at Menlo Ave. and left again at Pennybrook Rd., entering **Lynn Woods**

Reservation. Open dawn to dusk year-round. Pick up a map at the park entry station.

At 2,200 acres (890 h) the reservation is the second-largest municipal park in the country. It has over 30 miles of multiple-use trails and three reservoirs. The park also has horticultural gardens. The varied habitats mean great birding. Visit the park website before arrival for helpful birding tips.

Lynn Woods Reservation
P.O. Box 8216
Lynn, MA 01904
(781) 593-7773
www.flw.org

Return north to Hwy. 1, turn south, drive 0.5 mile (0.8 km), bear right at Lynn Fells Pkwy., and turn right at Forest St. to enter 640-acre (259-h) **Breakheart Reservation,** a state facility. Open dawn to dusk year-round. Admission fee is charged.

A visitors center, extensive trails, two freshwater lakes, the Saugus River, hardwood forests, and rocky hills attract both people and 140 species of birds. See buffleheads, ring-necked ducks, songbirds, and hawks.

Breakheart Reservation
177 Forest St.
Saugus, MA 01906
(781) 233-0834
**www.mass.gov/dcr/parks/met
roboston/breakhrt.htm**

Drive Lynn Fells Pkwy. southwest 3.8 miles (6.1 km) to Pond St. and arrive at the headquarters of **Middlesex Fells Reservation.** Open dawn to dusk daily; visitors center open 10 A.M. to 4 P.M. Friday to Monday in summer. Request a bird checklist and trail map.

Three reservoirs and two large ponds set in mixed hardwood forest make the park an ideal birding site for seeing both forest and water species. At Spot Pond concentrate on the

Crane Beach dunes are nesting grounds for thousands of piping plovers.

Dusk at Wellfleet means birds returning to wetlands to feed and rest.

islands using a spotting scope to see swans, herons, geese, ducks, and other waterbirds and shorebirds. On the many trails through forest areas, look for perching birds and songbirds, as well as owls, woodpeckers, and raptors.

Friends of the Fells
4 Woodland Rd.
Stoneham, MA 02180
(781) 662-2340
www.fells.org

Drive I-93 south from Middlesex to exit 32, go west on Salem St., cross the Mystic River, turn right on Hwy. 16 (Mystic Valley Pkwy. becoming Alewife Brook Pkwy.), drive 2.6 miles (4.2 km), turn west on Hwy. 2 (Concord Tpke.) to Pleasant St. (Hwy. 60), turn south, merge with Trapelo Rd., turn right at Mill St., and

approach the entrance to **Beaver Brook Reservation.** Visit the 59-acre (24-h) wetlands, woodlands, ponds, marshes, and fields on the north to see large flocks of ducks, geese, herons, and swans in fall.

Beaver Brook Reservation
Mill St.
Belmont, MA 02478
(617) 484-6357
**www.mass.gov/dcr/parks/
metroboston/beaver.htm**

Follow Trapelo Rd. west, merge onto Belmont St. and Mt. Auburn St., then follow Memorial Dr. (Hwy. 2) to I-90, cross under, turn left on Mountfort St., and turn right at Park Dr.

Bear right at Riverway, which becomes Jamaicaway, then exit the traffic circle onto Arborway, following it to become Morton St.

Turn right at Harvard St., go right at Walk Hill St., and enter **Boston Nature Center and Wildlife Sanctuary** on the right. Open dawn to dusk daily; center open 9 A.M. to 5 P.M. weekdays, 10 A.M. to 4 P.M. weekends and holiday Mondays. Donation for entry is appreciated.

The sanctuary has 2 miles (3.2 km) of full-access trails and boardwalks through 67 acres (27 h) of meadows and wetlands. See many migratory birds, wild turkeys, red-tailed hawks, red-winged blackbirds, and ring-necked pheasants.

Boston Nature Center and
Wildlife Sanctuary
500 Walk Hill St.
Mattapan, MA 02126
(617) 983-8500
www.massaudubon.org/boston

A final stop south of Boston is **Blue Hills Reservation.** Take Walk Hill St. southeast, turn right at Blue Hill Ave., and drive 4.2 miles (6.8 km) to Canton Ave. and the 7,000-acre (2,833-h) reservation, on the left. Open dawn to dusk daily; trailside museum open 10 A.M. to 5 P.M. Wednesday to Sunday and Monday holidays. Admission fee is charged.

See nature exhibits and hike 150 miles (241 km) of trails and paths. See wild turkeys, red-tailed hawks, and snowy owls, as well as migrant songbirds in spring in the woods and waterfowl in fall near the ponds.

Blue Hills Reservation
695 Hillside St.
Milton, MA 02186
(617) 698-1802
**www.mass.gov/dcr/parks/
metroboston/blue.htm**

❸ To Cape Cod

From Canton Ave. follow Washington St. (Hwy. 138) south to I-93, drive about 6 miles (9 km) east to exit 7 (Hwy. 3), and turn south for 11 miles (18 km) to exit 13 (Hwy. 53). Go north on Washington St., turn east on Hwy. 253, drive 5 miles (8 km) to Neal Gate St., turn south, drive to Hwy. 3A, and turn right. **North River Wildlife Sanctuary** is on the left. Open dawn to dusk daily; center open 8:30 A.M. to 5 P.M. Monday to Saturday. Admission fee is charged.

A red maple swamp and cattail marsh lead to a salt marsh with a platform overlooking the North River, all along a 0.5-mile (0.8-km) boardwalk with great bird viewing. See raptors such as sharp-shinned hawks, shorebirds, wading birds, and grebes, scaups, and other waterfowl.

In spring and summer Woodland Loop Trail turns up boreal birds such as scarlet tanagers, owls, and ovenbirds.

North River Wildlife Sanctuary
2000 Main St.
Marshfield, MA 02050
(781) 837-9400
**www.massaudubon.org/
northriver**

Follow Main St. (Hwy. 3A) south to Ocean St. (Hwy. 139), turn right on Webster St., and go left on Winslow Cemetery Rd., which leads to **Daniel Webster Wildlife Sanctuary.** Open dawn to dusk daily. Admission fee is charged.

On Pond Loop Trail visit observation blinds overlooking shallow wetlands to see herons, egrets, and shorebirds; it passes a purple martin colony on the west end of Webster Pond. On River Walk Trail a boardwalk over the Green Harbor River leads to a viewing deck. Another boardwalk on Secret Trail gives access to a red maple swamp. Both have waterfowl. Fox Hill Trail connects all of these paths, ending at an observation platform with views of marshy grasslands and large wading birds. Note hawks and falcons soaring overhead.

Daniel Webster Wildlife
Sanctuary/Mass Audubon
208 South Great Rd.
Lincoln, MA 01773
(781) 837-9400
**www.massaudubon.org/
danielwebster**

Go south on Webster St., turn west at Careswell St. (Hwy. 139), and turn right on Tremont St. (Hwy. 3A). Go south 2.3 miles (3.7 km) to Mayflower St., turn right, and go 1.2 miles (1.9 km) to **North Hill Marsh Wildlife Sanctuary.** Open dawn to dusk daily. Admission fee is charged.

A clearly marked trail system leads through the sanctuary's pine woodlands and wetlands to a 90-acre (36-h) pond that is a magnet to both migratory birds and shorebirds.

North Hill Marsh Wildlife
Sanctuary/Mass Audubon
208 S. Great Rd.
Lincoln, MA 01773
(781) 837-9400
**www.massaudubon.org/
northhill**

Return to Hwy. 3A, go south, join Hwy. 3, drive southeast for 14.5 miles (23 km) to Hwy. 6, and proceed east 13 miles (21 km) to exit 6 (Barnstable). Go left on Iyannough Rd., bear right on

A semipalmated sandpiper feeds along the shoreline.

Main St. (Hwy. 6A), drive east 4.1 miles (6.6 km), and turn left at Bone Hill Rd. to reach 110-acre (45-h) **Long Pasture Wildlife Sanctuary** and **Cape Cod Center for Bird Conservation.** Open dawn to dusk daily. The sanctuary has trails that lead through groves of tupelo, spruce, and holly trees with pond, swamp, and marsh habitats with wading birds. The site also has a good view of Barnstable Harbor.

Long Pasture Wildlife
Sanctuary/Mass Audubon
345 Bone Hill Rd.
Barnstable, MA 02637
(508) 362-7475
**www.massaudubon.org/
longpasture**

Return to Hwy. 6A, drive east to Willow St., turn right, and join Hwy. 6 east. Drive 21 miles (34 km), to the Orleans traffic circle and continue on Hwy. 6 for another 3.8 miles (6.1 km) to West Rd. and note the signs to **Wellfleet Bay Wildlife Sanctuary.** Open 8 A.M. to dusk daily; closes at 8 P.M. in summer; center hours change with season and day; see website. Admission fee is charged.

Wellfleet Nature Center has exhibits, two 700-gallon aquariums, and educational programs. The sanctuary's 5 miles (8 km) of trails include a boardwalk over a salt marsh, trails through pine-and-oak woodlands and two ponds, a heath bog, and a salt-marsh margin, one of the best spots for bird-watching.

See snowy egrets, greater and lesser yellowlegs, plus 15 other sandpiper species. Also see great horned owls, ospreys, northern harriers, whimbrels, warblers, and herons.

Wellfleet Bay Wildlife
Sanctuary/Mass Audubon
291 Hwy. 6
South Wellfleet, MA 02663
(508) 349-2615
**www.massaudubon.org/
wellfleet**

While on the Cape, also plan a visit to **Cape Cod National Seashore.** The shore's Salt Pond visitors center, with information about birding, is in Eastham.
www.nps.gov/caco

209

BIRDING 27 TOUR

New Haven, Connecticut, to Newport, Rhode Island

The rocky Connecticut and Rhode Island shores, with their many bays, inlets, ponds, and beaches, invite a potholing and backroads journey of bird-watching and discovery. Nooks and crannies from ocean to quiet cattail marshes display a wonderland of birds.

Forgo the metropolitan complex to the west and enjoy the rugged countryside as this birding route follows the coast from Bridgeport and New Haven to Newport and Bristol. Visit in spring to see tiny warblers finish their epic journeys of migration in the company of wading birds such as glossy ibis and snowy egrets, the soaring flight of ospreys and harriers, and the drumbeat of ducks and geese. Return in summer to see more than 100 nesting species, or follow the route again in fall, when birds answer their insistent urges and turn their wings south as the spectacle of migration repeats. Even in winter, when the sea smokes in the frigid air, seabirds and waterfowl abound. Discover a different way to see the familiar, looking through a bird's eyes.

A laughing gull in a solemn moment.

Connecticut Audubon Society's Coastal Center at Milford Point features a three-level viewing tower at its main facility. It sits within a wildlife sanctuary and is adjacent to a closed wildlife management area, both birding hot spots.

❶ Audubon Coastal Center at Milford Point

Start the birding tour west of New Haven on Long Island Sound at the Connecticut Audubon Society's **Coastal Center at Milford Point** and Smith-Hubble Wildlife Sanctuary.

Take I-95 south 12 miles (19 km) to exit 34 (Hwy. 1), turn east on Bridgeport Ave., drive to Naugatuck Ave., turn left, right on Milford Point Rd., and right on Seaview Ave. Drive 0.4 mile (0.6 km) to a fork, bear right, and enter the center. Open 10 A.M. to 4 P.M. Tuesday to Saturday, noon to 4 P.M. Sunday. Donation is appreciated.

Exhibits, a tide-pool demonstration tank, and an ornate 70-ft. (21.3-m) observation tower are centerpieces of the facility. It also has a boardwalk and viewing platform overlooking Wheeler WMA, a site closed to the public and a likely place to see nesting piping plovers.

The salt marsh at the mouth of the Housatonic River is a rest stop for migrating waterfowl and shorebirds and a shelter for seabirds during winter storms.

Connecticut Audubon Society's
Coastal Center at Milford Point
1 Milford Point Rd.
Milford, CT 06460
(203) 878-7440
**www.ctaudubon.org/visit/
milford.htm**

❷ New Haven Area

Return east 10.7 miles (17.2 km) on I-95 to exit 44 (Kimberly Ave.), turn left, drive to 1st St., turn left, and drive 1 mile (1.6 km) to **Sandy Point Bird Sanctuary,** on the left. Open 24 hours daily except for nesting closures; parking lot closes at 11:30 P.M. Admission fee is charged.

The site is a sandy beach with intertidal flats, marshes, wetlands, and river, all with views of Long Island Sound. A 1.7-mile (2.7-km) mixed-use walkway accesses 3.5 miles (5.6 km) of public beach.

See migratory waterfowl, seabirds, wading birds, and raptors from the trail and beach. In spring and fall large numbers of geese, swans, and ducks are

present. In winter birds collect at the park; birding after storms is particularly good for seeing unusual seabirds such as scaup and northern fulmars, as well as the waterfowl.

West Haven Parks & Recreation Dept.
355 Main St.
West Haven, CT 06516
(203) 937-3651
www.cityofwesthaven.com

Next, head north on 1st Ave. and continue 3.3 miles (5.3 km). It will become Forest Rd. Make a right turn at Edgewood Ave. leading to **Edgewood Park.** Open dawn to dusk daily.

Walking paths connect the West River and six ponds surrounded by mixed hardwood forest, especially good for seeing forest birds during spring and fall migration. The site also has a wetlands viewing platform, from which shorebirds such as herons, egrets, and smaller wading birds are visible. Also look for waterfowl, diving ducks, and loons.

Edgewood Park
720 Edgewood Ave.
New Haven, CT 06515
(203) 946-8028
www.cityofnewhaven.com

Drive 0.5 mile (0.8 km) east on Edgewood Ave., turn left at Sherman Ave, go right at Henry St., and continue as it changes to Munson St. and Hillside Pl. Turn right at Prospect St. for a short block, left at Edwards St., and left again at Whitney Ave. Go 0.8 mile (1.3 km) and turn right on East Rock St., leading to **East Rock Park.** Open dawn to dusk daily.

Trowbridge Environmental Center is to the south; ask staff for current birding information, see displays, or obtain a trail guide for the Nature Trail, a good place to see many types of spring warblers.

East Rock Park
720 Edgewood Ave.
New Haven, CT 06515
(203) 946-6086
www.cityofnewhaven.com

Take Whitney Ave. south to Willow St., turn east, enter I-91 south, transition to I-95 north, and take exit 50 (Woodward Ave.) and Main St. Turn right on Townsend Ave., drive 2.2 miles (3.5 km) to Lighthouse Rd., turn right, and enter **Lighthouse Point Park.** Open 7 a.m. to sunset daily. Nonresident parking fee is charged.

The point's location on the Atlantic Flyway is responsible for the many bird species seen here, though the favorites among local birders are the

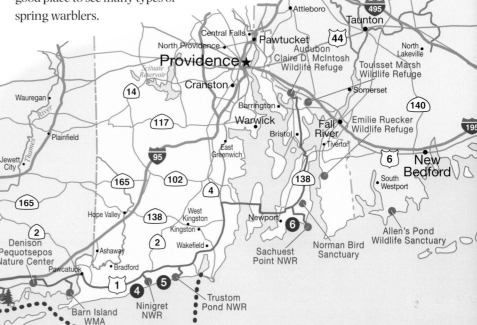

PIPING PLOVER
Charadrius melodus

Length: 6–7.5 in. (15–19 cm)

What to Look for: Pale sand-colored plumage with a partial neck band and orange legs. They blend motionless into the sand, but watch for head bobbing and listen for the plaintive whistle. Appear more plump and stout than other related birds.

Piping plover chick. Nesting adult male (opposite page).

Habitat: Beaches, often above high-tide line. Lay speckled eggs in shallow scrapes, hard to see. Nesting areas are usually closed to prevent loss of clutch in heavily visited areas. Rare and threatened throughout their range. Cooperate with restrictions imposed in nesting areas to help the birds survive.

hawks and butterflies. Visit in September to enjoy the annual celebration of Hawkfest at Lighthouse Point Park.

During migration many thousands of songbirds and raptors can be seen at Morris Creek wetlands, an estuary along the park's south border.

Lighthouse Point Park
2 Lighthouse Point Rd.
New Haven, CT 06512
(203) 946-8019
www.cityofnewhaven.com

❸ Connecticut's Southeast Shore

Return to I-95 N, drive east 11.2 miles (18 km) to exit 59 (Goose Ln.), turn left, then right at Clapboard Hill Rd. Drive 0.9 mile (1.4 km) and turn right on Meadowlands Rd., leading to **Guilford Salt Meadow Sanctuary** and a limited parking area. Open dawn to dusk daily. Respect the private property along Meadowlands Rd. by accessing the sanctuary only on the marked trail.

Follow the full-access 1-mile (1.6-km) loop trail or view the sanctuary from the East River by canoe or kayak. The site is a critical nesting habitat for Nelson's sharp-tailed sparrows, with more found at this location than anywhere else in the world.

The salt marsh also gives fine views of hawks and other birds of prey.

Guilford Salt Meadow Sanctuary
Audubon Connecticut
613 Riversville Rd.
Greenwich, CT 06831
(203) 869-5272
sanctuary: (203) 458-2582
**www.audubon.org/local/
sanctuary/guilford**

Consider extending a visit to the area by traveling inland to three woodland state parks ideal for seeing boreal birds: **Chatfield Hollow SP** and **Cockaponset SP** (off Hwy. 80), and **Devil's Hopyard SP** (north of Old Lyme off Hwy. 156). For additional information, visit the Connecticut State Parks website: **dep.state.ct.us/stateparks**

Return to I-95 N, drive 4.7 miles (7.6 km) east to exit 62 (Hammonasset Connector), go south for 1.2 miles (1.9 km), and follow posted signs to enter **Hammonasset Beach SP** and Meigs Point Nature Center. Open 8 A.M. to sunset daily; center open 10 A.M. to 5 P.M. Tuesday to Sunday, late June to Labor Day. Admission fee is charged (higher on weekends). Nature center staff conduct educational pro-

grams during summer; check with staff for upcoming events.

The park has 2 miles (3.2 km) of beach and wetlands, some with boardwalks. Some areas of the park are closed to the public, but most still have excellent views from the trails. On Willard Island, for instance, there are three trails passing between closed areas and a viewing platform on the island's far side.

See egrets, clapper rails, willets, owls, and osprey, as well as waterfowl in migration periods.

Hammonasset Beach SP
1288 Boston Post Rd.
Madison, CT 06443
(203) 245-2785
dep.state.ct.us/stateparks

Return to I-95 N, take exit 64 (Hwy. 145), turn south, and then left for 1 mile (1.6 km) on Old Clinton Rd. to the headquarters of **Stuart B. McKinney NWR Salt Meadow Unit.** Open 30 minutes before sunrise to 30 minutes after sunset daily.

The refuge has eight units dotted along the Connecticut coast; most are closed to public visitation. Salt Meadow is a recognized IBA, with over 280 recorded bird species. The unit has a self-guided trail through the river and tidal wetlands.

It's common to see wading birds, shorebirds, and songbirds, including endangered roseate terns. Several thousand common terns also nest at the site; the roseates can be distinguished by their all-black bills and long, protruding tails.

Stewart B. McKinney NWR
733 Old Clinton Rd.
Westbrook, CT 06498
(860) 399-2513
www.fws.gov

Return to I-95 N, drive east 12 miles (19 km), take exit 72, and follow the signs south to **Rocky Neck SP.** Open 8 A.M. to sunset daily; camping fee May to September. Admission fee is charged.

Bride Brook divides the park, and its west edge borders Fourmile River. Both have wetland margins. Follow the westside woodland-and-marsh trails and visit the beach. See hawks, cranes, herons, night-herons, and other raptors and wading birds. On the beach see gulls and shorebirds.

Rocky Neck SP
P.O. Box 676
Niantic, CT 06357
(860) 739-5471
dep.state.ct.us/stateparks/ parks/rockyneck.htm

Return to I-95 N, go east 10.7 miles (17.2 km), take exit 85 (Hwy. 1N), drive 3.1 miles (5 km) southeast, and turn right at Depot Rd., which leads to the entrance of **Bluff Point SP.** Open 8 A.M. to sunset daily.

This 800-acre (324-h) coastal reserve sits on a wooded peninsula overlooking Long Island Sound. It has both hiking trails and great bird-viewing spots from trails along its west side.. The southernmost loop trail overlooks a natural-area preserve to the east and a sandy spit to the west.

A vestige of the region's original habitat, it is a migrant trap for small perching birds and songbirds, as well as hawks.

Bluff Point SP
90 Walbach St.
New London, CT 06320
(860) 444-7591
dep.state.ct.us/stateparks

Return to I-95 N, drive east 3.6 miles (5.8 km), and take exit 90 (Hwy. 27). Turn right on Hwy. 27 and left on Coogan Blvd., drive 0.7 mile (1.3 km), turn right at Jerry Browne Rd., and go right on Pequotsepos Rd., which leads to **Denison Pequotsepos Nature Center.** Open 9 A.M. to 5 P.M. Monday to Saturday, 10 A.M. to 4 P.M. Sunday. Admission fee is charged.

Part wildlife sanctuary, part educational facility and tourist attraction, the 300-acre (121-h) site has exhibits and 8 miles (13 km) of trails in a wooded preserve. A boardwalk crosses wetland areas around Duck Pond; other trails wind through forest and meadow habitats with bluebirds, blue jays, woodpeckers,

and owls. A variety of hawks and owls are held in an outdoor flight enclosure, making it easy to closely examine their plumage and habits.

Denison Pequotsepos Nature Center
109 Pequotsepos Rd.
Mystic, CT 06355
(860) 536-1216
www.dpnc.org

At Jerry Browne Rd. turn southeast. Drive to Mistuxet Ave., turn left, bear right at both Deans Mill Rd. and Flanders Rd., and turn left at Stonington Westerly Rd. Drive 2.2 miles (3.5 km), turn right at Green Haven Rd. and immediately right again at Palmer Rd., which leads in 1.2 miles (1.9 km) to 1,013-acre (410-h) **Barn Island WMA.**

The area is a recognized IBA for two subspecies of sharp-tailed sparrows, willets, and king rails. It has 4.5 miles (7.2 km) of mixed-use coastal trails. Use caution when birding here in fall during deer hunting season; the site is popular with hunters.

See glossy ibis, great and snowy egrets, little blue herons, and other large wading birds. Also view least and common terns, black rails, Savannah sparrows, yellow-breasted chats, northern harriers, and short-eared owls.

Connecticut Wildlife Div.
Barn Island WMA
391 Rte. 32
North Franklin, CT 06254
(860) 642-7239
www.lisrc.uconn.edu/coastal access

This male piping plover is nearly invisible as it sits on its nest on a sandy beach. The bill becomes orange with a black tip for a short time during mating season.

A snowy owl has marble-eyed beauty and a stoic manner that never ceases to amaze those who get the chance to view one. This owl was photographed at Audubon Coastal Center at Milford Point, far south of its normal range.

Ninigret NWR
3679-D Old Post Rd.
Charlestown, RI 02813
(401) 364-9124
www.fws.gov

❺ Trustom Pond NWR

Follow Hwy. 1 south 6.2 miles (10 km) to Moonstone Rd., turn right, and go 1 mile (1.6 km) to Matanuck Schoolhouse Rd. and turn right, leading to 800-acre (324-h) **Trustom Pond NWR.** Open daily dawn to dusk.

More than 300 recorded bird species have been observed at this site, and ospreys nest here. The site is a favorite for local bird-watchers seeking neotropical migratory songbirds and perching birds in spring and fall.

Trustom Pond NWR
3679-D Old Post Rd.
Charlestown, RI 02813
(401) 364-9124
www.fws.gov

If time permits, take a maritime detour by ferry to **Block Island NWR.** The refuge has 32 miles (51 km) of trails. Board ferries at Point Judith; reservations are advised.
www.fws.gov

❻ Newport Area

Return to Hwy. 1, turn northeast, drive 11.7 miles (19 km) to Hwy. 138, turn east, and cross the Jamestown and Claiborne Pell bridges into Newport. Follow Admiral Kalbfus Rd. to become Mantonomi Ave., turn right on Valley Rd. (Hwy. 138A), and bear right on Purgatory Rd. Turn left where it becomes Paradise Ave. at its end; take a quick right on Sachuest Point Rd. and drive to its end, **Sachuest Point NWR.** Open dawn to dusk daily.

The point is an important stopover for migrating and wintering birds of all species. Over 200 birds have been recorded in the refuge, and over 150 reside here. They include snowy owls, peregrine falcons, northern harriers, and harlequin ducks.

There are 2 miles (3.2 km) of interpretive trails with viewing platforms. The refuge is popular for birding in all seasons.

Sachuest Point NWR
3679-D Old Post Rd.
Charlestown, RI 02813
(401) 364-9124
www.fws.gov

Return to Sachuest Point Rd., make a right turn at Hanging Rocks Rd., and turn left at Third Beach Rd., which leads to 450-acre (182-h) **Norman Bird Sanctuary.** Open 9 A.M. to 5 P.M. daily. Admission fee is charged.

The preserve has 7 miles (11.3 km) of trails that pass ponds, cross wetlands on boardwalks, wend through cattail marshes, and follow ridgelines. Both wetland birds and shore-

❹ Ninigret NWR

Return to Stonington Westerly Rd. (Hwy. 1), turn right, follow Hwy. 1 through the town of Westerly to Franklin St., turn right, and drive about 9 miles (14.5 km) southeast. Turn right from Hwy. 1 just prior to Ninigret Town Park, driving to the road's end and a parking lot at **Ninigret NWR.** Open dawn to dusk daily.

Over 250 bird species have been recorded at the refuge; 70 species nest there. The site is a former military airfield, and it is on the north shore of Ninigret Pond, a large salt pond. The site has a visitors center and a 3-mile (4.8-km) nature trail with interpretive kiosks and viewing platforms. Visit Foster and Coon coves to see wading birds and shorebirds; the main pond is where to view waterfowl.

⬅️⬅️ **Not to Be Missed!**

Birds of Connecticut at the Yale Peabody Museum
170 Whitney Ave., New Haven, CT 06511

The 722 mounted specimens in the Birds of Connecticut Hall provide a close examination of the state's common, rare, and threatened birds. The specimens are posed realistically, showing species' distinguishing marks, hybridization, plumage changes, and unusual plumages. Each species is represented by at least one male and female, showing age differences and breeding changes. The exhibit took five years to complete and opened to the public on May 12, 1972.

In New Haven take exit 3 off I-91, turn onto Trumbull St., and turn right onto Whitney Ave. at the second intersection. Follow the signs to the Peabody Museum visitors parking lot 22 at Yale University. Street parking is also available. Open 10 A.M. to 5 P.M. Monday to Saturday, noon to 5 P.M. Sunday. Admission fee is charged; discounts for seniors, children, and college students with school-issued identification cards.

For further information:
www.yale.edu/peabody/exhibits/ctbirds.html

Mounted specimens allow close views to examine each bird's distinctive markings, plumage, coloration, and size—all features that are sometimes difficult to discern in the wild.

Audubon Claire D. McIntosh
Wildlife Refuge
1401 Hope St.
Bristol, RI 02809
(401) 245-7800
www.asrieec.org

birds are seen in the marshes and ponds, while the woods hold ring-necked pheasants, woodcocks, and many species of songbird.

Norman Bird Sanctuary
583 Third Beach Rd.
Middletown, RI 02842
(401) 846-2577
www.normanbirdsanctuary.org

Take Third Beach Rd. 2.9 miles (4.7 km) north, turn right at E. Main Rd. (Hwy. 138), go 5.5 miles (8.8 km), bear left at Turnpike Ave., Bristol Ferry Rd., and Mt. Hope Bridge, and bear right at Metacom Ave. Drive 3.9 miles (6.3 km) north, turn left at Tupelo St., and turn right at Hope St. to arrive at **Audubon Claire D. McIntosh Wildlife Refuge.** Hours vary by day and season; consult the website. Admission fee is charged. The site offers educational programs, nature walks, and a walking trail with a 0.3-mile (0.4-km) boardwalk through both freshwater and saltwater marshes with views of Narragansett Bay. See shorebirds, wading birds, and waterfowl, as well as seabirds such as grebes, cormorants, and scoters.

If time permits, also visit these important sites:

- **Touisset Marsh Wildlife Refuge,** Warren, RI; marsh, meadow, and forest habitat with nature trails.
- **Emilie Ruecker Wildlife Refuge,** Tiverton, RI; great and snowy egrets, glossy ibis, and ospreys.
- **Allen's Pond Wildlife Sanctuary,** Dartmouth; 300 bird species.

New York City Area

Whet an appetite for birding by taking advantage of New York's Forever Wild preserves, nature centers, and parks before taking a quick subway ride to Jamaica Bay or a trip by car out to Montauk Point. The route maps the nearby and familiar, as well as hidden nooks and crannies along backroads and bays to chart a birding adventure to remember. Whatever the season, there are birds to be seen. Visit during migration and view tiny songbirds en route to their summer or winter range. Note birds that nest in the region in late spring and summer, and see others that endure the heart of winter's cold.

Home to millions, the metropolis and its surrounding regions is also an area filled with birds of many species. From moments of quiet contemplation in Manhattan's Central Park to the farthest shores of Long Island and Sandy Hook, visit and enjoy.

The Pool in Central Park, on the west side of the park between 100th St. and 103rd St., is a quiet sanctuary for birds in the midst of a busy city. Red maples and willow trees rest on the water's edge, frequently filled with songbirds.

A graceful and streamlined tree swallow at Jamaica Bay Wildlife Refuge can be distinguished from other swallow species by its blue-green back and head.

❶ New York City and Boroughs

Start a birding tour of New York in **Central Park,** an oasis for birds and people alike. Claims have been made that 300 bird species visit or inhabit the park,

but it's certain that at least 270 have been recorded there. Of that, 192 either reside or nest within the park's boundaries. Warblers are especially plentiful, with over 30 species noted; during migration their presence increases. Visit these hot spots:

- **Central Park Pond,** near 59th St.; waterfowl and shorebirds visit the pond's margins and island.
- **Wagner Cove,** just west of Cherry Hill fountain in the south end; a secluded corner of the lake. Also find

Hallett Nature Sanctuary, a 3.5-acre (1.4-h) preserve only open by reservation.

- **Strawberry Fields,** on the lake's southwest shore; a wooded area with a variety of songbirds, meadows for ring-necked pheasants.

- **Central Park Lake,** off W. 72nd St.; 18 acres (7 h) of meandering shore good for waterfowl and wading birds.

- **Central Park Ramble,** just north of the lake; a 38-acre (15-h) garden with the Gill (a stream). Over 230 birds have been recorded, and it is rated one of the top 15 bird-watching sites in the country.

- **Belvedere Castle,** in the Great Lawn section; papier-mâché birds on the second floor depict the park's birds, and recordings of songs helps to identify them.

- **Turtle Pond,** at Belvedere Castle's base; Turtle Island is a nesting and foraging site for birds. A blind overlooks the pond; use it to view herons perched atop dead trees.

- **The Reservoir,** the park's largest water body, north-central park; a jogging track around the reservoir gives good views of birds. See up to 20 species of waterfowl, plus gulls, loons, and grebes.

- **The Pool,** west side, near W. 102nd St.; small, quiet, with a small stream. See birds such as great egrets, herons, ducks, and other waterfowl.

- **Harlem Meer,** east side near 108th St.; an 11-acre (4.5-h) lake (*meer* means lake in Dutch) with woods. Watch for swans, grebes, night-herons, ducks, and geese.

- **The Ravine,** creek habitat linking the Pool with Harlem Meer; a 90-acre (36-h) area with woodlands, the Loch (a stream), and several waterfalls. Birds bathe in its waters; even glossy ibis come to this location.

Remember that Central Park, even its secluded sections, is part of a large urban city; use caution for personal safety and always bird in pairs or groups.

Central Park
14 E. 60th St.
New York, NY 10022
(212) 310-6600
www.centralparknyc.org

The Forever Wild Program has been implemented throughout New York City parks. Its aim is to protect and preserve the most ecologically valuable land in the five boroughs. Over 8,700 acres (3,521 h) comprising 48 sites have been placed into preservation status by the Forever Wild program, including:

- **Riverside Park,** at the Hudson River between 72nd St. and 155th St.; at 79th St. boat basin, Canada geese, ducks, and other waterfowl swim among the boats.

- **Inwood Hill Park** and **Shorakapok Preserve,** Henry Hudson Pkwy. and Riverside Dr.; the oldest stands of forest and last salt marsh in Manhattan on the Manhattan ridge. Good hiking and nature trails. Over 150 recorded bird species, such as hairy woodpeckers, black-capped chickadees, warblers, herons, egrets, and belted kingfishers.

- **Riverdale Park and Raoul Wallenberg Forest Preserve,** in the Bronx at Henry Hudson Pkwy. and

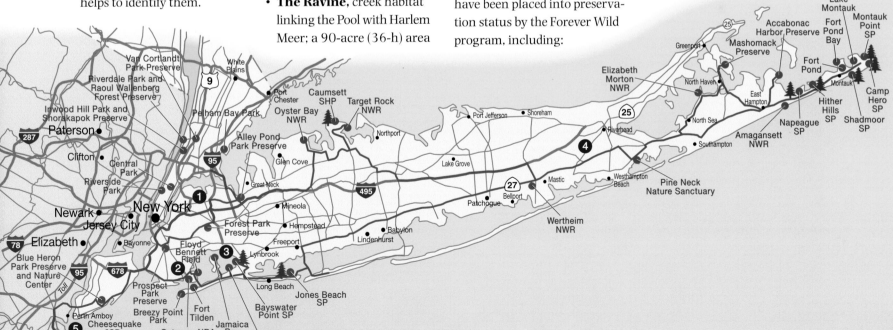

254th St., left at Independence Ave., and right on Spaulding Ln.; a haven for screech-owls, downy woodpeckers, red-tailed hawks, and white-throated sparrows. Yellow and other warblers and common yellowthroats nest at the forest.

- **Van Cortlandt Park Preserve,** Yonkers, off Major Deegan Expy. at Van Cortlandt Park W; third-largest park in the boroughs and an IBA. Bird-watch along Tibbet's Brook and the wetlands to see wood ducks, red-tailed hawks, barred owls, and eastern bluebirds. Several nature trails pass through wetland and forest habitats.
- **Pelham Bay Park,** Bronx, Hutchinson River Pkwy. at

Shore Rd.; the Thomas Pell Wildlife Refuge entrance is at the bridle path at the golf course. Also visit Pelham Bay Park Marine Sanctuary, Shore Rd. to Park Dr., left to Orchard Beach. Follow the boardwalk trail north past Orchard Beach Nature Center.

- **Alley Pond Park Preserve,** Queens, Long Island Expy. at Cross Island Pkwy.; abundant birdlife in and around wetlands and marshes. Osprey platforms were installed in Little Neck Bay to encourage nesting during late spring.
- **Forest Park Preserve,** Queens, Union Tpke. west from Grand Central Pkwy. to Forest Park Dr.; preserved hardwood forest is a bird-friendly habitat. See yellow-

throated, cerulean, and mourning warblers. Visit trails and observation areas at Strack Pond.

- **Prospect Park Preserve,** Brooklyn-Queens Expy. to Prospect Expy., east to Parkside Ave; 526-acre (213-h) park of ravine and wetland habitats. Visit the Audubon Center at the Boathouse for recent sightings. See ruddy ducks, white-throated and chipping sparrows, eastern towhees, warblers, and hermit thrushes plus shorebirds.

NYC Dept. of Parks and Recreation/the Arsenal
830 5th Ave.
New York, NY 10021
(212) 639-9675
www.nycgovparks.org

A chestnut-sided warbler's yellow crown and ruddy sides make it easy to identify and remember. The bird's song sounds like *tsee, see, see, see, swee-BEAT-chew.* As a memory jog, just remember, "I wish to see Miss Beacher."

❷ Gateway NRA

Take the Battery Tunnel from Manhattan to Brooklyn, follow I-278 south to Brooklyn Belt Pkwy., drive east to exit 11S (Flatbush Ave.), and enter the Floyd Bennett Field Unit of **Gateway NRA** on Jamaica Bay. Open dawn to sunset daily; visitors center open 8:30 A.M. to 5 P.M. daily. Obtain staff recommendations for birding spots and learn about recent sightings. Pick up a bird checklist at either visitors center.

The 9,155-acre (3,705-h) unit, which spans Queens and Brooklyn and encompasses most of Jamaica Bay, has recorded over 300 bird species. It is extremely diverse, with a full range of recreational opportunities, such as hiking, biking, swimming, boating, kayaking, canoeing, and other sports.

Golden-crowned kinglets are among the common migratory species found at the refuge, and peregrine falcons are making a comeback to their historic range. Visit these birding hot spots within the recreation area:

- **Floyd Bennett Field,** Brooklyn Belt Pkwy., exit 11S, south 1.1 mile (1.8 km) on Flatbush to the entrance. The North Forty area and pond along the north boundary and Raptor Point at the northeast corner are good for seeing wading birds, birds of prey, and shorebirds.
- **Fort Tilden and Breezy Point Park,** follow Flatbush

Ave. southwest to Rockaway Point Blvd. and Breezy Point Park. Parking fee is charged April to September; pay at Fort Tilden visitors center, open 9 A.M. to 5 P.M. daily. Threatened piping plovers nest on sandy beaches here in summer. Visit in winter to see gulls and waterfowl, fall and spring to view raptors and migrants.

- **Jamaica Bay Wildlife Refuge,** Brooklyn Belt Pkwy. north to exit 17 (Cross Bay Blvd.), south across the bridge, 1 mile (1.6 km) to the visitors center, open 8:30 A.M. to 5 P.M. daily. A self-guided walk on East Pond and West Pond trails and Upland trail provides promising birding, among the most diverse in the entire New York area.

Gateway NRA
Public Affairs Office
210 New York Ave.
Staten Island, NY 10305
(718) 354-4606
www.nps.gov/gate

❸ Jamaica Bay

Two other Jamaica Bay birding sites are not part of Gateway NRA. Drive Cross Bay Blvd. south to Beach Channel Dr., turn east to Beach 64th St., turn north to Decosta Ave., and turn east to **Dubos Point Wetlands Sanctuary.** Open dawn to dusk daily.

Limited public facilities are to be found here, but the birding is outstanding at this reclaimed dredge-spoils site raised in 1912 from wetlands around Jamaica Bay. See merlin and peregrine falcons, both endangered species. Other common sightings include herons, ducks, hawks, snowy egrets, and Nelson's sharp-tailed and seaside sparrows. The best trail access is along the north shoreline and to the east.

NYC Dept. of Parks and Recreation/the Arsenal
830 5th Ave.
New York, NY 10021
(212) 639-9675
www.nycgovparks.org

Return to Beach Channel Dr., turn east, drive 2.3 miles (3.7 km) to Mott Ave., turn north, and follow Mott Ave. to 12-acre (4.9-h) **Bayswater Point SP.** Open dawn to sunset daily, year-round.

The park is a prime location for seeing neotropical and other migrant birds in spring and fall, nesting birds in late spring to summer. Its habitats include beach, wetlands, and woodlands. Facilities are limited; the park is intended as a natural preserve.

Bayswater Point SP
c/o Gantry Plaza SP
50-50 Second St.
Long Island City, NY 11101
(718) 471-2212
nysparks.state.ny.us/parks

Cape May warblers have distinctive chestnut-colored cheeks. This bird perches in a flowering cherry tree in Central Park but is more common in conifers.

❹ Long Island

Return on Mott Ave. southeast for 1.6 miles (2.6 km), turn left on Frisco Ave., right on Beach 12th St. to Seagirt Blvd. Go east to Nassau Expy., turn south, then east on Park St. and follow the main streets of Long Beach for 8 miles (13 km) to Loop Pkwy., turn left, cross the bridge, and enter **Jones Beach SP.** Open dawn to sunset daily, year-round. Admission fee is charged. Consult staff for birding advice.

The park has several units on the barrier islands, with 6.5 miles (10.5 km) of ocean shore and a 2-mile (3.2-km) boardwalk. The northwest area is undeveloped and attracts migratory birds.

Jones Beach SP
P.O. Box 1000
Wantagh, NY 11793
(516) 785-1600
nysparks.state.ny.us/parks

Boreal owls are **rarely seen**, but **conifer forests** are good places to look for these **diminutive charmers**

Take Meadowbrook Pkwy. 6 miles (10 km) north to Southern Pkwy.; travel east 16 miles (26 km), merging with Hwy. 27; take exit 58S (William Floyd Pkwy.), and turn south. Turn west on Montauk Hwy. for 0.7 mile (1.1 km), turn south on Smith Rd., and drive 0.3 mile (0.5 km) to the entrance of 2,550-acre (1,032-h) **Wertheim NWR.** Open dawn to dusk daily; headquarters open 8 A.M. to 4 P.M. weekdays except major holidays.

Nearly 300 bird species have been seen in the refuge. They include black, bufflehead, and wood ducks; scaups and gadwall are the focus of refuge management. Nesting structures are in place for songbirds, barn owls, ospreys, and wood ducks to encourage reproduction.

The best time to visit is late winter, when waterfowl numbers peak and migration brings raptors and northern songbirds. Hike 4 miles (6.4 km) of trails, or canoe the refuge's waterways. Blinds and information kiosks are also available to visitors.

Wertheim NWR
360 Smith Rd.
Shirley, NY 11967
(631) 286-0485
www.fws.gov

Return to Hwy. 27, drive 14 miles (22.5 km) east to exit 64 (Lewis Rd.), turn south, and drive to a T intersection with Montauk Hwy. Turn east, south on Josiah Fosters Path, and west on Head

of Lots Rd., which leads to 15-acre (6.1-h) **Pine Neck Nature Sanctuary,** a Nature Conservancy preserve. Open dawn to dusk daily.

Trails through forest, wetlands, and shoreline offer good birding of migratory and nesting songbirds, shorebirds, great horned owls, and red-tailed hawks. Scan the tidal flats on incoming tides for wading birds.

The Nature Conservancy
322 8th Ave., 16th Flr.
New York, NY 10001
(212) 997-8451
**www.nature.org/wherewework/
northamerica/states/newyork/
preserves/art10993.html**

Return to Hwy. 27, go east 27 miles (43 km) to Amagansett (just past East Hampton), turn south on Atlantic Ave., and drive to 36-acre (14.6-h) **Amagansett NWR.** Open dawn to dusk daily; area closures may apply during nesting periods.

Directly bordering the Atlantic Ocean, it is an important rest stop for migrants. Visit April to May and September to October to see raptors and other migrating birds. Both threatened piping plovers and least terns have successfully nested here.

Long Island NWR Complex
360 Smith Rd.
Shirley, NY 11967
(631) 286-0485
www.fws.gov

Return to Hwy. 27 east and pass through **Napeague SP,** one of the largest remaining areas of undeveloped beach and dune ecosystems on Long Island. Over 30 species of birds breed in the park; if time permits, turn off on Napeague Meadow Rd., go right on Lazy Point Rd., and bird the western side of Napeague Harbor and Napeague Pond.

From Hwy. 27 east, take a left turn on Napeague Harbor Rd., which approaches the harbor from the southeast and enters **Hither Hills SP.** Open dawn to sunset daily, year-round.

The bay and harbor are an important area for a variety of wintering waterfowl, and there are hiking and nature trails overlooking the bay. Also visit Fresh Pond near the park's center, which frequently attracts wading birds and shorebirds. Staff at Hither Hills have birding pamphlets for both parks.

Hither Hills SP
50 S. Fairview Ave.
Montauk, NY 11754
(631) 668-2554
nysparks.state.ny.us/parks

Continue east a short way on Hwy. 27; note **Fort Pond** on the left side of Montauk Hwy. Still farther northwest is **Fort Pond Bay.** The two, along with **Lake Montauk,** are good locations to find wintering greater and lesser scaups, red-breasted and

common mergansers, American black ducks, buffleheads, and common goldeneyes. They are also nesting areas for least bitterns, mallards, and ospreys.

Continue east on Hwy. 27 through Montauk Village, turn right at Seaside Ave., and enter **Shadmoor SP.** Open dawn to sunset daily, year-round.

Two stairways lead from the bluffs to the beach. Paths and elevated viewing platforms make bird-watching the sea and offshore waters easy. The park is a flyover stop for migrant birds, and many songbirds stop and stay. Check the black cherry trees, often full of visiting warblers.

Shadmoor SP
50 S. Fairview Ave.
Montauk, NY 11754
(631) 668-3781
nysparks.state.ny.us/parks

Drive to land's end at the tip of Long Island where two state parks nestle—**Montauk Point SP** on Block Island Sound, and **Camp Hero SP** on the Atlantic side. Montauk Point is open dawn to sunset daily; Camp Hero is open 24 hours daily and is a registered National Historic Site.

The two parks contain nearly pristine habitats enjoyed by seabirds and land-dwelling species alike: heavily wooded maritime forest with seaside bluffs, wetlands, and meadows. Both parks are latticed with trails and paths. Overlooking all, Montauk

Pelham Bay Park, with its varied habitats from wooded to salt marsh to bay shoreline, is a popular birding site.

Lighthouse stands in majesty as the tidal race spills between the ocean and the sound.

In winter large flocks of surf, white-winged, and black scoters, common loons, common and king eiders, buffleheads, common goldeneyes, great cormorants, red-breasted mergansers, and harlequin ducks visit. At 125 to 135 species, the Christmas bird count here has among the highest totals in the Northeast. In the protected waters of Block Island Sound, see a variety of large and small waterfowl, wading birds, and shorebirds.

Visit Big Reed, Little Reed, and Oyster ponds for northern harriers, red-shouldered hawks, least bitterns, blue-winged teal, herons, egrets, and songbirds. Keep a watchful eye on the ocean, too. Sea turtles and whales and other marine mammals visit the point.

Montauk Point SP
50 S. Fairview Ave.
Montauk, NY 11754
(631) 668-3781
nysparks.state.ny.us/parks

Return 16 miles (26 km) via Hwy. 27 to East Hampton, turn right on N. Main St., bear right on Springs-Fireplace Rd., and drive 5.5 miles. Note the **Accabonac Harbor Preserve** sign on the right past the white church; this Nature Conservancy preserve is open dawn to dusk daily.

Paths wind through marsh and wetlands from the trailhead on Springs-Fireplace Rd.; close all gates after passage. Threatened piping plovers and locally threatened least terns nest on the site, as do other shorebirds, wading birds, and waterfowl. Also see nesting ospreys, hawks, harriers, and other raptors.

The Nature Conservancy
322 8th Ave., 16th Flr.
New York, NY 10001
(212) 997-8451
**www.nature.org/wherewework/
northamerica/states/newyork/
preserves/art10984.html**

Return to East Hampton, turn right on N. Main St., right on Newtown Ln., bear left on Railroad Ave., turn left on Race Ln., right on Gingerbread Ln., and left on Toilsome Ln. A final right turn onto Sag Harbor Rd. (Hwy. 114) and driving 9.2 miles (14.8 km) leads to the ferry to Shelter Island (fare required). Hours vary; visit the website at **www.southferry.com**

Disembark on Shelter Island; follow Hwy. 114 north for 1 mile (1.6 km) to **Mashomack Preserve,** another Nature Conservancy facility. Open dawn to dusk daily; the visitors center has trail maps. Donations are appreciated.

There are 11 miles (17.7 km) of hiking on four trails, including one full-access trail. The site has 80 known nesting species and 60 species of birds that winter at the preserve's oaks, shore, and sphagnum moss swamp wetlands.

Visit from mid-March to late summer to see nesting ospreys in great numbers. In fall waterfowl include hundreds of black ducks and Canada geese. Even ruby-throated hummingbirds visit the island and preserve.

The Nature Conservancy
322 8th Ave., 16th Flr.
New York, NY 10001
(212) 997-8451
**www.nature.org/wherewework/
northamerica/states/newyork/
preserves/art10992.html**

Return by ferry to North Haven, drive Hwy. 114 south, and continue straight 1.8 miles (2.9 km) on Short Beach Rd. (Hwy. 60). Bear right on Noyack Rd. and drive 2.2 miles (3.5 km) to **Elizabeth Morton NWR,** on the north side of the road opposite Noyack Golf Club. Open dawn to dusk daily; the sandy peninsula with piping plover nesting areas is closed April to August. Admission fee is charged. An information kiosk has trail maps.

The 187-acre (76-h) refuge has a widely varied collection of bird habitats, including saltwater beach and marsh, brackish lagoons, maritime oak and cedar forests, freshwater ponds, tidal flats, meadows, and shrub vegetation areas. It is of little surprise that several hundred bird species have been recorded on the refuge and that many birds nest here.

A nature trail winds from upland areas to the beach, which follows the jutting peninsula about 2 miles (3.2 km) into the Shelter Island Sound. See all types of migratory birds, waterfowl, shorebirds, and wading birds. In spring large numbers of neotropical migrant songbirds are also present at the refuge's forests and meadows.

Long Island NWR Complex
360 Smith Rd.
Shirley, NY 11967
(631) 286-0485
www.fws.gov

Return about 25 miles (40 km) west on Long Island, following Hwy. 27 to Shirley, turning north to join I-495, and proceeding east to exit 53 (Express Dr. N). Turn west on Northern Pkwy. to exit 42N (DeForest Rd.), turn left on Deer Park Rd., which becomes Park Ave., and drive 5.3 miles (8.5 km) to Main St. in Huntington. Continue through town, turn left on West Neck Rd., drive 4.4 miles (7.1 km), cross the neck to Lloyd Harbor Rd., and go east to Target Rock Rd., a right turn, and enter **Target Rock NWR.**

Open 30 minutes before sunrise to 30 minutes after sunset daily. Portions of the beach are closed to the public during nesting season every April to August to protect threatened piping plovers and bank swallows. Admission fee is charged.

Visit the headquarters to obtain a trail guide, or pick up brochures at the information kiosk at the trailhead.

The trail passes through hardwood forest to reach the Huntington Bay shoreline, where migratory waterfowl, wading birds, and shorebirds are plentiful. See neotropical migrant warblers, common yellowthroats, and other songbirds in spring and fall. Large numbers of hawks and other raptors also transit the park in fall. In winter look for diving ducks, scoters, grebes, and loons.

Target Rock NWR
12 Target Rock Rd.
Huntington, NY 11743
(631) 286-0485
www.fws.gov

Retrace west on Target Rock Rd. and Lloyd Harbor Rd. to **Caumsett SHP,** an adjacent facility. Open year-round from sunrise to sunset. Admission fee is charged.

Though the park is primarily a historical estate, its nature trails provide many additional miles of access to woodlands, meadows, rocky shorelines, and salt

marshes. The site also hosts the Volunteers for Wildlife Hospital and Education Center, a rehabilitation program for rescued wild birds and other animals.

For birders the area around Fresh Pond and the sand beach and bay on the northwest point provide the best opportunities to see birds.

Caumsett State Historic Park
25 Lloyd Harbor Rd.
Huntington, NY 11743
(631) 423-1770
**nysparks.state.ny.us/parks/info
.asp?parkID=68**

Take West Neck Rd. back to W. Main St., turn right, continue west on Lawrence Hill Rd. as it becomes N. Hempstead Tpke., then turn north on Oyster Bay Cove Rd. Follow Cove Rd., E. Main St., and W. Main St. to a right turn on W. Shore Rd., skirting the margin of **Oyster Bay NWR.** Open dawn to dusk daily.

A comprehensive visit to this refuge requires a boat; craft are available to rent locally. To sample the refuge from a vehicle, pull off on W. Shore Rd. to look for birds along the shore. In winter waterfowl fill West Harbor and it's common to see

An immature yellow-crowned night-heron at Jamaica Bay Wildlife Refuge.

223

This little vagrant bird caused quite a stir after it was photographed on Jones Beach. The still-controversial verdict: It's a male cross between a hermit and a Townsend's warbler—definitely an accidental in the northeastern states.

large flocks of Canada geese, greater white-fronted geese, snow geese, tundra swans, and many species of dabbling and diving ducks in rafts that speckle the water. Pay special attention to sheltered areas.

Long Island NWR Complex
360 Smith Rd.
Shirley, NY 11967
(631) 286-0485
www.fws.gov

❺ The North New Jersey Shore

Return via the Long Island Expy. (I-495) and Brooklyn-Queens Expy. (I-278) to the southwest tip of Long Island and the Verranzano Narrows

Bridge (toll). Cross the bridge, take exit 14 (Narrows Rd. N), turn left on Hylan Blvd., continue on Steuben St., and then rejoin Hylan Blvd. Drive 7.4 miles (12 km) southwest to Poillon Ave. and turn right, heading north to the entrance and parking lot of **Blue Heron Park Preserve and Nature Center.** Open 11 A.M. to 4 P.M. Tuesday to Saturday, noon to 4 P.M. Sunday.

The preserve is another site in New York's Forever Wild program. The visitors center is just off Poillon Ave. It has two viewing decks with bird feeders. Staff frequently demonstrate bird-banding techniques using a mist net to capture songbirds.

The 169-acre (68-h) park has six kettle ponds, steep-sided remnants of the glaciation that blanketed the region 15,000 years ago. Blue Heron Pond is crossed by a footbridge.

As the preserve's name suggests, it's common to see great blue herons here. Equally likely are glossy ibis, black-crowned night-herons, wood ducks, owls, and ospreys, among other wading birds, waterfowl, raptors, and songbirds.

NYC Dept. of Parks and Recreation/the Arsenal
830 5th Ave.
New York, NY 10021
(212) 639-9675
www.nycgovparks.org

Return to Hylan Blvd., turn right, drive to Huguenot Ave., turn right, and turn left at Drumgoole Rd. W, entering Korean War Veterans Pkwy. (Hwy. 440) and traveling west. Cross Outer Bridge, proceed to Garden State Pkwy. (Hwy 9), drive south 7.2 miles (11.6 km) to exit 120 (Matawan Rd.), bear right at the off-ramp, and turn right on Morristown Rd. Make another right turn at Gordon Rd. and proceed to the entrance of **Cheesequake SP,** noting its signs. Open daily year-round. Admission fee is charged Memorial Day to Labor Day; free otherwise.

A 1,361-acre (551-h) coastal salt marsh that transitions to upland forest, the park

has trails that pass through a natural-area preserve. The park's paths range from 1.5 miles (2.4 km) to 3.5 miles (5.6 km) and in difficulty from moderate to strenuous. All have excellent birding, especially in spring when migrants pass through the park and nearby waterways.

Visit the Interpretive Center near the trailhead parking to obtain a bird checklist with 186 recorded species of birds. Among the many birds likely to be seen are ospreys, egrets, marsh wrens, warblers, vireos, and double-crested cormorants.

Cheesequake SP
300 Gordon Rd.
Matawan, NJ 07747
(732) 566-2161
www.state.nj.us/dep/park sandforests/parks/

Return to the Garden State Pkwy., turn south, drive to exit 117 (Lloyd Rd.), cross under the parkway, turn right on Clark St., and turn left to enter Hwy. 36. Drive south 14 miles (22 km) toward Keyport and Sandy Hook, bearing right on Ocean Ave. and turning north to enter **Gateway NRA Sandy Hook Unit.** Open daily year-round. Admission fee is charged.

A 2,044-acre (827-h) peninsula thrusting into the Atlantic at the northern tip of New Jersey, the park is a popular birding site because of the large numbers of migratory waterfowl and other species that follow the seacoast as they fly through the region.

Also of interest at the park is Sandy Hook Lighthouse. Built in 1764, it is the oldest surviving lighthouse in the country. Take advantage of the 5-mile (8 km) multiuse pathway that extends the length of the peninsula.

A year-round birding site, the park is among New Jersey's best. Visit the Sandy Hook Bird Observatory, located at the park's far end near Fort Hancock, to consult staff on bird identifica-

tions, recent sightings and current hot spots. Also obtain a bird checklist and visit their website: **www.njaudubon.org/ centers/shbo**

Birding locations at Sandy Hook include Plum Island, Spermaceti Cove boardwalk by the visitors center, Horseshoe Cove salt marsh, North Pond, and the grassy fields at Fort Hancock. Also peruse the tidelands and dune areas, especially in late spring when birds exhibit their mating behaviors. Rare birds such as piping plovers and least terns sometimes nest in

the park. (Note that beach closures are enforced in some nesting areas.) In addition, ospreys nest, fish, and soar at Sandy Hook and in offshore waters, busily feeding and rearing their young from late spring through late summer.

Migration in spring and fall brings a peak in the number of bird species, from tiny songbirds to massive great blue herons and other waterbirds. The most commonly seen during these times are flycatchers and gnatcatchers, phoebes, warblers, sparrows, buntings, loons,

grebes, and gulls. Less frequently seen but always memorable are snowy owls and the Lapland longspurs. When strong storms blow in from the south, even rare birds, such as scissor-tailed flycatchers, Townsend's warblers, and swallow-tailed kites, have made appearances.

Gateway NRA/Sandy Hook Unit
P.O. Box 530
Fort Hancock, NJ 07732
(732) 872-5970
www.nps.gov

Ross's geese have short, stubby bills with irregular raised, darker areas. These features, along with their rounded heads, distinguish them from larger snow geese, birds with which they often flock. The bird seen here was photographed on Jones Beach in November with Canada geese in the background.

Philadelphia Area

BIRDING TOUR 29

Coastal Pennsylvania, Delaware, and New Jersey take the spotlight in this birding tour of the rivers, coastal estuaries, and seacoast that travels north from Philadelphia and swings back along the western shore of the Delaware River before crossing the river and venturing east to Cape May. En route, quiet parks, preserves, reserves, refuges, and sanctuaries celebrate the birds moving along the Atlantic Flyway. This horseshoe of a route is good luck for every bird-watcher that travels its path. Along the way, see rare and endangered birds, the annual prehistoric spectacle of horseshoe crabs spawning as shorebirds loot their eggs, and quiet nests camouflaged on the sandy dunes, grassy knolls, and rocky shores. Observe and enjoy the many wonders to behold.

The cradle of liberty and the Delaware River are hot spots for migratory songbirds, waterfowl, shorebirds, and seabirds plying the Atlantic coast. Visit areas within a two hours' drive of the city to enjoy beautiful birds answering nature's summons.

Ruddy turnstones are usually seen in small groups. They have shorter legs than most other members of the sandpiper family.

Manayunk Canal Towpath is the connecting link for the Schuylkill River Trail. A bike is leisurely transport for a little early morning birding.

Neshaminy Creek, has 4 miles (6.4 km) of trails. River Walk and Inner Loop trails are the most productive for birders, and both have trailheads on Logan Walk. They follow the riverine shoreline and the tidal marsh, entering the woodsy interior of the park.

See wading birds and shorebirds throughout the year, migratory waterfowl and neotropical migrant perching birds and songbirds in spring and fall. Many migrants nest in the park's forest areas. Also see kingfishers, gnatcatchers, and flycatchers near the rivers, especially in morning and evening after the hatches of flying insects.

Neshaminy SP
3401 State Rd.
Bensalem, PA 19020
(215) 639-4538
www.dcnr.state.pa.us/state
parks/Parks/neshaminy.aspx

❶ Bristol Area

Drive 14.5 miles (23 km) north on I-95 from Philadelphia to exit 37 (Street Rd.), turn southeast, drive to State Rd., and turn left to enter 330-acre (134-h) **Neshaminy SP.** Open dawn to sunset daily, year-round.

The park, which includes a 71-acre (29-h) natural area along the Delaware River and

To reach **Silver Lake Nature Center,** return to State Rd., turn northeast for 2.9 miles (4.7 km), make a left turn on New Rodgers Rd., a right on Otter St., a left on Bath St., and go 0.5 mile

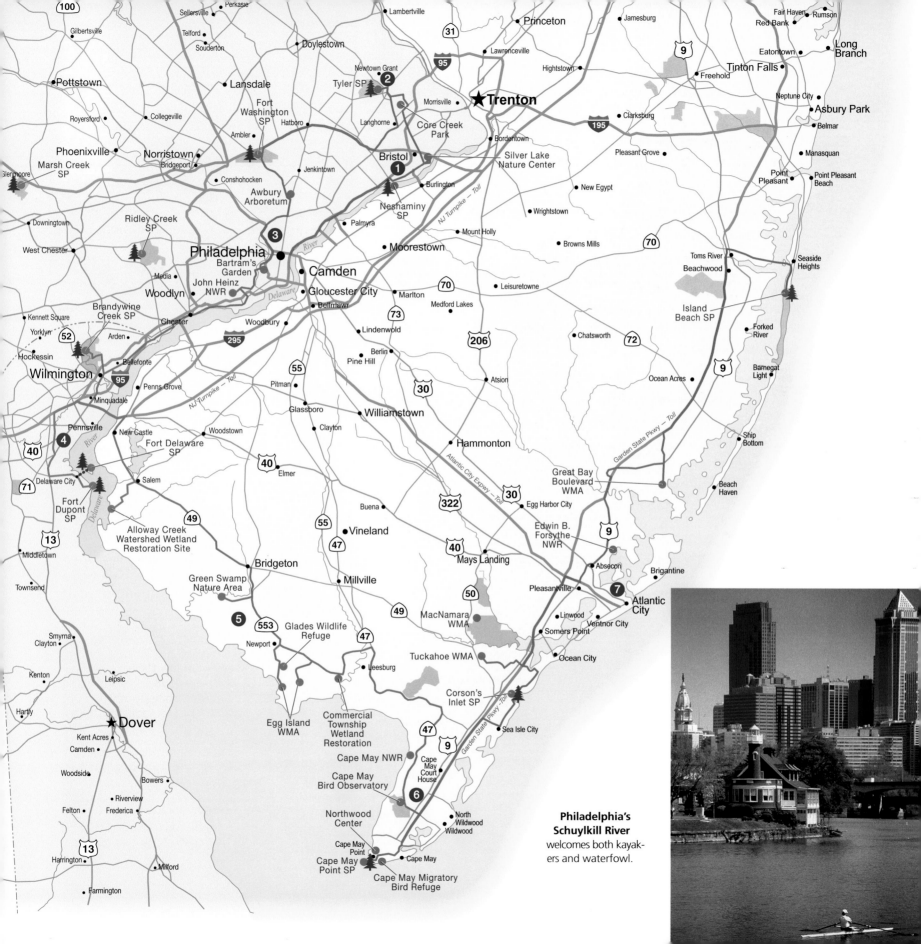

(100)
Gilbertsville
Sellersville
Perkasie
Lambertville
Princeton
Jamesburg
Fair Haven
Red Bank
Rumson

Telford
Souderton
Doylestown
(31)
Lawrenceville
Hightstown
(9)
Eatontown
Long Branch

Pottstown
Lansdale
Newtown Grant
Tyler SP
(2)
Morrisville
★ Trenton
(195)
Clarksburg
Freehold
Tinton Falls
Neptune City
Asbury Park

Phoenixville
Norristown
Fort Washington SP
Hatboro
Langhorne
Core Creek Park
Bordentown
Silver Lake Nature Center
Pleasant Grove
Belmar

Royersford
Collegeville
Ambler
Jenkintown
Bristol (1)
Burlington
New Egypt
Manasquan

Marsh Creek SP
Bridgeport
Conshohocken
Awbury Arboretum
Neshaminy SP
Palmyra
Wrightstown
Point Pleasant
Point Pleasant Beach

Glenmoore
Downingtown
Ridley Creek SP
(3) Philadelphia
Bartram's Garden
Camden
Mount Holly
Moorestown
Browns Mills
(70)
Toms River
Beachwood
Seaside Heights

West Chester
Media
John Heinz NWR
Gloucester City
Marlton
(70)
Leisuretowne
Island Beach SP

Woodlyn
Chester
Bellmawr
Woodbury
Medford Lakes
Chatsworth
(72)
Forked River

Brandywine Creek SP
Kennett Square
Arden
(295)
Lindenwold
Berlin
Pine Hill
(73)
(206)
Ocean Acres
Barnegat Light
(9)

Yorklyn
(52)
Bellefonte
Penns Grove
Woodstown
(55)
Pitman
Glassboro
(30)
Williamstown
Atsion
(9)
Ship Bottom

Hockessin
Wilmington
(95)
Minquadale
Clayton
Hammonton
Barnegat Light

Pennsville
(4)
New Castle
Fort Delaware SP
(40)
Elmer
Buena
Egg Harbor City
Great Bay Boulevard WMA
Beach Haven

(40)
(71)
Delaware City
Salem
(55)
Vineland
(322)
(30)
Edwin B. Forsythe NWR
(9)

Fort Dupont SP
(49)
Alloway Creek Watershed Wetland Restoration Site
(47)
Mays Landing
(40)
Absecon
Brigantine

(13)
Middletown
Bridgeton
Green Swamp Nature Area
Millville
(50)
MacNamara WMA
Pleasantville
(7) Atlantic City

Townsend
(5)
(553)
Glades Wildlife Refuge
(47)
(49)
Linwood
Ventnor City
Somers Point

Smyrna
Clayton
Newport
Leesburg
Tuckahoe WMA
Ocean City

Kenton
Egg Island WMA
Commercial Township Wetland Restoration
Corson's Inlet SP
Sea Isle City

★ Dover
Leipsic
Kent Acres
Camden
Hartly
Cape May NWR
(47)
(9)
Cape May Court House

Woodside
Cape May Bird Observatory
(6)

Bowers
Northwood Center
North Wildwood
Wildwood

Riverview
Frederica
Cape May Point
Cape May Point SP
Cape May
Cape May Migratory Bird Refuge

(13)
Felton
Harrington
Milford
Farmington

Philadelphia's Schuylkill River welcomes both kayakers and waterfowl.

(0.8 km). Trails are open dawn to sunset daily; visitors center open 10 A.M. to 5 P.M. Tuesday to Saturday, noon to 5 P.M. Sunday.

The center's setting is a 253-acre (102-h) county park with 4.5 miles (7.2 km) of trails, plus a 0.5-mile (0.8-km) full-access path. An observation platform overlooks the wetlands and lake. Also ask staff about guided walks to Bristol Marsh Preserve, a Nature Conservancy site with viewing platforms and nature trails to allow close looks at migratory waterfowl.

See typical wetlands birds plus migratory seabirds such as coots, mergansers, scaups, and loons. Merlins, falcons, and hawks also visit the lake.

Silver Lake Nature Center
1306 Bath Rd.
Bristol, PA 19007
(215) 785-1177
www.silverlakenaturecenter.org

❷ Tyler SP

Follow Bath Rd. south to Bristol Pike for 2.2 miles (3.5 km), bearing left as it splits from Oxford Valley Rd., and turn right on New Rodgers Rd. Drive 4.9 miles (7.9 km), turn right on E. Lincoln Hwy., go left on Woodburn Rd., and drive 2 miles (3.2 km). Here the road enters **Core Creek Park,** an excellent birding area for seeing warblers, vireos, and other migratory songbirds in spring around Lake Luxembourg.

The lake also attracts migratory waterfowl, wading birds such as herons, and shorebirds.

Continue 1.5 miles (2.4 km) north on Woodbourne Rd., turn left at Newtown Bypass, drive west 3 miles (4.8 km), and turn right on Swamp Rd. The entrance to 1,711-acre (692-h) **Tyler SP** on Neshaminy Creek is on the left, 500 feet (152 m) ahead. Open dawn to sunset daily.

Forests, fields, and wetlands provide habitats necessary for birds to thrive. In the hardwood forest areas look for warblers, tanagers, thrushes, and vireos. In meadows see bobolinks, grasshopper sparrows and meadowlarks. The Neshaminy Creek wetlands are favored by waterfowl, including wood ducks and several species of diving ducks. Visit these areas on 4 miles (6.4 km) of

hiking trails, 10.5 miles (11.2 km) of bike paths, and 9 miles (14.5 km) of bridle trails.

Tyler SP
101 Swamp Rd.
Newtown, PA 18940
(215) 968-2021
www.dcnr.state.pa.us/state
parks/parks/tyler.aspx

❸ Philadelphia Area

The first stop on the way back to the outskirts of Philadelphia is **Fort Washington SP,** off I-276 in Whitemarsh.

Take Newtown Bypass south and bear right at Newtown Langhorne Rd., go 3 miles (4.8 km) as it becomes N. Pine St., turn right at E. Maples Ave., left at

S. Bellevue Ave., enter Hwy. 1, and travel south for 3.5 miles (5.6 km). Take the Pennsylvania Tpke. (I-276) west 13 miles (21 km), and take exit 339 (Pennsylvania Ave.), go west 1.4 miles (2.3 km), and turn left at S. Bethlehem Pike, which leads to Fort Washington SP. Open dawn to sunset daily.

The park is a must-see for raptor lovers. All 16 East Coast species have been recorded here, and the park features an observation deck especially for viewing migrating raptors. Visit from September to November.

There are also 3.5 miles (5.6 km) of trails through forests and fields, and the raptor deck has full access. In spring visit the meadows to see warblers, vireos, tanagers, and thrushes, along with meadowlarks.

John Heinz NWR at Tinicum Marsh, just a stone's throw from the bustling city of Philadelphia, is host to Canada geese and a variety of other waterfowl.

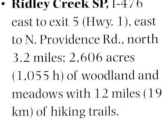

John Heinz NWR's observation platform gives the best views of the area's surrounding wetlands and birds.

Fort Washington SP
500 Bethlehem Pike
Fort Washington, PA 19034
(215) 591-5250
www.dcnr.state.pa.us/stateparks/parks/fortwashington.aspx

Follow S. Bethlehem Pike 0.6 mile (1 km) south to a left turn at Church Rd., drive to Hwy. 309, turn south for 4.2 miles (6.8 km), bear right at E. Washington Ln., and turn left at Chew Ave. The 55-acre (22-h) **Awbury Arboretum** is at Chew Ave. and Awbury Rd. Open dawn to sunset.

See the Secret Garden, a bird sanctuary and viewing blind.

Awbury Arboretum Association
1 Awbury Rd.
Philadelphia, PA 19138
(215) 849-2855
www.awbury.org

Next, visit America's oldest botanical reserve, **Bartram's Garden.** Open 10 A.M. to 5 P.M. daily except holidays.

Go southeast on Awbury Rd., turn right on E. Haines St., turn left at Germantown Ave., go right on W. Berkley St., and enter Hwy. 1 traveling southwest. Drive 1.6 miles (2.6 km), merge onto I-76 east, go 5.5 miles (8.8 km), take exit 346B (University Ave.), turn left onto S. 34th St., and turn right at Grays Ferry Ave.

Bear left at Paschall Ave. and left again at S. 49th St. Follow it as it becomes Grays Ave. and bear left onto Lindbergh Blvd., arriving at S. 54th St. and the garden.

River Trail Boardwalk winds through the Schuylkill River's floodplain, a 1.5-acre (0.6-h) wetland with bulrushes and marsh grasses that attracts many shorebirds. Trail maps are available at the Bartram Barn kiosk and in the museum shop.

Bartram's Garden
54th St. and Lindbergh Blvd.
Philadelphia, PA 19143
(215) 729-5281
www.bartramsgarden.org

Follow Lindbergh Blvd. 3.5 miles (5.6 km) southwest to **John Heinz NWR** at Tinicum Marsh and Mud Island. Open dawn to dusk daily; Cusano Environmental Education Center is open 8:30 A.M. to 4 P.M. daily except for major holidays.

The refuge has 10 miles (16 km) of trails with blinds, board-walks, and an observation tower; best for birding is Impoundment Trail. The 4.5-mile (7.3-km) canoe trail along Darby Creek is navigable for several hours near high tide. Canoe and kayak rentals are available locally.

More than 280 recorded bird species visit the confluence of the Schuylkill and Delaware rivers' freshwater marshes and wetlands, an Atlantic Flyway stop. The birds include 80 that nest. Migratory birds range from warblers to sandpipers, along with ducks, geese, swans, herons, night-herons, egrets, and other waterfowl and shorebirds.

John Heinz at Tinicum NWR
8601 Lindbergh Blvd.
Philadelphia, PA 19153
(215) 365-3118
www.fws.gov

The Philadelphia area is also richly endowed with state parks. Visit these during migration:

- **Marsh Creek SP,** 2 miles (3.2 km) south of exit 312 (Hwy. 100) from Hwy. 76; a 535-acre (217-h) lake with hiking trails through mixed hardwood forest. Exercise caution in hunting season.

- **Ridley Creek SP,** I-476 east to exit 5 (Hwy. 1), east to N. Providence Rd., north 3.2 miles; 2,606 acres (1,055 h) of woodland and meadows with 12 miles (19 km) of hiking trails.

PA Dept. of Conservation and Natural Resources
P.O. Box 8767
Harrisburg, PA 17105
(888) 727-2757
www.dcnr.state.pa.us

Great egrets, with their long legs, necks, and bills, are adept at silent, stealthy stalking to hunt their prey.

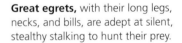

Barnegat Lighthouse is a picturesque landmark at Edwin B. Forsythe NWR, an ideal place to see migrating shorebirds.

❹ Lower Delaware River

Travel south from Philadelphia along the Delaware River's west bank, visiting these state parks, open 8 A.M. to sunset daily (admission fee is charged):

- **Brandywine Creek SP,** I-95 south to Hwy. 202, north to Mount Lebanon Rd., south to Rockland Rd.; 933-acre (378-h) park with 14 miles (22.5 km) of trails and the Brandywine Creek Nature Center, with an indoor observation deck complete with rocking chairs for civilized birding! Good for bluebirds at Freshwater Marsh.
- **Fort Delaware SP,** I-95 south to exit 4A (Hwy. 1), south to Wrangle Hill Rd., east to Delaware City; visitors ride a ferry to Pea Patch

Island (fare) and the park. Nature trails on the 288-acre (117-h) island lead to an observation tower with views of a heron rookery.

- **Fort Dupont SP,** south of Delaware City off Hwy. 9; 322-acre (130-h) park with a self-guided marsh-and-wetland trail by the Delaware River and the Chesapeake and Delaware Canal.

DE Div. of Parks and Recreation
89 Kings Hwy.
Dover, DE 19901
(302) 739-9200
www.destateparks.com

❺ Delaware Bay Area

Return via Hwy. 1 to I-95 north, drive 3 miles (4.8 km) to I-395 east, go 6.5 miles (10.5 km), and

turn south on Hwy 40 to Salem. Bear right on S. Front St., go 0.5 mile (0.8 km), turn right on Oak St., continue on Chestnut St., turn left on Amwellbury Rd., go 1.8 miles (2.9 km), and turn left on Money Island Rd., which leads to **Alloway Creek Watershed Wetland Restoration Site.** The property is owned by Public Service Electric and Gas and is open to the public. Open dawn to dusk daily.

Two trails lead to viewing platforms—one on the Delaware River, the other to the southeast, near electrical transmission towers. The site also has a birding blind near a small pond.

During spring watch migrating shorebirds that have nesting in mind. Raptors migrate through the site in fall. With winter come large flocks of snow and Canada geese, ducks, and waterfowl.

Wear protective clothing and use repellents; mosquitoes are bothersome along the river, especially when breezes die.

Alloway Creek Watershed
Wetlands Restoration Site
Money Island Rd.
Elsinboro, NJ 08038
(888) 627-7437
www.njwildlifetrails.org

If time permits, make a stop at **Green Swamp Nature Area,** another PSE&G site. Return to Salem, follow Hwy. 49 southwest 15.5 miles (25 km) to Bridgeton, turn right at S. Pearl St., bear right at Grove St. (Hwy. 609), and drive 3.2 miles (5.1 km) to Fairton Rd. (Hwy. 553). Turn right, then right again on Back Neck Rd., drive 2 miles (3.2 km), and arrive at the nature area on the right side of the road. Open dawn to dusk daily; unstaffed.

See waterfowl, wading birds, shorebirds, hawks, and nesting ospreys, as well as butterflies.

Public Service Electric and Gas/EEC
P.O. Box 236-N33
Hancocks Bridge, NJ 08038
(888) 627-7437
**www.pseg.com/environment/
overview.jsp**

Return to Hwy. 553, turn right, follow the curve as the name changes to Cedarville Rd., drive 6.4 miles (10.3 km) to Baptist Rd., and turn right. Go 1 mile (1.6 km), turn left at

Fortescue Rd, and drive 2 miles. A National Park Service office servicing the region has staff with information and directions for sites and trails at 7,113-acre (2,879-h) **Glades Wildlife Refuge,** a Natural Lands Trust site, and other local birding locations. Open dawn to dusk daily; the National Park Service office is open 9 A.M. to 5 P.M. weekdays except major holidays.

Wetlands, forests, and river shorelines are traced with trails; an observation tower provides good bird-watching. Spring migration feeding frenzies occur on the river when flocks of turnstones, Forster's terns, and plovers gather as horseshoe crabs lay their eggs at low tide. Glades is also a great place to spot bald eagles and northern harriers.

New Jersey Coastal Heritage
Trail Route/NPS Headquarters
389 Fortescue Rd.
Newport, NJ 08345
(856) 447-0103
www.nps.gov/neje

Ask NPS staff about these other unstaffed birding sites, also open dawn to dusk:

- **Egg Island WMA** (Turkey Point), south on Fortescue Rd. through Fortescue to end of New Jersey Ave.; alternate access via Hwy. 553 to Dividing Creek, west on Maple St., and south to end of Turkey Point Rd. Take footbridge to trails into salt marsh, and ponds. See marsh wrens, sparrows, northern harriers, gulls, and herons.
- **Commercial Township Wetland Restoration,** Hwy. 553 to Port Norris, south to end of Strawberry Ave.; another PSE&G site, with two boardwalks and other trails with viewing platforms. See egrets, neotropical migrants, shorebirds, and waterfowl.

❻ Cape May Peninsula

Drive 4.5 miles (7.2 km) north on Hwy. 649 from Port Norris to Morristown Byps. (Hwy. 670), turn east, drive 12.5 miles (20 km), and follow Hwy. 347 to Dennisville. Turn south at Hwy. 47, go 7.8 miles (12.6 km), turn right on Kimble Beach Rd., and arrive at the 5,000-acre (2,033-h) Delaware Bay Division of **Cape May NWR,** a Ramsar Wetland of International Importance. Open dawn to dusk daily; office open 8 A.M. to 4:30 P.M. weekdays. Two Mile Beach is closed April 1 to September 30 to protect nesting birds; hunting is permitted during season.

A mix of lowland swamp, salt marshes, beach, tidal flats, and upland maritime forest, the refuge receives hundreds of thousands of migratory birds of all species in spring and fall.

See plovers, red knots, ruddy turnstones, egrets, herons, and other wading birds converge on the horseshoe crabs during spring spawning. Designated viewing areas and decks are managed to provide access and take in all the action while protecting the birds.

Visit Headquarters Trail, Woodcock Trail, and Two Mile Beach, and ask staff about their recent sightings.

Cape May NWR
24 Kimbles Beach Rd.
Cape May Court House, NJ 08210
(609) 463-0994
www.fws.gov

Return to Hwy. 47 and drive south 4.6 miles (20 km) to arrive at **Cape May Bird Observatory,** a popular New Jersey Audubon Society site. Open 9 A.M. to 4:30 P.M. daily.

With a focus on backyard birding, it has an outside observation deck and informative staff, including guides for hire with knowledge of the area. See migratory neotropical songbirds, hummingbirds, shorebirds, songbirds, and hawks.

Cape May Bird Observatory
600 Rte. 47 N
Cape May Court House, NJ 08210
(609) 861-0700
www.njaudubon.org

Continue south on Hwy. 47 following Delsea Dr. for 3 miles (4.8 km) and enter Garden State Pkwy. (Hwy. 109S). Drive 4.2 miles (6.8 km) south on Hwy. 109, following Lafayette St. to Jackson St. Turn west, bear left

A seaside sparrow at Cape May delivers its mating song.

A Forster's tern **awaits the start**
of a horseshoe crab **feeding frenzy**

on W. Perry St., continue as it becomes Sunset Blvd., and drive 1 mile (1.6 km) just past Bayshore Rd. to the parking area of **Cape May Migratory Bird Refuge,** a Nature Conservancy preserve. Open 9 A.M. to 4:30 P.M. Thursday to Monday.

The site has meadows, ponds, dunes, saltwater marshes, and a mile (1.6 km) of shore. Trails lead to beach and dune nesting areas with endangered least terns and piping plovers; all of these nesting areas are protected.

William D. and Jane C. Blair Jr.
Cape May Migratory Bird Refuge
350 Rte. 47
Delmont, NJ 08314
(609) 861-0600
**www.nature.org/wherewework/
northamerica/states/newjersey**

Northwood Center, at the tip of Cape May, is the other Audubon-managed facility on the Cape. Continue west on Sunset Blvd. to Light House Ave., turn left, then left on Lake Dr. Open 9 A.M. to 4:30 P.M. daily.

The center has excellent shorebird viewing on Lake Lily.

Cape May Bird Observatory
701 E. Lake Dr.
Cape May Point, NJ 08212
(609) 884-2736
**www.njaudubon.org/centers/
cmbo**

If time permits, go south on Light House Ave. to **Cape May Point SP.** Open dawn to sunset daily, year-round.

It has trails to coastal dunes, ponds, marsh, and forest habitats, all providing a ringside seat at one of the most popular migratory bird sites in North America.

Cape May Point SP
P.O. Box 107
Cape May Point, NJ 08212
(609) 884-2159
**www.state.nj.us/dep/parksand
forests/parks/capemay.html**

❼ New Jersey Shore

Turn north from Cape May, returning to Garden State Pkwy., drive 19 miles (31 km) north to exit 17 (Sea Isle Blvd.), and go east, bearing left on JFK Blvd. Turn left on Landis Ave. (Hwy 617), drive 3.6 miles (5.8 km), and bear left to enter **Corson's Inlet SP.** Open 24 hours daily. Admission fee charged Memorial Day to Labor Day.

The park has a 98-acre (40-h) nature area with beachfront and sand dunes protecting nesting piping plovers, least terns, and black skimmers.

Trails and guided interpretive tours are available.

Corson's Inlet SP
c/o Belleplain State Forest
P.O. Box 450
Woodbine, NJ 08270
(609) 861-2404
**www.state.nj.us/dep/parksand
forests/parks/corsons.html**

Follow Hwy. 619 northeast, turn right on E. 55th St., left on Central Ave., and left on 34th St., which leads to Roosevelt Blvd. Drive 2.4 miles (3.9 km), bear right on Tuckahoe Rd. (Hwy. 631), and drive 5 miles (8 km) to the office of **Tuckahoe WMA (MacNamara WMA),** on the right. Open dawn to dusk daily. Obtain maps before proceeding.

Observe waterfowl, shorebirds, and waders on 14,599 acres (5,908 h) of woods and marshes. See Acadian flycatchers and prothonotary, hooded, and yellow-throated warblers.

Tuckahoe WMA
CR 631/Tuckahoe Rd.
Tuckahoe, NJ 08270
(609) 628-2436
www.njfishandwildlife.org

If time permits while traveling north, also visit:

- **Edwin B. Forsythe NWR,** Garden State Pkwy. north to Atlantic City Expy., east to Hwy. 9, north to Great Creek Rd., east to end; 43,000-acre (17,402-h), three-unit refuge: Brigantine, Barnegat Bay Estuary, and Holgate. All are subject to closures to protect nesting birds; consult staff. **www.fws.gov**

- **Great Bay Boulevard WMA,** Hwy. 9 north to Tuckerton, south 1.8 miles (2.9 km) on Great Bay Blvd.; unstaffed salt marsh with shorebirds such as red knots, dowitchers, curlews, plovers, willets, turnstones, and yellowlegs. Open dawn to dusk daily. **www.njfishandwildlife.org**

- **Island Beach SP,** Garden State Pkwy. north to Dover, east on Hwy. 37, south on Hwy. 35; barrier island ecosystem with a nature center, an interpretive center, trails, and boardwalk. Admission fee is charged. Nesting osprey. **www.state.nj.us**

Gulls on watch at the sand dunes on the New Jersey coast.

Washington, D.C., and the Chesapeake Bay

Begin south of the District of Columbia on the shores of the Potomac River, then trace the river upstream to Washington, D.C., where national parks offer refuge to shorebirds, songbirds, and waterfowl. Next, visit the Great Falls of the Potomac and head farther upstream on a historic canal trace before swinging east for a leisurely birding tour of the western shore of Chesapeake Bay. Finally, cross over to the rural eastern shore, where time is measured by the rise and fall of the tides and the seasonal clock of migratory birds flying the coastal route to winter in Chesapeake's sheltered barrier islands, bays, and rivers. Finish the drive on Chincoteague Island, where wild horses and restless sand dunes vie with over 300 bird species for a traveler's attention.

The national capital city and its surrounding region were born of water—the Atlantic, the Chesapeake, the Potomac, and endless acres of wetlands. The area has long been an important stopover for birds transiting the Atlantic Flyway or awaiting winter's end.

As the sun rises on a marsh at Blackwater NWR, waterfowl and birds of all kinds begin their day. The Wildlife Drive, a 6.5-mile (10.5-km) loop, is a good way to see this daily event from the warmth of a car used as a convenient blind.

Wilson's snipes prefer solitude or the company of only a few of their own kind.

❶ Mason Neck SP

Begin the birding route by going south on I-95 for 6 miles (9.7 km) from I-495 in Washington, D.C., and taking exit 163 (Hwy. 642). Cross under the interstate, turn right on Gunston Cove Rd., drive south and east 4.4 miles (7.1 km),

bear right at High Point Rd., and enter **Mason Neck SP.** Open 8 A.M. to sunset. Admission fee is charged. The park is also the entrance for **Mason Neck NWR.** Refuge trails open dawn to dusk daily.

Located on a peninsula in the Potomac River, the park and

refuge share a heron rookery, which, along with tundra swans, ducks, and bald eagles, are their main attractions for birding. There are 3 miles (4.8 km) of hiking trails, elevated boardwalks over the marsh, and a visitors center. Consult staff about recent bird sightings.

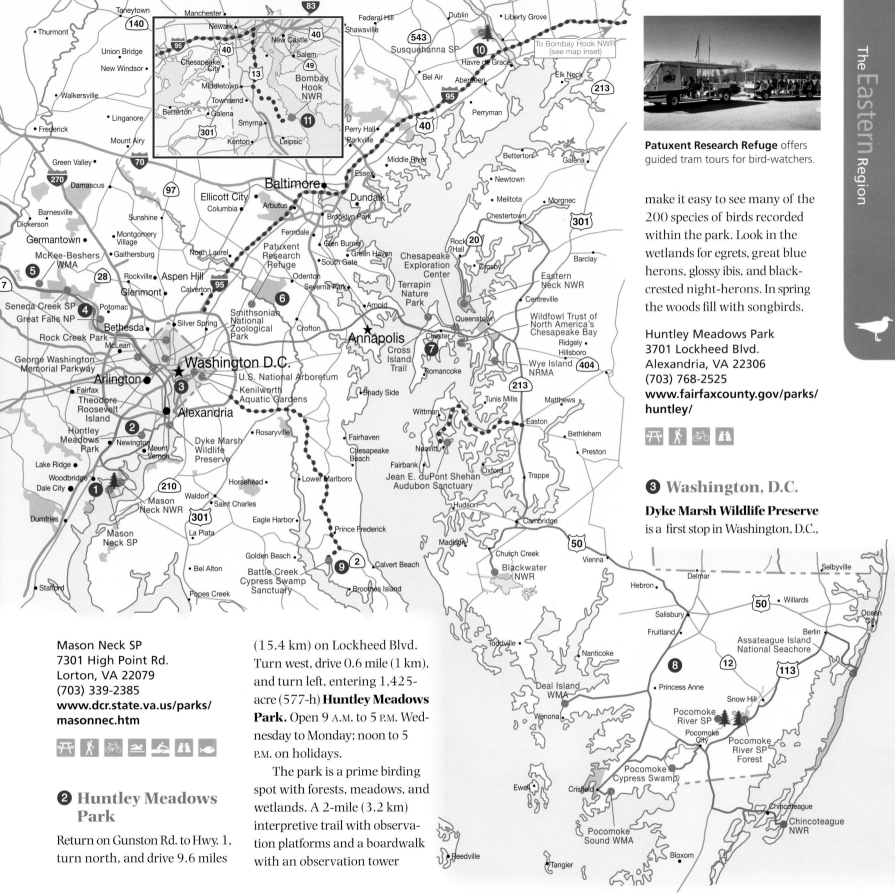

Patuxent Research Refuge offers guided tram tours for bird-watchers.

make it easy to see many of the 200 species of birds recorded within the park. Look in the wetlands for egrets, great blue herons, glossy ibis, and black-crested night-herons. In spring the woods fill with songbirds.

Huntley Meadows Park
3701 Lockheed Blvd.
Alexandria, VA 22306
(703) 768-2525
www.fairfaxcounty.gov/parks/ huntley/

❸ Washington, D.C.

Dyke Marsh Wildlife Preserve is a first stop in Washington, D.C.,

Mason Neck SP
7301 High Point Rd.
Lorton, VA 22079
(703) 339-2385
www.dcr.state.va.us/parks/ masonnec.htm

❷ Huntley Meadows Park

Return on Gunston Rd. to Hwy. 1, turn north, and drive 9.6 miles (15.4 km) on Lockheed Blvd. Turn west, drive 0.6 mile (1 km), and turn left, entering 1,425-acre (577-h) **Huntley Meadows Park.** Open 9 A.M. to 5 P.M. Wednesday to Monday; noon to 5 P.M. on holidays.

The park is a prime birding spot with forests, meadows, and wetlands. A 2-mile (3.2 km) interpretive trail with observation platforms and a boardwalk with an observation tower

one of many possible on George Washington Memorial Pkwy.

Go north 1 mile (1.6 km) on Hwy. 1, turn right on Beacon Hill Rd. for 1.7 miles (2.7 km) as it becomes Belle View Blvd., turn left on the George Washington Memorial Pkwy., and make a final right on Belle Haven Rd., which leads to Dyke Marsh Wildlife Preserve. Open dawn to dusk daily.

Some 300 species of birds visit these wetlands. Walk the haul road trail, a local favorite.

George Washington Memorial Pkwy. Headquarters/NPS
Turkey Run Park
McLean, VA 22101
(703) 289-2500
www.nps.gov/archive/gwmp/ dyke-marsh.htm

Follow George Washington Memorial Pkwy. north 9 miles (14.5 km). Just past the Theodore Roosevelt Bridge, turn into the parking lot for **Theodore Roosevelt Island.** Open dawn to dusk daily.

Use the footbridge to cross the Potomac River to the 88-acre (142-h) island. This bird sanctuary is dedicated to the 26th American president, renowned as an outdoorsman. Its 2.5 miles (4 km) of trails and boardwalks pass through wooded wetlands with many forest and river birds.

Theodore Roosevelt Island
c/o Turkey Run Park
George Washington Mem. Pkwy.
McLean, VA 22101
(703) 289-2500
www.nps.gov/this/

Reenter George Washington Memorial Pkwy., exit left at Spout Run Pkwy., make a left U-turn on the connector, and enter Washington Pkwy. southbound and cross Francis Scott Key Bridge (Hwy. 29). Turn right with Hwy. 29, go west to K St., and circle onto New Hampshire Ave. NW. Drive 0.7 mile (1.1 km), circle onto Connecticut Ave. NW, and drive to **Smithsonian National Zoological Park.** Open 6 A.M. to 8 P.M. April to October, 6 A.M. to 6 P.M. otherwise, except Christmas. Pick up *This Month's Birds* from visitors center docents.

The park has a number of good birding spots:

- **Wetlands by the Bird House:** Abundant food at the pond attracts wood ducks, mallards, gadwalls, northern shovelers, northern pintails, and teal. A colony of black-crowned night-herons nests, and other wading birds, such as great egrets and herons, are common from April to late October.
- **Rock Creek Bike Trail:** Riparian forest hosts nesting wood ducks, mallards, songbirds, woodpeckers, kinglets, owls, and raptors.
- **Olmsted Walk:** Tall oaks attract migratory warblers, vireos, and other songbirds.
- **Lemur Island:** Nesting Baltimore orioles and eastern kingbirds abound in spring.
- **Visitors center:** Sapsuckers are seen in winter.

Smithsonian National Zoological Park
3001 Connecticut Ave. NW
Washington, DC 20008
nationalzoo.si.edu

Return to Connecticut Ave., go 2 miles (3.2 km) north to Nebraska Ave. NW, bear right, then turn right on Military Rd. NW, which leads east to Glover Rd. and **Rock Creek Park.** Open 9 A.M. to 5 P.M. Wednesday to Sunday, except major holidays.

The Nature Center has information and exhibits about the park and its birds. An extensive system of trails and paths leads to good birding sites throughout this expansive park, and a pond near the center attracts songbirds, with an especially

A male red phalarope in breeding plumage is colorful. By fall its plumage turns to gray on top with white on its undersides. Note that the orange bill with black tip will also lose its color, becoming all black during winter.

large variety of redstarts and warblers, including magnolia, Nashville, black-and-white, and black-throated green.

Look for yellow-billed cuckoos, Swainson's thrushes, scarlet tanagers, great-crested fly-catchers, and other forest and river birds.

Rock Creek Park
3545 Williamsburg Ln. NW
Washington, DC 20008
(202) 895-6070
www.nps.gov/rocr/

Follow Military Rd. east to Georgia Ave. NW, jog right onto Missouri Ave. NW, bear left on Riggs Rd. NW, then bear right on South Dakota Ave. NE. Drive 1 mile (1.6 km), turn right on Sargent Rd. NE as its name changes to 13th St. NE, go 1.2 miles (1.9 km) to Girard St. NE, turn left, and make a right turn on 14th St. NE. After crossing Rhode Island Ave. NE, 14th becomes Montana Ave. NE and connects with New York Ave. NE (Hwy. 50). Turn east on Hwy. 50 and go 1 mile (1.6 km) to the 446-acre (180-h) **U.S. National Arboretum.** Open 8 A.M. to 5 P.M. daily except Christmas. No fee charged.

The arboretum is dedicated to specimen plants and trees in display gardens, but the variety of vegetation favors visits by many birds. Paths through the gardens, woods, and along the river produce good viewing opportunities. See woodpeckers,

Blackwater NWR is a scenic spot: Look closely to see the bald eagles roosting at sunset in the loblolly pines.

hermit thrushes, kinglets, warblers, eastern towhees, scarlet tanagers, and yellow-billed cuckoos. Near the river view ducks, geese, and wading birds.

U.S. National Arboretum
3501 New York Ave. NE
Washington, DC 20002
(202) 245-2726
www.usna.usda.gov

Drive east on Hwy. 50, turn south on Hwy. 295, exit at Pennsylvania Ave., and drive east to Prout St. Turn right, then right again on Nicholson St. SE, cross under the highway, make a right turn on Anacostia Dr. SE, and enter **Kenilworth Aquatic Gardens,** across the Anacostia River from the National Arbore-

tum previously visited. Open 7 A.M. to 4 P.M. daily.

Kenilworth Marsh, 77 acres (31 h) of riverine wetlands, surrounds the gardens. See long-billed marsh wrens, American bitterns, and other wading birds on a 0.7-mile (1.1-km) trail that leads through the marsh to a channel and the river.

Kenilworth Aquatic Gardens
National Park Service
1900 Anacostia Dr. SE
Washington, DC 20020
(202) 426-6905
www.nps.gov/archive/nace/keaq

❹ Great Falls NP

Next, travel west of the city by following Anacostia Dr. west,

rejoining Hwy. 295 west, and turning south on I-295. Drive about 5 miles (8 km), turn west on I-495, and drive 12.5 miles (35 km) to exit 44 (Hwy. 193). Go 4.2 miles (6.8 km) west on Hwy. 193, turn right on Old Dominion Dr., and enter 800-acre (324-h) **Great Falls NP.** Open 7 A.M. till dusk daily except Christmas; visitors center open 10 A.M. to 4 P.M. daily, longer in spring and summer. Admission fee is charged.

About 163 bird species have been sighted along the 15 miles (24 km) of hiking trails in this park named for 77-foot (23.5-m) Great Falls of the Potomac. They include waterfowl, songbirds, woodpeckers, hawks, vultures, and kingfishers.

Chincoteague NWR is a typical dune-studded sandy beach habitat.

Great Falls NP
9200 Old Dominion Dr.
McLean, VA 22102
(703) 285-2965 or (703) 285-2966
www.nps.gov/grfa

❺ McKee-Beshers WMA

Return to I-495, drive north to exit 39 (Hwy. 190, also called River Rd.), and turn west. Drive 15 miles (24 km) on River Rd., just past **Seneca Creek SP,** to **McKee-Beshers WMA** on the left. Open dawn to dusk daily.

A 2,000-acre (809-h) tract bordered by the historic Chesapeake & Ohio Canal NHP on the south and the state park to the east, the site has many trails in forest, meadow, and wetland habitats. They include the 185-mile (297-km) C&O Canal Towpath Recreational Trail that extends from Cumberland to Washington.

Over 200 species of songbirds, waterfowl, and upland game birds such as wild turkeys and woodcocks are present. Also see hawks, owls, and woodpeckers.

McKee-Beshers WMA
c/o Gwynnbrook Work Center
3740 Gwynnbrook Ave.
Owings Mills, MD 21117
(410) 356-9272
www.dnr.state.md.us/
publiclands/central/mb.asp

❻ Patuxent Research Refuge

Return to I-495, drive 13.8 miles (22 km) north and east, continue 3.8 miles (6.1 km) on I-95 south to exit 22A (Hwy. 295), and go north 3.7 miles (6 km) to Powder Mill Rd. Turn right on Scarlet Tanager Loop, arriving at the National Wildlife Visitors Center of **Patuxent Research Refuge.** Center open 10 A.M. to 5:30 P.M. daily except holidays, mid-March to October; closes at 4:30 P.M. November to March. Admission fee is charged.

See interactive exhibits on migratory bird routes, endangered species recovery programs, and wildlife habitats. More than 200 recorded bird species frequent the trails, which have views of Lake Redington, Cash Lake, and Goose Pond. Although there are other trails and roads, take the tram-only route, a 1.9-mile (3.1-km) motor tour through woodland and wetland areas with a guide. The tram fee is charged separately; buy tickets at the bookstore.

Patuxent Research Refuge
10901 Scarlet Tanager Loop
Laurel, MD 20708
(301) 497-5580
www.fws.gov

❼ Kent Island

Next, venture to Chesapeake Bay in search of birds. Return to Powder Mill Rd., turn right, then turn right again on Laurel Bowie Rd. Drive 7 miles (11.3 km), take Hwy. 50 east, and drive 25.5 miles (41 km) through Annapolis and across the Chesapeake Bay Bridge to exit 37 (Stevensville) on Kent Island. Go north, cross the highway, turn left at Skipjack Pkwy., and turn left on Log Canoe Cir. to enter **Terrapin Nature Park.** Open dawn to dusk daily, year-round.

The Terrapin Nature Center at the park is a trailhead for the 6.5-mile (10.5-km) **Cross Island Trail,** which extends all the way to the next waypoint. It crosses several creeks on wooden bridges and offers great views of the wetlands and waterfowl.

Trails totaling 3 miles (4.8 km) also wander through woodlands, sandy beaches, meadows, wetlands, and tidal ponds with two observation blinds. Benches on the boardwalk are inviting for soaking up views of birds plying Chesapeake Bay. Best birding takes place in autumn.

Terrapin Nature Park
191 Log Canoe Cir.
Stevensville, MD 21666
(410) 758-0835
www.discoverqueenannes.com/showrecreation.asp?rid=31

Take Hwy. 50 east 3.5 miles (5.6 km) to exit 41 (Main St.), turn left under the highway, and follow Piney Narrows Rd. north past the small-boat harbor to the **Chesapeake Exploration Center.** Open 8:30 A.M. to 4:30 P.M. weekdays, 10 A.M. to 4 P.M. weekends.

The horn-shaped peninsula is directly on the Kent Narrows channel at the Chester River, a good place to see mute swans, green and great blue herons, and many migrating shorebirds. Visit in fall and ascend the observation tower, which gives a clear view of river and bay.

Chesapeake Exploration Center
425 Piney Narrows Rd.
Chester, MD 21629
(410) 604-2100
www.qac.org

❽ Delmarva Peninsula

Enter the Eastern Shore on the Chesapeake Bay Bridge by continuing on Hwy. 50, taking exit 43B, and turning right on

Chester River Beach Rd. Turn left at Main St., right at Perrys Corner Rd., and right again at Discovery Ln. to reach the **Wildfowl Trust of North America's Chesapeake Bay** facility. Open 9 A.M. to 5 P.M. daily except major holidays. Admission fee is charged. There are 4 miles (6.4 km) of trails, two observation towers, a wetland boardwalk, viewing blinds, and a bird-feeding station. The visitors center has a panoramic view, making it easy to see the common waterfowl of the area. There is also a waterfowl aviary and a raptor mews, with non-releasable captive birds of prey and demonstrations.

Wildfowl Trust of North America
600 Discovery Ln.
P.O. Box 519
Grasonville, MD 21638
(410) 827-6694
www.wildfowltrust.org

Return to Hwy. 50 east for 2.7 miles (4.3 km), take the Ocean City exit to follow Hwy. 50 as Ocean Gtwy. for 2.9 miles (4.7 km), and turn right at Carmichael Rd. Drive 4.4 miles (7.1 km), turn right at Wye Island Rd., and proceed to

Jean E. duPont Shehan Audubon Sanctuary

Open to the public for self-exploration on selected Mondays and Sundays, the sanctuary also serves as the state headquarters of Audubon Maryland–DC. A 950-acre (384-h) peninsula bordered by 3 creeks, the site has 8 miles (13 km) of shoreline and 10 miles (16 km) of walking trails. Nearly 200 recorded bird species frequent the sanctuary, which offers year-round environmental science and experiential programs for school-aged children. For more information:

(410) 745-9283
www.audubonmddc.org/centers_JEDs.html

Wye Island NRMA, with 6 miles (9.7 km) of easy trails through wetlands and along bays and bluffs of the Wye River. Open dawn to dusk daily. Admission fee is charged.

See wading birds, bald eagles, ducks, and geese. Actively hunted in season; be prudent.

Wye Island NRMA
632 Wye Island Rd.
Queenstown, MD 21658
(410) 827-7577
www.dnr.state.md.us/publiclands/

Return to Ocean Gtwy., turn right, drive 1.6 miles (2.6 km), and turn north on Hwy. 213. Drive about 23 miles (37 km) to Chestertown, make a left turn at Chestertown Rd. (Hwy. 20), drive 4.9 miles (7.9 km) west, bear left as Hwy. 20 continues at Rock Hall Rd., then bear left again in Rock Hall at E. Sharp St. (Hwy. 445). Proceed south 5.6 miles (9 km) to enter **Eastern Neck NWR.** Open 7:30 A.M. to dusk daily; office open 7:30 A.M. to 4 P.M. weekdays. Subject to hunting season closures September to late November.

Roads and trails total 6 miles (9.7 km): four wildlife trails with

The observation deck at Chincoteague NWR provides a good vantage point for birders yet retains a comfortable separation from the birds.

Bombay Hook NWR is a migratory hot spot for snow geese, a place where there is always room for one more

boardwalks, observation towers, platforms, and photography blinds. The refuge is a major migratory stop for waterfowl and is home to the threatened southern bald eagle. See tundra swans, geese, songbirds, and large and small wading birds.

Eastern Neck NWR
1730 Eastern Neck Rd.
Rock Hall, MD 21661
(410) 639-7056
www.fws.gov

Return to Hwy. 50 in Wye Mills, drive 30 miles (48 km) south beyond Cambridge, and turn west on Hwy. 16. Drive 6.2 miles (10 km), turn south on Key Wallace Rd., and proceed to 27,000-acre (10,927-h) **Blackwater NWR.** Open dawn to dusk daily; visitors center open 8 A.M. to 4 P.M. weekdays, 9 A.M. to 5 P.M. weekends. Admission fee is charged. Subject to hunting season closures from September to late November.

Mostly tidal marsh, the refuge is a haven for osprey, peregrine falcons, and bald eagles. Over 85 bird species breed here.

The visitors center hosts a bird observatory overlooking the marsh with Osprey Cam—a web video feed on a platform—and spotting scopes.

The refuge has a 6.5-mile (10.5-km) loop drive and hiking trails, including an 80-foot (24-m) full-access boardwalk.

Blackwater NWR
2145 Key Wallace Dr.
Cambridge, MD 21613
(410) 228-2677
www.fws.gov

Southeast of Blackwater are several good birding stops:

- **Deal Island WMA,** Hwy. 50 to Salisbury, south on Hwy. 13 to Princess Anne, west on Deal Island Rd.; wetland forest with marsh trails. One of Maryland's

only two breeding populations of black-necked stilts.
www.dnr.state.md.us

- **Pocomoke Sound WMA,** Princess Anne, Hwy. 413 to Crisfield; boat access only; hire in Crisfield. Glossy ibis steal the show from April to September with a supporting cast of ospreys, barn owls, and herons.
www.dnr.state.md.us

- **Pocomoke Cypress Swamp,** Hwy. 13 west of Pokomoke City to Hwy. 371, southwest to Hickory Point Rd.; a well-known bald eagle roost, with up to 50 birds in a flock.
skipjack.net/le_shore/ worcestr/pocomoke.html

- **Pocomoke River SP and Forest,** east 6.5 miles (10.5 km) from Pocomoke City on Hwy. 113; popular spot for migrating warblers in spring. Several hiking and canoe trails for bird-watching.
www.dnr.state.md.us

Continue east on Hwy. 13 to Chincoteague Rd., cross to Chincoteague Island, and go east on Maddox Blvd. to **Assateague Island National Seashore** and **Chincoteague NWR;** alternate access at Ocean City. Open sunrise to sunset daily. Admission fee is charged.

Over 320 bird species visit the refuge. It is a year-round habitat for ducks, geese, and swans. Best viewing takes place in fall and winter. Follow nature trails to beach, salt marsh, and tidal-flat habitats. See glossy ibis, willets, rails, gulls, oystercatchers, terns, hawks, ospreys, egrets, and ibis rookeries. Mute swans also nest in the refuge.

Chincoteague NWR
P.O. Box 62
Chincoteague Island, VA 23336
(757) 336-6122
www.fws.gov

Great black-backed gulls await the changing tide.

Visit these sites along the way...

❾ Battle Creek Cypress Swamp Sanctuary
Calvert Co./Natural Resources Div.
175 Main St.
Prince Frederick, MD 20678
(410) 535-5327
www.dnr.state.md.us

Between the Patuxent River and Chesapeake Bay via Hwy. 4; the most northerly stands of bald cypress. See migrant Kentucky, prothonotary, and hooded warblers and northern parulas. A 1,700-foot (518-m) boardwalk gives easy access.

❿ Susquehanna SP and Lower Susquehanna Heritage Greenway Trail
3318 Rocks Chrome Hill Rd.
Jarrettsville, MD 21084
(410) 557-7994
www.dnr.state.md.us

At Chesapeake Bay's head. Visit 2.3-mile (3.7-km) floodplain trailheads at Deer Creek picnic area or Fisherman's Park at Conowingo Dam. See neotropical migrants, as well as its many hawks and other raptors.

⓫ Bombay Hook NWR
2591 Whitehall Neck Rd.
Smyrna, DE 19977
(302) 653-6872
www.fws.gov

Located on the northwest neck of Delaware Bay. One of the largest natural tidal salt marshes in the mid-Atlantic. Visit November to March, the peak season for waterfowl. Facilities include a visitors center, auto tour, and observation towers. Open sunrise to sunset. Admission fee is charged.

BIRDING TOUR

John James Audubon State Park & Nature Preserve

Born in 1785 on the West Indies island of Haiti, John J. Audubon, the son of a French merchant, went on to carve an immortal place in history as a naturalist painter of birds. He was among the first artists to depict birds in life-size form and in natural surroundings, giving insights into their habits and behaviors as well as details of their plumage. For avid bird-watchers the park, museum, and preserve are an avian mecca. There are indoor exhibits to entice curiosity, as well as wooded lakes and rivers filled with birds, reminding visitors of the vivid paintings of birds that Audubon created from this very spot.

A visit to Kentucky's state park and preserve honoring the famous bird artist recalls the nine-year span of Audubon's residence in the bluegrass town of Henderson. It also gives visitors a chance to see its museum and extensive collection of his avian paintings.

John James Audubon Museum exhibits memorabilia, personal effects, and, of course, the largest collection of the artist's works, both in originals and in his publications. Surrounding it is Audubon Nature Preserve.

John James Audubon SP

The park and nature preserve honoring John James Audubon are located on Hwy. 41 in the bluegrass country town of Henderson, Kentucky, south 25 miles (40 km) on I-164 from exit 29 on I-64. Henderson is roughly 95 miles (153 km) west of Louisville and 95 miles (153 km) east of St. Louis.

The park was first set aside in 1938 as a bird sanctuary and tribute to Audubon. It memorializes the period from 1810 to 1819 when the artist and ornithologist lived in Henderson, a time during which he painted and published some of his most famous works of wildlife art.

A self-taught naturalist and painter, he rose to world prominence with his artful and realistic paintings of birds, and he

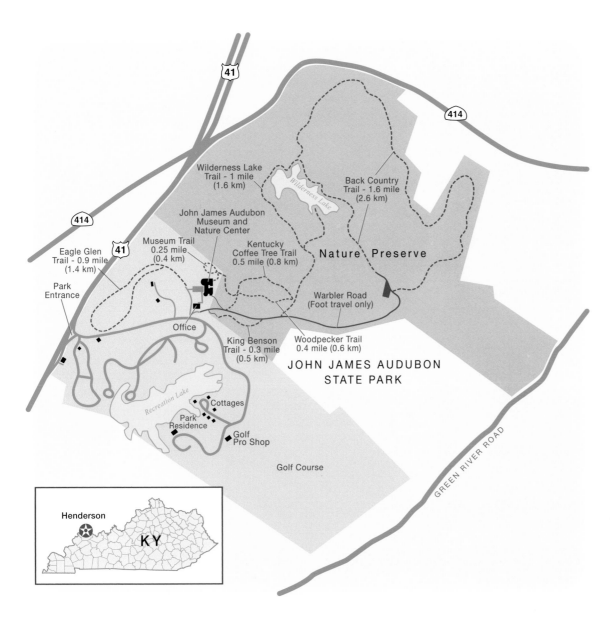

41

414

Wilderness Lake
Trail - 1 mile
(1.6 km)

Wilderness Lake

Back Country
Trail - 1.6 mile
(2.6 km)

414

John James Audubon
Museum and
Nature Center

Museum Trail
0.25 mile
(0.4 km)

Kentucky
Coffee Tree Trail
0.5 mile (0.8 km)

Nature Preserve

Eagle Glen
Trail - 0.9 mile
(1.4 km)

41

Park
Entrance

Warbler Road
(Foot travel only)

Office

King Benson
Trail - 0.3 mile
(0.5 km)

Woodpecker Trail
0.4 mile (0.6 km)

JOHN JAMES AUDUBON
STATE PARK

Recreation Lake

Cottages

Park
Residence

Golf
Pro Shop

Golf Course

GREEN RIVER ROAD

Henderson

KY

illustrating birds. She taught the children of the plantations along the river, and he painted.

Eventually, buoyed by the success of his book, he settled in New York. He issued his last print in 1838, began a slow slide into senility, and died in 1851 at the age of 65. His grave is far from the quiet Ohio River town of Henderson—he was buried at Trinity Cemetery in New York City.

In 1905, more than a half century after his death, the

A commemorative sign at the park details the life of John J. Audubon.

achieved a fame that has persisted long beyond his lifetime.

By 1820, when he was 35, Audubon had produced his epic work *The Birds of America*, much of it at Henderson. With 435 hand-colored engravings, he followed in Alexander Wilson's footsteps and attempted to pictorially depict every bird in North America. His genius was recognized, and the book quickly went into additional editions. Its quality was such that it remains a reference standard even today, one by which all bird paintings and field guides are still judged.

Audubon's stay in Henderson, while long in years, ultimately ended in tragedy. Though he married, became a father of two sons and a girl, and established a dry-goods store, his luck ran out. His daughter died, his business failed, and in 1819 he was imprisoned in the town jail for bankruptcy. Upon his release, he fled the town and its memories and traveled with his wife down the Mississippi River, always

National Audubon Society was founded in his honor; since that time, the organization has spawned many local chapters in the United States, and it has spread far and wide, becoming international in scope. As an ironic footnote, Audubon had no role in the founding of the organization that bears his name and that has made him familiar in every household.

Today the Audubon Society promotes the protection of birds and other wildlife through its many programs, foundations, and associations. It conducts educational seminars and outings, and it holds lands in trust for future generations.

The park's museum in Henderson houses the world's largest collection of Audubon memorabilia and the most extensive collection of his work found anywhere. The memorabilia collection provides valuable context for his paintings.

Equally important to visitors is the Nature Center, with its wildlife observation room and a Discovery Center with such hands-on exhibits as a giant bird nest, a perennial favorite for young bird-watchers.

The park is open 10 A.M. to 5 P.M. daily year-round, except on Thanksgiving and from Christmas to New Year's Day. Admission fee is charged.

John James Audubon SP
3100 U.S. Hwy. 41 N
Henderson, KY 42419
(270) 826-2247
www.parks.ky.gov

John James Audubon Nature Preserve

This 535-acre (216-h) preserve lies entirely within the state park. It was added to the park in 1979, and it has since grown through several additions.

The preserve protects old-growth hardwood forests on bluffs of loess (loess is a deposit of rich windborne river silt) overlooking the Ohio River Valley. Such habitats are scarce, and the abundance of birds that visit the preserve is testimony to the value that they hold for wildlife.

The preserve also has a quiet lake encircled by forest. Wilderness Lake is shallow, filled with cattails in some of its inlets, and attracts forest birds to its still waters. There they are joined by waterfowl and migratory shorebirds traveling the Mississippi and Ohio River flyways.

There are 6.5 miles (10.5 km) of trails, ranging from easy walks to moderately strenuous. Despite the nearby state park's many popular attractions, which include a golf course and other recreational facilities, the preserve is quiet, secluded, and a worthwhile birding spot. It receives visits each spring and fall by over 20 warbler species, including northern parula, black-throated blue, orange-crowned, yellow, chestnut-sided, magnolia, and Tennessee wood-warblers.

They are joined by many other species of forest-dwelling

Wilderness Lake Trail Boardwalk spans wetlands on the lake, bounded on all sides by dense mixed-hardwood forest. During spring migration colorful neotropical songbirds fill the woods with their songs.

Audubon Nature Preserve has several trails that lead through the wildlife refuge offering good opportunities to see some of the 20 warbler species that visit the park, along with woodpeckers, owls, and other forest birds.

Woodpecker Trail is a favorite with many bird-watchers. It passes through a boreal setting with open understory and a thick canopy that provides birds with cover from hawks flying overhead and access to food on the forest floor.

songbirds and perching birds, including vireos, summer and scarlet tanagers, eastern towhees, chipping, white-throated, and American tree sparrows, and ruby-throated hummingbirds. In deep forest there are also pileated and red-bellied woodpeckers, northern flickers, and yellow-bellied sapsuckers.

Plan to visit the preserve in early morning or stay overnight at the state park. During afternoons in summer, it becomes quite crowded, and only in late evenings and early mornings can one completely capture the mood and tenor that drew the artist to the Ohio's banks where he created his immortal draw-

ings of the birds that passed this way. At such times it's easy to imagine his footsteps traveling to the quiet margins of Wilderness Lake, his hands unfolding his easel, and his brushes laying down the first strokes of a painting now on display in the park's museum. Then, with a start, the actual bird appears.

Enjoy visiting Kentucky's well-regarded birding country.

John James Audubon Nature Preserve
3100 U.S. Hwy. 41 N
Henderson, KY 42419
(270) 826-2247
www.parks.ky.gov

Nashville to Knoxville

Venture into the Cumberland Mountains to see migrating birds in passage mingle with resident birds, all the time exploring Tennessee's handsome country, two great cities, and America's most popular national park, the Great Smoky Mountains.

The endless ridges and rivers of Tennessee fairly resonate with the sound of wings each spring as neotropical songbirds fill the area's forests with song. For a few short weeks in April and May, bird-watchers can see a passing parade of colorful birds, an opportunity to thumb the pages of field guides, commit birds to memory, and recall past sightings. Down the valleys and mountains come cascades of warblers—over 20 species in all—in the company of vireos, swallows, flycatchers, and sparrows. They pause at the region's many lakes and reservoirs, then settle to nest or fly farther north, depending on their habits. Cut a birding path across their journey, traveling between the home of country music and the Great Smokies, to enjoy bird-watching at its finest.

Long Hunter SP has all-weather piers on J. Percy Priest Lake with birdhouses to welcome purple martins.

Belted kingfishers are able to hover overhead before they plunge headfirst into the water after small fish.

❶ Nashville Area

The city of Nashville recognizes the importance of urban greenways. Besides providing recreational space, protecting plants and animals within the urban setting, and facilitating alternative transportation on walking and bicycle paths, they are great places to enjoy bird-watching. Visit one or more of Nashville's Greenways Trails in the central city to bird along the rivers and creeks.

From the I-65 and I-40 interchange, go north on I-65, exit east on Shelby Ave., turn right on S. 5th St. and left on Davidson St., to enter **Shelby Nature Park** and **Shelby Bottoms Greenway.** All the Nashville greenways are open dawn to sunset daily.

The greenway has 5 miles (8 km) of paved paths and 5 miles (8 km) of hiking trails with boardwalks, scenic over-

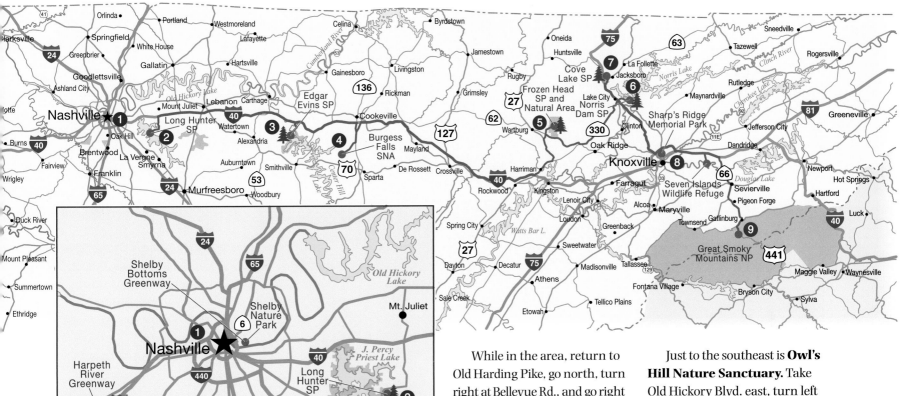

looks, seven rustic bridges, and interpretive signs. There are several ponds as well as hardwood forests, which are good habitats for shorebirds, waterfowl, and songbirds. See river birds during migration in spring and fall.

Nashville Greenway Projects
511 Oman St.
Nashville, TN 37201
(615) 862-8400
**www.nashville.gov/greenways/
projects.htm**

Harpeth River Greenway is on the southwest side of the city. Return on I-24 to I-40, drive southwest 11.4 miles (18.3 km) to exit 196 (Hwy. 70), cross under the highway, and drive to Sawyer Brown Rd. Turn right, go to Old Harding Pike, turn right, then turn right again on Morton Mill Rd. and the greenway. Open dawn to sunset daily.

It has a 1-mile (1.6 -km) trail with an 800-foot (244-m) boardwalk and scenic overlooks along the Harpeth River.

While in the area, return to Old Harding Pike, go north, turn right at Bellevue Rd., and go right at Old Hickory Blvd. Turn left at Hwy. 100, which travels on the north side of the **Edwin and Percy Warner Parks** and a nature center. Open from sunrise to 11 P.M. daily; center open 8:30 A.M. to 4:30 P.M. Tuesday to Saturday except major holidays.

The nature center has educational programs and maps of the two parks, with 12 miles (19 km) of hiking trails. On Hungry Hawk Trail are a bird blind and an observation platform. See owls, hawks, woodpeckers, and forest songbirds.

Warner Parks
511 Oman St.
Nashville, TN 37201
(615) 352-6299
**www.nashville.org/parks/
warner.htm**

Just to the southeast is **Owl's Hill Nature Sanctuary.** Take Old Hickory Blvd. east, turn left at Hillsboro Pike Rd., then turn left at Beech Creek Rd. to reach the 160-acre (65-h) preserve. Open 8 A.M. to sunset daily.

The pond at Owl's Hill is home to wood ducks and Canada geese, while wooded areas have owls, hawks, and smaller woodland birds. See great horned, barred, and barn owls and eastern screech-owls.

Owl's Hill Nature Sanctuary
545 Beech Creek Rd.
Brentwood, TN 37027
(615) 370-4672
www.owlshill.org

Follow Old Hickory Blvd. 3.4 miles (5.5 km) east to Granny White Pike, turn north, go 1.8 miles (2.9 km) to Otter Creek Rd., and turn right to enter into

Platforms, overlooks, and boardwalks like these at Burgess Falls SNA are features that make birding easy.

set daily, year-round. A camping fee is charged.

The park sits on the eastern shore of **J. Percy Priest Lake,** has several other units, and has many hiking trails. See Chuck-will's-widows, cedar waxwings, brown thrashers, white-eyed vireos, indigo buntings, eastern towhees, and prairie warblers.

Long Hunter SP
2910 Hobson Pike
Hermitage, TN 37076
(615) 885-2422
**state.tn.us/environment/parks/
LongHunter**

Radnor Lake SNA. Open dawn to dusk daily; visitors center open 8 A.M. Tuesday to Saturday and 9 A.M. Sunday and Monday, closes 5 P.M. Sunday to Thursday and 4 P.M. Friday and Saturday. Admission fee is charged. This is among the best birding spots available locally.

This 1,100-acre (445-h) urban haven attracts thousands of ducks and other waterfowl each winter. The ridges, with the highest elevation in the area, are good spots to look for hawks and other raptors migrating in spring before the trees leaf out.

Radnor Lake State Natural Area
1160 Otter Creek Rd.
Nashville, TN 37220
(615) 373-3467
**state.tn.us/environment/na/
natareas/radnor**

❷ Long Hunter SP

Continue east 16.8 miles (27 km) on Old Hickory Blvd., which becomes Bell Rd. (Hwy. 254); make a right at Morris Gentry Blvd., again at Murfreesboro Pike, and a left turn at Hamilton Church Rd. Go 1.8 miles (2.9 km), turn left at Hopson Pike (Hwy. 171), and note the signs for **Long Hunter SP.** Open 7 A.M. to sun-

❸ Edgar Evins SP

Return to Hwy. 171 and drive 4.3 miles (6.9 km) north to I-40, heading east. Drive 42 miles (68 km), take exit 268 (Hwy. 96), go south 3.8 miles, cross Hwy. 141, and continue straight on Edgar Evins State Park Rd. to 6,000-acre (2,428-h) **Edgar Evins SP.** Open 6 A.M. to 10:30 P.M. daily. A camping fee is charged.

The park has several hiking trails good for birding, with one starting at the visitors center and circling the lake's shoreline.

Among warblers, look for cerulean, yellow-throated, prothonotary, and hooded species. Hawks, osprey, and falcons visit the lake. Also see American redstarts, northern parulas, and hairy woodpeckers.

Edgar Evins SP
1630 Edgar Evins State Park Rd.
Silver Point, TN 38582
(931) 858-2446
state.tn.us/environment/parks/ EdgarEvins

❹ Burgess Falls SNA

Exit the park, turn east for 7.8 miles (12.6 km), enter I-40 east, go 14 miles (22 km), and take exit 287 (Hwy. 136). Drive south 3.1 miles (5 km) and take Old Kentucky Rd. to a right turn at Burgess Falls Rd. A short distance beyond is the entry to **Burgess Falls SNA.** Open 8 A.M. to 30 minutes before sunset daily. Park subject to closures for high water and snow.

Sheer bluffs, narrow ridges, memorable waterfalls, and mixed hardwood forests make this reserve a beautiful place to birdwatch. Hiking trails lead to several waterfalls; 70-foot (21-m) Burgess Falls is the highest and a good place to watch for swallows along the cliffs. Taking the gravel road to Burgess Falls, while not as scenic as the trail,

may provide better birding. At the dam and lake, see Acadian and great crested flycatchers, along with an assortment of waterfowl in winter. Louisiana waterthrushes appear in summer.

Burgess Falls SP
4000 Burgess Falls Dr.
Sparta, TN 38583
(931) 432-5312
state.tn.us/environment/parks/ BurgessFalls

❺ Frozen Head SP and Natural Area

Return north to I-40, go east 59 miles (95 km) to exit 347 (Hwy. 27), turn north, pass through Harriman, and drive 12 miles (19 km) to Clayton Howard Rd. Turn right, go to Liberty Rd., turn left, then left again on Hwy. 62 for 0.7 mile (1.1 km), and turn right at Flat Fork Rd., which leads in 4.2 miles (6.9 km) to 11,876-acre (4,806-h) **Frozen Head SP and Natural Area.** Open 8 A.M. to sunset daily.

Located in the Cumberland Mountains at 3,324 feet (1,013 m), it is a favorite spot in spring to see neotropical migrants begin their mating and nesting behavior, which includes melodious calls and songs.

Obtain a map of the park's 20 trails at the visitors center; they range from easy to very strenuous. Also consult staff on recent bird sightings in the park and current hot spots.

Burgess Falls SNA is striking in its beauty. Surrounded by layered rock, its river and forests are home to abundant wildlife and birds.

Frozen Head SP and Natural Area
964 Flat Fork Rd.
Wartburg, TN 37887
(423) 346-3318
state.tn.us/environment/parks/ FrozenHead

❻ Norris Dam SP

Drive back to Hwy. 62, turn east, drive 14 miles (23 km) to Oliver Springs, turn north on Hwy. 330, and drive northeast 18 miles (29 km) to Lake City. Turn left on N. Main Ave. (Hwy. 25), turn

Yellow-rumped warblers often sit on branches in an opening so they can quickly fly out to catch passing insects.

Return to I-75, drive 20 miles (33 km) south to **Knoxville,** turn east on I-640, and take exit 6 (Hwy. 441). Follow Old Broadway St. NE south, turn right on Ludlow Ave., then bear right at Sharp's Ridge Rd., which enters 111-acre (45-h) **Sharp's Ridge Memorial Park.**

Knoxville is a city with many trails that connect its residents with nature, and this park is one of its better places to see migrant songbirds in spring. The paths along creeks and wooded areas are especially handy for those with bird-watching in mind.

See a large sampling of warbler species, as well as tanagers, rose-breasted grosbeaks, vireos, thrushes, indigo buntings, Baltimore orioles, and both flycatchers and gnatcatchers. Use the turnouts along the ridge and the park's many walking trails. Also visit the J. B. Owen Overlook, a wooden observation deck with good views of metropolitan Knoxville.

Sharp's Ridge Memorial Park
329 Sharp's Ridge Memorial Dr.
Knoxville, TN 37917
(865) 215-1413
www.ci.knoxville.tn.us/parks/ sharpsridge.asp

Return to I-640, drive east and south 4.4 miles (7.1 km) to I-40, and go east 9.2 miles (15 km) to exit 402 (Midway Rd.). Drive south 2.6 miles (4.2 km),

right on Hwy. 441, and drive east 1.8 miles (2.9 km) to the entrance of 4,038-acre (1,634-h) **Norris Dam SP.** Open dawn to 10 P.M. daily; office open 8 A.M. to 4:30 P.M. daily.

Check out Songbird and River Bluff trails, and visit the lakeshore during migration. Birds seen here include red-breasted nuthatches, evening grosbeaks, seven woodpecker species, and pine siskins. Wooded areas also have a number of different owls.

If time permits, also visit the park's Lenoir Pioneer Museum, an 18th-century gristmill and threshing barn, which offers many fascinating insights into early Appalachian pioneer life.

Norris Dam SP
125 Village Green Cir.
Lake City, TN 37769
(865) 426-7461
state.tn.us/environment/parks/ NorrisDam

❼ Cove Lake SP

Follow Hwy. 441 west to I-75, drive 6.2 miles (10 km) north to exit 134 (Veterans Memorial Hwy.), turn east for 0.5 mile (0.8 km), and turn left at Cove Lake Ln., which leads to 673-acre (272-h) **Cove Lake SP.** Open 8 A.M. to sunset daily year-round. The park is within Caryville.

A mountain lake and paved hiking trails make this park a birding hit. It is home to a flock of Canada geese that forgo northern migration. In winter they are joined by mallards, wood ducks, ring-necked ducks, gadwalls, and hooded mergansers. In spring and summer warblers and flycatchers are found in the park's wetlands.

Cove Lake State Park
110 Cove Lake Ln.
Caryville, TN 37714
(423) 566-9701
state.tn.us/environment/parks/ CoveLake

turn left on Kodak Rd., drive 0.2 mile (0.3 km), and turn left at the church onto Kelly Ln. to reach a parking lot and trailhead for 360-acre (146-h) **Seven Islands Wildlife Refuge.**

The refuge is a remarkably restored tallgrass and shortgrass prairie that was farmland until 2002. See ospreys and bald eagles soaring over the French Broad River, pileated woodpeckers, wild turkeys and upland game birds in the forests, and screech-owls and eastern meadowlarks in the grasslands.

Seven Islands WR/L&N Station
401 Henely St., Ste. 5
Knoxville, TN 37902
(865) 525-9400
www.sevenislands.org

❾ Great Smoky Mountains NP

Return to I-40, turn east, drive 5 miles (8 km) to exit 407 (Hwy. 66), and go 8.8 miles (14.2 km) to join Hwy. 441 (Forks of the River Pkwy.). Hwy. 441 leads in 15.5 miles (25 km) to **Great Smoky Mountains NP.** Open daily year-round. Admission fee is charged.

Over 240 bird species have been recorded in the Smokies, and nearly 120 species breed in the park. Included among them are 52 neotropical species. The park and its varied habitats are also an important resting place for migrating birds in spring and fall, when shrubs, trees, wetlands, and waterways fill with traveling birds.

On the highest ridges where the spruce-fir forests flourish, look for chestnut-sided warblers in the thickets and dark-eyed juncos in wooded areas. Also note nesting nuthatches, saw-whet owls, vireos, black-capped chickadees, sparrows, warblers, and winter wrens.

The mid-to-low elevations have the greatest populations and the largest variety of bird species—more than can be listed. Favorites here include Carolina chickadees, indigo buntings, scarlet tanagers, belted kingfishers, more warblers, and the ever-present sparrows.

Beginning in mid-September broad-winged hawks start to group at the park in preparation for their impressive migration. Birders throughout the flyway await their passage overhead in large flocks once they depart Great Smoky Mountains NP.

Even as they move on, other flocks and species arrive, a clockwork schedule devised by nature acting through their instincts. From late April to early May, it is easy to add many unusual bird species to one's life list.

While in the park, visit these top birding areas:

- **Sugarlands Visitors Center.** Hike the Little River and Sugarland Mountain trails to contrast river birds with those of the upland ridges and forests. Also visit Laurel Falls and take the Roaring Fork motor nature trail, using turnouts to see the birds.

- **Cades Cove Visitors Center.** Just outside the park on Foothills Pkwy. is Look Rock Fire Tower parking area. Also drive 11-mile (18-km) Cades Cove Auto Loop through a lush valley. Best times to visit are early mornings, when visitor traffic is minimal.

- **Oconaluftee Visitors Center.** Hike Bradley Loop trail or enter the 2,175-mile (3,500-km) Appalachian Trail at Big Creek. It bisects the park following its east-to-west ridgelines.

Great Smoky Mountains NP
107 Park Headquarters Rd.
Gatlinburg, TN 37738
(865) 436-1200
www.nps.gov/grsm

American redstart males are easy to identify. They have distinctive black bodies with bright orange and yellow patches on their wings and tail.

Atlanta to Augusta

One of the secrets to great bird-watching is observing the route that birds follow in migration and visiting several sites across their path that have promising habitats. Such is the case found between the cities of Atlanta and Augusta at the South Carolina border. Birds flying from the Gulf of Mexico to Canada along the inland valleys and mountain ridges pass through the lakes, wetlands, and forests of this region at the peak of its spring wildflower bloom. Time a journey to discover these wayfarers and see scenic sights off the beaten path. The route visits locales with endangered species, but it's the neotropical migratory songbirds that steal the show.

From birding in the city suburbs to days spent watching majestic eagles and osprey take flight on rural wetlands, Georgia offers birders the opportunity to see both northern and southern birds in a convenient, enjoyable tour.

Augusta Canal Towpath is a historic water-transportation site with excellent birding. The hardwoods attract many forest-dwelling birds, while waterfowl and wading birds fill the canal and its shoreline.

Red-cockaded woodpeckers are endangered due to loss of habitat. It's easy to see their white cheeks and black-capped heads, but the red cockades—flashes extending backward from the eyes—are rarely prominent.

❶ Atlanta Area

From the intersection of I-85 and I-20 in downtown Atlanta, travel east on I-20 to exit 60B (Moreland Ave.), turn north, then east on Ponce de Leon Ave. NE, drive 2.2 miles (3.5 km), and turn right on Scott Blvd. Proceed for 2 miles (3.2 km) northeast to Medlock Rd., turn left, drive to Wood Trail Ln., and turn right to reach 28-acre (11-h) **Clyde Shepherd Nature Preserve.**

This Decatur preserve in sight of North Dekalb Mall has wetlands, a 4-acre (1.6-h) beaver pond, and an observation tower donated by the Atlanta Audubon Society. It also has boardwalks, a small bridge, and an observation deck.

See indigo buntings, wood thrushes, orchard orioles, catbirds, and waterfowl, including blue-winged teal, hooded mergansers, and ring-necked ducks.

Clyde Shepherd Nature Preserve
2580 Pine Bluff Dr.
Decatur, GA 30033
(404) 728-1411
www.cshepherdpreserve.org

Return to Scott Blvd., turn right, drive 1.5 miles (2.4 km), turn right at Coventry Rd., and turn left on Heaton Park Dr. to arrive at **Fernbank Forest** and Fernbank Science Center. Center open 2 P.M. to 5 P.M. Sunday through Friday, 10 A.M. to 5 P.M. Saturday. Access to the forest is through the center; register before entry.

This 65-acre (26-h) mixed hardwood forest has paved trails and has recorded sightings of 155 bird species. Songbirds are plentiful during migration, and many birds remain at the site year-round or nest here.

Fernbank Forest
Fernbank Science Center
156 Heaton Park Dr.
(404) 378-4311
Atlanta, GA 30307
**www.fernbank.edu/museum/
fernbankforest.html**

Drive south on Heaton Park Dr., turn left at Artwood Rd. NE, and turn right on Ponce de Leon Ave. NE. Follow it east 2.1 miles (3.4 km) to Moreland Ave. NE, turn south, drive to I-20, and drive west 15 miles (24 km). Take exit 44 (Thornton Rd.), go south to Skyview Dr. E, turn right at Mt. Vernon Rd., and enter **Sweetwater Creek SP.** Open 7 A.M. to 10 P.M. daily, office open 8 A.M. to 5 P.M.; trails close at dusk. Parking fee is charged.

Over 9 miles (14.5 km) of wooded trails follow Sweetwater Creek or circle George Sparks Reservoir. The lake hosts wintering waterfowl, and the hardwood forest and stream have wading birds, wood ducks, songbirds, woodpeckers, and owls. Boat and canoe rentals provide a unique way to see waterbirds on the reservoir.

Sweetwater Creek SP
P.O. Box 816
Lithia Springs, GA 30057
(770) 732-5871
www.gastateparks.org

Return to I-20, head east 9.3 miles (15 km) to I-285, turn north, drive 9 miles (14.5 km) to I-75, and turn north. Drive 11 miles (18 km) to exit 269 (Barrett Pkwy.), turn east, drive 2.2 miles (3.5 km) to Old Hwy. 41, turn left, go 1.2 miles (1.9 km), and turn right on Stilesboro Rd. NW. Follow the sign at Kennesaw Mountain Dr. to enter **Kennesaw Mountain National Battlefield Park.** Open dawn to dusk daily; visitors center open 8:30 A.M. to 5 P.M. daily except Christmas and New Year's Day. Obtain a bird checklist at the visitors center.

The park is a hot spot for neotropical migrants from early April to mid-May and again from late August to October. At these times see many species of warblers, tanagers, thrushes, and vireos. Also visit the mountaintop to watch hawks circle. Trails total 18 miles (29 km).

Kennesaw Mountain NBP
900 Kennesaw Mountain Dr.
Kennesaw, GA 30152
(770) 427-4686
www.nps.gov/kemo

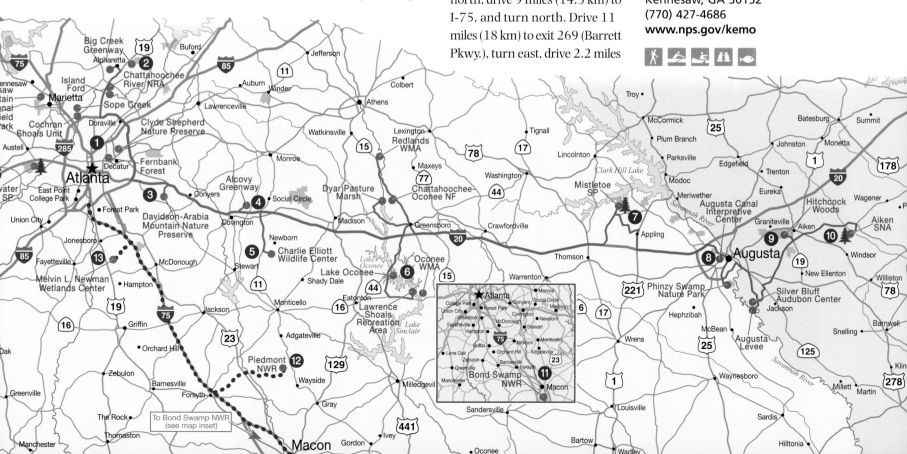

Return to I-75, go south to to I-285, turn east for 6 miles (9.7 km), and take exit 27 (Hwy. 400). Go north 5.2 miles (8.4 km) to exit 6 (Northridge Rd.), cross under the highway, make three successive right turns on Dunwoody Pl., Roberts Dr., and Island Ford Pkwy., and note the sign leading to **Chattahoochee River NRA.** Open dawn to dusk daily; visitors center open 9 A.M. to 5 P.M. daily except Christmas. Admission fee is charged.

With 16 park units spread over 48 miles (77 km) of the Chattahoochee River and 50 miles (80 km) of hiking trails, opportunities for bird-watching abound. Obtain trail maps and consult park staff for recent bird sightings.

Reliable park locations in the vicinity worth birding include:

- **Island Ford,** from park headquarters follow Island Ford Pkwy. south; hill and ridge trails through mixed hardwood forest along the river yield many migrant and resident birds.

- **Cochran Shoals Unit,** I-25 to exit 22, north on Northside Dr.; daily bird counts during migration exceed 50 species. Trails range from easy to strenuous and pass through woods and wetlands. See Lincoln's sparrows, herons, Connecticut warblers, olive-sided flycatchers, and water-fowl, plus hawks overhead and most species of wood-pecker found in Georgia.

- **Sope Creek,** I-25 to exit 24, north on Riverside Dr. to Johnson Ferry Dr., southeast

2.2 miles (3.5 km) on Paper Mill Rd.; multiuse trails lead through woods along creeks. See woodpeckers, owls, and songbirds.

Chattahoochee River NRA
1978 Island Ford Pkwy.
Atlanta, GA 30350
(678) 538-1200
www.nps.gov/chat

❷ Big Creek Greenway

Return to Hwy. 400, drive north 4 miles (6.4 km) to exit 8 (Mansell Rd.), turn right, drive to North Point Pkwy., and turn right. **Big Creek Greenway** has a parking lot 800 feet (243 m) south of North Point Mall across from Haverty's Furniture; walk behind the shops to a stairway, which leads to the wetlands trail. Open daily dawn to dusk.

At the southern edge of the swamp is a boardwalk, where songbirds, finches, eastern blue-birds, and other perching birds are seen. During nesting, look at the birdhouses just past the bridge. The trail connects to a park along Big Creek, a water-way that feeds into the Chatta-hoochee River. The park has 6.1 miles (9.8 km) of paved paths.

Alpharetta Recreation
and Parks Dept.
1825 Old Milton Pkwy.
Alpharetta, GA 30004
www.alpharetta.ga.us

❸ Davidson-Arabia Mountain Nature Preserve

Follow Hwy. 400 south to I-285, head east and south 19 miles (31 km), join I-20 east for 6.8 miles to exit 74 (Evans Mill Rd.), and go south. Drive 0.9 mile (1.4 km) as Evans Mill Rd. turns into Woodrow Dr., then turn right on Klondike Rd., which leads to **Davidson-Arabia Mountain Nature Preserve.** Open 7 A.M. to sunset daily.

The preserve has a nature center and trails that include a wooden boardwalk and several granite bridges. The best birding is on the South Lake and Forest trails, which lead to Arabia Lake. See migrants that include song-

Chattahoochee River NRA Nature Center is a good starting point to find birding sites at this wide-flung park complex.

birds, wading birds, and water-fowl, as well as many resident birds of the forest. Look for raptors, owls, and woodpeckers on the Mountain Loop Trail.

Davidson-Arabia Mountain
Nature Preserve
3787 Klondike Rd.
Lithonia, GA 30038
(770) 484-3060
www.arabiaalliance.org

❹ Alcovy Greenway

Return to I-20 east, drive 19 miles (31 km) to exit 93 (Hwy. 142), cross over the highway, and drive north to Hazelbrand Rd. Turn right and go 1.8 miles (2.9 km) to arrive at 115-acre (47-h) **Alcovy Greenway** and conservation center on the road's right side. Center open 8 A.M. to 5 P.M. Monday to Friday.

Woodlands, wetlands, and meadow habitats make up this preserve on the Alcovy River. Walk Dogwood Trail and listen for songbirds—their serenade is heard long before the birds are seen. Also see wood ducks, red-bellied and pileated woodpeckers, barred owls, and red-shouldered hawks. The greenway stretches north and south.

Alcovy Conservation Center
11600 Hazelbrand Rd.
Covington, GA 30014
(770) 787-9229
www.gwf.org/facilities.htm

❺ Charlie Elliott Wildlife Center

Return to I-20, drive east 4.1 miles (6.6 km) to exit 98 (Hwy. 11), turn south for 6.2 miles (10 km), and then turn left into 6,400-acre (2,590-h) **Charlie Elliott Wildlife Center** at the sign. Open dawn to dusk daily; center open 9 A.M. to 4:30 P.M. Tuesday to Saturday.

A nominated IBA, the site has recorded more than 190 bird species. Follow the self-guided auto tour or hike 3 miles (4.8 km) of trails. View American redstarts, summer tanagers, and assorted warblers, vireos, gnatcatchers, and flycatchers. Sightings on the center's trails also include anhingas and yellow-billed cuckoos.

Charlie Elliott Wildlife Center/
Georgia DNR Wildlife Division
543 Elliott Trail
Mansfield, GA 30055
(770) 784-3059
georgiawildlife.dnr.state.ga.us

❻ Lake Oconee Area

Return to I-20, drive east 32 miles (51 km) to exit 130 (Hwy. 44), and turn south for 8 miles to **Lake Oconee.** Continue 2.2 miles (3.5 km) on Hwy. 44 to Old Phoenix Rd., turn left, go 4 miles (6.4 km) to New Phoenix Rd., turn left, and drive to Hwy. 16. Turn left, drive 5 miles (8 km), make a left turn on Wallace

Davidson-Arabia Mountain Nature Preserve is a peaceful setting for birds and other wildlife, with both forests and wetlands.

Dam Rd. and another left on Lawrence Shoals Rd. Entry for **Lawrence Shoals Recreation Area** and a trailhead to **Oconee WMA,** is 300 feet (92 m) to the right. Open dawn to dusk daily.

There is good birding on the trail and at an observation deck near the shoreline of the lake. See waterfowl, including teal, ring-necked ducks, and mallards, as well as sandhill cranes and bald eagles. Also see vireos, warblers, woodpeckers, and hawks.

Lawrence Shoals Recreation Area
125 Wallace Dam Rd. NE
Eatonton, GA 31024
(706) 485-8704
www.southerncompany.com

Return north on Hwy. 44, cross I-20, and enter Greensboro. Turn west at W. Broad St. (Hwy. 278), drive 11.4 miles (18 km) to Farmington Rd., turn right, enter Greshamville, and turn

Prothonotary warblers are on the threatened list. Refuges and preserves are managed to retain their necessary habitats.

right for 2.1 miles (3.4 km) on C. M. Copeland Rd. Just past Greenbriar Creek Bridge, turn right on Greenbriar Dr. to reach the trailhead for **Dyar Pasture Marsh.** Unstaffed.

The proximity of this tributary to Lake Oconee provides opportunities to see kingfishers, bald eagles, ospreys, peregrine falcons, and other fish-eating birds. An impoundment attracts little blue and great blue herons and other shorebirds, including sandhill cranes. The pine and hardwood forest is a good spot to see songbirds. Wood storks have also been noted in fall.

Georgia DNR Wildlife Division
2070 U.S. Hwy. 278, SE
Social Circle, GA 30025
(770) 918-6400
georgiawildlife.dnr.state.ga.us

Return to Greensboro, turn north on Hwy. 15, and drive about 12 miles (19 km) to enter **Chattahoochee-Oconee NF,** with many trails suitable for bird-watching. The forest is home to endangered red-cockaded wood-peckers, and **Redlands WMA** protects their habitat. Forest open daily except during periods of extreme fire danger. Camping fee is charged.

Chattahoochee-Oconee NF
1755 Cleveland Hwy.
Gainesville, GA 30501
(770) 297-3000
www.fs.fed.us/conf

❼ Mistletoe SP

Return to I-20 through Greensboro, drive east 45 miles (72 km) to exit 175 (Hwy. 150), go north 8.1 miles (13 km) to Mistletoe Rd., turn right, and drive 2.8 miles (4.5 km) to arrive at **Mistletoe SP.** Open 7 A.M. to 10 P.M. daily. Admission fee is charged.

The park on Clarks Hill Lake has a 3.5-mile (5.6-km) nature trail and a wildlife observation area, plus a nature center with informative displays. Also try Cliatt Creek Trail. See eastern bluebirds, pine warblers, screech-owls, nuthatches, and yellow-billed cuckoos in the forests, and view waterfowl, shorebirds, and wading birds in and along the creek and lake.

Mistletoe SP
3723 Mistletoe Rd.
Appling, GA 30802
(706) 541-0321
gastateparks.org

❽ Augusta Area

Go back to Hwy. 150, turn east, drive 0.5 mile (0.8 km) to Dozier Rd., turn right, drive 5.6 miles (9 km), cross White Oak Rd., and continue straight on Schucraft Rd. Turn right at Hwy. 221, drive south to I-20, go east 16 miles (26 km) to exit 199 (Washington Rd.), turn right, proceed to Calhoun Expy., turn left on 15th Ave., and go right on Greene St., which leads to **Augusta Canal Interpretive Center.** Open 9:30 A.M. to 5:30 P.M. weekdays and Saturday; 1 P.M. to 5:30 P.M. Sunday. Admission fee is charged.

Obtain a self-guided tour map at the center.

This working power canal on the Savannah River was constructed in 1845 and gives interesting historical perspectives. Of interest to bird-watchers are its towpath and nature trails, which offer excellent views of river and wading birds. An undeveloped wetlands provides an urban wildlife refuge between the canal and the river along the upper first level.

Augusta Canal Interpretive Center
1450 Greene St.
Augusta, GA 30901
(706) 823-0440
www.augustacanal.com

Go east on Greene St., turn right at 13th St., and turn left at Walton Way. Drive 1.1 miles (1.8 km), turn right on Hwy. 1, go 2 miles (3.2 km), turn left at Doug Barnard Pkwy., and turn left on Lock & Dam Rd., which leads in 0.6 mile (1 km) to a left turn at **Phinzy Swamp Nature Park.** Open noon to dusk Monday to Friday; dawn to dusk Saturday, Sunday, and holidays.

The park has several trails worth birding: Beaver Dam Trail passes an active beaver pond, a meadow, a lake, and a swamp; look for wading birds, songbirds, and wild turkeys. Cattail Trail is short and accesses Floodplain Boardwalk over Phinzy Swamp and an observation deck; look for wading birds and waterfowl.

Also see Constructed Wetland Trail, a water-treatment marsh that is a favorite stopping point for migrating waterfowl, marsh birds, and wading birds.

The 1.1-mile (1.8-km) River Scar Trail visits cypress-tupelo swamp and has a deck overlooking an ancient river scar; see double-crested cormorants, pied-billed grebes, warblers, ring-necked ducks, and wood storks.

Southeastern Natural Science Academy
1858 Lock & Dam Rds.
Augusta, GA 30906
(706) 828-2109
**www.phinizyswamp.org/
PhinizySwamp.htm**

Two other birding locations are worth a visit:

- **Augusta Levee,** I-520 to exit 16 (Hwy. 28), south to Old Jackson Hwy., south to Silver Bluff Rd., and turn right; Bird the swamp area on the right

at **Silver Bluff Audubon Center** or continue to the road's end and the **Augusta Levee.** Bird only from the road, respecting private property. Streams, lakes, fields, upland pine forest, and hardwood bottomlands make up this 3,000-acre (1,214-h) working-forest preserve with over 200 bird species recorded, including endangered wood storks. The center has limited hours and reservations are required; call ahead.

Silver Bluff Audubon Center
4542 Silver Bluff Rd.
Jackson, SC 29831
(803) 471-0291
sc.audubon.org/silverbluff.html

❾ Hitchcock Woods

Follow Silver Bluff Rd. north 16 miles (26 km), bear left at Whiskey Rd., and turn left on Hitchcock Dr. SW. Follow the

signs to 2,000-acre (809-h) **Hitchcock Woods.** Open dawn to dusk daily. Donations are appreciated.

The forest has 65 miles (105 km) of trails through wetlands, upland forests, streams, and rivers. See ruby-crowned kinglets and other forest birds. Obtain a trail map at the entrance.

Hitchcock Woods
P.O. Box 1702
Aiken, SC 29802
(803) 642-0528
www.hitchcockwoods.org

❿ Aiken SNA

Take Whiskey Rd. south to E. Pine Log Rd. (Hwy. 302), drive east 15.5 miles (25 km) to Salley Rd., turn right, and drive south to 1,067-acre (432-h) **Aiken SNA.** Open 9 A.M. to 9 P.M. during daylight saving time, 9 A.M. to 6 P.M. otherwise. Admission fee is charged.

The park includes four lakes, portions of the South Edisto River, swamps, and pine and hardwood bottomland forest, with a 3-mile (4.8-km) nature trail to a wetlands boardwalk.

See southern bald eagles, plus endangered red-cockaded woodpeckers and wood storks. During spring the area fills with neotropical migrant birds. In winter waterfowl visit the lakes and river, and shorebirds are common year-round.

Aiken SNA
1145 State Park Rd.
Windsor, SC 29856
(803) 649-2857
www.southcarolinaparks.com

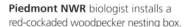

Piedmont NWR biologist installs a red-cockaded woodpecker nesting box.

Visit these sites along the way...

⓫ Bond Swamp NWR
718 Juliette Rd.
Round Oak, GA 31038
(478) 986-5441
www.fws.gov/bondswamp

Located 6 miles (9.7 km) south of Macon on Hwy. 23; a recognized IBA in forest wetlands of the Ocmulgee River floodplain. Several trails offer views of waterfowl, small and large wading birds, nesting pairs of bald eagles, woodpeckers, owls, and neotropical songbirds.

⓬ Piedmont NWR
718 Juliette Rd.
Round Oak, GA 31038
(478) 986-5441
www.fws.gov/piedmont

Take I-75 south to Forsyth, east on Juliette Rd. for 18 miles (29 km); over 200 recorded bird species, including endangered red-cockaded woodpecker. Convenient trails lead to marshes, lakes, and forest habitat areas, each populated with different bird species.

⓭ Melvin L. Newman Wetlands Center
2755 Freeman Rd.
Hampton, GA 30228
(770) 603-5603
**www.ccwa1.com/facilities/
wetlands.center.aspx**

Take I-75 south to exit 235, go south to Freeman Rd., and go east; over 130 recorded bird species on a 32-acre (13-h) preserve with wetlands trails and a boardwalk. See shorebirds on Lake Shamrock and ponds.

Savannah, Georgia, to Charleston, South Carolina

Follow the sun-drenched coast north from Georgia to South Carolina, stopping for a while at coastal bird-watching hot spots. This is a land of blackwater swamps, tupelo gums, and bald cypresses filled with birds both rare and memorable.

The lowland plains that stretch from south of Savannah to north of Charleston are cut by meandering rivers, filled throughout the winter with waterfowl. When spring arrives, so do migrating songbirds, gulls, and seabirds of all species. Even as the ducks and geese begin their trek to the North, moss is tweaked from the cypresses and magnolias to build nests, and the marshes and wetlands resound with the songs of mating birds and the strident calls of territorial challenges. Visit this special land ruled by the rhythms of nature and the tides rather than by human needs and schedules. See the pageant performed by Nature each year, seemingly unchanged in any way since time began.

Tybee Island beach and pier are just outside the closed national wildlife refuge. They provide a good platform for seeing many species of birds that reside in or visit the preserve.

Common terns have prominently forked, swallowlike tails, black-capped heads, and dark fringes along the ends of their wingtips.

❶ Melon Bluff Nature Preserve

Drive south 22 miles (35 km) on I-95 from I-16 to exit 76 (Hwy. 84). Go east and bear right on Colonels Island Rd. for 3.2 miles (5.1 km) and arrive at 3,000-acre (1,214-h) **Melon Bluff**

Nature Preserve Visitors Center. All visitors must register at the visitors center, open 9 A.M. to 4 P.M. Tuesday to Sunday. Admission fee is charged.

This private sustainable forest was once a plantation. Its coastal shore, river, wetlands, and moss-draped ancient oaks are alive

year-round with songbirds, wading birds, and marsh birds. In winter also see waterfowl and birds of prey. Wood storks, roseate spoonbills, and painted buntings sometimes visit, too.

The 2.5-mile (4-km) Devendorf Birding Trail starts at the nature center. It was built by the

American Forest Foundation's Forested Flyways program.

Melon Bluff Nature Preserve
2999 Islands Hwy.
Midway, GA 31320
(912) 884-5779
www.melonbluff.com

If time permits, also visit **Harris Neck NWR** by returning to I-95, driving south to exit 67, and going south on Hwy. 17, then 7 miles (11.3 km) east on Harris Neck Rd. Open dawn to dusk daily.

Just one imot of the wide-flung Savannah Coastal Refuges Complex, the refuge is among the best location locally to see painted buntings each year from April to September. Drive

Tybee Island lighthouse is an easy-to-recognize landmark.

the 4-mile (6.4-km) auto tour for the best opportunity to view these birds with their vivid red, green, and blue plumage. Also see endangered wood storks.

Savannah Coastal Refuges Complex also manages **Blackbeard Island NWR,** to the south; boat access only. Known for its endangered piping plovers, bald eagles, and wood storks.

Savannah Coastal Refuges
1000 Business Center Dr., Ste. 10
Savannah, GA 31405
(912) 832-4608
www.fws.gov/harrisneck

❷ Savannah Area

Return north on I-95 to I-16, turn east, drive to exit 165 (37th St.), bear left to follow 37th St., turn right on Martin Luther King Jr. Blvd., and turn left on W. Victory Dr. (Hwy. 80). Go 9.5 miles (15.3 km) east and cross the Wilmington River to **Fort Pulaski NM.** Open 9 A.M. to 5 P.M. daily, Memorial Day to Labor Day; 9 A.M. to 5 P.M. daily otherwise. Admission fee is charged.

About 200 recorded species of birds have been noted on the islands and salt marshes that make up this Civil War historic site. Trails ranging from 0.3 to 6 miles (0.4 to 9.7 km) in length give birders good views of migratory songbirds in spring and fall; shorebirds are common year-round, while waterfowl peak during winter.

Tampa and St. Petersburg Area

Florida's Gulf Coast offers birders the beauty of the tropics combined with birds only seen in southern waters. From a base in the twin cities on Tampa Bay or in Orlando, see birds of the Gulf's shores, mangroves, rivers, and many tempting isles.

Like an arm thrust into the Caribbean Sea, Florida is the first landfall in spring for many birds that island-hop from South America. Beginning in March and continuing to May, waves of migrating birds stop to rest in the pine flatwoods of the West Coast. They join resident birds that seem exotic to those accustomed to northern birds—smooth-billed anis, swallow-tailed kites, roseate spoonbills, American anhingas, and a fistful of egrets and herons. If a personal watercraft is available, bring it along on the trip. Some of the most spectacular bird-watching is reserved for hidden keys, islets, and barrier bars best seen from boats, but there are many fascinating birds to see at every stop.

A green heron, intent on hunting for a crustacean or fish meal in the plentiful swamps and marshes of Florida.

Roseate spoonbills swish their wide bills in the murky waters of Florida's swamps.

❶ Lower Suwannee NWR

Begin the birding route by driving I-75 north toward Gainesville, taking exit 354 (Hwy. 27), driving northwest 22 miles (35 km) to Williston, and continuing on Hwy. 27 Alt. for 27 miles (43 km) to Chiefland. Turn west on Hwy. 345 for 11.9 miles (19 km), bear left at Hwy. 347, go 5.8 miles (9.3 km), and turn right at N.W. 31st Pl. to arrive at **Lower Suwannee NWR.** Refuge open dawn to dusk daily; office open 7:30 A.M. to 4 P.M. weekdays except major holidays. Obtain brochures, maps, and information at the office.

The refuge consists of wetlands with 20 miles (32 km) of Suwannee River frontage and coastal marsh habitat on the Gulf of Mexico. More than 250 bird species have been recorded here, 90 of which nest in the refuge. Ospreys and bald eagles nest in early spring, swallow-tailed kites nest from March through July, and thousands of knots, dowitchers, oystercatchers, sandpipers, turnstones, and

At **Homosassa Springs Wildlife SP** a snowy egret shares the water's edge with a pair of wood ducks.

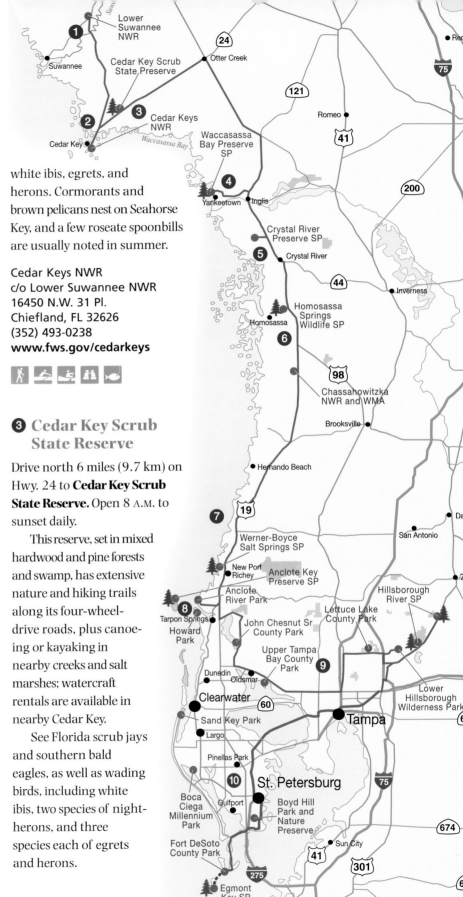

plovers arrive in March and April. Many migrate farther south for the winter, passing through again in fall. In summer see white ibis, egrets, herons, endangered wood storks, or rare limpkins. Also see neotropical migrants.

Bird by canoe or kayak on the Demory Creek canoe trail near the town of Suwannee. The coastal estuary is great for sea kayaking or hikes on its trails and boardwalks with observation decks and towers. Also consider visiting:

- Fishbone Creek Trail, with an elevated viewing deck
- Salt Creek Boardwalk
- River Trail and boardwalk
- Dennis Creek Trail, with boardwalks and benches
- Shell Mound Trail

Another option is to drive the nearly 50 miles (80 km) of refuge roads, using an automobile as a birding blind, especially the 9-mile (14.5-km) Dixie Mainline Rd.

Lower Suwannee NWR
16450 N.W. 31 Pl.
Chiefland, FL 32626
(352) 493-0238
www.fws.gov/lowersuwannee

❷ Cedar Keys NWR

Take Hwy. 347 south 14.4 miles (23.2 km) to Hwy. 24, bear right, and follow Hwy. 24 south to Cedar Keys and **Cedar Keys NWR.** The refuge's 13 coastal islands are only reachable by boat, but rentals and tour boat operators provide services in Cedar Keys. The refuge site is unstaffed; service kiosks on the trails and beaches provide trail and habitat information.

The center of Atsena Otie Key—one of the few places on the gulf where magnificent frigatebirds are easily seen—is closed to protect fragile plants; its beaches are open. Some 20,000 wading birds nest, breed, and feed in the refuge, with 10,000

white ibis, egrets, and herons. Cormorants and brown pelicans nest on Seahorse Key, and a few roseate spoonbills are usually noted in summer.

Cedar Keys NWR
c/o Lower Suwannee NWR
16450 N.W. 31 Pl.
Chiefland, FL 32626
(352) 493-0238
www.fws.gov/cedarkeys

❸ Cedar Key Scrub State Reserve

Drive north 6 miles (9.7 km) on Hwy. 24 to **Cedar Key Scrub State Reserve.** Open 8 A.M. to sunset daily.

This reserve, set in mixed hardwood and pine forests and swamp, has extensive nature and hiking trails along its four-wheel-drive roads, plus canoeing or kayaking in nearby creeks and salt marshes; watercraft rentals are available in nearby Cedar Key.

See Florida scrub jays and southern bald eagles, as well as wading birds, including white ibis, two species of night-herons, and three species each of egrets and herons.

Crystal River Preserve SP is a good place to use binoculars or a spotting scope to view waterbirds and shorebirds.

❻ Homosassa Springs Wildlife SP

Drive south 9.1 miles (14.6 km) on Hwy. 19 to **Homosassa Springs Wildlife SP** visitors center. Open 9 A.M. to 5:30 P.M. daily. Allow approximately four hours to see the park. Admission fee is charged.

A boat tour, included in the price of admission, takes guests from the visitors center to the entrance of Wildlife Park on Pepper Creek. Here a 1.1-mile (1.8-km) paved and elevated boardwalk provides many opportunities to see birds and wildlife, including manatees and an underwater observatory in the main spring.

The park's Pepper Creek Birding Trail, serviced by a tram as well as by foot, is part of the Great Florida Birding Trail.

Homosassa Springs Wildlife SP
4150 S. Suncoast Blvd.
Homosassa, FL 34446
(352) 628-5343
www.floridastateparks.org/ homosassasprings

If time permits, visit nearby 30,500-acre (12,343-h) **Chassahowitzka NWR** or 33,919-acre (13,727-h) **Chassahowitzka WMA.** The refuge, with headquarters 4 miles (6.4 km) south of Homosassa on Hwy. 19, is accessible only by boat. To visit the WMA, drive 2.5 miles (4 km) south on Hwy. 19 to Thrasher Rd.; an auto tour

---

Cedar Key Scrub State Reserve
P.O. Box 187
Cedar Key, FL 32625
(352) 543-5567
www.floridastateparks.org/ cedarkeyscrub

❹ Waccasassa Bay Preserve SP

Stay in the boat used to visit the prior two waypoints, because **Waccasassa Bay Preserve SP** is also accessible only by boat, and Cedar Key is one of three places to launch. The preserve encompasses the entire crescent-shaped beach and bay south from Cedar Key to Yankeetown, on Hwy. 98. Open 8 A.M. to sunset daily. Rental boats and guided tours are also offered in Yankee-town and in Gulf Hammock, or use a personal watercraft.

Bald eagles, ospreys, egrets, herons, gulls, and brown pelicans are some of the attractions. In spring neotropical migrant song-birds and shorebirds are abundant. Also keep an eye out for swimming manatees.

Waccasassa Bay Preserve SP
P.O. Box 187
Cedar Key, FL 32625
(352) 543-5567
www.floridastateparks.org/ waccasassabay

❺ Crystal River Preserve SP

Take Hwy. 24 east to Hwy. 98, turn south, drive for 32 miles (52 km), turn right on State Park Dr., and enter **Crystal River Preserve SP.** Open 8 A.M. to sunset daily.

There are 9 miles (14.5 km) of seaside and forest trails, a 2.5-mile (4-km) interpretive trail, and canoe trails. Obtain a park trail map and inquire about recent bird sightings at the visitors center, which also has exhibits.

Birds range from threatened bald eagles to endangered wood storks, plus hundreds of species of wading birds and shorebirds.

Crystal River Preserve SP
3266 N. Sailboat Ave.
Crystal River, FL 34428
(352) 563-0450
www.floridastateparks.org/ crystalriverpreserve

starts at the intersection, and all visitors must enter and exit here or at Hwy. 550 a short distance south. Obtain a driving-tour guide at the check station.

Bird-watchers should exercise caution because the area is open to hunters. Avoid visits in hunting season, especially November to early January, late March to April 1, and September to October.

Extensive areas of hardwood forest swamp make sightings of large wading birds, hawks, bald eagles, and songbirds likely. Also see chuck-will's-widows, ospreys, swallow-tailed kites, limpkins, and northern bobwhites.

FL Fish and Wildlife Conservation
Office of Recreational Services
620 S. Meridian St.
Tallahassee, FL 32399
(850) 488-5520
**www.floridaconservation.org/
recreation/chassahowitzka**

❼ Werner-Boyce Salt Springs SP

Drive 13 miles (21 km) south on Hwy. 19 to Port Richey and turn west just before Ridge Rd., the entry to **Werner-Boyce Salt Springs SP.** Open 8 A.M. to sunset daily.

This newly established park preserves 4 miles (6.4 km) of untouched gulf coastline. Walk the 0.5-mile (0.8-km) nature trail or explore some of the 170 recorded bird species that the park has noted, including

raptors, wading birds, shorebirds, and migratory songbirds. During migration see anhingas, several species of egrets and herons, night-herons, ospreys, and white ibis.

Also visit the salt spring; while small in diameter, it is 320 feet (98 m) deep.

Werner-Boyce Salt Springs SP
P.O. Box 490
Port Richey, FL 34673
(727) 816-1890
**www.floridastateparks.org/
werner-boyce**

❽ Anclote Key Preserve SP

Continue 8 miles (12.9 km) south on Hwy. 19, turn right on Anclote Blvd., and bear right on Bailey's Bluff Rd. to enter **Anclote River Park.** Located offshore 3 miles (4.8 km) is **Anclote Key Preserve SP,** accessible only by boat and home to at least 43 different types of birds. Many of these birds are beach-nesting species such as piping plovers and American oystercatchers. Open 8 A.M. to sunset daily.

Boats can be hired in Tarpon Springs. Those without access to watercraft may view river birds and shorebirds from Anclote River Park or at **Howard Park,** on the peninsula to the south.

Avoid disturbing nests or birds; park staff will advise visitors of restrictions and closures in nesting areas in coastal parks.

The best time to visit is at low tide, when herons, egrets, dowitchers, plovers, white ibis, and other shorebirds feed. Winter visitors will see bald eagles on their nests along Bailey's Bluff Rd. from December until May. The shoreline parks also offer views of ospreys, gulls, terns, and double-crested cormorants.

Anclote Key Preserve SP
1 Causeway Blvd.
Dunedin, FL 34698
(727) 469-5942
**www.floridastateparks.org/
anclotekey**

❾ Tampa Area

Bird-watchers traveling south on Hwy. 19 will notice the increasing suburban development that announces the entry into **Tampa** and its surroundings.

Unlike its peninsula-bound neighbor St. Petersburg, this mainland city has sprawled east, north, and south along Old Tampa Bay and Hillsborough Bay. Seen from the air, the city is pocked with countless small ponds, lakes, creeks, and rivers, making it an excellent birding habitat of urban forests, wetlands, swamps, and grasslands.

Homosassa Springs Wildlife SP excels in its interpretive program.

American anhingas have body forms similar to cormorants.

Return to Hwy. 19, drive south 2 miles (3.2 km), turn east for 2.9 miles (4.7 km) on E. Tarpon Ave., which becomes Keystone Rd., turn south on E. Lake Rd., and follow it to the entrance of **John Chesnut Sr. County Park,** on the road's west side adjacent to Lake Tarpon. Open 7 A.M. to dusk daily.

The 255-acre (103-h) park also encompasses Brooker Creek, cypress swamps, and pine flats,

the home or resting places of brown pelicans, gulls, ospreys, bald eagles, cormorants, and anhingas. Birds such as hawks, American kestrels, and many species of songbirds nest in the woods beside the lake.

There are 3 nature trails:

- North Trail goes through a cypress swamp and accesses a canoe trail.
- Peggy Park Trail is a self-guided walk; see the park

brochure for additional information and route.

- An elevated boardwalk by the boat ramp leads to an observation tower.

The park is heavily visited, especially during summer. Best times to bird are early morning and late in the day, after crowds thin and a peaceful quiet settles over the park.

John Chesnut Sr. County Park
2200 E. Lake Rd.
Palm Harbor, FL 34685
(727) 669-1951
www.pinellascounty.org/park/ 04_Chesnut.htm

Follow E. Lake Rd. south to the Oldsmar Ramp to Tampa Rd. (note its name change to W. Hillsborough Ave.). Turn east, drive 4.3 miles (6.9 km) to Double Branch Rd., and turn right to enter **Upper Tampa Bay County Park.** Open 8 A.M. to 6 P.M. daily.

A 2,144-acre (868-h) preserve with ponds, pine flatwoods, salt marshes, oyster bars, oak hammocks, and mangrove forests, the park is located on Old Tampa Bay. It has a nature center, several trails, a boardwalk, and a canoe trail on Double Branch Creek.

See rufous-sided towhees, catbirds, brown pelicans, egrets, herons, night-herons, terns, white ibis, and ospreys. Use caution and remain vigilant on the trails; American alligators

and occasional rattlesnakes, coral snakes, and cottonmouths have been noted. Those with canoes or kayaks can see waterfowl, roseate spoonbills, and kingfishers while paddling silently in the mangrove swamp.

Upper Tampa Bay Park
8001 Double Branch Rd.
Tampa, FL 33635
(813) 855-1765
www.hillsboroughcounty.org/ parks/parkservices

Return to W. Hillsborough Ave., turn east, drive 11.9 miles (19 km) to I-275, go north 4.9 miles (7.9 km), take exit 52 (Fletcher Ave.), drive east 5.4 miles (8.7 km) to a left turn at Lettuce Lake Ave., and enter 240-acre (97-h) **Lettuce Lake County Park.** Open sunrise to sunset daily.

Audubon Resource Center at the park offers visitors programs and information. Two boardwalks—one 3,500 feet (1,067 m) long—and a viewing tower offer views of birds going about their daily routines.

See migratory warblers in spring, waterfowl in winter, and wood ducks, wading birds, and shorebirds year-round.

Lettuce Lake County Park
6920 E. Fletcher Ave.
Tampa, FL 33592
(813) 987-6204
www.hillsboroughcounty.org/ parks/parkservices

Turn east on Fletcher Ave., drive 1.3 miles (2.1 km), and turn right into a parking area for 16,000-acre (6,475-h) **Lower Hillsborough Wilderness Park.** Open sunrise to sunset daily. Additional access is available on Fletcher Ave.'s north side.

With over 60 miles (97 km) of trails, boardwalks, and canoe paths, this regional park is worth taking time to explore. It includes 13 miles (21 km) of the Hillsborough River, bald cypress swamps, wetlands, and riverine mixed-hardwood forest.

See an endangered wood stork rookery, roseate spoonbills, several species of herons and egrets, white ibis, and numerous other shorebirds and waterfowl. Also see American anhingas and double-crested cormorants. Neotropical migrant songbirds such as warblers, vireos, tanagers, and others can be seen in the wetlands and marshes in spring and fall.

Lower Hillsborough
Wilderness Park
12702 Hwy. 301
Thonotosassa, FL 33592
(813) 987-6200
**www.hillsboroughcounty.org/
parks/parkservices**

Return to I-75, go south to exit 265 (E. Fowler Ave.), drive east 2.3 miles (3.7 km) to Hwy. 301, and go north 9.5 miles (15.3 km) to enter **Hillsborough River SP,** on the left. Open 8 A.M. to sunset daily; interpretive center open 8 A.M to 5 P.M. daily. Admission fee is charged.

Start at the park's interpretive center for exhibits and information. The park has four nature trails totaling 7.3 miles (11.7 km) passing through swamps, river floodplains, and oak hammock forest along the Hillsborough River. A scenic suspension bridge crosses the river. Canoes are available for rent.

The forests are good places to see woodpeckers, kingfishers, perching birds, hawks, and boreal songbirds. The fast-flowing river margins have large wading birds, while swamp areas have catbirds, blackbirds, and many smaller wading species.

Hillsborough River SP
15402 U.S. 301 N
Thonotosassa, FL 33592
(813) 987-6771
**www.floridastateparks.org/
hillsboroughriver**

❿ St. Petersburg Area

From the prior waypoint, turn south on Hwy. 301, drive 13.7 miles (22 km), and take the on-ramp for I-4 heading west. Drive 6.6 miles (10.6 km) to I-275 south, cross Tampa Bay, and take the left exit 22 (I-175). Exit at

Lettuce Lake Park has both extensive boardwalks (left) and a viewing tower (below).

Cattle egrets first nested in Florida in 1952; today they are found nearly everywhere

9th St. S to join 5th Ave. S, turn right on Dr. Martin Luther King St. S, drive south 2.8 miles (4.5 km), noting that the road's name changes to Country Club Way S, and enter **Boyd Hill Park and Nature Preserve.** Open 9 A.M. to 8 P.M. Tuesday to Thursday, 9 A.M. to 6 P.M. Friday and Saturday, and 11 A.M. to 6 P.M. Sunday. Closed Mondays and major holidays. Admission fee is charged.

The preserve comprises 245 acres (99 h) on Lake Maggiore, with 3 miles (4.8 km) of trails and boardwalks. Staff conducts interpretive programs, guided tours, and animal rescue. Visit the birds-of-prey aviary, which houses captive raptors with permanent injuries.

Lake Maggiore is a great spot within the city to see migratory birds, shorebirds, ospreys, and eagles, plus many larger wading birds and raptors.

Boyd Hill Park and Nature Preserve
1101 Country Club Way S
St. Petersburg, FL 33705
(727) 893-7326
www.stpete.org/explore.htm

Go east on Country Club Way S, turn south on Fairway Ave. S, right on Alhambra Way S, proceed as it becomes 16th St. S, and turn right on 54th Ave. S. Drive west 2.7 miles (4.3 km), continue as it becomes Pinellas Bayway S, drive 6 miles (9.7 km) south, and cross the toll bridge to **Fort**

DeSoto County Park. Open sunrise to sunset daily; office open 8 A.M. to 5 P.M. daily.

The park, which hosts more visitors than any other Pinellas County park, is made up of five islands. It has a 2,200-foot (671-m) interpretive trail, a 6.8-mile (10.9-km) paved recreation trail, and both a 1-mile (1.6-km) and a 0.8-mile (1.2-km) nature trail at Soldier's Hole and Arrowhead picnic area.

Because the park is the first landfall for birds migrating from South and Central America after crossing the Gulf of Mexico, it sometimes sees heavy concentrations of neotropical birds during spring. A condition known as "fallout" occurs when northerly and easterly headwinds tire the birds. At such times trees at the park may hold dozens of exhausted birds too tired to fly on.

Check out the wooded section of the park east of the pier and Arrowhead Picnic area for warblers, which arrive from mid-March to early May. Brown pelicans, herons, egrets, roseate spoonbills, double-crested cormorants, oystercatchers, black skimmers, and various gulls and plovers are year-round residents of the islands.

Fort DeSoto County Park
3500 Pinellas Bayway S
Tierra Verde, FL 33715
(727) 582-2267
www.pinellascounty.org

Werner-Boyce Salt Springs SP protects fragile coastal habitat.

Standing atop the fort and looking southwest, **Egmont Key SP** is visible 3 miles (4.8 km) farther offshore. Open 8 A.M. to sunset daily. There are no services or concessions.

Accessible only by private boat, the key is a historic site where gun batteries were built in 1898; it also houses a 150-year-old operating lighthouse. The island is a wildlife refuge and home to many species of birds, as well as sea turtles, box turtles, and gopher tortoises.

Several marinas in St. Petersburg offer ferry services. A visit offers the chance to see magnificent frigatebirds, tropicbirds, pelagic and double-crested cormorants, American anhingas, and other rarely seen waterbirds.

Egmont Key SP
4905 34th St. S, Ste. 5000
St. Petersburg, FL 33711
(727) 893-2627
www.floridastateparks.org/egmontkey

While in St. Petersburg, also visit these parks:

- **Boca Ciega Millennium Park,** I-275 to Gandy Blvd. N, west 8 miles (12.9 km) to 125th St. N, south to park; a viewing tower overlooks pine-flatwood and coastal-oak hammock forests, mangrove swamp, and meadows with shorebirds, wading birds, birds of prey, waterfowl, and upland game birds.

- **Sand Key Park,** I-275 to Roosevelt Blvd. N (Hwy. 686), northwest and west 12.4 miles (20 km) over Belleair Beach Cswy., north on Gulf Blvd.; benches at a salt marsh with herons, roseate spoonbills, anhingas, American moorhens, and great horned owls.

Pinellas County Parks
631 Chestnut St.
Clearwater, FL 33756
(727) 464-3347
www.pinellascounty.org/park

Miami, the Everglades, and the Florida Keys

BIRDING 35 TOUR

Throw out preconceptions of other locales with a visit to the bird-rich southern tip of Florida. Picture-postcard views of ranked flamingos and roseate spoonbills on sandbars vie for attention with smaller birds of every species. This is the promised land for bird-watchers, where spring brings trees full of almost every warbler and vireo species imaginable, the waves are punctuated by rafts of pelicans and anhingas, and it's possible to hear the soft sounds of birds on their nests beside bald cypresses and mangroves. Start in the north at Port St. Lucie and travel south until the route reaches the first of Florida's Keys, but finish the tour in its haunting Everglades.

Venture to a place where sparkling sand meets the Gulf Stream's endless blue waters and enjoy birding from sunrise to sundown before trekking inland to the primordial Everglades or taking a first step off the mainland to Key Largo.

At Anne Kolb Nature Center trees filled with white ibis make an arresting sight.

The greater flamingo is nearly an icon for the state of Florida, and yet even there they are rare except in zoos.

❶ St. Lucie Inlet Preserve SP

From I-75 take exit 101 (S.W. Kenner Hwy.) and go east 0.5 mile (0.8 km) toward Coral Gardens. Turn right on S.E. Cove Rd., drive 4.3 miles (9.7 km) to S.E. Dixie Hwy., and turn left.

St. Lucie Inlet Preserve SP, an offshore barrier island opposite the foot of S.E. Cove Rd., is accessible only by private boat. Several marinas on the east side of S.E. Dixie Hwy. have rental craft and launch facilities. Open daily from 8 A.M. until sunset. Admission fee is charged.

A 3,330-foot (1,015-m) boardwalk on the island passes mangrove forests, live oaks, cabbage palms, paradise trees, and wild lime trees to the beach. In summer rare Ridley and other sea turtles use the park's beach to lay their eggs. The shore is constantly scanned by gulls and

other scavenger birds between their offshore fishing trips.

See wading birds, shorebirds, brown pelicans, white ibis, and purple plovers. In fall the annual raptor migrations bring ospreys, hawks, peregrine falcons, and American kestrels. American bald eagles and merlins accompany them.

St. Lucie Inlet Preserve SP
4810 S.E. Cove Rd.
Stuart, FL 34997
(772) 219-1880
**www.floridastateparks.org/
stlucieinlet**

❷ Hobe Sound NWR

Drive south 5.7 miles (9.2 km) on S.E. Dixie Hwy., joining Hwy. 1 by S.E. Pettway St., and arrive at the office of 1,035-acre (419-h) **Hobe Sound NWR.** Open dawn to dusk daily. Admission fee is charged. Obtain a refuge map and bird checklist, and ask staff about recent birding hot spots.

While the refuge office is on Hwy. 1, much of the refuge is on Jupiter Island. Before going to

the island, walk the 0.4-mile (0.6-km) nature trail through scrub-oak and sand-pine forest.

Return north on Hwy. 1 to S.E. Bridge Rd., turn right, drive to S. Beach Rd., and turn left. This road leads to a parking area and trailhead. The 2.5-mile (4-km) Beach Trail leads north to Peck Lake. There are trails, a viewing platform, and 3.5 miles (5.6 km) of beach.

A total of 183 bird species have been recorded here, including scrub jays, white ibis, and belted kingfishers.

Hobe Sound NWR
P.O. Box 645
Hobe Sound, FL 33475
(772) 546-6141
www.fws.gov/hobesound

❸ Jonathan Dickinson SP

Across Hwy. 1 from Hobe Sound NWR is **Jonathan Dickinson SP.** Open 8 A.M. to sunset daily.

The park has a new Environmental Education and Research Center, with staff that can assist with bird identification and recommend areas with high activity. Hiking, canoeing, kayaking, and boat tours are bird-watching options at this park, which has boardwalks and an observation tower.

Over 140 bird species have been noted, including endangered Florida scrub jays. Best birding is on Kitching Creek or the main Loxahatchee River, where wading birds and shorebirds gather. Also note woodpeckers and owls.

Bill Baggs Cape Florida SP offers tours of its lighthouse, which overlooks the park.

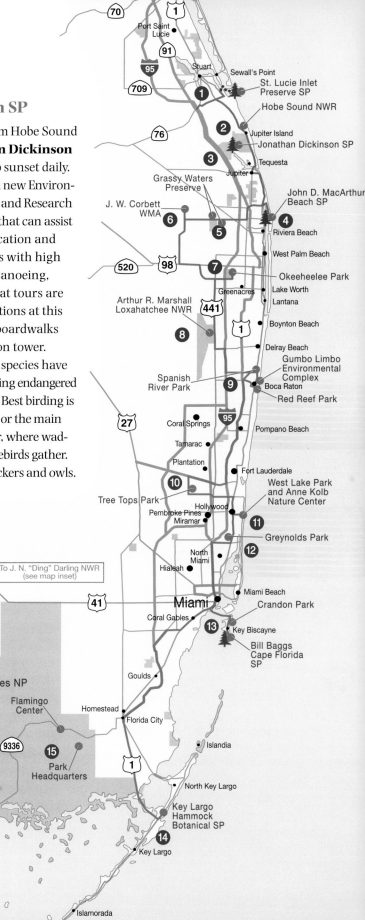

At Tree Tops Park the observation tower offers good views of the canopy's birds.

plovers, sandpipers, brown pelicans, herons, and other shorebirds and wading birds. Roseate spoonbills sometimes visit in summer, nesting in the nearby mangrove swamps.

John D. MacArthur Beach SP
10900 S.R. 703 (A1A)
North Palm Beach, FL 33408
(561) 624-6950
**www.floridastateparks.org/
macarthurbeach**

❺ Grassy Waters Preserve

Return 2.2 miles (3.5 km) west on PGA Blvd. to I-95, take the southbound on-ramp, go 2.4 miles (3.9 km) to exit 77 (Northlake Blvd.), and head west. Drive about 5 miles (8 km) to **Grassy Waters Preserve,** with sites north and south of Northlake Blvd. Open 8 A.M. to 4 P.M. Monday to Saturday, 9 A.M. to 5 P.M. Sunday. Hours extended to dusk on Wednesday.

Everglades Pavilion is at 8537 Northlake Blvd., and Charles W. Bingham Wilderness Pavilion is at 8264 Northlake Blvd. The north site has a lake and two trails through uplands and wetlands. The south site has a nature center surrounded by a 1,500-foot (457-m) raised boardwalk in sawgrass prairie and bald cypress marsh.

See great blue herons, great egrets, limpkins, ibis, turkey vultures, hawks, bald eagles, ospreys, waterfowl, and wading

birds at the eastern edge of the vast Everglades wetlands.

Grassy Waters Preserve
8264 Northlake Blvd.
West Palm Beach, FL 33412
(561) 804-4985
**www.cityofwpb.com/park/
grassy.htm**

❻ J. W. Corbett WMA

Continue 7 miles (11 km) west on Northlake Blvd. to Seminole Pratt Whitney Rd. and turn north to arrive at **J. W. Corbett WMA.** Open dawn to dusk daily. Admission fee is charged.

Obtain a trail map at the kiosk. Walk the 1.2-mile (1.9-km) Hungryland Boardwalk Trail through pine flatwoods, sawgrass marsh, oak-cabbage palm hammock, bald cypress swamp.

See pileated woodpeckers, barred owls, and screech-owls. Pairs of sandhill cranes nest here in winter, and mixed warblers trill melodious songs in spring. Also see endangered wood storks, along with herons, egrets, common yellowthroats, and other wading birds.

Birders should avoid the facility during hunting season, late August to early April.

FL Fish and Wildlife Commission
8535 Northlake Blvd.
West Palm Beach, FL 33412
(561) 625-5122
**myfwc.com/recreation/
jw_corbett**

Jonathan Dickinson SP
16450 S.E. Hwy. 1
Hobe Sound, FL 33455
(772) 546-2771
**www.floridastateparks.org/
jonathandickinson**

❹ John D. MacArthur Beach SP

Next head south 13.8 miles (22 km) on Hwy. 1 to PGA Blvd., turn

left, bear right at N. Ocean Dr., and enter174-acre (70-h) **John D. MacArthur Beach SP.** Open 8 A.M. to sunset daily. William T. Kirby Nature Center is an excellent resource for information, viewing displays, and viewing live-animal exhibits.

The park consists of subtropical coastal habitats on a barrier island. There are three nature trails and a 1,600-foot (488-m) boardwalk spanning Lake Worth Cove. See gulls, terns,

❼ Okeeheelee Park

Drive 10 miles (16 km) south on Seminole Pratt Whitney Rd., turn east on Southern Blvd. for 3.9 miles (6.3 km), turn south on W. Forest Hill Blvd., drive 6.6 miles (10.6 km), and turn left into **Okeeheelee Park.** Open dawn to sunset daily. Visitors center hours vary; see website.

Okeeheelee Nature Center has 2.5 miles (4 km) of nature trails in 90 acres (36 h) of wetlands and pine flatwoods. See common moorhens, ring-necked ducks, coots, teal, wood ducks, pied-billed grebes, ospreys, and hawks. The center has exhibits, birds-of-prey demonstrations, and guided walks.

Okeeheelee Nature Center
7715 Forest Hill Blvd.
West Palm Beach, FL 33413
(561) 233-1400
**www.co.palm-beach.fl.us/parks/
locations/okeeheelee.htm**

❽ Arthur R. Marshall Loxahatchee NWR

Drive west on W. Forest Hill Blvd., turn south on Hwy. 441 for 10.5 miles (16.9 km), and turn right at Lee Rd. to enter **Arthur R. Marshall Loxahatchee NWR.** Open sunrise to sunset daily. Visitors center hours vary; see website. Admission fee is charged.

The 143,874-acre (58,224-h) refuge preserves Everglades habitat and hosts 257 recorded bird species, including endangered snail kites.

A 0.4-mile (0.6-km) boardwalk behind the visitors center passes into the swamp, ending at an observation tower. A 5.5-mile (8.8-km) canoe trail accesses a floating platform equipped with a restroom.

Arthur R. Marshall Loxahatchee NWR
10216 Lee Rd.
Boynton Beach, FL 33437
(561) 732-3684
www.fws.gov/loxahatchee

❾ Boca Raton Area

Go south to W. Atlantic Ave. (Hwy. 806) on Hwy. 441, turn east to I-95, and go 4.4 miles (7.1 km) south to exit 48 (Hwy. 794). Cross the interstate on 51st St., go east to a right turn at Hwy. 1, a left at N.E. 40th St.,

West Lake Park and Anne Kolb Nature Center (below) offer several ways to experience birds. Walking trails, boat tours, or a stroll on the covered dock (right) may yield a good birding experience. For the fortunate birder, perhaps a roseate spoonbill or snowy egret sighting will be the reward.

and a right at N. Ocean Blvd. Drive south to **Gumbo Limbo Environmental Complex** on the left in **Red Reef Park.** Open 9 A.M. to 4 P.M. Monday to Saturday, noon to 4 p.m. Sunday except major holidays. Donation.

See exhibits, interpretive displays, aquariums, a 40-foot (12.2-m) observation tower, and an elevated boardwalk through hammock and mangroves.

Gumbo Limbo Environmental Complex
1801 N. Ocean Blvd.
Boca Raton, FL 33432
(561) 338-1473
www.gumbolimbo.org

Red Reef Park is a 67-acre (27-h) oceanfront park. Open 8 A.M. to 10 P.M. daily. Birds include brown pelicans, osprey, ring-billed and laughing gulls, and migrant warblers.

Red Reef Park
1400 N. State Rd. A1A
Boca Raton, FL 33432
(561) 393-7974
**www.ci.boca-raton.fl.us/parks/
redreef.cfm**

Just north, between Red Rock Park and N.E. 40th St., is **Spanish River Park,** with similar birding.

❿ Tree Tops Park

Drive south on N. Ocean Blvd., turn right at E. Palmetto Park Rd., go 3 miles (4.8 km) to I-95, drive south for 17 miles (28 km), and take exit 26 (I-595). Drive west 6 miles (9.7 km) to exit 3 (Hwy. 84), turn south on Nob Hill Rd., and go 2.5 miles (4 km) to **Tree Tops Park.** Open 8 A.M. to 6 P.M. daily in winter, 8 A.M. to 7:30 P.M. in summer. Admission fee is charged on weekends.

Nature trails, a 1,000-foot (305-m) boardwalk through the wetlands, and viewing platforms at the marshes make easy work of seeing waterfowl such as American coot, teal, and mottled ducks. Common moorhens and pied-billed grebes nest in the park. Egrets, herons, and anhingas are present year-round. See varied migratory songbirds in spring.

Tree Tops Park
3900S S.W. 100th Ave.
Davie, FL 33328
(954) 370-3750
www.broward.org/parks

⑪ West Lake Park and Anne Kolb Nature Center

Drive south on Nob Hill Rd. to Griffin Rd. (Hwy. 818), turn east, and drive 8.7 miles (14 km) to a right turn at Hwy 1.

Go south 2 miles (3.2 km), turn right at Sheridan St., and turn left after 1.4 miles (2.3 km) into **West Lake Park,** site of **Anne Kolb Nature Center.** Open 8 A.M. to 6 P.M. daily October to March, 8 A.M. to 7:30 P.M. April to September; center open 9 A.M. to 5 P.M. daily year-round. Admission fee is charged.

The center offers 2-hour-long nature specialist–narrated boat tours on West Lake and its tidal creeks for an additional fee.

Walking trails, an observation tower, and three marked canoe trails make the park an ideal birding site. See roseate spoonbills, white ibis, yellow-crowned night-herons, Wilson's plovers, and spotted sandpipers.

Anne Kolb Nature Center
751 Sheridan St.
Hollywood, FL 33019
(954) 926-2480
www.broward.org/parks

At Jonathan Dickinson SP the best way to go birding is in a kayak.

⑫ Greynolds Park

Return to Hwy. 1, turn south, drive 7.9 miles (12.7 km), and turn right at N.E. 179th St. with an immediate left at W. Dixie Hwy. to arrive at 249-acre (101-h) **Greynolds Park.** Open dawn to sunset daily.

This former rock quarry has mangrove wetlands and a wading bird rookery with trails to provide good views from the start of courtship in February through fledglings leaving the nest in summer. Visit near sundown to see the birds return to roost in large flocks. Species such as herons, double-crested cormorants, anhingas, white ibis, and cattle and great egrets are common here.

Greynolds Park
17530 W. Dixie Hwy.
North Miami Beach, FL 33160
(305) 945-3425
www.miamidade.gov/parks

⑬ Key Biscayne

Go south on Hwy. 1, turn east 3.1 miles (5 km) on N.E. 163rd St. (Hwy. 826), enter I-95 south, and go 12.3 miles (19.8 km) to exit 1A (S.W. 25th Rd.). Turn left onto Rickenbacker Cswy. and drive over the causeway to **Key Biscayne** and **Crandon Park,** the first of two stops on Key Biscayne. Open 8 A.M. to sunset daily; nature center open 9 A.M. to 5 P.M. daily.

Drag your eyes from the scenic grandeur of the island, note the park's nature center, take its guided nature tours, hike its trails, or walk the mangrove boardwalk to a fossilized reef overlook. See seabirds, wading birds, neotropical migrant songbirds, and colorful butterflies.

Crandon Park
6767 Crandon Blvd.
Key Biscayne, FL 33149
(305) 361-5421
www.miamidade.gov/parks

Continue on Crandon Blvd. to its end at **Bill Baggs Cape Florida SP.** Open 8 A.M. to sunset daily. Admission fee is charged.

Start with a tour of the lighthouse—its lofty height gives a good overview of the park.

Birding is best along the sea wall and the nature trails on the park's west side. To the north a trail leads through mangroves.

Bill Baggs Cape Florida SP
1200 S. Crandon Blvd.
Key Biscayne, FL 33149
(305) 361-5811
www.floridastateparks.org/capeflorida

⑭ Key Largo Hammock Botanical SP

Return to Hwy. 1 on the mainland, go south 7.6 miles (12.2 km), turn right at the on-ramp